THE POPE AGAINST NUREMBERG

THE POPE AGAINST NUREMBERG

HOW THE VATICAN HELPED NAZIS ESCAPE POSTWAR JUSTICE

GERALD J. STEINACHER

New York University Press

NEW YORK

NEW YORK UNIVERSITY PRESS
New York
www.nyupress.org

Please contact the Library of Congress for Cataloging-in-Publication data.

ISBN: 9781479845248 (hardback)
ISBN: 9781479845279 (library ebook)
ISBN: 9781479845262 (consumer ebook)

This book is printed on acid-free paper, and its binding materials are chosen for strength and durability. We strive to use environmentally responsible suppliers and materials to the greatest extent possible in publishing our books.

The manufacturer's authorized representative in the EU for product safety is Mare Nostrum Group B.V., Doelen 72, 4831 GR Breda, The Netherlands. Email: gpsr@mare-nostrum.co.uk.

Manufactured in the United States of America

10 9 8 7 6 5 4 3 2 1

Also available as an ebook

„Wo immer ernste Forschung sich bemüht, die Wahrheit zu finden und ein gerechtes Urteil zu fällen, soll und darf sie ihre Ergebnisse und Kritik bis zum Letzten bekanntgeben.“[1]

—Bishop Johannes Neuhäusler

“Wherever serious research endeavors to find the truth and render a fair judgment, it should and must disclose its findings and criticisms to the fullest extent.”

CONTENTS

PREFACE

I feel very strongly that my work, in addressing difficult questions of guilt and responsibility, must also always reflect my commitment to remembering and honoring victims. For as long as I can remember, I have wanted to be a historian, but the specific motivations for my research focus are even clearer: I grew up next to the site of a former Nazi concentration camp near the Austrian–Italian border. My natural childhood curiosity about the events that had taken place there were met with silence and denial by the grown-ups in my (perpetrator) society in the 1970s and 1980s. A controversy in Austria, sparked by Kurt Waldheim's 1986 presidential campaign, reignited these questions and led me to shift my historical interests from the Middle Ages to more recent history. Waldheim, a former UN Secretary General, faced scrutiny over his Nazi past, including his knowledge of war crimes during his service in Hitler's army. His defense—claiming he was merely following orders—was rejected by many, and especially along the generational divide that marked Austrians who had lived through the war versus those born later. Austria is by no means the only European country troubled by its fascist legacy. For almost 15 years, I called Austria's southern neighbor, Italy, my home[1]—a country that, like Austria, continues to struggle with coming to terms with its fascist past.

By 2014, I had started my intensive research for this book. In the intervening years, I have traveled to more than 60 archives housed in Europe, the United States, Israel, and Australia. These research efforts culminated in a two-month stay at the Vatican archives in Rome in 2021, to which I have returned several times since. This study therefore stands on a wide and deep archival foundation that informs and structures the narrative I offer in the following pages. In particular, this story does not come just from the top (Church leadership) or just from below (individual, "ordinary" priests). Nor is it primarily the story of a national church (e.g., Germany, Italy). Instead, it reveals how vast numbers of diverse actors and elements interacted. For example, the various initiatives undertaken to undermine the Nuremberg trials and postwar justice did not result solely from directives from the Vatican or efforts by German clergy. Rather, they reflected the interactions of these actors. The various sources I have collected for this study illustrate these connections well.

My findings and the story I aim to tell in these pages have resulted from an extensive, major research project that consumed much time and energy. I could not have undertaken it without the help of others, some of whom I acknowledge briefly here.

Most important, I thank all the Holocaust survivors who shared their time and experiences with me, sat down for interviews, and enlightened younger generations by visiting my classes. I also am very grateful to Benjamin Ferencz, one of the prosecutors in the Nuremberg trials. A short exchange I had with him in 2021, just a short time before he died at the age of 103, will stay with me forever. I also appreciate my encounters and exchanges with witnesses of the time, such as the Catholic monsignor who witnessed firsthand, as a young priest in Rome, men like Bishop Alois Hudal helping Nazi perpetrators escape Allied justice. These interviews and encounters helped me to understand the views of this generation, the complexity of which I could not have comprehended solely from documents. It also helped me to clarify for myself that understanding does not mean justifying. I certainly do not justify the actions of these clergy.

Many colleagues and friends also have provided valuable feedback and helped me to identify sources. I particularly wish to thank Suzanne Brown-Fleming and her colleagues at the United States Holocaust Memorial Museum (USHMM) in Washington, D.C.: Elizabeth Anthony, Peter Black, Rebecca Erbelding, Jan Lambertz, Juergen Matthaeus, and Anatol Steck. A 2014 research workshop at the USHMM, on "Moral Dilemmas and Moral Choice in the Holocaust: Dietrich Bonhoeffer and Pius XII as Case Studies in Religious Leadership," also enabled me to narrow my research focus. Uki Goñi (Buenos Aires) has generously provided expert advice, ever since we first met in Buenos Aires in 2009. My long-time mentor Guenter Bischof (New Orleans, La.) inspired me to be the best advisor I can be to my own graduate students. He also helped me with this book. Heartfelt thanks go to: John Q. Barrett (New York City), Olof Bortz (Uppsala), Winfried Garscha (Vienna), Roland Kostics (Uppsala), David I. Kertzer (Providence, R.I.), Kevin P. Spicer (North Easton, Mass.), Eward Westermann (San Antonio, Tex.), Kerstin von Lingen (Vienna), Valentina Ciciliot (Venice), Mark Gudgel (Omaha, Neb.), Michael Laurence Miller (Vienna), Matteo Sanfilippo (Viterbo), Philippe Sands (London), Susanna Schrafstetter (Burlington, Vt.), Alan Steinweis (Burlington, Vt.), Bob Moore (Sheffield), Michael Germer (Lincoln, Neb.), Stefan Schulte (Cologne), Malte Rehbein (Passau), Kevin Madigan (Cambridge, Mass.), Hubert Wolf (Muenster), Olof Bortz (Stockholm), and Nina Valbousquet (Paris).

In support of this book, I received a number of prestigious fellowships and held visiting professorships, all of which were invaluable to my efforts to complete this ambitious research. I am deeply indebted to the Center for Holocaust Studies at the Leibniz Institute for Contemporary History and the *Historisches Kolleg* Institute for Advanced Study in History, both located in Munich. For their hospitality in Munich, I thank Andreas Wirsching, Andrea Löw, Thomas Schlemmer, Maximilian Strnad, and Christof Mauch. The Vienna Wiesenthal Institute for Holocaust Studies (Éva Kovács, Jochen Boehler, and Marianne Windsperger); the International Institute for Holocaust Research at *Yad Vashem* in Jerusalem; the Center for Holocaust and Genocide Studies at the University of Uppsala, Sweden; the Bogliasco Foundation in Genoa, Italy; the Universities of Passau and Venice; the Australian National University in Canberra; and the Central European University in Vienna, Austria, all provided resources and assistance. I particularly thank my own institution, the University of Nebraska–Lincoln, for its constant support since 2011 and for naming me James A. Rawley Professor in History in recognition of my work in the field of Holocaust studies. I consider myself lucky to have wonderful colleagues there, with whom I can work productively on both research and teaching, including Ari Kohen, Bedross Der Matossian, Alex Vazansky, James Le Sueur, Margaret Jacobs, Dawne Curry, Carole Levin, and Will Thomas. A special thank you also goes to the staff and faculty at the University Library at the University of Nebraska–Lincoln. Their interlibrary loan service was priceless for this project.

In drafting this manuscript, I am grateful for the support of the copy editors Dillon Rockrohr, James Reilly, and Elisabeth Nevis; the team at New York University Press, especially Jennifer Hammer and Brianna Jean; and my agent, Rita Rosenkranz. I also thank everyone who helped transcribe the many archival sources cited herein or assisted in other ways. I am indebted to my supportive siblings—Alfred, Tina, and Werner—and to my strong and loving mother, Annemarie. Finally, my deepest gratitude goes to my wonderful wife, Stas, for her unwavering support and patience throughout the process of writing another major book.

INTRODUCTION

Without hesitation I described myself as Catholic. In fact, I did not belong to any church, but the help I received from the Catholic priests had remained deep within my memory, so I decided to honor the Catholic Church by becoming its honorary member.[1]

This is how Adolf Eichmann, one of the key organizers of the Holocaust, later recalled with surprising fondness the support he received from clergy during his escape from justice. His flight from Europe to Argentina in 1950 was facilitated by the help of Catholic priests affiliated with both the Vatican and Nazi networks. A network of former Nazis, Argentine officials, and Catholic clergy provided Eichmann with food, shelter, transportation, and forged documents. He was far from alone: thousands of Nazi fugitives followed similar routes, crossing the Alps into Italy and departing from European ports for South America and beyond. Along the way, they relied heavily on the assistance of Catholic clergy and institutions, which furnished them with false identities, travel papers, and safe passage out of Europe.

While the Allies were establishing mechanisms of postwar criminal justice, including the Nuremberg war crimes trials, many Nazi perpetrators and collaborators quietly slipped away, aided by escape routes commonly referred to collectively as the "Ratline." The Church's involvement in the Ratline, as evidenced in Eichmann's remark, raises pressing and complex questions about the part played by the Catholic Church during that postwar period. Were these acts the work of a few rogue priests acting independently, or did they reflect a broader, more systemic pattern? More provocatively, did elements within the Church hierarchy—including the pope himself—know about or even sanction these efforts? And if so, what motivated such actions? Were they driven by ideological sympathies, Cold War pragmatism, or a desire to protect the institutional Church?

These questions about the Vatican's role in aiding Nazi fugitives prompted me to broaden the scope of my research, which had been initially focused on the stories of Nazi escape. The Ratline, however, became the starting point for a wider investigation into the Vatican's stance on postwar justice as a whole. To grasp these dynamics fully, I examined the Holy See's response to Nazi war crimes trials and its attitude toward the emerging postwar order. I soon discovered that the Vatican was highly critical of Allied projects that were focused on retributive justice—and it made that criticism heard, backing it up with manifold actions in support of Nazi war criminals. Ultimately, I found that the Vatican's interventions on behalf of Nazi war criminals—whether they were awaiting trial, imprisoned, or fleeing overseas to escape justice—must be understood as part of a larger, interconnected strategy. I argue that these acts were not isolated incidents but were deeply embedded in the Vatican's broader approach to postwar geopolitics, justice, and the preservation of institutional influence in a rapidly changing world.

"Forgive Germany, Pope Urges World," noted *The New York Times* headline on April 16, 1948. The call to forgive and help rebuild Germany—rather than punish it—came from the global leader of the Catholic Church just three years after the end of the deadliest military conflict in human history. Of the estimated 60 million lives lost, the majority were civilians. The victims included six million Jews murdered in a coordinated, systematic, and industrialized genocide—the Shoah, or Holocaust. Millions more were wounded, and those who survived were left traumatized for life. The cultural and infrastructural losses, as well, were immeasurable. Nazi Germany and its allies, particularly Japan and Italy, ultimately bore responsibility for all of these costs. After the defeat of these Axis powers, the world grappled with the question of how to deal with those responsible for the dictatorships, war, and genocide that had been unleashed in such catastrophic ways. Pope Pius XII gave his answer in an argument to German Catholic leaders: The world needed to forgive and forget Germany's war crimes and help rebuild the country.[2]

The pope did not limit himself to public appeals. He and his closest advisors also tried to derail initiatives by Allied powers to bring Nazi perpetrators to justice, offered appeals for clemency, and actively obstructed criminal justice efforts. Catholic leadership helped finance the defense of Nazi war criminals, managed public relations campaigns on behalf of the accused, coordinated diplomatic interventions for clemency and impunity, and actively opposed extraditions. This all begs the question: Why would the Catholic Church and its leadership so vigorously oppose punishing war crimes and applying criminal justice? This book draws on a wealth of documents from once-secret Vatican archives to delve into the Vatican's responses to the postwar Nazi war crimes trials, as well as the rationales offered for their efforts on behalf of the accused.

Beyond the immediate implications of Pope Pius XII's call to forgive and forget, this book deals with a series of difficult but important questions that it raises. How can and should a society move forward after war, genocide, and dictatorship? Can it build lasting peace in such a situation? What is essential, and what is beneficial, for accomplishing vast objectives like ensuring justice and moving forward on individual, community, and societal levels? The Catholic Church's emphasis on unlimited forgiveness creates challenging problems for consideration related to the possibilities, conditions, and limits of reconciliation in the immediate postwar years. Many of the questions raised and intensely discussed during that postwar period remain relevant today, because they are intrinsic to the human condition and transcend time.

The issues at stake during the postwar period share many common elements with what we nowadays study in the field of "transitional justice." The UN defines this concept in the following way: "Transitional justice covers the full range of processes and mechanisms associated with a society's attempt to come to terms with a legacy of large-scale past conflict, repression, violations and abuses, in order to ensure accountability, serve justice and achieve reconciliation."[3] The postwar years involved a complex transition from war to peace and also, in some societies like West Germany, Italy, and Austria, from dictatorship to democracy. The architects of the Nuremberg war crimes trials called for punitive justice as a way of dealing with the past and of enabling a new beginning. U.S. legal scholar Ruti Teitel succinctly outlines the questions that also troubled the minds of the architects of Nuremberg justice: "The debate over transitional criminal justice is marked by profound dilemmas:

Whether to punish or to amnesty? [...] Who properly bears responsibility for past repression? To what extent is responsibility for repression appropriate to the individual, as opposed to the collective, the regime, and even the entire society?"[4] The international conflicts of the twenty-first century, including the war in Ukraine, emphasize the continued urgency of these issues. With that said, I freely acknowledge from the outset that there are no simple answers to these complex questions, and this book does not claim to provide definitive solutions. Furthermore, though its central focus is on the leaders of the Catholic Church, its objective is not to pass judgment on the Church but rather to comprehend, without justifying, the actions the Church chose to take during the postwar years.

Since German author Rolf Hochhuth premiered his 1963 play *The Deputy*, which criticized the pope for his public silence during the Holocaust, the role of Catholic Church leadership and the actions of Pope Pius XII during the Nazi regime have inspired heated debates. For some, Pius XII was "Hitler's pope," remaining silent on the genocide; for others, this "Vicar of Christ" did everything possible to help Jews and other Nazi victims.[5] The ongoing push for his canonization has further churned the waters, as did the decision to open the archives of his pontificate, which hold over 16 million documents, in 2019. When announcing this long overdue decision and the loaded expectations it raised, Pope Francis firmly stated that the "Church is not afraid of history."[6]

This remark likely alludes to the controversies surrounding his mid-century predecessor on the throne of St. Peter. Pius XII presided over the Catholic Church from March 1939 until his death in October 1958—highly challenging times. Soon after his election, World War II commenced, along with its many horrors. Pius XII's reign also included the immediate postwar years and the transition from wartime alliances to the new global Cold War. The newly opened Vatican archives help fill many of the gaps that have remained regarding Vatican history during that tumultuous period, including the crucial, unanswered questions about the Vatican's postwar treatment of Nazi and Axis war criminals.

Notably, even before the conclusion of World War II, the Allies recognized the need to hold Nazi Germany accountable for their heinous acts of aggression, war crimes, and mass crimes against civilians. They were resolute that such atrocities should not and could not go unpunished. Nevertheless, the enormity of the crimes committed by the Axis nations meant that ensuring that justice was served effectively represented a difficult task. The Allied nations eventually agreed to prosecute Nazi perpetrators at Nuremberg and other war crimes trials, with the aims of establishing a firm rule of law, drawing clear dividing lines between former dictatorships and a new era, and contributing to the destruction of Nazism in Germany.

Pope Pius XII held views on guilt and punishment that differed markedly from those of the victorious Allies. He advocated a measured and restrained approach toward the German people and firmly opposed radical measures, such as widespread purges of former Nazis from society or the permanent weakening of Germany. In his view, such policies would prove counterproductive and ultimately play into the hands of what he regarded as "godless communism." The involvement of influential Church officials, including the pope's main spokespeople in Germany, reached a peak in the form of calls for a generous amnesty for war criminals. Such an amnesty would essentially have nullified the efforts of the Allies to bring the perpetrators to justice, as duly observed by U.S. government officials. The case of the convicted Nazi criminal Ernst von Weizsäcker offers a clear example of how Pope Pius XII intervened, both directly and personally, thus toeing (and arguably crossing) the line of obstruction of Nuremberg justice. Based on new evidence I have uncovered in the Vatican archives, this book specifies just how much the pope exerted his influence to seek impunity for one of Hitler's top diplomats.

The Church's call for almost unlimited forgiveness through amnesty may seem surprising; as we will see, the perpetrators of the Holocaust did not meet even the minimum standards for forgiveness according to Catholic doctrine. They rarely admitted personal guilt, let alone repenting or asking for forgiveness. However, they were forgiven by Catholic clergy anyway, apparently reflecting the Vatican's broader aims of strengthening the influence of Catholic teachings and the Church in society. The "re-Christianization" of European secular societies had become a crucial goal. In this context, Catholic leaders' responses to Nuremberg justice might be understood, at least partially, as an attempt to save as many souls as possible by bringing former Nazis back to the Church. The case of SS General Oswald Pohl, a prominent Holocaust perpetrator, offers a telling example: In prison, Pohl converted to Catholicism, prompting the pope to bless him and the Vatican to intervene to save him from the gallows. For Pius XII, the harvest of souls was worth any sacrifice.

As I argue herein, the Church's various responses represent points on the same spectrum, ranging at times from cautious critiques of the chosen methods of criminal punishment to, at other times, full-on smear campaigns against war crimes trials and, ultimately, to obstructions of justice. The Vatican's efforts to aid Axis war criminals must also be understood within the broader context of its postwar priorities during the early Cold War. Saving the souls of former Nazis, re-Christianizing society, promoting *caritas* (love, or charity) and forgiveness for the vanquished nations, and combating the imminent threat of "atheistic communism" functioned as powerful motivations driving the Vatican's responses to the enormous challenges of the postwar years. This mentality effectively blurred the distinction between Nazi victims and Nazi perpetrators, to the point that some clergy would end up portraying Nazis, after their defeat, as "victims" of Allied revenge. From this perspective, the actions that Catholic clergy undertook on behalf of Nazis appear neither as anomalies nor as the acts of individual rogue priests. Instead, they represent an essential part of the pope's critical stance toward postwar justice—a stance that must be understood in the context of the massive refugee crisis in the aftermath of the war and in line with early Cold War logics.

Very few scholars have examined the Vatican's stance on the Nazi war crimes trials and postwar justice. Some literature examines the opposition of the German Christian churches (both Lutheran and Catholic) to the Nuremberg trials and the wider Allied denazification program; one of the most notable books on this subject is Frederic Spotts's *The Churches and Politics in Germany*.[7] However, the Vatican's stance can be glimpsed only through fragmentary or indirect evidence provided in these prior studies. Another pertinent work comes from Suzanne Brown-Fleming, whose *The Holocaust and Catholic Conscience* investigates the papal nuncio in Germany in the postwar years; her insights helped me to clarify the role of the U.S. Catholic Church in those years.[8] Religious and theological teachings also need to be taken into consideration when studying the Vatican and the Catholic Church. For this purpose, Katharina von Kellenbach's *Mark of Cain* and Rainer Bendel's edited volume *Kirche der Sünder–Sündige Kirche?* [*Church of Sinners, Sinful Church?*] provided valuable resources for this book, though again, they both focus on German churches rather than the Vatican.[9]

Despite extensive research on Nazi escape networks, relatively few studies have systematically investigated the role of the Catholic Church and its representatives in facilitating these escapes. For example, Uki Goñi's crucial book *The Real Odessa* focuses on Argentina and the role of the Argentine government under Juan Perón in recruiting German experts, including many Nazis and war criminals.[10] In my 2011 book *Nazis on the Run,* I provided a comprehensive history of the Italian Ratline, revealing the structures and various institutions that facilitated the escape of Nazis and war criminals from Italy overseas within the context of the early Cold War.[11] In that work, I dedicated only one chapter to the role of Catholic clergy. As an expansion of that research, this book delves much deeper into the topic. Michael Phayer's 2007 book *Pius XII, the Holocaust, and the Cold War* examines the pope's involvement during the Holocaust and the Catholic Church's role in the early years of the Cold War.[12] Phayer stands among the few scholars who have contextualized the Ratline within the broader framework of the Vatican's early Cold War policies. With the recent opening of the Vatican archives, scholars now have the opportunity to delve into the inner workings and rationales of the pope and his closest collaborators. This book represents a concerted effort to do just that.

Finally, I must note that the inspiration for this book came not only from the opening of the Vatican archives but also from my own personal history. The question of how to reckon with the Nazi past has been with me since I was a child, growing up in a perpetrator society that also was deeply shaped by Catholicism. In addition to that broader connection to these questions, a specific trigger sparked my interest in this particular topic. In the early 2000s, I conducted interviews with Nazi victims for the U.S. Holocaust Memorial Museum in Washington, D.C. In that role, I interviewed a Catholic woman who had been imprisoned in a Nazi concentration camp in Northern Italy. When asked to testify against one of her tormentors in a 1990s trial, she refrained from speaking about the cruelty of the accused. When I asked her, later and off record, why she had refused, her answer resonated with me deeply: The judges, the lawyers, the police, and the historians, too—they can all leave this behind them, she said. But she must go home, knowing that the perpetrator lives in the neighboring village, as he has for the past decades. She had run into him before, and she might do so again. I was speechless. How could victims, bystanders, resisters, and perpetrators all go on living in the same society after mass violence and dictatorship? Whereas I had no answer, the woman's local Catholic priest offered her one. He demanded that the woman forgive and forget. Forgive she could, but how, she asked, could she forget her own suffering? This interaction has stayed with me, and in my attempt to address her questions, and others related to it, I offer this book.

PART 1

NUREMBERG

1

JUDGMENT DAY

May 1945. My beloved Reich lay in ruins. Defeated. As I stood on the shore of a little Austrian lake, I became aware that I, SS-*Obersturmbannführer* Adolf Eichmann, was now nothing but a hunted deer, not better off than the deer in the forest that I saw before me. . . . [My family] would stay here in the safety of the cottage on the Aussee in Ischl, my uncle's chalet. I, though, had no option but to flee.[1]

This reflection by one of the most notorious organizers of the Holocaust, Adolf Eichmann, describing the moment of Nazi Germany's defeat, offers an idealized, disturbing view. But as it reveals, for Nazi perpetrators, Germany's unconditional surrender on May 8, 1945, represented a potential moment of reckoning with their wartime deeds.

During the course of the war, the Allies repeatedly made it clear to the Nazis and their collaborators that the acts they were committing were so heinous, so enormous, so unprecedented, that the world needed to address them. They could not go unpunished. The Allies issued multiple public statements to this effect, printed in newspapers and broadcast on radio in Allied and neutral countries. Many Germans secretly listened to these broadcasts, and Eichmann and other leading Nazis were fully aware of their contents, which emphasized the acts for which they would be held liable.

Specifically, Nazi Germany, Imperial Japan, and fascist Italy, along with their allies, were responsible for the deadliest war in human history, resulting in over 60 million deaths and many millions more wounded and scarred by the traumas of modern warfare. The Nazis and their collaborators had organized the systematic murder of 6 million Jews in what we call the Holocaust or Shoah. Millions more fell victim to a "master race" ideology; any opposition or resistance was brutally repressed, and slave laborers were starved or worked to death. The Nazi worldview contained no novel elements. Eugenics, racism, racial antisemitism, ethnic nationalism, and militarism had been prevalent in Europe and beyond since at least the nineteenth century. But the Nazi regime stands out in history for its unprecedented embrace of total dictatorship, total war, and total genocide. It is often regarded as the embodiment of absolute evil, serving as a benchmark against which other atrocities and genocides are measured.

The Nuremberg trials also stand tall in our collective memory. They represent a moment of reckoning with the Nazi regime. Some of the main war criminals sat in the dock while the civilized world judged some of the worst atrocities ever committed. "Justice served" is a common sentiment among people who look back on Nuremberg. As this chapter acknowledges, this perspective holds some validity. But I also explicitly acknowledge that criminal justice, like life, is never perfect. Nor was punishment through due process of vanquished leaders of the Nazi regime a foregone conclusion. On the contrary, the road to Nuremberg was long, twisting, and uncertain, and the realization of the trials required a fortunate convergence of circumstances. This chapter explores how the Allied war crimes trials against Axis leaders came to be and the challenges the prosecutors faced. Because the Vatican's stance on the Nuremberg trials can be understood only by grasping the basics of the trials' history, it is important to understand some of those foundations. Indeed, key legal concepts that remain fundamental to society, such as the meaning of genocide and crimes against humanity, have their roots in the ashes of the Third Reich.

GAZING INTO THE ABYSS

By April 1945, it had become apparent to the world that the total defeat of Nazi Germany was only a matter of time—weeks, or mere days, away. The Third Reich no longer had a tenable military path: Soviet forces were closing in on Berlin from the east; U.S. and British forces had taken over the Rhineland in the west; and in northern Italy, German forces had already begun negotiating a surrender. The remaining German forces would have little choice but to follow suit. German cities lay in ruins after massive Allied air raids, while Adolf Hitler ranted in his bunker, as depicted in the film *Downfall* (2004), and refused to consider surrender. In his last public appearance, available in a propaganda newsreel, Hitler decorated members of the Hitler Youth outside his bunker. Some of them were barely 12 years old. Women were being trained to use anti-tank weapons, and anyone who could carry a weapon was thrown into the fight against the advancing Allied armies. German losses reached their peak in 1944–45. The untrained soldiers served as mere cannon fodder.

Once Soviet forces approached Hitler's bunker, following heavy fighting and overcoming defenses raised by German, French, and Belgian members of the SS, the end became a question of hours. On April 30, 1945, Hitler and his longtime mistress Eva Braun chose suicide. His remains were burned in a courtyard outside the bunker. Many of his closest associates and other Nazi leaders in Germany followed his example and ended their lives. They had gambled everything, lost everything, and faced a future of reckoning. Both they and the German civilian population particularly feared the prospect of Soviet revenge for the brutal warfare and atrocities the Nazi army had committed in the East.

Although these suicides garnered a lot of attention, the majority of the defeated Nazis chose life. After years of receiving and following orders, Nazi officials were left to their own devices, and the sense of *Verlorenheit* (lostness) this situation created is evident in Eichmann's memoirs. High-ranking Nazi and SS leaders tried to blend into the millions of German POWs, by changing their uniforms, procuring false papers, and, like Eichmann, seeking to become anonymous. Recognizing these attempts to evade justice, the Allies invested significant effort in screening the masses of prisoners to identify high-ranking Nazis and members of the notorious SS, which was deeply complicit in Nazi crimes. Thus for example, Heinrich Himmler, one of the highest-ranking Nazi leaders and key perpetrator of the Holocaust, was quickly recognized and captured by British forces; he died after swallowing cyanide on May 23, 1945. However, the Allies generally did not categorize or treat ordinary German soldiers as war criminals. Instead, they were usually classified and treated as POWs. Considering the vast numbers of people involved, the task of identifying war criminals was enormous.

It was also crucial. When the war ended, and the concentration and extermination camps were liberated, the entire world confronted the devastating moral abyss created by the Nazis. The concentration camps were never a secret. Since Hitler's regime first opened Dachau in 1933, the Nazis made no real attempt to hide their actions. On the contrary, they actively publicized the camps as part of their purposeful, strategic terror campaign. Initially used to imprison and suppress political opponents, the camps later expanded as mass arrests and incarceration of Jews began. Their precise purpose and nature also evolved, such that different types of camps emerged as the Nazis' tactics expanded.

In addition to the shifting nature of these sites of evil, their full extent could often not be truly captured in written reports. Seeing their full horror, depicted in images and film reels, was a profoundly different experience. Dwight D. Eisenhower, Supreme Commander of the Allied Expeditionary Force in Europe, wrote about his first encounter with a concentration camp:

> The same day [April 12, 1945] I saw my first horror camp. It was near the town of Gotha. I have never felt able to describe my emotional reactions when I first came face to face with indisputable evidence of Nazi brutality and ruthless disregard of every shred of decency. Up to that time I had known about it only generally or through secondary sources. I am certain, however, that I have never at any other time experienced an equal sense of shock.[2]

Other people's reactions to encountering these experiences similarly ranged from shock, disbelief, and anger—to lust for revenge. Such a desire was understandable among the victims. When the Dachau concentration camp was liberated by U.S. forces in late April 1945, some of the liberated prisoners immediately killed their tormentors. American soldiers, uncovering the grotesque evidence of the atrocities committed by Nazis, summarily executed some of the SS guards rather than taking them as prisoners. In eastern parts of Germany, Soviet soldiers exacted revenge by looting German towns and cities and committing mass rapes against German women and girls, often with little interference from Soviet military authorities.

But the shock of these liberations were also felt deeply by regular people throughout the world. It provided a further push to establish the Nuremberg trials, as well as to expand denazification efforts to purge all national, regional, and local administrations of anyone with Nazi Party membership. This goal represented a monumental effort, given the party's millions of members and pervasive influence at every level of society—from justice departments and police forces to town mayors, university professors, and high school teachers. In parallel with the massive effort involved in denazification, there arose substantial fears of a power vacuum and the potential for chaos. Dismissing millions of people from their jobs would bring society to a standstill. Thus, the Allies needed to find and establish a delicate balance between delivering justice and maintaining order.

Yet when Germany surrendered unconditionally in May 1945, the Nazi regime was completely dissolved. There was no leadership and no central German government; the German state had essentially ceased to exist. Its furthest eastern parts were granted to the Soviet Union and Poland, triggering a massive wave of German refugees fleeing those areas. The rest of Germany was divided and occupied by the United States, United Kingdom, Soviet Union, and France.

As we might expect in hindsight, chaos reigned. The Allies had to address some immediate priorities: establishing law and order, organizing a new local civil administration, and preventing a hunger crisis in a war-torn country where many cities had been reduced to rubble. But empathy for the German civilian population was limited. With Germany's criminal warfare came the ruin of its former reputation as a cultured nation. In the ruins of the Third Reich, anything German was suspected of being complicit, criminal, or evil. Germany became a pariah nation.

PUNISHMENT FOR AXIS CRIMINALS

As noted above, even before the end of World War II, the Allies had determined that the atrocities committed by the Axis powers—particularly their war of aggression, war crimes, and the systematic mass murder of European Jews—should not go unpunished. But when measured against the magnitude of the Axis crimes, how could justice be served? With the Moscow Declaration of November 1, 1943, the Allies announced their intention to try the perpetrators in the places where they committed their crimes. However, a thorny question remained: How would the Allies deal with Nazi criminals whose crimes could not be specified or limited to a single country?[3] The appropriate nature and design of the courts to try Axis criminals also remained disputed among the Allies. The vanquished war criminals claimed the trials represented an overreaching expression of victors' justice; the Allies believed that through discussions and planning, they could ensure "the greatest trial in history," as described later by the well-known English jurist Sir Norman Birkett.[4] According to its planners, this trial would draw a clear line under the Nazi past and create conditions for a new beginning. And indeed, the Nuremberg trial represented the first international war crime trial in history.

* * *

It is not easy to pinpoint the exact moment when the idea of trying Nazi criminals first arose, but it clearly was closely tied to postwar planning by the Allies. At a meeting aboard a warship off the coast of Newfoundland, U.S. President Franklin Roosevelt and British prime minister Winston Churchill put to paper their common aims, summarized in the Atlantic Charter. It included the liberation and self-government of currently occupied nations, equal access to trade and raw materials, the "destruction of Nazi tyranny," and a just peace where all nations could live safely and without fear. Great Britain and the United States declared no interest in territorial conquest and maintained that no territorial changes should be made that were contrary to the wishes of the people affected. The Charter contained ideas for a future security system that might help prevent future wars by disarming aggressors. Reflecting the parties' hopes for a better future, it is reminiscent of President Woodrow Wilson's Fourteen Points, articulated at the end of World War I. The meeting between Roosevelt and Churchill occurred in August 1941, when the United States had not yet entered the war but was helping the British war effort with loans and material support. After the Japanese attack on Pearl Harbor in December, though, the United States joined the worldwide conflict and mobilized all its forces.[5] Burdened by these pressing concerns, the question of how to deal with Nazi leaders and Axis war criminals once the war ended was not a priority at first. Yet as news about Nazi atrocities spread, the Allies' attention increasingly shifted back to such considerations.

A particularly crucial event occurred in the small Czech town of Lidice in June 1942, just 20 kilometers away from the Czech capital of Prague. During a Holocaust conference in 2023, I took the opportunity to tour Lidice and Theresienstadt—both places infamous for Nazi terror in that part of Central Europe. What left a deep impression on me was what was not evident in Lidice: the old town, which no longer exists. It was wiped out by the SS as a reprisal against the Czech resistance that had, with the help of British intelligence, successfully assassinated the "Butcher of Prague" Reinhard Heydrich, second in command in the SS hierarchy.

When Nazi forces rolled into Lidice on the morning of June 10, 1942, they killed all the men and buried them in a mass grave. They gathered up the women and children to be deported. Few survived. The houses were burned and razed to the ground. Today, Lidice is a memorial town, with green fields, modest markers, and a small museum nearby. The total absence of the old town and its people instill immeasurable horror—at least, that is what I felt on that day in Lidice.[6] The Czechoslovakian government, which had fled to London, urged their British hosts to make sure these crimes and clear violations of international norms would not go unpunished. Churchill reportedly suggested bombing German towns as a reprisal, but this tactic never materialized.[7] Instead, the decision was made to document the Nazi atrocities systematically. Even as the atrocities grew in number and intensity, however, concrete preparations for trials or punishment were slow to emerge. Everyone's energies remained devoted to winning the war first.

More information about Nazi atrocities kept piling up, including mounting evidence of the systematic mass murder of Jews. In contrast with the pope, who remained very cautious even in the face of ample, first-hand information, the Allies spoke out clearly and publicly. In a joint public statement dated December 17, 1942, the Allied nations condemned the "bestial policy of cold-blooded extermination" of the Jews in Europe and warned the Nazi perpetrators and their collaborators that they would "not escape retribution" once the war was over. This powerful statement gained attention. However, the declaration provided little more than a promise of retribution. Actual Allied efforts to rescue Jews and other Nazi victims still trapped in Europe were initially minimal.[8]

In January 1943, at a meeting in Casablanca in then-French Morocco, Roosevelt and Churchill agreed on some key decisions: The war would continue, and the Allies would accept nothing less than unconditional surrender from Germany, Japan, and Italy. These nations' war powers needed to be undermined completely and their current regimes ousted. In other words, the Allies would not broker negotiated peace agreements with the Nazis or any other Axis power. Hitler, Benito Mussolini, and the Japanese Emperor Hirohito had to be removed. When Churchill and Roosevelt met later that year, in Quebec City in August, they also seemed to agree on a plan for the summary execution of top Nazi leaders. But this question took up little space in their meeting; they still had a war to fight, and the Axis had not yet been defeated.

Once Allied forces landed in Sicily, however, prompting the surrender of Italy in September 1943, the defeat of Nazi Germany seemed like only a matter of time, and more time and resources gradually were directed to postwar planning. An early, concrete step toward the Nuremberg trials came in October 1943, with the creation of the United Nations War Crimes Commission (UNWCC), which was tasked explicitly with collecting evidence and preparing for trials. Shortly after its creation on October 26, the UNWCC met in London, though without any Soviet participation. The lawyers and diplomats in attendance initially focused on war crimes in a narrow sense, that is, crimes that violated the Geneva or Hague Conventions. These conventions had regulated warfare since the nineteenth century, and they defined tactics such as killing, torture, or depriving prisoners of war (POWs) of life's necessities as war crimes. These protections for wounded soldiers and POWs had been extended in 1929.[9] But the protections largely apply to soldiers, not civilians, and the conventions seemed outdated in light of the "total war" the Nazis waged against overwhelmingly civilian victims.[10]

On November 1, 1943, shortly after the first meeting of the UNWCC and immediately following the Moscow Conference of foreign ministers, the Allies declared their joint intention to try perpetrators in the places where they committed their crimes. They reached no decision on how to deal with the top Nazi leaders whose crimes could not be attributed to any single country, but they affirmed their intention to punish them. The Moscow Declaration represented a stark warning to the Axis perpetrators:

> Let those who have hitherto not imbrued their hands with innocent blood beware lest they join the ranks of the guilty, for most assuredly the three allied Powers will pursue them to the uttermost ends of the earth and will deliver them to their accusers in order that justice may be done. The above declaration is without prejudice to the case of the major criminals, whose offences have no particular geographical localization and who will be punished by the joint decision of the Governments of the Allies.[11]

The Allies were making it clear that no war criminal would be let off the hook, regardless of the legal challenge associated with international or non-localizable crimes.

When Roosevelt, Churchill, and Josef Stalin met for the first time in person in Tehran in late November 1943, they made some further critical decisions. Stalin promised to join the war against Japan once the war in Europe was over. The Western Allies promised to open a major second front in Europe, attacking Germany from the West. They also agreed that Germany should never again be allowed to raise a military power that could threaten world peace. During one dinner, Stalin was in high spirits and suggested that the program for weakening Germany for good should include the execution of 50,000–100,000 German officers. The violent recommendation reportedly made Stalin's British and American dinner partners uneasy, uncertain if the dictator was serious or not. Stalin had executed thousands of his own officers in the 1930s purge and would likely not have hesitated to shoot thousands of his captured enemies. Roosevelt "jokingly said that he would put the figure of the German Commanding Staff which should be executed at 49,000 or more," according to the minutes of the meeting. Churchill strongly rejected the idea of summarily executing soldiers who had done their duty and followed orders, but he believed Nazi war criminals needed to be punished for their barbarous acts.[12] Even if Churchill rejected mass executions on that occasion, it did not mean the British opposed shooting some number of Nazi leaders instead of granting them trials.

Stalin's radical suggestions also seemingly echoed the dramatic reality unfolding in the Soviet Union. The country had faced the Nazi onslaught since June 1941, and vast areas of its territories had been conquered by Nazi forces and their allies. The German occupation was brutal, showing no respect for international norms. Hitler made clear early on that the war in the East would be different—a total war, a racial war, a war of extermination against "the enemy." Soviet POWs died in vast numbers in German captivity, having been systematically starved or left without shelter in harsh weather conditions, in clear violations of international agreements. But it was not only Soviet soldiers who were deliberately killed; Soviet civilians suffered tremendously too. During the war, an estimated 27 million Soviets were killed, the highest death toll of any nation in World War II (with the possible exception of China), and most of the casualties were civilians. To offer some perspective, the United

States suffered 400,000 casualties, nearly all of whom were members of the military. Citing the atrocious crimes committed on its soil, against its people, the Soviet Union demanded retribution. It wanted punishment by an international court and mandates that would outlaw aggressive war as a "crime against peace." Considering this view, it is not surprising that Moscow initially played a very active role in rewriting the legal norms for warfare.[13]

Stalin made clear the kind of trial he had in mind, in the form of an initial public war crimes trial of German criminals that the Soviets organized.[14] The first war crimes trial unfolded at the Kharkov Theatre in December 1943, with 6,000 people in attendance. Three German *Einsatzkommando* officers and one Soviet collaborator were found guilty and publicly hanged. Their corpses remained on display for days. The men accused were likely complicit in the murder of thousands of civilians (most of them Jews), but the judgments appeared preordained, and the defense counsel was strictly restrained. Still, Stalin's propaganda depicted the trial as a victory for justice, and he ensured that it was widely covered by filming the trial and inviting Western journalists to observe the proceedings.[15] In justifying these trials, the Soviets explicitly cited the Moscow Declaration, which as noted previously, required that Axis soldiers involved in atrocities be judged in the countries where they had committed their crimes.[16]

Around the same time, Roosevelt came under increased pressure to articulate some basic guidelines for postwar policies on Germany. In answer, his 1943 Christmas message tried to speak to the moment. The United Nations had no intention of enslaving the German people, Roosevelt said, and the United States wanted Germany to grow in peace, as a useful and respectful member of the community of European nations. Germans deserved to live in peace, he said, but he also made clear that the Allies would strip them "once and for all" of Nazism, militarism, and racism. The President, and by extension the American people, rejected the "idea of a master race doctrine" in which the powerful should dominate the weak.[17] What Roosevelt did not mention was the deep-seated racism and antisemitism among many Americans, and the reality of Jim Crow laws for racial segregation in the American South.

When German troops marched into its former Axis ally Hungary and started to deport the country's Jews in March 1944, Roosevelt followed up his Christmas message with another powerful public statement. On March 24, he openly denounced the murder of European Jews and defined their slaughter as one of the darkest crimes in all of history. In turn, he underlined the determination of the United States to bring the leaders and their conspirators to justice, not just in Germany but in all Axis countries: "It is therefore fitting that we should again proclaim our determination that none who participate in these acts of savagery shall go unpunished."[18]

PLANS FOR PUNISHMENT

By the summer of 1944, various branches of Roosevelt's government had begun detailing plans to ensure that the perpetrators would not escape punishment. George Kennan, the U.S. diplomat who later articulated the Cold War containment strategy, suggested that the top Nazi leaders should be executed on the spot. For him and others, legal formalities seemed out of place.[19] Henry Morgenthau Jr., the U.S. Secretary of the Treasury, proposed a radical and harsh treatment for Germans, reflecting concepts of collective guilt and responsibility.[20] Morgenthau was a secular Jew, and by 1944, he was deeply engaged in protecting the remaining Jewish population in Europe. Through his efforts to help Jews trapped in Axis-controlled Europe, he knew better than most the massive extent of Nazi crimes.[21] Beyond punishing just the Nazi war criminals, Morgenthau argued that Germany as a whole had to pay a high price. For him, an appropriate solution would be to return Germany to an agricultural state without access to heavy industry, such that it arguably would be incapable of ever starting another war. Morgenthau also called for German POWs to be used as laborers to rebuild Europe.[22] Nazi leaders were to be executed without trial, and only "small-fry" Nazis would be subject to judgment by "military commissions."[23]

Morgenthau's ideas sparked resistance. Secretary of War Henry L. Stimson was convinced that his plan would be disastrous for the reconstruction and future stability of Europe, so he called instead for Nazi criminals to be brought to trial and suggested leveraging German industry to rebuild Europe. This stance rejected the idea of Germans' collective guilt and specifically cited the importance of a prosperous Germany for Europe. Stimson's and Morgenthau's ideas represented a diametric contrast within the same government administration. Although Roosevelt initially leaned toward Morgenthau's ideas, he eventually gave in to more moderate voices. Ultimately, it was Stimson's perspective that dominated the approach, thereby "setting the course for the elaboration of an entirely different American approach to Nazi war criminals"[24] and opening the way for the War Department to develop a strategy to prosecute Nazi war criminals.

In addition to indicting for war crimes, legal experts on Roosevelt's team, together with the Soviets, proposed adding indictments for any "conspiracy to commit aggressive war," as outlawed by the Kellog-Briand Peace Pact of 1928. Within this framework, starting a war is a crime. But the Kellogg-Briand Pact did not specify any sanctions for violators, so many experts remained unconvinced by this legal strategy. The British worried that trials of major criminals, such as Hitler and Goebbels, would be unpractical and potentially create a dangerous forum for them to spew Nazi propaganda. A memorandum by the British Lord Chancellor Sir John Simon, dated September 4, 1944, neatly illustrates the British view:

> It is much to be hoped that the principal criminals may, before the end, be disposed of by the people whom they have led to destruction, or may take their own lives—but if they fall alive into the hands of the Allies, what is to be done with them? I am strongly of the opinion that the method of trial, conviction, and judicial sentence is quite inappropriate for notorious ringleaders such as Hitler, Himmler, Göring, Goebbels and Ribbentrop. Apart from the formidable difficulties of constituting the Court, formulating the charge, and assembling the evidence, the question of their fate *is a political, not a judicial, question.*[25]

For Sir Simon, "how they [were] to be disposed of" was a question that would be completely up to Allied discretion.[26]

Despite such uncertainty and conflicting views, though, U.S. planners translated the basic guidelines into a concrete instructional handbook that applied at least to second- and third-tier Nazi criminals. By the fall of 1944, the U.S. War Department's *Handbook for Military Government in Germany* made clear who would be subject to automatic arrest and then screening for war crimes: members of the Gestapo and the SS, police officers, officers of the *Waffen* SS, functionaries of the Nazi Party of the rank *Ortsgruppenleiter* and above and other regional and local officials of the Nazi state. The War

Department anticipated that these different categories would apply to more than 220,000 Nazi officials who would need to be arrested and interned. What would be done with them after their arrest and internment was left unsaid. Organizing and holding trials of 220,000 individuals was not a realistic goal, but it also seemed nearly impossible to draw clear lines among them.[27] The Americans proposed that introducing a conspiracy doctrine would make prosecution easier. According to this doctrine, once a court determined that a Nazi organization was criminal, the prosecution only needed to demonstrate that a person had been a member of that organization to establish legal guilt.[28]

Punishing Axis collaborators seemed less controversial. Their respective national governments would have to deal with them after the war. Yet their treatment deserves special mention; the Axis allies of Nazi Germany are often overlooked. Hungary was a close ally of Nazi Germany, as was Romania, and both nations sent large military forces to fight alongside the German Wehrmacht and against the Soviet Union. Both governments also were deeply complicit in the Holocaust. Puppet states and regimes led Croatia, Slovakia, and Norway, to name a few. As this list implies, there was no shortage of Nazi collaborators, recruited from the pool of fascists that spread across many nations. I highlight this point as a reminder of a basic but often overlooked fact: Not all Germans were Nazis, and not all Nazis were German. Nazism came in many languages. And Fascism was popular in many European countries and even in the Americas throughout the 1930s.

The outcomes for Nazi collaborators varied. The name of the Norwegian fascist leader Vidkun Quisling lives on as a synonym for a traitor or collaborator, but the man himself was executed by the postwar Norwegian government, as were many other quislings. Others got away, like the fascist leader Ante Pavelić of Croatia. As we know, many Nazis escaped postwar punishment through various means. For the Soviet Union, fleeing Nazi collaborators created a particular issue; in contrast with the situation in Britain or the United States, large numbers of Soviet citizens had sided with Nazi forces, for various reasons.

In February 1945, Roosevelt, Stalin, and Churchill met again, in the spa town of Yalta in Crimea, a meeting that produced far-reaching decisions. Stalin pushed for Soviet influence over Poland; the Soviet dictator reaffirmed his promise to declare war on Japan. The treatment of Germany was discussed widely. After the Allied victory, they agreed that the central German government would cease to exist, the country would suffer large territorial cuts in its Eastern part, and it would pay substantial reparations. The defeated nation was to be divided into occupation zones and run by the main three Allies, with their junior partner, France, added later. Despite its occupation by the Allies, Germany would remain one economic unit. The Big Three leaders, which included a seriously ill Roosevelt at that point, agreed to judge all Axis criminals after the war in Europe.[29] The idea of some type of trial of surviving Nazi leaders was accepted as a possibility. After Yalta, White House advisor Samuel Rosenman also went to London to discuss details of a possible military trial.

President Roosevelt died on April 12, 1945, while Soviet forces were closing in on Berlin and Hitler was ranting in his bunker. Weeks later, Roosevelt's successor Harry S. Truman arrived with a large delegation to San Francisco, where Allied representatives were hammering out the last details of the charter for the United Nations, designed to ensure future peace. In parallel, some participants regarded the war crimes trials as another way to contribute to future peace.[30] These considerations are critical; the policies towards vanquished enemies can either contribute to a durable peace or trigger new conflicts.[31] As demonstrated by current events and recent cases, such as in Afghanistan, Libya, Syria, and Gaza, we still lack any easy recipe for how to achieve lasting, stable peace following conflict and war. Still, when the Nazi forces in Berlin surrendered on May 2, Truman grabbed the opportunity to finalize postwar plans. Without checking with his allies, he told the gathered international press in San Francisco about the creation of an international military tribunal for top Nazi leaders.[32]

In the same press conference, Truman announced his appointment of Robert H. Jackson to represent the United States as chief prosecutor, making him the main figure in the U.S. effort at Nuremberg.[33] This prosecutorial pick and decision to announce the tribunal without approval from the other Allies did not sit well with Stalin or ease any of the growing tensions with the Soviets. Justice Jackson was a Democrat who had worked for the Roosevelt Administration since the 1930s and been named to the Supreme Court in 1941. Michael Marrus describes him in this way: "Dignified, brilliant, and capable of masterful oratory, Jackson was also an erratic performer, hot-tempered, and suffering, perhaps, from a streak of insecurity."[34] Within a matter of weeks,

Jackson formed his team, which went to work further on a detailed and practical plan for organizing the trial. In a report to President Truman dated June 6, 1945, Jackson described his tireless efforts to meet the tight deadline, such that he

> worked out a plan for preparation, briefing, and trial of the cases; allocated the work among the several agencies; instructed those engaged in collecting or processing evidence; visited the European Theater to expedite the examination of captured documents, and the interrogation of witnesses and prisoners; coordinated our preparation of the main case with preparation by Judge Advocates of many cases not included in my responsibilities; and arranged co-operation and mutual assistance with the United Nations War Crimes Commission and with Counsel appointed to represent the United Kingdom in the joint prosecution.[35]

Jackson's report was widely published and read—including by Pope Pius XII.

Notably, Jackson rejected a Soviet-style "show trial." He regarded the rule of law as non-negotiable for the planned trial. If someone appeared before the court whose guilt could not be proven, the court must be prepared to declare them not guilty. The war crimes trials could function to punish culprits, but they could not—nor could any other type of criminal proceeding—undo the massive crimes committed or the damages they inflicted.[36] No trial could bring back the millions of people killed or redress the suffering of millions more or reverse the immense material destruction caused by Hitler's war. The past could not be changed.

However, future aggressors might be deterred, and Jackson's stance was accordingly very forward-looking, even if also marked by some degree of wishful thinking. He believed that law must be universal, so that it would apply not only to Nazis but also to future violators of international law and, especially, potential perpetrators of aggressive war. Jackson was in many ways an idealist, as argued by German historian Annette Weinke. He wanted to use the trials to create an international peace order, based on universal principles of law and justice, and he was not alone in this desire. Various U.S. politicians and public figures described a vision of a *Pax Americana* for the world, in language often imbued with "a missionary rhetoric."[37] The Nuremberg trials were largely a

U.S. undertaking, driven by American initiative, personnel, and resources. Jackson was well aware of this influence, and for the sake of appearances and to assure British support, he later proposed that a British judge should preside over the trial, instead of an American one.[38]

As much as he was forward-looking, for Jackson and other Allied planners, the lessons of the first "war to end all wars" loomed large. In the early days of World War I, German forces had shot several thousand civilian hostages in France and Belgium, as "reprisals."[39] Following their victory in World War I, these allies compiled lists of German war criminals and considered putting the German Kaiser to an international trial. Ultimately, they pressured the German state to take on the responsibility for judging some German nationals who had engaged in war crimes. The *Reichsgericht* (Germany's Supreme Court) in Leipzig held just 17 trials, of which 10 resulted in (prison) sentences. The rest of the defendants were acquitted. Preliminary proceedings in hundreds of other cases went nowhere. The trials were widely considered a fiasco at the time, and as lessons for the future, they indicated that the Germans were not willing to judge themselves.[40] But these proceedings also reflect more general questions about what happens when national courts are expected to judge their own citizens and soldiers for war crimes. Arguably, such a scenario makes the trial a matter of military, personal, and national honor, as much as anything else. In Germany, the Leipzig trials came to be viewed as a form of victors' revenge, much like the harsh Treaty of Versailles.

With these lessons from history clearly in mind, the Allies determined that after World War II, there could be no escape from punishment or the judgments of history for the Germans. The German nation had to face the full extent of the crimes committed in its name. To achieve this goal, and to avoid a repetition of similar mistakes, the Allies would hold these trials.

In a meeting at Cecilienhof Castle in Potsdam, near Berlin, on August 1, 1945, the future of the international tribunal hung in the balance, especially in relation to the Soviets' participation. Stalin, Truman, and Churchill (later replaced at the Potsdam meeting by Clement Attlee) again discussed the postwar borders of Europe and the treatment of a defeated Germany. On two points, they readily agreed: Germany should never again be in a position to wage another world war, and the failures of Versailles after World War I should not be repeated. The Allies also concurred on five Ds: demilitarization, denazification, democratization, decentralization, and deindustrialization. Despite such demonstrations of unity, the leaders did not agree on *how* to implement these principles. Democratization, for example, meant something very different for Stalin than it did for Truman. Similar differences in interpretations applied to the other four principles as well. Their different perspectives became clearer as Stalin strengthened his grip over Poland, and the Allied joint administration of occupied Germany proved increasingly unrealistic. Yet the Allies eventually agreed, in a communique, to hold a joint international tribunal for the main German war criminals and to do so as soon as possible.

FIREWALLS AGAINST BARBARITY

Following extensive discussion and disagreement, on August 8, 1945, U.S., Soviet, British, and French representatives signed an agreement "for the prosecution and punishment of the major war criminals of the European Axis."[41] Legal scholars declared and defined the main crimes that fell within the court's jurisdiction. Although "war crimes" were well established as violations of the international treaties that had regulated the basic rules of warfare since the nineteenth century, the indictments contained some novel international law concepts, including "crimes against peace" and "crimes against humanity," norms that were first introduced in the context of Nuremberg. In detail, "crimes against humanity" referred to deporting, enslaving, and killing civilians, and "crimes against peace" covered wars of aggression. Both are now criminalized by the international community.[42] The Americans, under Jackson's leadership, also introduced the conspiracy concept, formalized as follows in the charter of the trials: "Leaders, organizers, instigators, and accomplices participating in the formulation or execution of a common plan or conspiracy to commit any of the foregoing crimes are responsible for all acts performed by any person in execution of such plan."[43] Jackson focused on the conspiracy charge, using it to link the various allegations and to include prewar violations such as Germany's annexation of Austria and the takeover of Czechoslovakia.

In addition to Jackson, Jewish jurists and refugees, including Hersch Lauterpacht and Raphael Lemkin, contributed to introducing these novel, and enduring, legal concepts. British scholar Philippe Sands offers a detailed history of these men and their work in his brilliant book *East West Street*.[44] Briefly, Lauterpacht grew up and started law school in Lemberg, in the Province of Galicia at the eastern corner of the Austro-Hungarian Empire (now the western Ukrainian city of Lviv). He received law degrees after studying under Hans Kelsen at the University of Vienna. Lemkin's origins instead involved the Russian Empire, in what is Belarus today. He received his law degree in Lemberg, in 1926. Both men lost family members in the Holocaust.

Lauterpacht, with others, made crimes against humanity a major principle in Nuremberg, and this contribution prevailed in the legal discourse. Lemkin instead argued that the systematic mass murder of Jews was "genocide," and though the term was used in court a few times, it was absent from the final Nuremberg judgments.[45] Still, the crime of genocide came to be introduced into international law after the Nuremberg trials, and in 1948, the United Nations issued the "Convention on the Prevention and Punishment of the Crime of Genocide," which defines genocide as

> any of the following acts committed with intent to destroy, in whole or in part, a national, ethnical, racial or religious group, as such: (a) Killing members of the group; (b) Causing serious bodily or mental harm to members of the group; (c) Deliberately inflicting on the group conditions of life calculated to bring about its physical destruction in whole or in part; (d) Imposing measures intended to prevent births within the group; (e) Forcibly transferring children of the group to another group.[46]

Lemkin's perspective suggested an even wider definition of genocide, to include cultural dimensions as well.

The introduction of these new crimes and legal concepts marked clear expansion in international law. However, the concepts also challenged long-established traditions of legality. Some of them arguably conflicted with basic principles of Western law, such as *nullum crimen sine lege* and no *ex post facto* laws—that is, the assertions that no crime can be punished without a previously existing law and that no retroactive law can be applied. According to these legal standards, people should not be punished for a deed that was not criminal, by law, at the time the deed was committed. This principle remains in force as part of the constitutional law of many Western democracies (e.g.,

Art. 103 Abs. 2 of the German Constitution, the *Grundgesetz*). By challenging, arguably, these principles, Nuremberg raised questions; defense lawyers especially criticized its ethics on this basis.[47] A similar judicial tension arose in 1989, surrounding the historically comparable controversy following the fall of the Berlin Wall. In this case, the ethical and legal challenges revolved around how to persecute killings committed by members of East German security forces at the intra-German border. These questions ultimately were resolved by the German Constitutional Court, in favor of the victims.[48]

As such considerations make clear, "Crimes against humanity was the most innovative and controversial of the three counts," according to historian Elizabeth Borgwardt, but the new legal concept also revealed the tenuous moral accountability offered by postwar justice.[49] Furthermore, prosecutors did not apply the crimes against humanity indictment to crimes by the Nazi government against German Jews in the 1930s, that is, to crimes against Germany's own citizens. Doing so arguably could have set a precedent for legal action in other countries with oppressed minorities, something the Allies wanted to avoid.[50]

Legal norms were not the only controversial element of the Nuremberg trials. Some think that the participation of Soviet judges and prosecutors undermined its moral authority.[51] Even if we could ignore the criminal nature of Stalin's dictatorship—which offers enough evidence of Soviet moral hypocrisy—a specific critique of Soviet participation in the tribunals arises from the crimes against peace and war crimes that the Soviets committed during World War II. Both Nazi Germany and the Soviet Union attacked Poland in 1939, one from the west, the other from the east, and these actions represented the primary catalyst of World War II in Europe. Following Poland's defeat, the Soviets and the Nazis divided up the once-sovereign, conquered nation. When defense lawyers for the Nazi Foreign Minister Joachim von Ribbentrop raised these questions and challenges during his trial at Nuremberg, it deeply embarrassed the Soviets.[52]

And then there was Katyn. The Soviets massacred thousands of Polish POWs, officers, and police in the forests around Katyn in 1940. The massacres constituted an obvious war crime, even by traditional legal standards. The Soviets falsely blamed the atrocities on Nazi forces.[53] The British and Americans worked to keep mentions of the Katyn massacre out of the indictment, apparently because they knew that the Soviets had perpetrated the crime. In the end, the Soviets failed at Nuremberg to pin the murder of Polish officers in Katyn on the Germans, at least officially. And to this day, Katyn has not been forgotten in Poland. Its memory contributes to the deep animosity between that country and Russia.

JUDGMENT IN NUREMBERG

Beyond such ethical and moral challenges, the Nuremberg Charter also had to overcome political and legal difficulties. Its promoters had to protect their Allied counterparts but still serve justice, and do so under new legal standards. Some of Stalin's crimes, such as mass starvations in Ukraine, gulags, and mass executions in the Soviet Union and Poland in the 1930s and 1940s, qualified as crimes against humanity under the new standards. Even outside the Soviet Union, we find ethically and legally questionable actions, including mass bombings of civilian targets and cities. Debates that persist even today include convincing arguments that indiscriminate bombing is a war crime. Plenty of other actions could be considered crimes too. The French military massacred an estimated 40,000 Algerian rebels in May 1945 but never was held responsible for it.[54] In their efforts to keep the focus on Nazi crimes and criminals, prosecutors limited any discussions of Allied violations of international law as much as possible,[55] choices that provided the bases to criticize the trials as simply an exercise in "victors' justice."

Those leading the Nuremberg trials also wrestled with choosing which Nazi leaders to prosecute. By the end of the war, the Allies had arrested hundreds of top Nazis; few were able to hide for long. Hitler, Himmler, and Goebbels would have been obvious picks, but they had cheated justice through suicide.[56] Practical constraints, including limited seating in the small courtroom, time, and judicial resources, meant that some top Nazis would be brought to trial, but others were not. The selection process also was subject to clear political considerations, such as when certain criminals were spared prosecution because they were deemed useful to the Allies.[57] The International Military Tribunal eventually selected 24 German and Austrian individuals for prosecution, including infamous figures like Hermann Göring, Joachim van Ribbentrop, and Martin Bormann (tried in absentia; as it later turned out, he had been dead since May 1945).[58] More people were charged in later trials, but in total, they represented only a very small selection of Nazi perpetrators.[59] In this sense, according to one scholar, Nuremberg represented a form of "symbolic justice for all victims" by punishing a few top leaders.[60]

Another crucial decision involved the location of the trials. The city of Nuremberg was chosen for several reasons. The city's court building had a prison that had survived the Allied bombing largely intact. Nuremberg also was located in the U.S. occupation zone of Germany. Last but certainly fittingly, Nuremberg had hosted annual Nazi Party rallies, so it held symbolic meaning.[61] Nazi history would end in defeat and disgrace in the same place it had once celebrated its biggest triumphs.

Even with all these controversies and challenges, the Nuremberg Charter ultimately was signed on August 8, 1945. On November 21, Robert Jackson's big moment arrived: He delivered the memorable opening statement to the trials, a speech that would go down in history. Reflecting his roles as both a chief prosecutor at Nuremberg and a justice of the U.S. Supreme Court, he emphasized the pursuit of justice, not revenge, as an imperative for the historic trial: "That four great nations, flushed with victory and stung with injury, stay the hand of vengeance and voluntarily submit their captive enemies to the judgment of the law is one of the most significant tributes that power has ever paid to reason." These iconic opening sentences capture Jackson's sense of the importance of the trials. The opening statement also clearly resisted the idea of German collective guilt, with the statement, "We would also make clear that we have no purpose to incriminate the whole German people." Jackson carefully distinguished German militarists and reactionaries from the mass of the ordinary German people. He cited the many Germans who had opposed the Nazi regime and paid a price for their opposition, including their imprisonment in early concentration camps like Dachau. In this way, Jackson defined Germans—resisters, Jews, and other targeted minorities—as among the first victims of the Nazi regime, a notion, as we will see, very much in line with the pope's beliefs.[62] Finally, Jackson sought for Nuremberg to set an important precedent that would improve the world: "We must never forget that the record on which we judge these defendants is the record on which history will judge us tomorrow. To pass these defendants a poisoned chalice is to put it to our lips as well."[63] These powerful words clearly were written with a deep sense of history. "In my opinion," wrote U.S. prosecutor Telford Taylor in his memoirs, "nothing said at Nuremberg thereafter matched [the opening statement's] force, perception, and eloquence."[64]

Jackson's profound awareness of the historical moment came not just from his judicial background but also his careful investigation of Nazi atrocities, which triggered his deep reflections about humanity. In another speech, Jackson addressed the monumental nature of the crimes, which served to shatter any naïve belief in human progress or Western superiority:

> It is common to think of our own time as standing at the apex of civilization from which the deficiencies of preceding ages may patronizingly be viewed in the light of what is assumed to be progress. The reality is that in the long perspective of history the present century will not hold an enviable position unless the second half is to redeem its first.[65]

Jackson seemed committed to doing his part in this redemption effort. Thomas J. Dodd, who became the leading counsel on Jackson's prosecution team, wrote to his wife Grace from Nuremberg and reflected this religiously informed view:

> Grace my dearest one . . . I feel that we are doing something so important that it is awesome—it is almost purifying, it has a deep religious meaning, of that I feel certain. Surely it is God's wish that men not wage wars of aggression. The proof here is absolutely overwhelming. I would never have believed that men could be so evil, so determined on a course of war; of murder; of slavery; of dreadful tyranny. Never before has such a record been written and men will read it for a thousand years in amazement and wonder how it ever happened.[66]

Beyond its existential weight and historic gravitas, the practical demands of the International Nuremberg Tribunal also were massive and unprecedented.[67] In just one year, it featured 403 open sessions, involving 94 witnesses who spoke in the courtroom (61 for the defense and 33 for the prosecution), as well as thousands of documents.[68] As these numbers indicate, the trial relied largely on documents, and witnesses had a lesser role. The Vatican archives include an impressive photo of the Nuremberg courtroom, from a bird's-eye perspective, showing the defendants in the dock, their lawyers, the prosecution, and the audience. But even more noteworthy are the massive piles of papers in front of the lawyers, staff, and defendants.[69]

Much of this written evidence came from seized German records, so the descriptions of events in court often reflected the perpetrators' perspective. Following the trials closely, Jewish communities across Europe, the Americas, and Palestine/Israel insisted that more attention be granted to the victims, their experiences, and their demands. One way to achieve such insights, Jewish leaders suggested, would have been by introducing more survivor statements.[70]

Instead, the prosecution showed documentary films as evidence—a novel tactic for such proceedings, which left a lasting impact. Some of the indelible scenes—such as video of a bulldozer in Bergen-Belsen moving mountains of corpses into mass graves—became "icons of extermination."[71] The Allies made most of these films, in April and May 1945, during the liberation of the concentration camps. For Jackson, these powerful media also offered a way to attain the Allied goal of re-educating the German people, in accordance with the principles agreed to at Potsdam: demilitarization, denazification, democratization, decentralization, and deindustrialization. In this context, the British historian Richard Evans effectively summarizes Jackson's aims for Nuremberg: "It was as much a means of public education in Germany as an instrument of justice in the world community."[72]

By turning the courtroom into a public forum for education, the Allied prosecution sought not only to deliver justice but also to expose the conditions that had precipitated the downfall of a major Western society.[73] The Allies believed that the Germans had committed horrible crimes and betrayed Western standards, but that they could be reformed, such that "The very notion of a fair trial was based on the idea that Germany was *not* beyond reform, that Germans *could* learn from the Allies and improve on their historical record."[74] The trial also created an important (albeit misleading) postwar distinction: The SS was declared a criminal organization, but the German army (Wehrmacht) was not.[75] This distinction laid one foundation for the myth that the Wehrmacht had nothing to do with the Holocaust. In turn, millions of German men who had served in the Wehrmacht got essentially a legal and moral free pass for decades to come.

The trials included some focus on the murder of an estimated 6 million European Jews, yet it was not actually the center of attention. The full nature of the Holocaust had not yet entered the consciousness of the world. But the trial revealed details underlying the Nazis' murder program, such as the names of many key perpetrators. Adolf Eichmann's name repeatedly appeared during the proceedings and even in the final judgment. Citing his culpability, members of the World Jewish Congress urged Jackson to put Eichmann on trial too; close observers already had identified him as a key organizer of the Holocaust.[76] But Eichmann, believed by the Allies to be dead, actually was on the loose, hiding under a false name, and carefully watching the proceedings while his role in the mass murder program was mentioned.

Those who stood accused in person showed little remorse. They all pleaded not guilty. The Nazi defendants claimed that they had played small roles and had no knowledge of the crimes. They assigned most of the blame to Hitler, Himmler, and Goebbels—all of whom were conveniently dead. Hermann Göring, second in command in the Third Reich, claimed to be appalled when presented with the Germans' mass atrocities; he condemned them, while claiming personal ignorance. His lies were far from convincing, especially in the face of court documents that proved his deep involvement in the genocide. But with the possible exceptions of Rudolf Hess, whose mental health was dubious, and Julius Streicher, the only defendant designated mentally unstable, the men in the dock did not live up to the world's expectations of them. They were responsible for monstrous crimes, unheard of in world history, and yet the trial showed clearly that they were neither clinically insane nor two-headed monsters. The humans standing trial seemed incredibly small compared with the scope of the horrors they had unleashed.

Furthermore, three days after the trial began, the court required that all evidence be read aloud in the courtroom and translated, which significantly slowed down proceedings. As some journalists in attendance made clear, following the proceedings was frustrating—and not a little boring as well.[77] Away from the spotlight and in addition to the public demands of the courtroom, Jackson was carrying a heavy load. The nature and immense burden of the work—entailing the review of thousands of harrowing photographs of mass execution sites and numerous atrocity reports—must have weighed heavily on him.

After eight intense months of proceedings, Jackson made his closing remarks at Nuremberg in July 1946. In so doing, he seemingly mocked the once-powerful leaders of the Third Reich:

> These men saw no evil, spoke none, and none was uttered in their presence. This claim might sound very plausible if made by one defendant. But when we put all their stories together, the impression which emerges of the Third Reich, which was to last a thousand years, is ludicrous. If we combine only the stories of the front bench, this is the ridiculous composite picture of Hitler's Government that emerges. It was composed of: A No. 2 man [Göring] who knew nothing of the excesses of the Gestapo which he created, and never suspected the Jewish extermination program although he was the signer of over a score of decrees which instituted the persecution of that race; A No. 3 man [Hess] who was merely an innocent middleman transmitting Hitler's orders without even reading them, like a postman or delivery boy; A Foreign Minister [Ribbentrop] who knew little of foreign affairs and nothing of foreign policy; A Field-Marshal [Keitel] who issued orders to the armed forces but had no idea of the results they would have in practice. . . . If you were to say of these men that they are not guilty, it would be as true to say that there has been no war, there are no slain, there has been no crime.[78]

As this closing statement indicated, the accused never denied wholesale that crimes had been committed under Hitler's regime. They just denied any personal involvement in those crimes.[79] Göring's defense was notably strong, in that he spoke eloquently and highlighted an obvious shortcoming of the trial, namely, that no Soviet crimes were being prosecuted, including its war of aggression against Poland in 1939. Furthermore, Göring questioned why the prosecutors, judges, and executioners of the court hailed from the four main victorious powers, with no representatives from neutral nations. In his final statement on August 31, 1946, Göring rejected the idea of a Nazi conspiracy to commit crimes. He claimed instead that circumstantial events simply developed over time, all while denying knowledge of mass crimes, particularly genocide against Jews, asserting, "I stand up for the things that I have done, but I deny most emphatically that my actions were dictated by the desire to subjugate foreign peoples by wars, to murder them, to rob them, or to enslave them, or to commit atrocities or crimes."[80] All his protests were objectively weak, but this last claim totally collapses under historical scrutiny: Göring signed the order, given to SS leadership in the summer of 1941, to bring about "the final solution of the Jewish question."

The International Military Tribunal handed down sentences on September 30 and October 1, 1946. It took the entire first day to read the 50,000-word general judgment. Then on October 1, the judges moved to the individual verdicts and the trial's conclusion. Of the 22 accused (of the original 24, one took his own life and another was declared unfit to stand trial), 12 were sentenced to death (Göring, Ribbentrop, Rosenberg, Frick, Keitel, Jodl, Kaltenbrunner, Frank, Streicher, Sauckel, Seyss-Inquart, and, in absentia, Bormann). Three of the accused were sentenced to life in prison (Hess, Funk, Raeder), whereas others got limited prison sentences (Doenitz, Schirach, Speer, Neurath).[81] Von Papen, Schacht, and Fritzsche were acquitted.[82]

The final act concluded with the execution of 10 Nazi criminals on October 16, 1946. In the lead-up to the executions, security around the prison and the city of Nuremberg was significantly tightened, reflecting concerns about potential civil disturbances and rescue attempts. Some of these former Nazi leaders submitted clemency petitions, all of which were rejected. In their final days, the men were allowed to say goodbye to their families, often a traumatic experience, especially for their children. After they were given their last suppers, the executions started soon after midnight. Göring cheated the hangman by poisoning himself just hours before his scheduled execution. With Göring's body lying in the prison morgue, the other 10 convicted Nazi criminals were led to wooden gallows, which had been prepared days ahead in the gymnasium of the Nuremberg prison.[83] One after the other was hanged in short succession. By the early morning hours, it was over. The bodies were cremated and the ashes scattered into the Isar River.

CONCLUSION

Nuremberg represented a triumph of the rule of law and due process, an alternative to revenge killings or collective punishment. The Nuremberg trials were not perfect (as is true of similar war crimes tribunals), but they were much different—and arguably better—than previous attempts at just reckoning after war. Allied leaders had considered summary executions for not just the top Axis leaders but also thousands of state officials and military officers. For most of the war, the possibility of the Nuremberg trials was not at all certain. They ultimately resulted from circumstances and the insistence of a few visionaries like Justice Robert Jackson, and in turn, they represent a critical moment in history, still studied today and still serving as a major inspiration.[84] Otto Kirchheimer, a German émigré and part of the wider Nuremberg think tank, was very aware that the International Nuremberg Tribunal would contribute to a new and better society through its capacity "to confirm the defeat of Hitlerism" by exposing the criminal nature of the regime, as well as by judging and assigning individual responsibility.[85] For Kirchheimer, the crimes were so immense that humanity could not move on without a reckoning. Nuremberg set a clear endpoint for the Nazi dictatorship. By documenting and publicizing the crimes, it also helped to discredit fascism and demonstrate that heads of state, even fascist ones, are not immune to punishment. They can be held responsible by the world community for their violations of basic international laws and norms.

In terms of its legacy, Nuremberg provided an inspiration for the International Criminal Tribunal for the former Yugoslavia, the International Criminal Tribunal for Rwanda, and the permanent establishment of the International Criminal Court (ICC).[86] Notably, all these tribunals were established in the early 1990s, after the end of the Cold War. During the course of the Cold War, international criminal justice remained mostly on ice. Arguably, Nuremberg was possible only because it happened so soon after the war, when the wartime Allies were still allies, a period that Jeffrey Herf has called "the brief Nuremberg interregnum between the end of the war and the crystallization of the Cold War."[87]

For all the international attention it drew at the time and its continued historical importance today, for both its discourses about jurisprudence and its exemplification of societal efforts to achieve moral reckoning with war, there is surprisingly little consideration in the existing literature of the Vatican's response or the pope's stance on the issues raised by Nuremberg or similar trials. Yet as it turns out, Pope Pius XII was not silent when it came to issues of retributive justice in the form of war crimes trials. On the contrary, questions of war, peace, and justice deeply troubled the head of the Catholic

Church, which could claim 2,000 years of experience in societies struggling to move on after war and other forms of mass violence. Pius XII was a powerful player in his own right, serving as both a head of state and a religious leader, and he was determined to wield this power by making sure that the victors heard his voice, loud and clear. Even as most of the world decried Germany's crimes, Germany retained an influential friend and advocate in the "Vicar of Christ." Pope Pius XII's decision to remain one of the few allies Germany could count on reflected not only his own personal experiences, as we will see in the next chapter, but also the overarching goals that he adopted for the universal Catholic Church.

2

THE VICAR OF CHRIST

Pope Pius XII today is best known for his decisions and actions during the Holocaust and WWII. As we have seen, critics accuse Pius XII of maintaining public silence in the face of the Nazi genocide against European Jews. Others come to his defense, asserting that he actually took decisive actions to rescue Jews and other victims of the Nazis during those dark times. His biographer Robert Ventresca summarizes it well: "In death, much more so than in life, Pius XII has become an intensely polarizing figure—to some he is a venerable saint, and to others he is a damnable silent witness to unimaginable atrocities in the heart of Europe."[1] Regardless of whether people view Pius XII as morally virtuous or morally culpable, he remains a significant figure in history.

Millions of Catholics embraced Pius XII as the "Vicar of Christ"—a traditional papal title denoting the pope as Christ's deputy on Earth. This role confers immense moral authority, raising the standard by which papal actions are judged. That moral weight helps explain the enduring controversy surrounding Pius XII's legacy. Efforts to canonize him have only intensified the debate. The controversies surrounding his conduct during the Holocaust—expressed in numerous publications, public statements, and documentaries, and sometimes referred to as the "Pius Wars"—have been extensively documented. This book instead focuses on the broader arc of Pius XII's papacy (1939–1958), which extended well beyond WWII into the early Cold War. It is the first crucial postwar years, however, on which this book mainly zooms in. Before and during the war, Pius XII sought to navigate the era's dictatorships through neutrality and cautious diplomacy, while intervening on behalf of Catholics and other persecuted groups when possible. In assessing Pius XII's efforts in this regard, it is useful to have a sense of his personality and career up to 1945.

EUGENIO PACELLI

Pius XII was born Eugenio Pacelli on March 2, 1876, in the historic city center of Rome. The Pacelli family had served the pope and the Vatican for multiple generations; they were part of what has often been referred to as the "black nobility." These Italian families owed their careers to the papacy and were steadfast in their loyalty to the Catholic Church. Eugenio was born only a few years after the Papal States—which for centuries had comprised large parts of central Italy and the city of Rome—were forcefully occupied by Italian troops in 1870. The pope at the time famously referred to himself as a prisoner in the Vatican. The loss of worldly power by the pope was a serious blow for the Pacelli family, and it sparked their resentment toward the new Italian nation-state. Still, Eugenio grew up a proud Roman, comfortable in the stability of a middle-class family, and he would spend most of his life a stone's throw away from where he was born. As far as we know, he had a rather quiet childhood, typical of his peers.[2]

When it came to serving the Church, Eugenio's path was, in a sense, predetermined. He was a talented student and good athlete, and his deep religiosity manifested early. He shared his family's strong tradition of venerating Saint Mary, the mother of Jesus, which would become one of the central features of his pontificate. However, he eventually deviated from family tradition by choosing to serve the Church as a priest, rather than as a lawyer. In 1899, he was ordained, then pursued degrees in law, philosophy, and theology before being named a monsignor in 1904. His enormous personal discipline and dedication were evident from the start, and he received multiple diplomatic assignments.[3] After the Papal States were lost in 1870, the Holy See no longer held sovereign territory.

A brief history: the Papal States existed for centuries and comprised most of central Italy. The pope was both head of state and religious leader. The secular power of the pope was real, with his own army and an active interest in territory and power politics. The Papal States resembled one of the many principalities that existed on Italian territory. But the Italian unification changed that. However, even after the papacy lost its territories, it maintained diplomatic relations with major powers, such as the Austro-Hungarian Empire, Prussia, and France. The pope also preserved many of the ceremonial traditions of the papal court like coronation, audiences, etc., which continued to endure.[4] Vatican diplomats began promising permanent neutrality toward all nations and a role for the Holy See as a "peaceful sovereign" as early as the Congress of Vienna in 1815–16, which decided the European political order for decades. Over time, this function became a hallmark of the Holy See.

When World War I erupted—the deadliest military conflict the world had experienced up to that point, fueled by the widespread use of modern weapons like machine guns and tanks—it claimed the lives of millions. The wartime Pope Benedict XV (1914–22) became known as "the great neutral." He had just been elected to be the new "Supreme Pontiff," and he formally declared the Holy See's neutrality in the conflict. Practical considerations played a role, in that Catholics fought on both sides. Pope Benedict XV publicly prayed for peace and a quick end to the fighting; internally, he appeared to hope to serve an intermediary role in peace negotiations. For example, he intervened (albeit unsuccessfully) with the U.S. government to prevent the dissolution of the Austro-Hungarian Empire, though this intervention also may have reflected his own interests. Historian John F. Pollard highlights Pope Benedict XV's neutrality in response to accusations of war crimes committed by Russia and Germany: "To have pronounced one way or another on alleged war crimes could inevitably have compromised the Vatican's claims to neutrality and impartiality, so in public, Benedict limited himself to generic condemnations of all atrocities."[5] In efforts to appear neutral, and thereby potentially mediate a peace that would end the slaughter, the pope sent Eugenio Pacelli on peace missions to the Austrian emperor and the German kaiser, ultimately in vain.

In 1917, Pope Benedict XV had ordained Pacelli as bishop and sent him as his envoy (nuncio) to the Bavarian capital of Munich.[6] Bavaria, the Catholic heartland of Germany, eventually became Pacelli's second home. It was the only place he lived for any length of time apart from Rome, specifically in Munich; he later spent time in Berlin. It helped that Pacelli had a talent for languages and spoke German fairly well. German priests and nuns joined his staff, and some of them remained his closest advisors until his death. During his time in Munich, Pacelli connected closely with Michael Faulhaber, the city's powerful bishop. During his time in Germany, Pacelli became well known for his distinctive presence. Contemporary descriptions emphasize his tall, spare build and distinctive aquiline nose, often noting the round eyeglasses that contributed to an impression of distance and intellectual severity. At the same time, personal recollections complicate this image, recalling a man capable of warmth, approachability, and dry humor.[7]

The beginning of Pacelli's tenure as a nuncio coincided with a dramatic, chaotic moment in Germany's history. In November 1918, the German army collapsed, along with its empire. The Kaiser went into exile, and chaos reigned in the defeated nation. The newly born German Republic slipped into civil war-like violence, involving various political factions. Munich even was run briefly by two Soviet-style governments, and Kurt Eisner, a far-left leader, openly opposed the Catholic Church. At some juncture, Pacelli departed Munich for Switzerland, seeking refuge from the chaos and the threats to his safety, possibly in response to a warning from his friend Cardinal Faulhaber, who recognized the danger. Pacelli eventually returned, only to have his residence stormed by radical leftists from Munich. During the incident, Pacelli reportedly found himself at gunpoint, an episode that his friends and admirers frequently shared when recounting his life. In any case, these Munich experiences and interactions with Bolshevik revolutionaries left a deep impression on Pacelli,[8] as indicated by his expressed attitudes toward Kurt Eisner.[9]

Notably, Pacelli referred to Eisner as an Eastern European Jew, assigning him to a group often stereotyped by Central Europeans as uneducated, backward, and Yiddish-speaking (in contrast to "proper German" speakers, like German and Austrian Jews). Eisner was in fact not from Eastern Europe; he had been born in Berlin. Furthermore, Eisner's family had Jewish roots, but he was a secular socialist who did not identify with religious Judaism. Among the conservative elites, a bigoted and widespread view alleged that Bolshevist chaos was merely the front for a worldwide, active conspiracy of Jews pulling the strings. Citing several far-left leaders who actually were of Jewish descent was proof enough for right-wingers and antisemites to see Jews and Bolsheviks as one and the same. A widespread, antisemitic trope referred to "Judeo-Bolshevism" and, when applied to smear Eisner, portrayed him as a foreigner who was not and could never be part of the German nation.[10] Such depictions likely emboldened the far right-wing German extremist who murdered Eisner in February 1919. Antisemitism was rampant, and deep-seated fears of communism, in a context marked by deep unrest and chaos, created an ideal breeding ground in Munich for right-wing agitators, including a young Adolf Hitler.

As this tumultuous period subsided, Pacelli expressed apprehension about a harsh peace treaty that arguably could destabilize Germany. He held out hope for a genuine lasting peace, but the Treaty of Versailles ending World War I failed to achieve it. Instead, a sentiment of despair arose in Germany, which Pacelli feared could favor the resurgence of communism.[11] As he was acutely aware, a significant number of Germans resented the Treaty of Versailles for its perceived unfairness.[12] Many regarded it as a dictate of the victors, who unfairly and falsely put all the blame for World War I on Germany. Others even believed that Germany had been cheated out of its victory, "stabbed in the back" by Jews and communists. This persistent myth and resentment famously gave rise to radical revanchist and nationalist movements.

While communism failed to gain a lasting foothold in Germany, it briefly rose to prominence in Hungary and, very importantly, throughout the former Russian Empire. Bolshevik forces, led by Vladimir Lenin, emerged victorious in Russia's civil war, and by 1922, the Soviet Union had become a tangible reality. The biggest country on the European continent, in terms of landmass, was now dominated by a strongly anticlerical regime and its famous maxim (introduced by the German philosopher Karl Marx) that "Religion is the opium of the people." Communists decried organized religion as a tool that wealthy classes used to hold down farmers and workers. It thus should come as little surprise that Pacelli was strongly anti-communist. He regarded a united, strong, Christian Germany as a critical bulwark against the spread of communism toward Central and Western Europe—a conviction he maintained throughout his life.

Despite his bitter, first-hand experiences with Bolshevik revolutionaries, it appears that the Vatican called on Pacelli to find a *modus vivendi* with the newly established Soviet communist regime in Russia so that the Catholic Church could operate there. Pacelli attempted to pursue contacts with Russia in 1924. After an earlier unsuccessful effort to enter into direct talks—carried out under the guise of a Vatican Relief Mission to Russia in 1922–23 led by Monsignor Edmund Walsh of Georgetown University—it fell to Pacelli to explore another attempt. Pacelli himself did not travel to Russia, however, but instead negotiated indirectly through contacts in Germany. Pacelli's mission was delicate and important, as indicated by a letter of the Holy See, and its goal was to enable access to churches and to provide a bare minimum of religious assistance for Catholics in Russia.[13] These efforts were apparently part of a wider, long-term goal, namely, to bring Orthodox Christians closer to the Roman Catholic Church.

The Vatican also called for missionary work among Russian exiles in Germany and the education of priests for that purpose, such as at the Pontifical Oriental Institute in Rome. "The [Russian] souls have become receptive to the kind word of such a merciful mother, as the Roman Church would like to be towards this people especially," Pacelli stated in a letter to the German bishops.[14] To improve the situation of Catholics in Russia, Pacelli also used his connections to the German chancellor to intervene on behalf of the Vatican with the Soviet government.[15] Germany and the Soviet Union, both international pariahs at the time, worked together in several areas. Yet it seems that not much came of these talks. Instead, Soviet communism emerged as a powerful and challenging opponent to the Holy See.[16]

Back in Germany, the relationship between Church and state after the fall of the Kaiser had to be redefined and rebuilt. A new liberal democratic order in Germany prompted skepticism among the Catholic clergy towards the new democratic state, driving the bishops to work hard to safeguard the Church's interests. In a 1924 letter, the senior German bishop told Pacelli that Catholic politicians, representing centrist conservative Christian parties in Germany, were the most logical partners for the Church. Cardinal Adolf Bertram, archbishop of Breslau, claimed that German democracy and its constitution had serious shortcomings (likely in reference to its secular character) but that the Catholic politicians were trying their best, after the "overthrow" (*Umsturz*) of the monarchy, "to create a structure that is compatible with Christian principles."[17] He added that other political parties (likely meaning those on the left) supported media that "very often swims in anti-Church waters."[18] The resulting alliances between the Church and conservative Christian parties in Germany seemingly worked for a while.

As a nuncio in Berlin from 1925 to 1929, Pacelli witnessed these stable years. The Weimar Republic hosted the Roaring Twenties in Berlin, a city known for its rich cultural life, cabarets, clubs, theaters, and lively movie industry, so well captured in the German historical film drama *Babylon Berlin*. Pacelli, the monkish ascetic, was less interested in this side of Berlin; he focused on defending the interests of the Church in this key European capital. In his free time, however, he took genuine pleasure in living among Germans—conversing in their language, participating in daily life, and immersing himself in the rhythms of their culture. When he was recalled to Italy in 1929, he was not eager to leave Germany. As Monsignor Giovanni Montini, one of his future confidants, noted retrospectively, "the Holy Father left his heart in Germany."[19] There is much truth to this statement, yet duty called. Back in Rome, Pacelli began to serve as the Vatican's cardinal secretary of state, a powerful position that made him one of Pius XI's (pope from 1922 to 1939) closest collaborators.

While Pacelli was in Germany, though, Benito Mussolini, the leader of the Italian Fascist Party, had been appointed Italy's prime minister, in 1922. Fascism as a political force first emerged in Italy, then spread through similar movements elsewhere. Mussolini's fascism served as an early model for other aspiring nationalist dictators, including the younger Hitler. It was characterized by militarism, extreme nationalism (usually focused on ethnicity), machismo, racism, sexism, and the glorification of a strongman leader. *Il Duce* (Italian for "leader") sought to unify the nation under a dictatorship, with imperial ambitions. In his younger years before World War I, Mussolini was a vocal anti-clerical and atheist socialist, a background that created tensions with the Catholic Church when he became Italy's head of government. His rise to power as prime minister posed serious challenges in a country that was overwhelmingly Catholic. While nationalist movements in Italy—including Mussolini's—were largely secular and often hostile to the Church, many Italians remained practicing Catholics. As a result, citizens often sensed a dilemma, torn between their allegiance to the Catholic Church and their loyalty to the Italian state.

By 1929 though, the papacy had signed the Lateran Pacts with Mussolini's government. The agreement consisted of two parts: the Lateran Treaty, which addressed the status of the Vatican City state, and a concordat that regulated state–church affairs. The Pacts assigned compensation to the Church for its loss of territory in 1870; reestablished its status as an independent, sovereign state (Vatican City); and affirmed its permanent neutrality. Rather than a nation-state, the Vatican was established as a state administration, designed to provide a basis for the universal mission of the Church.[20] According to Article 24 of the Lateran Treaty, which created the Vatican city-state,

> The Holy See declares that it desires to take, and shall take, no part in any temporal rivalries between other states, nor in any international congresses called to settle such matters, save and except in the event of such parties making a mutual appeal to the pacific mission of the Holy See, the latter reserving in any event the right of exercising its moral and spiritual power.[21]

The exact meaning of this text is a matter of interpretation, but it indicated generally that, even if the Holy See was to be neutral in rivalries between states, it could take a stance on "moral and spiritual" matters. The neutral territory of Vatican City and its state bureaucracy provided a basis for this role. To be precise, the terms "Vatican" and "Holy See" are not identical. The Vatican refers to the city-state and its administration, while the Holy See refers specifically to the papacy. Diplomatic relations are established with the Holy See, not with the Vatican City State. However, in practice, "Holy See" and "Vatican" are often used interchangeably.[22]

By recognizing the sovereignty of the tiny territory of Vatican City as an independent country, separate from Italy, the Lateran Treaty also ended a longstanding dispute over the annexation of the papal states. Furthermore, it established Catholicism as the official state religion of Italy and granted the Church various privileges. The Vatican, in turn, recognized the Kingdom of Italy, ending its historical opposition to the Italian nation-state, which had been fully unified in 1870/71. Church officials swore an oath of allegiance; the Italian government gained the right to offer a say in the appointment of bishops. Despite some conflicts, as when the fascist state sought to dissolve Catholic youth organizations, the compromise worked well, and the fascist government and Catholic Church coexisted relatively smoothly for almost a decade.

After all, they had much in common. They held shared ideals about traditional family and gender roles and an authoritarian form of government, and they were united by common ideological enemies, such as communists, socialists, and liberals.[23] Furthermore, the pope, the king, and Mussolini were all Italians. All the parties thus seemed to profit from the agreement, but it was particularly beneficial for Mussolini, who succeeded in what Italian governments had failed to achieve for almost 60 years. To this day, the creation of the Via della Conciliazione (Conciliation)—an avenue commissioned by Mussolini that leads from Castel Sant'Angelo to Saint Peter's Square in Rome—serves as a reminder of Il Duce's diplomatic victory.

Meanwhile, the political situation in Germany was changing rapidly. The Nazi Party gained great momentum. Catholic leaders in Germany initially condemned aspects of Nazi ideology, and the Bavarian Conference of Bishops made clear that Catholics should avoid joining the Nazi Party. In November 1930, at a gathering of the archdiocese of Munich, Cardinal Faulhaber called national socialism (Nazism) "a heresy" that "cannot be brought into harmony with the Christian worldview."[24] Faulhaber correctly identified the Nazis as not just a political party but a secular religion, with ambitions to replace Christianity with a cult centered around blood and a celebration of the pre-Christian Germanic past. Yet he was unwilling to go so far as to excommunicate Catholics or exclude them from the sacraments for their Nazi Party membership—a constraint that the Vatican pushed aside when dealing with Catholic communists years later.[25] By 1933, Hitler, the leader of the German fascists, had been appointed chancellor of Germany, and the bishops adapted to this new situation.

THE POPE AND THE NAZIS

Although from one perspective, the Catholic Church historically has remained indifferent to which worldly governments rule society, as long as it has been able to continue to operate, the Church itself is an absolute monarchy, with strict male-dominated hierarchies. It therefore might not be surprising that the Church also traditionally has favored authoritarian regimes—usually monarchies—over liberal democracies, which encourage freedom of all religions and no special privileges for the Catholic Church.[26] In teachings about the state, the Catholic Church consistently asserts that the authority of both the state and the Church are God-given, such that both demand individual obedience. The Church's mission, its "essential role, after all, was to save souls" and to spread the gospel of Jesus, yet, as author Mark Riebling points out, "in practice, the spiritual purpose entailed a temporal one: the achievement of political conditions under which souls could be saved."[27] Therefore, for Pacelli and the Holy See, contemporary political and social conditions related closely to their ecclesiastical teachings and principles.[28]

For Pacelli, a top priority was to negotiate with Hitler, the new strongman leader of Germany. His superior, Pope Pius XI, also hoped that reaching a compromise with the Nazis would benefit the Church. Hitler had been born and raised Catholic; his first vice-chancellor was a Catholic, Franz von Papen, who also was keen on making a deal with the Church. After all, Hitler seemed like "merely" another fascist, a German version of Mussolini, with whom the Vatican had successfully made a pact. As the Vatican's cardinal secretary of state, Pacelli had a key role in negotiating a concordat in 1933 with Germany, which then served as the basis for the continued working relationship between the Catholic Church and the German state. An iconic official photo of the signing ceremony features Vice-Chancellor von Papen, Pacelli, and Monsignor Giovanni Montini, with von Papen and Pacelli portrayed deeply focused on the documents in front of them, backed by assistants. The photo clearly aims to underscore the significance of the moment.

While the Holy See hoped the deal would safeguard the Church, Hitler celebrated the diplomatic agreement as a huge propagandic success, a demonstration to German Catholics that the pope had given his blessing to the Nazi regime. Accordingly, many ordinary German and Italian Catholics considered fascism and national socialism natural allies of the Church, joined in fighting their common enemies of communism and liberal democracy.[29]

This initial accommodation of the Nazis did not last. The relationship between the Nazi state and the Catholic Church hierarchy soon deteriorated, in large part also because of the central role that racial antisemitism played in Nazi ideology. Yet even if he embraced this form of hatred as few had before him, Hitler did not invent antisemitism. Its roots go back throughout history, even to the earliest forms of Christianity and beyond. Christian antisemitism (sometimes called anti-Judaism), a form of religious animosity toward Jews, stemmed from Jews' rejection of Jesus as the Messiah. For almost 2000 years, Christians had falsely accused Jews of the killing of Jesus, or deicide, and propagated malicious blood libel accusations, wrongfully attributing the death of Christian children to Jews as well. These hateful views were officially revoked only in 1965, with the Second Vatican Council's *Nostra Aetate* ("In Our Time") declaration. In other words, this Catholic break with anti-Jewish traditions didn't come until twenty years after the Holocaust.[30] To put into perspective the centuries-old alleged "Jewish threat," we might consider a simple demographic fact: Even as the intensity of antisemitic claims about the actions and influence of Jewish people rose to fevered heights, in much of Europe, Jews represented a tiny minority. In Germany and Italy, they never made up more than 1 percent of the population.[31]

The Church may have been inclined to discriminate against Jews, but endorsing overt violence and murder was decidedly contrary to official Christian teachings. The Church wanted to convert Jews, not kill them. In the nineteenth century, an emerging form of antisemitism classified Jews as a "separate race" and connected them with ancient accusations and stereotypes, albeit in secular form. Jews started being depicted as a threat to the "purity" of bloodlines. This bigoted ideology suggested that Jews introduced corruption, sexual deviancy, and harmful foreign influences into gentile society. Religious affiliation could be altered, such as through conversion, yet racial antisemites fantasized about the segregation, expulsion, and murder of Jews.[32]

In an era dominated by Mussolini and Hitler, the Vatican attempted to distinguish the Church's brand of antisemitism from the racial antisemitism of those fascist dictators. However, for many ordinary Catholics and priests, the distinction was far from clear. Racially antisemitic language appeared in Church circles and publications.[33] The antisemitic trope that communism ("Bolshevism") was a Jewish world conspiracy also crept into the religious sphere. As the Italian historian Lucia Ceci writes, the "Catholic press was invaded by the image of the Bolshevik Jew, the fomenter of every revolution and ferocious in his anti-Christian hatred precisely because he was a Jew."[34] On the one hand, Catholic discourse about the Judeo-Bolshevik threat echoed nearly identical claims in some Nazi propaganda. On the other hand, the Church sought to distance itself from contemporary proponents of racial antisemitism, stressing conversion as a solution to the so-called Jewish question. This position required walking a very fine line. The Church did not formally condemn Hitler's influential *Mein Kampf*, often referred to as the Nazi bible.

However, the Vatican condemned *The Myth of the 20th Century*, by Alfred Rosenberg, another prominent figure in the Nazi hierarchy.[35] This nuanced decision exemplifies the Vatican leadership's attempt to maintain a delicate balance, asserting its principles without overtly antagonizing the Nazi regime.

In September 1935, the Nazi government had enacted the infamous Nuremberg Laws, which aimed to define Judaism as a "race" and forbade "intermarriage" between German Jews and "German blooded" citizens (sometimes referred to in Nazi lingo as "Aryans"). This first step toward subjecting Jews to second-class status initiated a sequence that started with discrimination and progressed to persecution, confiscation of property, and forced emigration, and culminated in systematic mass murder. Both German Catholic bishops and the Vatican refrained from voicing any public protests against the discriminatory laws. The Church noted some concerns about the laws' impact on Jews who had been baptized and on Christians with Jewish heritage, but it offered no principled opposition. It is worth recalling that, for centuries, the Church already had confined Jews to ghettos and discriminated against them to diminish their allegedly negative influence on Christians. The former Jewish ghetto in Rome—which persisted until the dissolution of the Papal States in 1870 and remains a tourist destination for many today—is a clear testament to this history.[36]

On March 14, 1937, Pope Pius XI issued an encyclical letter, addressing breaches of the concordat and rejecting Nazi racial ideologies. Munich's Cardinal Faulhaber, together with Pacelli, helped shape drafts of the document ultimately known as *Mit Brennender Sorge* ("With Burning Concern"). They kept its preparations secret from Nazi authorities and surprised them by reading it aloud in German churches on a chosen Sunday mass. The document, written in German rather than Latin (as would be typical), made the conflict public and encouraged its widespread consumption. *Mit Brennender Sorge* marks one of the few public protests by the Church against the Nazi regime and its anticlerical policies. Yet it also appeared as a central tool in the Church's efforts to defend itself and its record in the postwar years. Notably, this letter and its contents spread almost simultaneously with the Church's endorsement of *Divini Redemptoris* ("The Promise of a Divine Redeemer"), a document written in Latin that condemned communism.[37] That is, both *Mit Brennender Sorge* and *Divini Redemptoris* were published in 1937, illustrating the Church's simultaneous stance against atheistic and materialist ideologies, as well as Pius XI's willingness to confront powerful regimes in an effort to defend fundamental Church interests and teachings. The Holy See took a stance on ideological matters.

Just a year later, the introduction of antisemitic laws in Mussolini's Italy hit close to home for Pius XI. The laws included restrictions on "mixed marriages" between Catholics of Jewish descent and "Aryan" Catholics—a clear violation of the Lateran Pacts of 1929, which protected Catholic marriages. The pope pushed for exemptions for baptized Jews, to no avail. In turn, the relationship between the Vatican and Italian fascists suffered notably; in early September 1938, Pius XI remarked to a group of Belgian pilgrims that Christianity had its roots in Judaism and that therefore, "Spiritually, we are Semites," hinting at an effort to dissociate the Church from racial antisemitism.[38] Fundamentally, teachings that identified "higher" versus "lower" human races posed a significant challenge to the core ideology of the Church, which emphasized the universal nature of humanity—all were created in the divine image. During the last months of his life, Pius XI worked on an encyclical against racism, but he died before it could be made public, and Pacelli, his successor as Pope Pius XII, quickly shelved it.[39]

Pacelli's election by the cardinals gathered in Rome did not come as a surprise, but neither was it a foregone conclusion. On March 2, 1939, from the great balcony of St. Peter's Cathedral, the cardinal dean proclaimed in Latin that Pacelli, the new pope, had chosen the name Pius. Despite their similar names, Pius XII exhibited a deeply different personality from his predecessor, who had not shied away from fighting with state leaders to defend Church interests. Pacelli, as cardinal state secretary, already had established a reputation for his cautious, diplomatic approach, seeking to avoid conflict whenever possible. As Pius XII, he continued to rely on cautious diplomacy and official neutrality to steer the Church through the stormy waters of war.[40] In navigating this course, he had little reprieve. Just six months after his ascension to the throne of St. Peter, German armies invaded Poland from the west, and the Soviets soon marched in from the east. World War II had begun.

THE POPE AT WAR

The challenges and necessary decisions that arose during World War II took a huge toll on Pius XII. As the war progressed, more detailed information about its horrors reached the Vatican. His German housekeeper and close confidante, Sister Pascalina Lehnert, asserted that the papal crown became "a crown of thorns" for the pope, due to the war.[41] Following the German–Soviet invasion of Poland in the fall of 1939, the pope was subject to desperate pleas and calls to speak out publicly against the atrocities committed against Jews, Polish clergy, and ordinary Catholics. Instead, he remained silent, arguably because he was convinced neutrality would best serve the Church and its potential future role in peace negotiations. When Hitler invaded the "godless" Soviet Union in 1941, many Catholic priests prayed for the victory of his "anti-Bolshevik crusade." The Vatican was more restrained. Pius XII had few illusions about the nature of the Nazi regime, but communism still arguably held primacy as the main enemy. Perhaps he hoped that God would allow the atheistic regimes to destroy each other in their deadly conflict, but that would have been wishful thinking. Ultimately, his uppermost priority was to navigate the Church, as an institution, safely through the storm.

By adopting a cautious stance, however, the Church left Catholics without clear guidance for how to react to the challenges of totalitarian dictatorships. They looked to tradition for answers. Church teachings promoted loyalty to the state, and in turn, many German soldiers expressed confidence that "God is with us," as their belt buckles proclaimed. German military chaplains—Protestant and Catholic—reassured them of the validity of this belief.[42] However, some minority of Catholics looked instead to their conscience and rejected service in Hitler's war. A prominent case is Franz Jägerstätter, a deeply religious Austrian farmer who maintained the deep conviction that he could not serve evil and kill innocent people as a soldier in Hitler's army. In his emergency of the soul, Jägerstätter turned to the local Catholic bishop for advice, who told him to obey God-given authorities, like everybody else. Jägerstätter disagreed. Convicted as a traitor, he was beheaded in 1943.[43]

Unlike Jägerstätter, Pius XII had access to secret information that documented the true extent of Nazi crimes all over Europe. It is well documented that the Holy See had early, detailed knowledge about the systematic mass murder of Jews in Nazi-dominated Europe.[44] One of the pope's most important informants was Don Pirro Scavizzi, a Roman priest who served as a chaplain on Italian hospital trains and gained firsthand knowledge about the ongoing mass executions of Jews in occupied Ukraine. In private audiences, Scavizzi reported this knowledge to the pope directly, starting in November 1941. The reports, preserved in the Vatican archives, did not mince words when it came to mass shootings of women, children, and men in ditches. "I saw him crying like a child and praying like a saint," recalled Scavizzi when describing the pope's reaction. During their meeting in January 1942, Scavizzi told the pope that perhaps 1 million Jews already had been murdered.[45] Pius XII reportedly was deeply moved, a reaction that does not align with the cynical portrayal of Pius XII presented in Rolf Hochhuth's influential 1963 play *The Deputy*. During the course of 1942, even more reliable, additional documentation of the Nazis' mass murder of Jews came from Allied governments and activists.[46] By the latter part of 1942, Pius XII began considering a less diplomatic stance, as reflected in his Christmas address that year.

Specifically, after the Allies denounced the ongoing mass murder of Jews in a joint declaration on December 17, 1942, the pope included, in his 24-page Christmas radio message, a vague and carefully worded sentence about "the hundreds of thousands who, without personal guilt, are doomed to death or to a progressive deterioration of their condition, sometimes for no other reasons than their nationality or descent [*stirpe*]."[47] The pope did not use the terms "Jews" or "non-Aryans," nor did he name the German government as the perpetrator of these crimes. Despite this vagueness, Pius XII achieved one of his objectives: The 1942 Christmas message helped bolster the papacy's moral authority. Still, as a diplomat and holder of the papal throne, Pius XII avoided public confrontation. He worried that an open break with Germany would worsen the Church's situation. He likely feared that directly opposing the Nazis could lead to reprisals and threaten the integrity of the Church as an institution. Without the Church, its clergy, and its rituals, the salvation of souls for Christ would be at risk. The 1942 documentary *Pastor Angelicus*, produced by the Catholic Cinematographic Center, presented him as an "Angelic Pastor," dedicated to his mission as the "Universal Father in a tragic period of human history," according to the film's opening description. This might be indicative of how he saw himself.

Less than a year later, his moral authority was tested again as the Nazi onslaught on Italian Jewish communities intensified. In the fall of 1943, the Holocaust reached the pope's city. The Jews of Rome were rounded up and deported to Auschwitz. After the Allies landed in Sicily in July 1943, the Wehrmacht came to occupy most of Northern and Central Italy, including Rome. Italy had become a battleground. The Germans did not touch the pope, and they respected the sovereignty of tiny, neutral Vatican City. But Italy's Jews were in mortal danger. On October 16, the Nazi SS began mass arrests of Roman women, children, and men in the old Jewish Quarter—a clear challenge to the pope's function as bishop of Rome and its population's traditional protector. Church officials met with German officers and diplomats, protested informally, and asked for the arrests to stop. Alois Hudal, an Austrian Catholic bishop in Rome , a strong proponent of a Vatican–Nazi alliance, pleaded with German authorities to back down, so as not to provoke the pope. Fearing an open break with the Vatican, Hudal and other representatives of the Holy See warned that the pope might not remain silent forever. An agitated German ambassador, Ernst von Weizsäcker, added to the warning, writing to Berlin that "The Curia is dumbfounded, particularly as the action took place under the very windows of the Pope, as it were."[48] Still, Weizsäcker expressed the hopeful and ultimately accurate prediction that Pius XII would not denounce Nazi Germany publicly. And indeed, the pope remained silent regarding the arrest of his fellow Romans.

A remarkable document describes the situation. A group of prominent Roman Jews, on the morning after the first round-up, wrote a letter from a hideout, in which they begged for the Holy Father's intervention to prevent the deportation of imprisoned Jews. The pope read the appeal the next morning and decided that not much could be done.[49] The Vatican instead intervened with German authorities specifically for the benefit of baptized Jews and those married to Christians. The SS carefully reviewed a list that had been hastily drawn up by Vatican officials and released those prisoners. As historian David Kertzer writes, "This was Rome, not Poland or Russia, and the Germans did not want to unduly provoke the Vatican."[50] On October 18, 1,007 remaining Jews were pushed onto trains and deported to Auschwitz. Most of them were murdered in the gas chambers upon arrival. Others would perish in slave labor camps. Only 16 survived.[51]

However, efforts by Vatican officials and other clergy to provide some forms of refuge ramped up. Monasteries and other institutions in the Vatican, Rome, and their surroundings opened their doors to Jews and others persecuted by the Nazis and Italian fascists.[52] Monsignor Domenico Tardini, a top Vatican official, later said that, in the period between September 1943 and June 5, 1944 (the date of the Allies' arrival in Rome), approximately 180 Catholic religious homes and institutions offered asylum to Jews and others, who were rescued from the Nazis and fascists. Monsignor Giovanni Montini also added, "Our priests and nuns, at the peril of their lives, helped these people just as the Holy See helped many Allied prisoners of war for the sake of doing good, not for any earthly reward."[53] The varied efforts to save Jews by Catholic clergy in Nazi-occupied Italy and elsewhere clearly were brave actions. But they were based on individual initiatives, rather than coordinated by the Vatican. Furthermore, even if new evidence of wider rescue episodes were to emerge, they could not fundamentally change the fact that Pius XII never clearly and publicly condemned the murder of millions of Jews. When the Vatican organized efforts to rescue and aid emigration, it focused them on converted Jews. The pope might have abhorred the atrocities, but rescuing Jews was not a Vatican priority.[54]

In countries such as Slovakia and Croatia, prominent Catholic clergy also were actively complicit in the Holocaust. As a Nazi puppet state, Slovakia was run by a Catholic priest.[55] The genocidal fascist regime in Croatia worked closely with local Church officials to make the country an "ethnically pure" Catholic nation through the genocide of Serbs, Jews, and Muslims.[56] In addition, some German Catholic clergy openly supported the Nazi cause.[57] When the Holocaust reached Hungary, in 1944, the Vatican intervened, following much Allied encouragement, to discourage the Hungarian government from acceding to deportations: "not from a false sense of compassion, but on behalf of thousands of Christians [converts]; it once again appeals to the Hungarian government not to continue this war against the Jews beyond the limits prescribed by the laws of nature and the commandments of God [. . .]."[58] The pope reportedly was troubled by reports of atrocities against the Jews in Budapest, but also worried about crimes committed by advancing Soviet communist forces and about the overall fate of Hungary, which for centuries had stood as a Catholic stronghold against Christianity's enemies from the East.

FUTURE JUSTICE AND PEACE

With a major defeat of the Axis armies at the Battle of Stalingrad in 1943 and advances by Soviet forces toward Central Europe, Pius XII grew increasingly concerned. In his view, Russian communism was a manifestation of devilish forces, and he opposed U.S. military support for their Soviet allies. A total defeat of Germany and its occupation by the communists was not in the interest of the Church.

Accordingly, the pope made it clear that he opposed the Allies' unconditional surrender formula for Germany.[59] As Monsignor Tardini phrased it, such a surrender seems "likely to arouse fears of all kinds of humiliations for the vanquished peoples, and so to rekindle hatred and stir up resentment."[60] To the pope, this strategy would prolong the war. It also provided no incentive for internal opposition to the Nazi regime in Germany. Thus, in response to the "radical" plan by U.S. Secretary of the Treasury Henry Morgenthau Jr. to permanently weaken Germany by dismantling its heavy industry, the papal officials wrote a memorandum to the U.S. representative at the Vatican in September 1944, expressing serious concerns:

> As to the fate of Germany after the military operations, it is pointed out to the Holy See that the Allied Authorities are examining the possibility not only of dismembering and suppressing several industries, but also deporting five million men, supposedly for the purpose of labor, and probably for all their life, to Russia. It is also pointed out, following upon the sad events frequently deplored in territories occupied by the German Armed Forces, there is a great deal of talk in America as to the necessity of reducing the number of the German population and using severe coercive measures. Although these indications do not appear worthy of belief to the Secretariat of State of His Holiness which is well aware of the humanitarian principles so often affirmed by the Anglo-American Authorities, this Secretariat would deeply appreciate any information relative to this matter.[61]

In addition to revealing the concerns of the Holy See about the fate of the German nation, this document contains another interesting piece of information: A handwritten note on the document indicates, "MCT told

Pope No foundation."[62] Apparently, during his meeting with the pope, U.S. Representative Myron C. Taylor dismissed the suggested plans for postwar Germany as mere rumor. Yet the German question continued to play on Pius XII's thoughts, as did the fate of Rome amid a total war.[63] As the war dragged on, the pope also hoped to broker a peace settlement through secret talks with German anti-Hitler opposition circles. No major successes ever materialized, however.

As bishop of Rome, Pius XII must have been deeply relieved when, in June 1944, the holy city was liberated by British and American troops without any major destruction. Much credit was given to the pope for making Rome a de facto "open city." Roman citizens celebrated the pope as *defensor civitatis,* or protector and savior of the city; street signs near the Vatican still refer to Pius XII with this title. The pope's moral authority in Italy reached an all-time high, as signified in an iconic photo that depicts Pope Pius XII, arms outstretched, embracing and protecting the people of Rome amid the rubble following an Allied air raid.[64] With the country in disarray and the fascist state quickly disintegrating, the papacy was one of the few stable authorities left in Italy. The Church's good standing and powerful reputation during 1945 and 1946 was aptly captured by the claim that "The pope basked in the sun of the hour of the Church."[65] The Italian population, particularly in newly liberated areas, looked to the papacy for guidance and support, and the Allies saw the Church as an important partner in Italy.

With the Americans in Rome, Pius XII also embraced the United States as a new superpower and acted accordingly. Once again, the Church worked to adapt to the changing times and make beneficial arrangements with the new sheriff in town. In his Christmas 1944 speech, Pius XII defined Western democracy, including its foundational belief in religious freedom for all, as compatible with Catholicism. He also warned against and condemned any form of collective guilt or punishment.[66] Furthermore, the Vatican continued to use its influence to emphasize the dangers of Soviet communism. In a meeting with U.S. General Mark Clark at the Vatican, Pius XII cited communism as one of his main concerns, on par with his worries about the ongoing safety of Rome. In his 1950 memoir, General Clark wrote, "The Pope inquired whether I had had any contact with the Russians and expressed concern over the possible effects of Communism in central Europe."[67] In taking a clear side on this conflict, the pope sought the support of the United States against Soviet communism. As historian Giuliana Chamedes puts it, "As a result of helping invite the United States to grow its presence in Europe, Pius XII acquired the epithet 'Coca Cola pope'—a booster for American military might and American economic assistance."[68] When U.S. forces undertook their atomic bomb attacks on the Japanese cities of Hiroshima and Nagasaki in August 1945, the Vatican newspaper *Osservatore* commented that a "new era" had begun. The new era featured nuclear weapons and war; it was also the American age.[69]

In anticipation of postwar guilt and punishment, Pope Pius XII made his thoughts public, though always diplomatically and in vague language. He repeatedly spoke out against all forms of revenge and for the necessity of "a bearable peace for all nations." Time and again, the Catholic Church stressed that forgiveness and love should come before punitive justice, to overcome the great moral catastrophe and evils born from war. Claiming a role as a "mother" for all, the Church defined Christianity as central to any just postwar world order.[70] As the end of the war came in sight, the pope pleaded for mild treatment of the vanquished nations, such as in his 40-minute audience with British Prime Minister Winston Churchill in August 1944. Describing the meeting, *The New York Times* reported that "the Pope expressed deep concern over the terms of peace to be offered Germany and her satellite nations and that he urged the Prime Minister to consider at the peace table the principle of nationalities on the thesis that nationalities do not die."[71] During the meeting, the pope also reportedly agreed that he was not against war crimes trials in principle, yet he believed Italians should be spared that fate. The pope's plea for his fellow Italians might not have been surprising, but at the same time, he expressed deep concern about the fate of his beloved German people too. He warned that a totally defeated and starving Germany would create new injustices and stir up hatred.[72]

Reflecting the extent of war-related devastation and the Church's felt responsibility to intervene in postwar decisions, Pius XII engaged with concerns across the European continent, yet his foremost focus remained close to home. At the war's end, Italy was on the brink of anarchy. It had become deeply divided and marked by hatred between fascist and anti-fascist forces. Revenge killings, better known as *vendetta*, were widespread. Mussolini and his mistress were shot by Italian partisans in April 1945, without any formal trial, and then their bodies were hung upside down at a gas station in Milan and mutilated. An estimated 12,000 former fascists and suspected collaborators shared a similar fate, executed in cold blood by fellow Italians between 1943 and 1948.[73]

This wave of intense hatred must be understood according to the background of Italy's recent history. When Germany occupied it in the fall of 1943, it became a battleground between Nazi forces and the Allies, as well as simultaneously the scene of a civil war between fascist and anti-fascist Italians. Mussolini's Nazi puppet regime in Northern Italy, which lasted for 20 months, was famous for its brutality and extremism.[74] The deep rift divided families, and the war's end did not heal those rifts. The violence simply did not stop.

Lynchings took place a stone's throw from the Vatican, including the brutal public beating and drowning of a former deputy prison director named Donato Carretta in the Tiber River. Revenge thus became a major concern for the pope. The Vatican was appalled by postwar killings, often committed by socialist and communist partisans, and condemned them in no uncertain terms. In parallel, criminal justice efforts by the Italian courts included hundreds of death sentences for Italian fascists and war criminals, reflecting the heated postwar climate.[75] Italian clergy, from cardinals to village priests, tirelessly wrote letters seeking mercy for fascists on trial. Many Italian clergy, including the curia of Milan, became active protectors of ex-fascists and Nazi collaborators.[76] The Holy See intervened with the Italian government, seeking clemency for these "unfortunate persons" on death row.[77] When the Italian government decreed widespread amnesty for crimes committed under fascism in 1946, it meant that most fascist perpetrators went unpunished, but it also represented a move that the Holy See must have welcomed as a way to overcome the deep divisions in the country. Administrative purges and trials against Italian fascists and Nazi collaborators ended after about two years, with few tangible results.[78]

Attempts to establish an "Italian Nuremberg," or an international tribunal to put Italian fascism on trial, also failed.[79] Yet fascist Italy had been Germany's closest Axis partner. It engaged in aggressive wars and committed war crimes in the Soviet Union, Yugoslavia, Greece, and particularly Ethiopia. Noting these acts, the Allies called for punishments. Justice

Robert Jackson, the main prosecutor at Nuremberg, met several times with U.S. officials about Italian war criminals. However, as Jackson soon learned, the postwar situation in Italy differed from that in Germany, marked as it was by the execution of Mussolini and widespread reprisal killings of many other fascists, "particularly in the north where they have been pretty ruthlessly treated," as Jackson noted in his diary.[80] The U.S. officials in Italy told Jackson that there was little left for the Americans to do regarding Italian fascists and that he should focus his energies on Germany. Furthermore, the Italian royal government switched sides in the fall of 1943 and fought alongside the Allies for the remainder of the war. This and other emerging Cold War logics prevented further reckoning with fascism in Italy. The Vicar of Christ offered no objections.

CONCLUSION

Leading the Catholic Church through a time of global upheaval, Pius XII was regarded by millions as a moral guide. Yet his earlier role as the Vatican's top diplomat shaped a cautious and measured leadership style. Highly educated and determined to steer the Church through the perils of fascism and communism, he prioritized institutional preservation over public confrontation with oppressive regimes. Though not a friend of the Nazis, Pius XII viewed communism as the greater threat and was prepared to compromise with fascist powers. As secretary of state, he brokered the 1933 concordat with Nazi Germany—a fragile agreement that soon unraveled.

Upon becoming pope in 1939, Pius XII was informed of Nazi atrocities early on, including the mass murder of Jews. Although reportedly disturbed by these crimes, he avoided public condemnation of Hitler, concentrating instead on the Church's security and spiritual mission and discrete interventions and aid operations for Nazi victims. His approach remained basically unchanged even when Jews were deported from Rome in 1943. Nevertheless, he is credited with shielding the city from becoming a battlefield, and after its liberation in 1944, his standing reached a peak. He then sought to strengthen ties with the United States and championed an anti-communist agenda.

With the war's end, Pius XII grew increasingly alarmed by Soviet expansion in Europe. Believing that a stable Germany was essential to resist communism—a conviction rooted in his experience of the German Empire's collapse in 1918—he opposed calls for unconditional surrender and urged leniency toward the German people. In his view, rebuilding Germany was vital to prevent it from falling under "godless" communist rule. This stance, however, clashed with the retributive justice pursued at the Nuremberg trials, prompting questions about whether Allied postwar tribunals aligned with the pope's vision for lasting peace.

3

THE POPE AND NUREMBERG

On June 2, 1945, just a few weeks after Germany's unconditional surrender, Pope Pius XII gave one of his most important speeches, detailing his views on both the Nazis and what would constitute a just postwar order.[1] He raised four main points. First, the Catholic Church had been a victim of the Nazis too, and it had spoken out against and condemned Nazi aggressions. Second, the Germans were not collectively guilty as a nation. Once the guilty parties had been punished, Germany would need to be welcomed back into the family of nations. Third, the Soviet Union and its allies occupied or dominated several smaller nations, with communist forces committing violence against civilians and clergy, particularly in Central and Eastern Europe (with explicit mentions of Slovenia and Croatia). Fourth, looking toward the future, the Church would be needed to ensure and consolidate true peace after the catastrophic war.

These views of the Church's role during the Nazi regime and its ideas for the future, as summarily provided by this speech, reflect the critical context created by Nuremberg-oriented concepts of justice. For example, the pope provided an explanatory background for his views on Germany, noting that he had worked there as a nuncio and was well acquainted with the country. In his years in Germany, Pius XII explained, he had learned to appreciate "the great qualities" of the German people and grew close with many of their leaders. Thus he asserted that a rebirth and reestablished dignity were possible for Germany, "after it has rejected the satanic spectrum exhibited by National Socialism and after the guilty . . . will have atoned for the crimes they have committed."[2] In turn, he proposed mild treatment for the German people, rejecting radical options like widespread purges or a permanent weakening of the country, as proposed by U.S. Secretary of Treasury Henry Morgenthau, Jr.. Anything remotely resembling collective punishment was rejected out of hand. The pope's deeply held goals for Germany had remained consistent since World War I: "a stable and unified Germany, fully integrated into the family of European states and acting as a spiritual, cultural, and political bulwark against Communism," as historian Robert Ventresca puts it.[3] Finally, the pope warned that a defeated and starving Germany would create new injustices, "rekindle hatred and stir up resentment."[4]

In addition to citing his own experience and sense of Germany as possessing great qualities, Pius XII justified his position by stressing the victimhood of the Catholic Church and its faithful under the National Socialist regime. He cited 2,800 Polish priests and hundreds of Austrian and German clergy who had been imprisoned in the Dachau concentration camp alone. As the pope announced, in an oddly triumphal tone, the Nazis had sought to destroy the Church but had not succeeded. In retrospect, we can discern that the pope downplayed many early compromises by the Church with fascist regimes, in not just Italy but also Nazi Germany. Before, during, and immediately after the Shoah, none of the hateful teachings of Christian antisemitism—still official doctrines at the time—were rejected or even critically reflected on, at least not yet by the Vatican.

Although most audiences, certainly in non-communist societies, reacted positively to the pope's speech, some U.S. observers raised questions about his neutrality, noting that "he had waited until Germany had been defeated before attacking the Nazis in public."[5] Such early criticisms of the pope's silence regarding Nazi crimes multiplied in the 1960s, "with the rise of 'Holocaust consciousness,'" and they have not stopped emerging and expanding in the years since.[6]

THE POPE AND THE PROSECUTOR

As the premises laid out in the June address made clear, the Vatican had reservations about the International Nuremberg Tribunal. But beyond this public statement, Pius XII had an opportunity to express his views directly to

Justice Robert Jackson, in a meeting that has gained little attention until now. In preparing for the Nuremberg trials, Jackson included the systematic persecution of Christian churches in Germany within the wider Nazi conspiracy to spark war and achieve conquest.[7] Seeking to make this case more powerfully, Jackson reached out to the Vatican to request further documentation.[8] At first, he did not believe the request would be met: "Most of my staff and most of the others with whom I discussed it said that I never would get any help from the Vatican, that the Vatican would stand aloof from any such thing as this. I had discussed the matter with the President and he had thought that it was a good thing to make the effort."[9] Thus, undeterred by naysayers and with President Truman's support, Jackson leveraged his close connections, such as with the powerful Archbishop of New York Francis Spellman and Father Edmund Walsh at Georgetown University, to reach out to the Vatican.[10]

His decision paid off: On August 28, 1945, Jackson had an audience with Pius XII in Rome. He detailed this interaction in his diary immediately after the meeting. As his first impression, Jackson described the pope as "a rather tired looking, hardworking ascetic." The rest of the diary entry focuses intensely on Nuremberg. I discovered this account of the meeting between the pope and the judge in Jackson's papers at the Library of Congress in Washington, D.C., during my extensive research time spent there. According to the diary, the two men first shared compliments to break the ice. Jackson told Pius XII that he was inspired by the pope's June 2 address to the cardinals about future peace; the pope returned the courtesy by stressing his positive attitude toward the United States. As Jackson recalled, "He expressed great enthusiasm about the United States."

But they quickly cut to the chase. The pope acknowledged that the United States would strongly influence future developments in Germany, and he expressed deep concerns about the limitations on religious freedom imposed in the Soviet occupation zone of Germany. Asserting that "what little news he had was bad," Pius XII alleged "that dictatorship was not over and religion not free."[11] In detailing his serious concerns about one of the main Allies, he described the Soviet government as an anti-religious dictatorship. It is hard to dispute these allegations. Yet even if they are accurate, by opening the meeting with these complaints about the Soviets, Pope Pius XII was adopting a strategic approach. On these topics, he assumed that Jackson would likely agree with him. Jackson had growing concerns about working with the Soviets at

Nuremberg, and he was keenly aware of the hypocrisy of placing representatives of a brutal dictatorship in a position to sit in judgment.[12]

Having set the stage this way, the pope indicated his concern and empathy for the German people. He also offered some personal history: As the former papal nuncio in Germany, he explained, he had always opposed the Nazis but had sought, through the concordat, to make life endurable for German Catholics. The concordat had not succeeded as he had hoped, because Hitler's government violated it constantly. Next, the pope welcomed Jackson's plan to include the persecution of the Church by the Nazis in the Nuremberg trial, but he reemphasized that his primary concern was the fate of the defeated German nation. Jackson's summary of the main points the pope raised reveals:

> . . . he was especially concerned that the whole German people should not be charged with criminality. He thought that was unwise and unfair, for he knew that many people had incurred considerable risk in opposing the Nazi regime. I said that I have never considered that all of the German people were criminals and would not make such a charge, and that I hope to prove that the German people were the first people to be betrayed. . . . He expressed great satisfaction that we were not accusing all Germans of being criminals.[13]

As these diary notes make clear, the pope continually and strongly rejected any notion of Germans' collective guilt. In sensing the pope's relief, Jackson also shared some of the basic strategy he had in mind for the planned war crimes trial: "I told him [the pope] in general of our plan for the trial of a few of the men who plotted the whole war and the whole persecution, particularly the plan to adjudge the S.S. and the Gestapo criminal organizations. He agreed that these were the core of Nazism."[14]

The pope thus was satisfied with the meeting. In Jackson's diary, he reports that a few hours after the meeting, Harold Tittmann, the U.S. diplomat to the Vatican,

> who had been waiting for me in the ante-room[,] was asked to go in and reported to me that the Pope had said that he was greatly pleased with the audience, was happy that the work was in good hands and had been impressed with my fairness and sense of justice. He repeated to him that he wanted to be of help.[15]

Jackson left the meeting satisfied too.[16] As an unobservant Protestant, he "did not really believe in God or practice religion, but he was tolerant of others who did and how they chose to do so," according to his biographer.[17] His notes reflect this assessment: Jackson did not see Pacelli as the Vicar of Christ but seemed impressed by the ascetic man's work ethic and dedication to his calling. Furthermore, Jackson got what he came for; the Vatican agreed to share some documents, sending them through Tittmann. Thus from Jackson's perspective, Pius XII was doing what he could to cooperate with the preparation for that historic trial, such that

> I was greatly pleased to find that the Pope not only had given me an audience but had taken so much interest in the matter that he had prepared a memorandum of the persecutions of the Church at the hands of the Nazis. While it was somewhat general, it was the kind of summary that was extremely useful for it drew together all the complaints from different parts of the country. He also had sent translations of certain correspondence with Ribbentrop damaging in its recitals of the persecutions and false promises.[18]

In promising to provide Vatican documentation of the Nazi persecution of the Church, Pope Pius XII also achieved several of his purposes. A central one was self-serving. At the time, the Vatican was actively seeking every opportunity it could find to reinforce the narrative of its own victimhood and early resistance to the Nazis. By pushing the narrative that only a handful of Nazi thugs had been responsible for the war and its crimes, the Vatican also could present the notion that the Nazis had held the German people hostage, so the Germans had been victims too. Jackson generally agreed with this view, establishing some common ground from which the two men could build their cooperation.

Jackson and the pope also shared three more ideals in common: They favored the rule of law over revenge; they wanted to emphasize the victimization of the Church by the Nazis; and they were critical of the Soviets. Jackson hoped that these common beliefs, along with the possession and presentation of the promised documents during the trials, could strengthen his prosecution effort, by giving it the indirect imprimatur of the Church's moral authority. Years later, in the early 1950s, in oral history interviews with

Columbia University historian Dr. Harlan B. Phillips, Jackson returned to his encounter with the pope. Notably, the *reminiscences* are closely based on his diary notes but also differ from them somewhat. In this particular case, the terminology and analogies that Jackson uses when considering the question of collective guilt have somewhat shifted, such that in the oral history, called "Reminiscences" in its final but never-published form, Jackson stated,

> He [the pope] wanted to know if I intended to charge the whole German people with criminality. I told him that I didn't and pointed out to him that I said that I didn't in my [June 1945] report to the President. He had seen that report and was familiar with it. He said that he had understood that was not my purpose and that he was greatly concerned that we should not do, what the Nazis had done, simply charge a whole race with guilt. He thought that was unwise and unfair.[19]

Thus, according to Jackson's recollection years later, the pope warned that what the Allies were doing to the vanquished Germans could be viewed as similar to what the Nazis had done to the Jews, condemning them to collective punishment as a race. Such a comparison as that offered by the pope would have been particularly problematic.

In the Columbia oral history, Jackson also recalled that the pope had offered concrete critiques of the Nuremberg trial's legal foundations:

> Among other things, he said to me that the [German and Catholic] legalists, as he called them, had some difficulty with some aspects of the trials, perhaps referring, though he didn't say so to *ex post facto* [retroactive laws]. But he said that if we gave these men a full and fair hearing before any of them were punished, it would be a moral step forward.[20]

According to Jackson, he had received some documents previously, which prompted his strong motivation to meet with the pope:

> We obtained, through that source, a large number of documents concerning the persecution of the church, certified by the Papal Secretary of State. These documents were not only intrinsically valuable as evidence, but the fact that we

> were able to get them from the Vatican had a strong moral influence in many quarters. The introduction of Vatican documents, showing that at least we had a degree of Vatican cooperation, was a powerful influence in Bavaria where the people were so largely Catholic.[21]

Despite some differences between the diary and the subsequent memoirs, the overall impression we can take from this assessment is that Jackson wanted more than just evidence from the Vatican that he could use in his prosecution. He sought the documents as a signal of moral authority, granted by the pope (at least indirectly) to the Nuremberg project. Jackson returned from Rome pleased with the pope's apparent interest in dealing with the war crimes.[22] In return, according to a report by the U.S. Military Government in Germany, the Catholic clergy were "pleased with Justice Jackson's determination to convict those guilty of crimes against natural law and the law of conscience."[23]

These glowing assessments seemingly were too optimistic. The Vatican's distrust of Nuremberg and its alleged assumption of collective German guilt lingered. But at the time, both the pope and Justice Jackson were able to pronounce their meeting a success. Jackson received documents from the Vatican; even more important, he received the moral support of the pope for the project, even if only conditionally and indirectly. The pope in turn gained a channel through which he could lobby for the mild treatment of the vanquished German nation while also inserting a "Church-as-victim-only" narrative into the Nuremberg proceedings.

Still, the Church sought to appear neutral. Although Jackson's audience with the pope coincided with one of the first *Osservatore Romano* reports about the Nuremberg trials, the article only briefly mentioned Jackson and his efforts. That is, in "The Headquarters of the International Military Tribunal," published August 10, 1945, the Vatican's official newspaper informed readers that the trial "will judge the big war criminals" and that Justice Jackson would head up the proceedings, which would be based on the principle of individual responsibility.[24]

In line with its promises, shortly before the trial opened in Nuremberg on November 20, the Vatican submitted verified copies of various documents to the International Military Tribunal. They detailed the persecution of the

Catholic Church, and specifically the violation of the concordat and crimes against the Church in the annexed Warthegau province (of Poland), where persecution of Catholic clergy, who arguably served as a bulwark against Germanization, was particularly ruthless.[25] They also included inquiries about the concentration camps.[26]

The American Jesuit Edmund Walsh, from Georgetown University, served as the go-between for Jackson and the Vatican.[27] He arrived in Nuremberg on November 3 with another precious document from the Vatican:[28] the text of the pope's June 2 speech, in which he had vividly depicted the Catholic Church as a victim of Nazi persecution.[29] Parts of the speech were read out loud in the Nuremberg court, creating a depiction of the Vatican as a voice for peace. The pope must have been delighted. Nuremberg provided a world stage on which to present his ideas about guilt and punishment. Ironically though, those views actually were on a collision course with Allied efforts to achieve widespread criminal justice. For the time being, with only a handful of the worst Nazi criminals in the dock, the pope acceded to the Allied approach to trying them. He knew political currents had shifted toward the United States and that he needed to accept this rising world power to protect the interests of the Church. Officially, as ever, the pope tried to remain neutral, appearing neither opposed to nor in support of the trial, but rather focused on saving souls.

Perhaps as an effort to affirm its status as a voice for peace, the Vatican also sought to connect the Nuremberg trials with broader notions of a world "between war and peace." In December 1945, its official newspaper published a commentary on a statement by the U.S. Catholic bishops, which emphasized that the guilty must be punished, but ordinary people needed to be helped back onto their feet. The Church condemned vengeful policies of hatred and supported the call to determine guilt or innocence on the basis of individual responsibility rather than collective punishment. The *Osservatore* referred specifically to the Nuremberg trials: "The trial against the German war criminals is now being held at Nuremberg. This is a trial which in itself is just and exemplary. Among the documents of the crushing responsibility of Hitler there is the disclosure of a diabolical plan for the extermination of all the Polish people"—likely a reference to the murder of Poles in general, the majority of whom were Catholic.[30]

Unsurprisingly, the Church signaled its significant interest in this particular aspect of the Nuremberg proceedings; it established its own victimhood. In the Vatican papers, I uncovered part of the Allies' indictment, with the section about the "Participation of Leadership Corps of Nazi Party in Persecution of Christian Church and Clergy" highlighted.[31] This section describes the Catholic Church as a victim of the Nazis, without acknowledging the many compromises or support by some clergy for Hitler's regime. Furthermore, these papers repeatedly refer to *Reichsleiter* Martin Bormann, the head of the Nazi party Chancellery and Hitler's private secretary, as particularly anti-Church. Included with these papers are Vatican reactions to reports suggesting that Bormann had evaded postwar justice by using a Vatican passport. A thorough, internal Vatican investigation was conducted in 1972, which included inquiries of the papal nuncio in Buenos Aires, and it did not provide any support for these claims.[32] Ultimately, the allegations proved untrue; Bormann had died in May 1945 and thus could not have been helped by the Vatican. But in Nuremberg, his fate was still unknown, and Bormann was tried in absentia.

It might not have aided Bormann, but the Vatican did intervene in favor of other accused Nazi war criminals during Nuremberg. The Holy See showed particular interest in the fate of the ex-Foreign Minister Konstantin von Neurath and former Vice-Chancellor Franz von Papen, both of whom had been essential to bringing about the concordat between the Nazi government and the Vatican in 1933. The difference in how the Church sought to assist these men highlights how its own interests defined the extent to which it would intervene.

Notably, the Vatican sought to distinguish "good" versus "bad" Germans. The "good" Germans included Catholic resisters, understandably, but also Nazi officials who upheld their religious faith and furthered the Church's interests. The "bad" Germans were guilty and likely unredeemable because they were unwilling to embrace Christ. Both von Neurath and von Papen belonged to the former category, at least in the Vatican's eyes.[33] In turn, von Papen's wife Martha called on this distinction when she asked for "the intervention of the Holy Father, who personally knows [von Papen's] fervently Catholic sentiments and his excellent intentions," on behalf of her disgraced husband, as revealed in internal Vatican notes.[34] Upon receiving this request, the

Vatican Secretariat of State, led by Giovanni Montini, reached out to British and U.S. diplomats to forward her plea, with the added note that Martha von Papen had received no news from her husband since April 1945, when he was taken into Allied custody. In response, Jackson informed the Vatican that von Papen had been allowed to communicate with his son, who also served as his counsel, and that no communications between son and mother had been interrupted.[35]

Although von Papen was acquitted in Nuremberg, in 1947 he was sentenced by a Bavarian denazification court to eight years of hard labor. Martha von Papen then appealed to the Vatican again,[36] prompting the Vatican Secretariat of State to instruct Bishop Aloisius Muench, the papal emissary in Germany, to look into the case. The Secretariat of State turned to U.S. diplomats, seeking for them to encourage the Bavarian government to exhibit clemency toward von Papen and release him from prison while his appeal was pending. It appears that U.S. authorities took notice of the strong interest of the Holy See in this matter. They responded by suggesting to Bavarian authorities that von Papen be moved to a hospital in the beautiful Garmisch area in southern Bavaria while he awaited the decision on his appeal. Bishop Muench's office also reported to the Vatican Secretariat of State, detailing his meetings with the Bavarian Bishop Johannes Neuhäusler. However, Bavaria's Minister of Justice Josef Mueller stated that the timing of such an intervention was not ideal. Instead, Mueller promised that he would see if something could be done for von Papen the following year. Bishop Muench specified to his Vatican superiors that his talks had been "private and completely confidential" [*"carattere privato e in via del tutto confidenziale"*].[37] As these reports of the behind-the-scenes dealings make clear, Vatican diplomats engaged carefully in secret diplomacy, but with great persistence. Their persistence paid off; by January 1949, the Catholic Franz von Papen had been released from prison.

The Church did not always enjoy the same degree of success in its endeavors on behalf of accused war criminals, though. Whereas von Papen was exonerated at Nuremberg, Konstantin von Neurath had been sentenced to 15 years' imprisonment.[38] His wife Marie had appealed to Pius XII early on to come to her husband's rescue in Nuremberg, in case he was sentenced to death.[39] This preemptive request proved unnecessary; his life was spared by the courts. When von Neurath instead received a prison sentence, Montini assured Frau von Neurath of the fatherly interest and concern of the "Holy Father," who had told Montini "to offer [her] his sympathy and understanding."[40] I reiterate this point for the remarkable fact it conveys: The sympathy and understanding of the Vicar of Christ centered on the family of a convicted Nazi criminal. With this encouragement, Marie von Neurath and her daughter followed up with another letter to the pope, in which they complained bitterly that von Neurath was being treated like a criminal rather than as a "political prisoner." The family of the Nazi foreign minister pleaded with the pope to intervene for him to be transferred from a prison in Berlin-Spandau to one in the American zone of Germany.[41] The request was unrealistic, in that both Western Allies and the Soviets would have had to agree to such a move. In July 1948, Muench advised caution to Montini, explaining that "Furthermore, I have been confidentially informed also that it would not be wise for the Representative of the Holy See to intervene because such intervention would be misconstrued and exploited for Sovietic propaganda."[42] The U.S. authorities agreed and suggested to Muench that nothing could be undertaken in this matter, due to the Soviets' veto power.

A NAZI WAR CRIMINAL IN HEAVEN

The Vatican's support for von Papen and von Neurath is not totally surprising; both were close to the Catholic Church. Vatican interventions on behalf of Holocaust perpetrators who exhibited a strong anti-Catholic record, in contrast, raise many more questions. One such war criminal was Hans Frank, the General Governor of Nazi-occupied Poland. Nicknamed the "Butcher of Poland," he was responsible for the suffering and death of hundreds of thousands of Poles, Jews and Catholics alike. His case was a top priority for the Polish government, which pushed for his extradition to Poland.[43] Instead, he ended up in the Nuremberg dock. On October 30, 1945, while on trial in Nuremberg, Frank converted to the Catholic faith, under the spiritual guidance of the U.S. military chaplain Father Sixtus O'Connor.[44]

During the Nuremberg proceedings, Frank learned that some of the evidence against him had come from the Vatican, and in response, he reportedly began ranting against the Church in the courtroom, as described by Justice Robert Jackson in his memoirs:

> The use of these documents was highlighted by Hans Frank, whose counsel demanded dramatically to know whether these documents had come from the Vatican, which was answered promptly by pointing to the [papal] certification. Frank announced that in that case he was going to leave the Catholic Church. The courtroom laughed aloud at the idea that the Catholic Church would be much shaken by the loss of him.[45]

Yet Frank's courtroom outburst does not appear to have been held against him by his Catholic shepherds.[46] In prison, at least initially, Frank admitted partial guilt, yet he never expressed regret for his crimes or asked his victims for forgiveness. Rather the opposite—at the conclusion of his trial, Frank retracted his prior limited admission of guilt and stated that German guilt had been more than paid off, given the brutal ethnic cleansing of Germans in the East.[47] At the end of the trial, Frank was found guilty for his participation in war crimes and crimes against humanity, and he was sentenced to death in Nuremberg. Hans Frank's wife Brigitte had recently returned to the Catholic faith of her youth, and she approached the powerful Cardinal Michael Faulhaber of Munich, who in turn appealed to the pope to save the Nazi criminal's life.[48] Faulhaber specifically advised Brigitte Frank to submit a clemency appeal for her husband and reassured her that his "intervention to highest Church authority [is] on the way."[49] The pope had been called to come to the rescue.

The recently opened Vatican archives offer new evidence about how events unfolded once the Vatican received Faulhaber's message. Cardinal Faulhaber had left Munich and was passing through Switzerland when next he communicated with Rome. Monsignor Walter Carroll, from the Vatican's Secretariat of State, happened to be traveling with him, which provided a direct line of communication to Rome. On October 7, 1946, Carroll cabled from Bern that Brigitte Frank had asked Cardinal Faulhaber to intervene and save her husband from the gallows. The cardinal offered emphatic support for such an intervention by the Vatican, citing the convicted criminal's good attitude as a reason. Therefore, the "*Cardinale raccomanda vivamente supplica*" ["Cardinal strongly recommends the plea"], Carroll noted.[50] When this plea reached the Vatican Secretariat of State, an intimate of the pope, Monsignor Domenico Tardini, warned against public or official support for Frank, which would damage the Church "more or less everywhere, especially in Poland." A note preserved in the Vatican archives indicates that the "Holy Father" agreed with Tardini's caution and suggested that Allied diplomats in the Vatican should be informed about Carroll's telegram "*a voce*" (with an oral message). No official intervention in writing would come from the Vatican. Such caution might have been triggered by critical press reports about Faulhaber's initial telegram to the Vatican, whose content had been leaked already.

A note dated October 11, 1946, offers proof that these precautions were followed, even as the cardinal's and the pope's wishes were achieved. That is, British, American, and French representatives received information verbally, in the "execution of the venerable orders of the Holy Father" ["*in esecuzione dei venerati ordini del Santo Padre*"].[51] A draft text of the communication with the Allied diplomats also is preserved in the archives; dated October 10, 1946, this handwritten note shows that the carefully worded text was communicated orally ["*a voce–non ufficiale*"], during an in-person meeting with the diplomats. The Secretariat of State, acting on the pope's direct orders, informed them that Cardinal Faulhaber recommended that the Vatican support the clemency appeal of the war criminal's wife. The Vatican also asked the diplomats to forward the plea to the appropriate Allied authorities.[52] Then Monsignor Giovanni Montini, representing the Vatican Secretariat of State, informed Faulhaber about these steps taken to help Frank in an official letter, composed carefully in an effort to protect the reputation of the Vatican against "unnecessary attacks":

> The State Secretariat of His Holiness accepted the request for approval of the clemency petition wished by the Frank family and recommended by Your Eminence and therefore we immediately approached the American representatives here as well as the British and French ambassadors for intervention. The step was taken firmly, but without official formalities in order to prevent unnecessary attacks, even if it was foreseeable that the outcome desired by the relatives could hardly be achieved.[53]

Even with such cautions, Frank's clemency plea went public and triggered negative press coverage, especially from the Left. The (Soviet-backed) Polish Provisional Government of National Unity expressed particular outrage. The

Vatican and Faulhaber quickly engaged in damage control. Faulhaber may have been proud of his efforts to ensure Frank's conversion and spiritual salvation, but he downplayed his involvement and explicitly denied the Vatican's intervention for Frank.[54] Despite its actual intervention with Allied diplomats, the Vatican also denied any direct action in Frank's favor. Asked for a comment after an Italian press article in the *Giornale della Sera* reported on the Vatican's intervention, the Vatican Secretariat of State denied any official action on Frank's behalf. This response deliberately avoided any mention of the conversation about Frank that the Vatican had undertaken with U.S., British, and French representatives, as indicated by a handwritten note from the State Secretariat dated October 12, 1946: "I said nothing of what the Secretariat of State had communicated the day before regarding Frank to H. E. Osborne, Mr. [William E. W.] Gowen and Mr. Bourdeillette" [*"nulla ho detto di quanto la Segretaria di Stato aveva communicato il giorno innanzi a riguardo di Frank a S.E. Osborne, al signor Gowen e al signor Bourdeillette"*].[55]

Ultimately, Frank's request for clemency was denied; he was executed with other Nazi criminals at Nuremberg. In his final words from the gallows, Frank asked the Lord for acceptance and mercy on his soul: "My Jesus, mercy!"[56] According to Frank's son Norman, the prison chaplain Father O'Connor had urged Frank to utter these last words.[57] Father O'Connor later wrote Norman, "I am sure that your father went straight to heaven and that he found a fair judgment at the judge seat of God."[58]

Noting such appeals for clemency, and despite the failure of interventions on Frank's behalf, lawyers for other Nazis on death row considered adopting such a "Hail Mary" tactic. A last-minute appeal for clemency to the pope seemed like a possible opportunity. Thus, the lawyer for Arthur Seyss-Inquart lost no time in asking Faulhaber for the pope's intervention for his client, too. The Austrian-born Seyss-Inquart had committed numerous crimes, especially during his reign as Nazi governor of the Netherlands. While in prison, Seyss-Inquart presented himself as a repenting Catholic. His lawyer used the same register to appeal to the Cardinal, informing Faulhaber of his own Catholic faith and mentioning that his brother served as a monk.[59] Despite the similarity of the tactics adopted by Seyss-Inquart's lawyer, I find little evidence that Faulhaber responded with any efforts to save Seyss-Inquart's life. It appears that Faulhaber's support for Nazi war criminals was not unlimited. In some cases, he even opposed Church interventions.[60] Later, during a 1952 meeting with a U.S. official, Cardinal Faulhaber seemingly expressed support for punishment, reportedly asserting that a convicted war criminal is a sinner who must atone for his sins. By that time, of course, the postwar momentum for trying Nazi war criminals had largely dissipated.[61]

Another example revealed in the Vatican archives involves Hans Laternser, a prominent defense lawyer at the Nuremberg trials, who requested papal interventions on behalf of several convicted Nazi generals. He wrote to the Vatican Secretariat of State, asking it to offer confirmation that these generals had respected the rules of war in Italy. Laternser stressed that such an intervention would be "in the interest of historical truth and justice." A note in the Vatican archives, apparently written by the influential Monsignor Angelo Dell'Acqua, recommended caution, though: "In my humble opinion, it is appropriate for the Holy See to remain uninvolved: we do not have all the elements to make a judgment on the conduct of the German generals during the war in Italy."[62] Such advice reflects the occasional consideration of caution and "non-involvement." In my assessment, though, it also indicates that the Vatican was engaged in ongoing cost-benefit analyses. A crucial concern was the reputation of the Holy See.

Such caution is understandable. The Catholic Church's interventions did not go unnoticed in the media.[63] Cardinal Faulhaber already had gained a public reputation by 1946, courtesy of the satirical magazine *Der Simpl* from Munich, which was known for its striking caricatures. On the cover of its July 1946 issue, a huge hen ("The Faithful Broody Hen") protects little chicks, dressed in Nazi uniforms wearing iron crosses, under her wings. The hen seemingly sports a party badge of the Christian-Social Union and a cardinal's hat, leaving little doubt about whom the chicken represented. The caption reads, "And she spread her wings protectively over them."[64] Beyond just Faulhaber, the artists of *Der Simpl* mocked the idea of Christian general absolution, while also alluding to and critiquing the clergy's pro-Nazi stance. For example, another cartoon shows brown Nazi sheep marching toward a "Denazification" machine that transforms them into white, innocent-looking sheep—with a high-ranking Catholic clergy giving them a final blessing. A large flag with the Bavarian coat of arms flies overhead, and a man depicted on the honor pulpit wears a crown, likely a reference to the royal Wittelsbach dynasty, which still had many supporters in Bavaria. Above the scene, a banner reads, "There is more joy over one repentant sinner than over ten righteous people!"—a reference to Luke 15:7.[65] Yet the magazine's satire was not limited to the Church; a label on the denazification machine read, "Patent H. Schmitt." Heinrich Schmitt (1895–1951), a politician from the Communist Party of Germany (KPD), served as the first Bavarian Special Minister for Political Liberation and was responsible for denazification.

Even among these varied critiques, though, Faulhaber's intervention on Frank's behalf stood out and caused clear damage to the reputation of the Church, and not just in Poland. Yet what upset the Vatican the most was not its own questionable intervention or reactions to it, but rather the fact that its intervention had been leaked to the press. On October 17, 1946, Faulhaber sent a long letter to the pope, apparently through Father Robert Leiber, in which he justified his actions. He complained that Frank's lawyer had leaked the information to the press, but he persisted in arguing that Frank and his family had deserved help, because of Frank's conversion to Catholicism and his religious life while in prison. Frank's last words, asking for mercy from Jesus, left the cardinal even more firmly convinced that the "heavenly Father" had transformed the Nazi: "Here has been the descendent grace of God at work, which We have observed in many other cases over the past few years of this bloody decade and now also under the gallows." Furthermore, Faulhaber used religious grounds to justify his support for the Frank family to the pope: "As the bishop of this family, which had become Catholic again, I had observed that the Lord's hand of grace had touched this family. I am still convinced today that the death of the father will bring the mother with the children closer to God."[66] As he could show, Hans and Brigitte Frank and their children returned to the bosom of Mother Church. After emphasizing this successful harvest of souls, Faulhaber signed off his letter with the phrase, "Your Holiness' most devoted servant."[67]

The justification represented a winning strategy, it would appear. Faulhaber later shared with Brigitte Frank a letter from Pope Pius XII, in which the Vicar of Christ wrote, "We took notice with emotion of the last utterances [under the gallows] of the executed Dr. Frank. We can only wish that such a change of attitude would become known among those who were previously caught up in the same errors and that it would give rise to reflection and imitation."[68]

A similar sentiment appears in Vatican reporting about the executions at Nuremberg. On the day after they occurred, the *Osservatore* rejoiced that nine of the eleven executed Nazi leaders had rediscovered their Christian faith, confessed to a priest, and reconciled with God: "Only two remained stubborn in the false teachings, atheists, and they could not save their souls," the Vatican newspaper asserted.[69] Considering the Church's interventions in support of Hans Frank and other defendants at Nuremberg, it clearly was not just the grace of God that was at work.

These Catholic appeals for clemency—which usually advocated for life imprisonment instead of execution—were notably not part of any principled movement against the death penalty. Up until 1969, the legal code of Vatican City included capital punishment as a penalty for attempted assassination of the pope. Only since then has the Church's position changed. In 1983, Pope John Paul II visited Mehmet Ali Ağca in prison—the man who had attempted to kill him—in a remarkable gesture of forgiveness. Today, the Church opposes the death penalty in principle.

Yet even in the period that it still allowed for executions, the Vatican stressed forgiveness, mercy, and dignity. On October 18, 1946, just two days after the Nuremberg executions, *L'Osservatore Romano* published a commentary titled "Nuremberg Chronicles" that sharply criticized the moral decadence of a sensationalist press reporting the executions in graphic detail. Rather than emphasizing justice or closure, the article highlights the troubling atmosphere surrounding the hangings, marked by widespread curiosity and media sensationalism. It condemns a morbid fascination with the mechanics of death and argues that such coverage reflected a deeper moral decay after years of war—what it described as "the poison of violence, of cruelty, of the atrocious, of the horrifying, inoculated by the habit of massacres."[70] This mouthpiece of the Vatican echoed the Holy See's desire to see an end to violence and retribution, all of which it labeled, rather indiscriminately, as "revenge."

INTERVENING FOR NAZI CRIMINALS

The Vatican's efforts to extend clemency to Nazi criminals were not limited to Nuremberg; they extended to war crimes trials and denazification proceedings throughout Europe. Among the accused were some of Frank's closest accomplices and prominent Holocaust perpetrators in occupied Poland. Arthur Greiser had been in charge of the Warthegau district, a Polish region annexed by Nazi Germany. SS *Obergruppenführer* Greiser oversaw the deportation of approximately 630,000 Jews and Catholic Poles, many of whom perished. His district was the site of the notorious first-test gassings, in Chelmno/Kulmhof.[71] As an instrument of the Nazis' ethnic cleansing policy, Greiser implemented hardline persecutions of the Catholic Church, thereby implementing Hitler's goal of destroying any remnants of a national Polish identity. As his SS file, kept in the U.S. National Archives, reveals, Greiser had been raised Protestant but broke with Christianity in 1939 and declared himself a Nazi "*gottgläubig*," therefore fully committed to Nazi teachings.[72] The Vatican knew of his beliefs but still sent a last-minute appeal in July 1946 to save Greiser's life, referring to him as

> one of the most severe foes of the Church in the Warthegau, where he was Governor. Despite this His Holiness, following the divine example of our Lord, who, on the cross, prayed for his executioners, grants the sentenced man's request and addresses to the proper authorities his paternal request to spare his life.[73]

This intervention is really remarkable. Among the documentation and evidence that the Church provided to Jackson regarding its persecution by the Nazis, much of it focused on the Warthegau. This raises the question: What could have been motivating the pope in Greiser's case? Was he hoping that Greiser would convert to the Catholic faith at the last minute? Whatever the reasons for it, though, the Poles angrily rejected the pope's intervention. Greiser was publicly hanged before a crowd of 15,000 observers.

Another telling example of Catholic interventions beyond Nuremberg again involves Faulhaber and his efforts on behalf of Dr. Josef Bühler. He was a close aide to Hans Frank in the *Generalgouvernement* and participated in the notorious Wannsee Conference, which coordinated the mass murder of Jews. At war's end, Bühler was arrested by U.S. forces and held as witness in Nuremberg, before being handed over to Poland for trial.[74] Once the Polish court had handed down his death sentence, Cardinal Faulhaber asked for clemency, with the argument that Bühler "always remained a faithful son of the Catholic Church and repeatedly helped members of religious orders and priests in Poland."[75]

Just as Frank and Greiser were, Albert Forster, the Nazi *Gauleiter* of Gdańsk/Danzig, was responsible for a regime of murderous occupation in Poland. Also like them, he sought out papal intervention. His wife Gertrude appealed to Pius XII in November 1946, asking for help for her husband, imprisoned in a Polish cell: "My husband, who has always been a devout Catholic, will be grateful for this help from the Church."[76] The Vatican Aid Commission in charge of war *victims* received instructions to look discreetly into the case of this war criminal. In a message to the Polish Cardinal August Hlond, the request noted, "But that's all, without getting into the business of the trial at all."[77] Cardinal Hlond answered, in a message to Montini, that there was no access to the prisoner, and further that his would be a major trial, similar to those held for Greiser and Rudolf Höss (the commandant of Auschwitz). Hlond further cautioned the Vatican that "The accusations brought against Forster are very serious, because his government in Danzig was cruel and bloody." As Primate of Poland and the country's leading bishop, Hlond had witnessed the atrocities firsthand; he knew what he was talking about.[78] The Vatican Secretariat of State still showed great interest in ensuring Forster had access to a Catholic priest, "to secure him the comforts of our holy religion."[79] It requested that Forster's wife receive information about her husband's situation and his treatment in prison. Nor did the Vatican leave it at this; it also appealed for clemency in his case.[80] A fair trial held by a Polish court sentenced Forster to death instead.[81]

In this case too, the question emerges: What were the Church's motivations for working so actively to intervene on behalf of these defendants, both in Nuremberg and at other war crimes trials beyond Nuremberg? One answer might come from signals that Catholic leaders came to see in Jackson's efforts in Nuremberg, and then even more in subsequent war crimes trials, an increasing threat to postwar peace and stability. The Vatican's newspaper repeatedly expressed concern about the fundamental ideas undergirding punitive justice, international law, and the adjudication of war crimes. Its reporting on the Nuremberg trials in particular highlighted their imperfections. Its main criticism was that victors, along with the defeated, needed to be punished for crimes they committed.[82] Related concerns regarding the dangers of "victors' justice" were prominent in continued attacks by the Catholic Church on the Nuremberg trials and denazification programs.

Another answer to the question reflects the concepts underlying criticisms of "collective punishment." Critics alleged that just because someone had been a member of the Nazi Party or the SS, or even a citizen of Germany, they had come to be seen as automatically guilty. The Church shared such concerns, and the defense lawyer Georg Boehm even ended his arguments in Nuremberg with a quote from one of Pius XII's speeches:

> Erroneous ideas are circulating in the world which declare a man guilty and responsible solely because he was a member of or belonged to a specific community, without making any effort to examine or to investigate whether there really exists a personal responsibility on his part for such acts of commission or omission.[83]

Pius XII's sometimes vague and purposefully diplomatic language certainly was open to different interpretations. But there can be little doubt that the Vatican rejected, from the beginning, anything resembling collective punishment and "victors' justice."

Through my further research into the actual speech that Boehm quoted, I learned that the pope gave it on the occasion of the promotion of 32 new cardinals on February 20, 1946. This ceremony serves to elevate Catholic bishops who have served the Church dutifully into the Sacred College, the body that elects future popes. Jackson attended the 1946 ceremony at the Vatican, at the invitation of his friend Archbishop Francis Spellman, who was being promoted as one of the new cardinals.[84] The pope granted Jackson a second audience at the time, during which he again stressed his concerns about the anti-religious politics of the Soviets.[85]

But something else stood out to me in the reports about this major Vatican event: Among the bishops elevated to cardinals, we find three Germans—Josef Frings of Cologne, Clemens August Count von Galen of Münster, and Konrad von Preysing of Berlin. Compared with other nations, Germany was thus remarkably well represented. All three priests had been considered steadfast defenders of Catholic interests during the Nazi regime. In elevating these new German cardinals, the pope sent a clear message: He still loved and supported German Catholics and their leaders. The *Osservatore Romano* reported prominently on the high mass celebrated by the new German cardinals in the

Santa Maria dell'Anima Church in Rome. Cardinal Faulhaber, assisted by the Austrian bishop Alois Hudal, led the ceremony and thanked Pius XII for his support of German Catholics. Citing the motto "*Opus Justitiae Pax*" ["Peace Is the Result of Justice"], Faulhaber stated that the pope opposed the expulsion of Germans from the eastern territories of the former Reich. The publication of the sermon would indicate that the pope approved of Faulhaber's views.[86]

With the exception of Frings, who would be put up somewhere else, all were hosted at the guest house attached to the Church, the Anima College, which was run by the Nazi-friendly Hudal. Hudal was certainly not a persona non grata among the German cardinals at the time. A 1946 group photo shows Hudal, Faulhaber, von Preysing, and von Galen, along with their assistants, in good spirits in the courtyard of the Anima Institute in Rome.[87]

Among those who received the promotion, perhaps the pope's most favored bishop on that day in Rome was von Galen.[88] When he first received the news, he thanked the pope for the honor, which he accepted on behalf of himself and the German people:

> That our poor German people, left in ruins by the war, humbled by defeat, hated and vengefully treated on all sides, have not been overlooked, but rather shown great respect by the calling of three German bishops to the College of Cardinals: for this the German Catholics with their bishops and priests, and also many non-Catholic Germans, thank the Vicar of Christ on earth from hearts that have been deeply moved.[89]

When von Galen received the red hat of cardinal and approached the papal throne, Pius XII embraced him strongly and whispered, "God bless you, and God bless Germany!"[90] In exhibiting this close connection with von Galen, and with the German people, Pius XII revealed his allegiances, while also holding up von Galen as a showcase for German Catholic clergy's resistance to Nazi policies.

But von Galen's political activities were neither straightforward nor single-minded. He had been an early and vociferous critique of Allied policies toward Germans. Considering that Faulhaber never fully embraced Nuremberg, it emerges that the pope elevated two of the most outspoken critics of Nazi war crimes trials as the newest members of the Sacred College. The opinions of the new cardinals were echoed by many other Catholic leaders, who felt encouraged by the pope's choices and the messages they signaled. Thus at the conclusion of the Nuremberg trials, another of the newly elevated cardinals, Joseph Frings, who remained one of the highest-ranking Catholic leaders in Germany, demanded an immediate "end of revenge."[91] In July 1946, he wrote directly to the Nuremberg tribunal, accusing them of ascribing collective guilt and alleging that the court was punishing people merely because they had been members of the Nazi Party or Nazi stormtroopers.[92] The apostolic nuncio to Switzerland joined in the chorus, referring to Nuremberg as a "questionable process."[93] Bishop Hudal cynically rejected the entire proceedings as "a really strange kind of justice."[94]

In turn, Catholic opposition to further Nazi war crimes trials—in Nuremberg and elsewhere—intensified. In May 1946, U.S. diplomats at the Vatican received notification of the concerns of German Catholic leaders like Faulhaber and Frings, who argued that denazification policies were based on assumptions of collective guilt and ignored the innocence of most Germans. They asserted that the Nuremberg trials would denigrate the reputation of the German nation as a whole. Furthermore, they claimed most Germans had known nothing about the crimes and, even if they had known, could not have prevented them. Thus, the bishops' position came to be that only a small clique of Nazi leaders was guilty and should be held responsible, whereas most Germans had been victims themselves. In these communications, the Vatican hinted to the Americans that the Holy Father shared such concerns about the flawed, unfair principles driving the proceedings.[95] The pope's patience with Nuremberg was running out.

CONCLUSION

The Vatican had reservations about the International Military Tribunal in Nuremberg, where only a handful of top Nazi leaders were tried; nevertheless, it ultimately accepted the proceedings. A pivotal, often overlooked event was a meeting between Justice Robert Jackson, the main prosecutor at Nuremberg, and the pope. As we have seen, the pope expressed his concerns and reservations about the trial during this meeting, but the parties also found some common ground. Pius XII did not formally praise or endorse the trial and instead carefully navigated between Vatican neutrality and avoiding tension with the American superpower. At one point, the Pope reportedly stated during an audience with a U.S. Navy officer in early 1946 that he found the conduct of the international Nuremberg trial was fair and that he "wanted to see justice done."[96] But as war crimes programs expanded, across other countries and over the years, the Vatican's concerns intensified. In the immediate postwar period, Pope Pius XII emphasized the importance of a stable, strong Germany as a defense against Soviet communism and advocated leniency toward the German people. He feared that severe punishments or prolonged weakness would leave Germany—and Christian Europe—vulnerable to "godless communism." These important considerations, pertinent to the history of Nuremberg and beyond, have been largely neglected before now. The Church's stance at Nuremberg revealed a broader postwar outlook: one of forgiveness, selective memory, and a growing narrative of Germans as victims.

During the Nuremberg Trials, the Vatican actively intervened in support of some Nazi defendants. It coordinated with defense lawyers, lobbied Allied authorities, and provided assistance to the families of the accused. The case of Hans Frank, Nazi governor of occupied Poland, exemplifies this approach. After converting to Catholicism in prison, his repentance was celebrated by Church officials as a spiritual triumph. The Vatican lobbied to save him from execution, and priests later assured Frank's children that he had gone to heaven. The Holy See also intervened on behalf of Frank's closest collaborators, opposing their extradition to Poland and continuing to appeal for clemency even after convictions—notably when the Nazi criminals had embraced the Catholic faith.

While the sincerity of such conversions is uncertain, the Church's efforts drew criticism, especially from the Polish press, which accused it of aiding fascists—a claim that dovetailed with communist propaganda. Media in communist countries joined in the attacks on the Vatican, soon followed by the communist press within Italy itself. Aware of the potential damage to its reputation, the Vatican tried to keep these interventions quiet. Yet, in the eyes of the pope, the Christian mission of mercy and the salvation of souls ultimately took precedence. Particularly favored by the pope's grace and protection were German Nazis who held views similar to his on Germany, emphasized their Christian convictions, or had assisted the Church during the Hitler regime. Chief among them was Ernst von Weizsäcker.

4

THE GOOD NAZI

The case of Ernst von Weizsäcker shows that Pope Pius XII personally and knowingly intervened on behalf of a wanted and ultimately convicted high-ranking Nazi official, and that the pope did so of his own free will and as a personal commitment. Pope Pius XII did so in ways that arguably obstructed the efforts of the Nuremberg courts. Why? Who was Weizsäcker that the pope threw in his full weight to save this allegedly "good Nazi" from postwar justice?

In his role as State Secretary of the Nazi Foreign Office, Baron von Weizsäcker was one of the highest-ranking diplomats of the Third Reich, second only to the Foreign Minister Joachim von Ribbentrop. Similar to his contemporaries—old-school diplomats socialized under the Kaiser—Weizsäcker was a member of the nobility, with vast ambitions and a diplomatic mindset. He never warmed to the Weimar democracy and expressed his preference for an authoritarian state instead. When Hitler came to power, Weizsäcker stayed in his post in the Foreign Office rather than resign. Many of this generation of German diplomats embraced the new regime, whether opportunistically or actively. There is some evidence that Weizsäcker actually disliked the radical Nazis and their methods; late in the war for example, he interacted with members of the anti-Nazi opposition and indicated his disapproval of Hitler's criminal policies. Yet he persisted in his high-ranking official position and worked for the regime, never exhibiting any outright resistance. The ambitious Weizsäcker was also a member of the Nazi Party,[1] and when he joined the SS in 1938, he vowed, "to promote and support the [Nazi] movement with all my powers."[2] By 1942, the diplomat had earned himself a promotion to the honorary rank of SS general, or SS *Brigadeführer*.[3] Perhaps because of his reputation as a cautious foreign policy strategist, though, Weizsäcker was pushed aside by Ribbentrop, and in 1943, he was appointed German ambassador to the Vatican.

Still demonstrating his diplomatic savvy, and perhaps fear for his own neck, Weizsäcker worked to get close to Pius XII. As one of his first ambassadorial acts, the practicing Protestant asked to take lessons on Catholic religion and culture, a move that certainly won him points with the Vatican.[4] Currying such favor was growing increasingly important, considering that at this point in the war, Germany was suffering a series of military defeats. After the murderous Battle of Stalingrad in early 1943 and the Allied landing in Sicily that summer, the looming Axis defeat was becoming ever more obvious. Furthermore, Weizsäcker and the pope shared some common ground: They both sought to end the war sooner rather than later, and neither had any interest in a totally destroyed Germany. Accordingly, Weizsäcker embraced the efforts to shift the narrative and focus, away from Nazi crimes and toward the threat of communism In the diplomatic credentials that he presented in June 1943, Weizsäcker both forwarded the greetings of the *Führer* to Pope Pius XII and stressed Germany's historic mission to defend the civilized world against the Bolshevist danger.[5] Displaying such dedication to Catholic interests and making a pledge for a Christian Europe, Weizsäcker came to personify, for the Vatican, "the good Nazi."[6] These moves would pay off after the war, when the pope powerfully expressed his appreciation for Weizsäcker's advocacy for Catholics, namely, by protecting him against the outcomes of his legal conviction in Nuremberg as a Nazi criminal.

GUEST OF THE POPE

When U.S. forces liberated Rome in June 1944, Weizsäcker moved himself and his family, as well as some (but not all) embassy staff, into the formally neutral territory of the Vatican. They were granted safe haven by the pope, which was not unusual; the Vatican had previously offered similar protections for Allied diplomats. For Weizsäcker, the move represented a wise precaution. Bishop Alois Hudal in Rome was disgusted by the mob, which seemed ready to go after Weizsäcker at the German embassy. As the Americans entered Rome, the pope asked citizens to replace "hate, revenge and persecutions with brotherly love," but despite this appeal, German officials were allegedly hunted down.[7] Staff from other Axis embassies, including those of Japan, Romania, Slovakia, and Hungary, also moved into the neutral Vatican territory. What sets Weizsäcker and his family apart is the pope's personal interest in their well-being. The Vatican proved exceptionally hesitant to hand over Weizsäcker and his embassy staff to the Americans, who repeatedly pressed for their transfer. Starting in the summer of 1944 and for the ensuing two years, the Vatican persisted in grappling with U.S., French, and British diplomats over Weizsäcker.

Following the German surrender in May 1945, though, Weizsäcker's protected status as a diplomat in the Vatican became increasingly unsustainable. On the very day of Germany's unconditional surrender, May 8, a U.S. diplomat explained to the Papal Secretariat of State that "No German Government exists from today and consequently the extraterritoriality of the German Mission has lapsed."[8] German diplomats became de facto private guests of the pope, and the British and Americans wanted those guests to be moved into their custody as soon as possible. The Vatican observed how other neutral states—especially Switzerland—were dealing with their German diplomats. According to a collection of newspaper clippings at the Vatican, it also took careful note of Allied denazification policies. Italian newspaper reports, predicting that Weizsäcker would end up in a "concentration camp," and an article in *Stars and Stripes* that reported on the arrests of more than 50,000 Nazis by U.S. security forces, did little to reassure the Vatican.[9] The assumption that Weizsäcker and his staff "would be harshly treated" by the Allies guided the months of stalling and negotiating that followed.[10]

In his memoirs, Weizsäcker described his demand for a promise that he would be treated with respect and not arrested when he returned home to Allied-occupied Germany.[11] In support of these wishes, and to save him from disgrace and prison, the Vatican tried several tactics. Its Undersecretary of State[12] Giovanni Montini suggested that Weizsäcker and other German diplomats should be granted de facto political asylum in the Vatican instead of being handed over, but U.S. diplomats held firm in their demands. They told Montini that privileged treatment for Weizsäcker and further delays in handing him over was "wholly inacceptable,"[13] noting that "The Government of the United States wishes to make it clear beyond all doubt that it would not concur in any exceptions whatsoever involving high German officials no matter what the circumstances"—while still also stressing, "of course, persons suspected of war crimes or subject to security arrest will receive treatment in accordance with their status."[14]

The British position aligned with the Americans', such that U.K. representatives also met with resistance from the Vatican. Sir Darcy Osborne, the British minister to the Holy See, reported to Winston Churchill in July 1945, "I have been unable to make any progress towards a settlement."[15] This stalemate revealed how dramatically the two sides' views differed. Montini repeatedly asked the Allies to make concessions for German diplomats—and Weizsäcker in particular. For example, Montini's office made the remarkable request of Osborne, to allow Baron Weizsäcker and his wife to leave the Vatican for a weeklong vacation on the Italian island of Ischia.[16] Encouraged by such support, Weizsäcker pressed for special treatment too and tried to negotiate his freedom of movement, such as trips to Switzerland.[17] Neither the British nor the American diplomats gave Montini or Weizsäcker any such assurances or pleasant vacations. In November 1945, the Allies specifically warned Montini that any German former diplomats found outside the Vatican would be arrested.[18] The pope's protection of the Nazi diplomat Weizsäcker is remarkable, yet as this book documents, it was not an isolated case.

From his safe haven behind Vatican walls, Weizsäcker also continued to act as a spokesperson for the Germans, asking the Vatican for expansive assistance and numerous interventions. A few examples must suffice here. In line with the Vatican's existing efforts, Weizsäcker strongly supported the defense of Franz von Papen and Konstantin von Neurath in Nuremberg.[19] But his particular attention centered on those members of his former embassy staff who had not moved into the Vatican in 1944 and instead had been interned by the Allies. Weizsäcker repeatedly asked Montini for money, clothing, and assurances of good treatment for his colleagues and their families. Through Weizsäcker's efforts, and with the collaboration of Bishop Hudal, the Holy See helped his former colleague at the Vatican, Karl Gustav Wollenweber, while he was in detention in Italy. The Vatican stressed that Wollenweber had converted to Catholicism while in internment, news that the pope received with delight.[20]

When the remaining diplomats were repatriated from Italy to Germany, their luggage ended up in Munich; Montini instructed Johannes Neuhäusler to store it for them. But protecting their belongings was only the start of what the future auxiliary bishop of Munich would do for former Nazis.[21]

As he raised these requests and demands, Weizsäcker also confronted some challenges. For example, responding to Allied accusations, Weizsäcker admitted that the German embassy had been running a secret radio transmitter from inside the Vatican. Weizsäcker claimed it was used only for diplomatic business, not for espionage. A handwritten note tells the rest of the story: "Seen by the Holy Father 8.6.45. Please ask Baron W. to hand over the device."[22] One of his former staff was accused of having been a Nazi spy, under the cloak of a diplomat, which Weizsäcker denied. Despite such alleged violations of the Vatican's hospitality, it continued to stand firmly with Weizsäcker.

Allied diplomats struggled to understand why. Recall that at the time, the public viewed Pope Pius XII as an unwavering moral authority and heroic figure, standing steadfast against the war and the Nazis. Given this public perception, the diplomats struggled to understand the motives behind the pope's support for Nazi officials and war criminals wanted by the Allies. In the words of the U.S. diplomat Harold Tittmann, "The Vatican is concerned only with appearances and with its own prestige as a charitable and impartial institution especially in the eyes of the German Catholic population to which the Vatican looks for assistance in future rehabilitation work for Germany."[23] British diplomats shared similar views, though they seemed less worried, because "what happens to them after their arrival in Germany is not the Vatican's concern, or even interest."[24] This prediction ultimately proved inaccurate; the Holy See maintained a close interest in what happened to the diplomats after they arrived in Germany.

For months, Montini continued to negotiate with the Allies, seeking privileged treatment for Weizsäcker and his staff. Some of the demands achieved success. In early 1946, the British embassy at the Vatican reported it had made concessions of honorable treatment, but "if the Vatican expected a formal guarantee that members of the [German] Mission would in no circumstances be arrested or interned, they would not get it."[25] Throughout the negotiations, the pope continuously assured Weizsäcker of his support. For Easter 1946, the pope sent Weizsäcker and his wife a personal, handwritten note in German, wishing them God's blessing for the holiday and promising inclusion in his prayers.[26] While the pope was writing this note, Weizsäcker was testifying at the Nuremberg International Military Tribunal on April 23, 1946, as a witness for the defense for Admiral Erich Raeder, commander of the German navy, who participated in war crimes. To enable him to give such testimony, the Vatican Secretariat of State insisted to U.S. authorities that when Weizsäcker went to Nuremberg, he would "be accompanied by an American officer, not as a guard, but as a company of honor."[27] Not only was Weizsäcker flown to Germany in an U.S. plane, but he also received a promise of his own freedom and return to the Vatican.

THE POPE'S PROTECTION

Finally, in August 1946, Weizsäcker and his wife left the Vatican for their family estate in Lindau, Germany, at Lake Constance in the French zone of occupation. Their trip took place in a Vatican limousine, courtesy of the pope.[28] After Weizsäcker returned to Frankfurt to be interrogated by the Americans as part of the Nuremberg trials, he was free to stay at his residence until further notice. His arrest and possible trial were not yet on the table, and Weizsäcker was understandably optimistic, prompting him to even ask the Allies for "immunity from arrest," with the pope's ongoing support.[29] As Montini wrote Weizsäcker as he was leaving Rome on August 23, "[I]n the moment of your leaving the Vatican, the Holy Father wants to express his gratitude and respect. Best wishes to your safe journey and that you can reunite soon with your family. His Holiness prays for your protection." Montini ended the letter by noting his own high respect for Weizsäcker.[30] But the letter was not the only gift Montini had to offer Weizsäcker; he also penned a letter of protection for him and his wife, in English, Italian, and French. It requested that any the competent civil and military authorities provide any assistance required by the Nazi ex-diplomat. For anyone reading the document, there could be little doubt that he was under the protection of the Vatican.[31]

After his initial interrogation, Weizsäcker remained at his estate, where he received a longer letter from the pope, dated March 1, 1947. Written in German, the letter recounted Pius's fond memories of their time spent together behind the Vatican's walls but also offered a view of the future of Germany:

> Please be assured that Our ongoing concern remains directed towards the development of a true European peace. Within the large framework of a renewed Europe, Germany can always count on Our understanding and support in its endeavor to find the basis for its resurgence while at the same time being conscious of its proper place foreseen by providence.[32]

With the expressed hope that Germany's misery would soon end, the letter concluded, "Your and your whole family's well-being, warmly recommending you to God's protection in prayer, we convey to you and your wife the expression of Our benevolence and special wishes," right above the signature of Pope Pius XII.[33] It was highly unusual for the pope to write a letter, in his own hand, to a diplomat; secretaries normally managed such tasks. It is also noteworthy that the pope wrote the letter in German, a personal touch, signaling his comfortable, close relationship with Weizsäcker. Beyond the distinctiveness of its authorship and language, this letter is also notable for its outcomes; Weizsäcker made good use of it soon thereafter.

When Weizsäcker was arrested by the Allies, on July 25, 1947, for his involvement in Nazi crimes, the Vatican expressed surprise and offense. It thought Weizsäcker's immunity had been assured. The pope, closely following every new development in the case, intervened immediately, accusing the Allies of breaking their alleged promises of de facto immunity to Weizsäcker. Offended that its interests were not prioritized, the Vatican expressed grave displeasure. The U.S. and British representatives firmly stated that Weizsäcker never had been given any assurances.

Once he was arrested, his family began appealing to the pope for further assistance. One of Weizsäcker's sons had married into a powerful pro-German Swiss military dynasty. This Swiss family connection proved very helpful, especially for financing and coordinating the legal defense.[34] These Swiss relatives asked that Bishop Aloisius Muench, the Papal representative in Germany, help Weizsäcker's lawyer Hellmut Becker.[35] A response came from the Vatican Secretary of State, indicating that the request was answered by the Holy See itself. In September, Bishop Aloisius Muench wrote to the Vatican, to provide an update about Weizsäcker's defense and a meeting with Weizsäcker's lawyer Becker. Muench described the prosecutor as a German "Jew, who emigrated back then from Germany to the USA" and now had returned. The prosecutor intended, according to Becker, to focus on Weizsäcker's time at the Vatican. Muench then shared questions that Becker had for the Vatican: "Would a step by the Holy See at the U.S. State Department be possible in order to avoid a trial of Mr. Weizsäcker?" The report also contains assurances that the accusations against Weizsäcker were light, in a legal sense, mainly alleging that he had worked for the Nazi government, not that he was personally guilty of any wrongdoing. In asserting that it would be better if no trial took place, Becker accused the German-Jewish prosecutor of being driven by prejudice against Weizsäcker, as well as against the Holy See. Muench referred to such bias as common knowledge.

Becker also asked if the Vatican would be willing to answer questions by the tribunal, whether indirectly or through official questionnaires from the court. Remarkably, this in-depth, informative letter never once asks for clemency. Instead, the demands it raises suggest that the Vatican helped with the impunity of an accused Nazi criminal. Nor does Muench question or challenge Becker's insinuations of a vengeful Jewish prosecutor and trial.[36] The Holy See apparently accepted all these aspects, ordering Muench to assist with Weizsäcker's trial, based on the rationale that Weizsäcker had behaved well in difficult times and was against the war.[37]

During his trial in November 1947, Weizsäcker faced charges of (1) aggressive war/crimes against peace; (2) plans and conspiracy to commit crimes against peace; (3) war crimes; (4) crimes against humanity; (5) systematic plunder of countries; (6) slave labor; and (7) membership in a criminal organization. He became the chief defendant in one of the subsequent Nuremberg trials (known as the Ministries case), organized by the Americans. The prosecution, led by Robert Kempner, confronted Weizsäcker with reports from the SS *Einsatzgruppen*, the mobile killing squads in the occupied Soviet Union, which left no doubt about the fate of the Jews: "The areas newly occupied by the commandos were made free of Jews. 4891 Jews were liquidated in the process." Reports about systematic persecutions and deportations also reached Weizsäcker's desk when he was still at the Nazi Foreign Office headquarters in Berlin. In a particularly damning piece of evidence, Weizsäcker indicated he had "no objections" to the deportation of 6,000 French and stateless Jews from France to Auschwitz in March 1942. Imprisoned in Nuremberg, Weizsäcker cynically blamed the Jews who had not fled from German troops and had instead "let" themselves be captured.[38]

The accusations leveled against Weizsäcker never deterred the pope. As the newly released documents in the Vatican archives reveal, the pope's great personal interest in Weizsäcker never stopped. I identified two large folders, in separate locations in the archives; together, they amount to more than 1,000 pages documenting the Vatican's step-by-step defense of the Nazi diplomat.[39] Briefly, once the trial began, Weizsäcker's Swiss family lobbied both the Papal nuncio and the Commandant of the Papal Swiss Guard.[40] They forwarded every Swiss newspaper story about the case to the Vatican, including an opinion piece from November 1947 that expressed great sympathy for the Nazi defendant while simultaneously slamming the Jewish prosecutor Kempner as a "manhunter [*Menschenjäger*] . . . who is sitting on his [Weizsäckers'] heels and wants to bring him to Ribbentrop's gallows." A handwritten note on the article, indicating "seen by the Holy Father" ("*visto dal S. Padre*") and dated November 11, 1947, suggests the pope kept up with the latest developments.[41]

On November 17, Marianne Weizsäcker, the ex-ambassador's wife, wrote directly to Pius XII and asked for his help. In her ongoing support for her husband,[42] Marianne stressed that the Nuremberg trials would not serve the much needed peace and begged the pope to "put in a good word" for her husband with the U.S. diplomat Myron Taylor, because "Such a word of your holiness would be of immeasurable value to my husband."[43] Apparently in response to her request, the Vatican Secretary of State soon thereafter sent a message to Taylor, reminding him of Allied assurances allegedly made to Weizsäcker when he left Vatican City.[44] The U.S. diplomats rejected this claim; they denied again that any "promises were made that had any impact on the current developments."[45] Although giving public testimony initially seemed inopportune, because the accusations against Weizsäcker referred to the period prior to his time in Rome,[46] even these reservations eventually were overcome, and the Holy See's activities on Weizsäcker's behalf reached yet another level.

Specifically, it started to provide evidence for his defense. Weizsäcker's former secretary, the Baron Sigismund von Braun, kept busy in Rome collecting affidavits for his old boss. In a letter written in December 1947, he asked the Holy See to provide a testimony for Weizsäcker's defense that addressed three themes: (1) Weizsäcker's views on war and peace and his contacts with the pope's wartime nuncio in Germany, Cesare Orsenigo; (2) Weizsäcker's role as mediator between the Nazi government and the Church in Germany; and (3) his behavior as ambassador to the Holy See. According to von Braun, the Nazis had planned to kidnap the pope and hold him hostage in Liechtenstein, but Weizsäcker prevented the abduction. At the end of the letter, von Braun asked for a meeting with Monsignor Tardini, which took place, according to a handwritten note.[47]

Still at the Vatican, von Braun wrote the pope directly on January 9, 1948, again characterizing Weizsäcker as a practicing Christian who had tried to prevent the war. Although both Cesare Orsenigo and the Italian ambassador Bernardo Attolico allegedly confirmed these efforts, both of them had died, such that they could not testify for Weizsäcker's case. Instead, von Braun asked the pope to help him find Vatican documents that would aid the defense team, composed of von Braun, Becker, and an American lawyer,[48] Warren Magee, who also was a close friend of Bishop Aloisius Muench. In the archival papers, I found notes that the Vatican Secretary of State systematically searched its own archives for "concrete facts in favor of Baron von Weizsäcker." Little material emerged to back the defense lawyers' claims, though, especially regarding Weizsäcker's peace work—"little to nothing came out" ("*poco o nulla risulta*"), indicated a frustrated-sounding Vatican clerk.[49] Undeterred, though, the efforts intensified. The archival paper trail reveals that the Holy See invested enormous effort, time, and human resources in seeking anything to help Weizsäcker—so much so that it would be impossible to cover all of those efforts in a single book chapter.

In the interest of space, I instead offer a single, representative example. Papal delegate Cicognani in Washington, D.C., wrote to Tardini in December 1947, informing him of an idea from a renowned personality to defend Weizsäcker: a news story, put out by the powerful Catholic Church in the U.S., detailing Weizsäcker's efforts to save the Holy City from destruction. With the recognition that the Vatican was encouraging the U.S. Catholic Church to support Weizsäcker, Cicognani took on an active role in encouraging such efforts, telling U.S. Church officials to work for Weizsäcker, in line with what the pope wanted. Cicognani had talked already with Monsignor Howard Carroll, the Secretary General of the American National Catholic Welfare Conference

(NCWC), who promised that the NCWC would follow and assist the trial. Carroll also promised to inform the Vatican about any new developments.[50]

Meanwhile, the Vatican collected any evidence in favor of Weizsäcker, such as statements from Vatican diplomats who had worked with him in Berlin. One general statement described Weizsäcker as a more "moderate" Nazi official and acknowledged that he had helped prevent a total break between the Catholic Church and the Nazis.[51] But among the vast wave of letters from the Vatican and Catholic institutions in Rome and beyond, all in defense of Weizsäcker,[52] one of the most powerful came from Father Anton Weber, the head of the Roman branch of St. Raphael's Society, a group that helped thousands of Jews and Catholics of Jewish descent, persecuted by the Nazis for belonging to the "Jewish race," escape by emigrating overseas. Father Weber wrote that Weizsäcker had protected the society from the Gestapo, though he knew the religious order was hiding Jews.[53] Clergy from Germany and elsewhere also came to the defense of the man standing trial. Dr. Paul Georg Berndorff, the *Geheimsekretär* and chaplain for Cardinal Frings of Cologne, wrote in April 1948 that Weizsäcker had opposed the attacks of the Third Reich government against the Catholic Church and that his private life was based on Christian values.[54] Bishop Hudal claimed, "Ambassador von Weizsäcker has repeatedly and openly expressed to me his deepest regret about the terror of the Nazi party inflicted on both religious denominations."[55] Affidavits came from a wide range of prominent secular personalities too, both former Nazis and anti-Nazis. Even the presidents of the International Red Cross, Max Huber and Carl Jacob Burckhardt, gave up their neutrality and wrote in Weizsäcker's defense.[56]

DEFENDING A WAR CRIMINAL

In an April 1948 handwritten letter, Weizsäcker's children appealed directly to "His Holiness" Pius XII, thanking him for providing material for their father's defense, through Bishop Muench. Writing in German, they claimed their father was standing in for many Germans who, in difficult times, refused to abandon their post, in an attempt to limit the damage, yet who were being painted unfairly by the same brush: "Anyone who is found in a crowd of madmen and criminals cannot escape the suspicion that he is one of them himself." Much would depend on the Holy Father, they wrote, because the world "looks to the judgment of Your Holiness as a guide." The children acknowledged their gratitude for the pope's willingness to relay a positive message about their father to Myron Taylor, the U.S. representative to the Holy See, but they asked for more, specifying "A very brief personal letter from Your Holiness to our American attorney, Mr. Magee, or to our mother, showing Your Holiness' personal appreciation for our father, would suffice."[57] It appears that Weizsäcker's U.S. lawyer Magee delivered the children's letter himself to the Vatican; facilitated by Bishop Muench, Magee received a private audience with the pope, during which he repeated the request for a note in favor of Baron Weizsäcker. The pope did not pen such a note immediately, so Magee hinted to Monsignor Walter Carroll that he would be leaving Rome soon.[58] But the lawyer worried for naught: The pope's note arrived in time. The short, handwritten note, addressed to Marianne Weizsäcker, reads in translation,

> We gladly welcomed your writing (sent to us in due time), in which You asked for help in the fate of your husband. Your esteemed family can be sure of Our sympathy as well as of Our prayer so that God's blessing will reign over them. From the Vatican, 2 May 1948.[59]

Thus on May 3, 1948, a thrilled Magee wrote Pius XII, using a postcard from the Roman Hotel Excelsior:

> Holy Father, I could not leave Rome without expressing on behalf of Baron von Weizsäcker, his dear wife, his children and myself our heartfelt and undying gratitude for the great help your Holiness has so generously given us. Your letter will be treasured and will come to this stricken family like the "voice crying in the wilderness." I personally shall carry with me always the memory of your presence. Most gratefully respectfully yours Warren Magee.[60]

Magee's excitement was well-warranted. As mentioned earlier, autographs from a pope were rare and special. When the news hit that the Holy See would release a statement in defense of Weizsäcker, Taylor called Monsignor Carroll from Florence. Carroll's notes about the conversation on June 4, 1948, are preserved in the Vatican archives. Taylor noted his displeasure upon reading about such revelations in the *Rome Daily American* newspaper, then reminded Carroll of the incident, during his time in Rome (1944–45), when U.S. Intelligence Services became aware of the enemy radio transmitter in the Vatican that belonged to Weizsäcker. Taylor indicated that he did not want to influence the Nuremberg court but also cautioned that, if a Vatican statement was forthcoming, Taylor would have to say something, because "the fact constituted a violation of the hospitality offered by the Holy See."[61]

The delicate situation seemingly was not lost on the Vatican. A handwritten note, apparently penciled by Monsignor Montini, tells Carroll, "[L]et's see to inform Mr. Taylor of the tenor of the letter,—of the cautious nature—of [the Vatican's] declarations made."[62] But the Vatican's attempt to walk the thin line between supporting Weizsäcker and angering the Americans was made far more difficult by the defense's ready use of the pope's autographs on defense affidavits entered into the trial records.[63]

In June 1948, Muench sent the opening statement by the defense to Tardini. Internal notes suggest the main takeaways for the Church: Weizsäcker was a true German patriot, good Christian, and honest diplomat.[64] A report by the NCWC News Service on July 19, 1948, also identified an important witness: Jesuit Father Ivo Zeiger, an intimate confidant of the pope and rector of the German College in Rome, who appeared in a special Nuremberg hearing. Zeiger recounted the defendant's consistent, valiant endeavors to cooperate with the Holy See to shorten the war and counteract Nazi persecution of the Church. The Catholic news service also stressed the importance of Zeiger's testimony and offered hope of an acquittal.[65]

In October 1948, Cicognani, the pope's envoy to the United States, also alerted Tardini to another article, published in the Washington newspaper *The Evening Star*, in which the noted Washington columnist Constantine Brown presented a very positive view of Weizsäcker. Cicognani underlined: "The journalist complains about the position of judge entrusted to a certain Dr. Kempner, who could allow himself to be guided by partisan sentiments, 'at the expense of the prestige of American justice.'"[66] Brown also alleged that Kempner was driven by hatred and vindictiveness. For antisemites, such language offered barely hidden clues to Kempner's Jewish background, reflecting the prejudicial attempts by Weizsäcker's lawyers Magee and Becker—as well as Bishop Muench—to demonize Kempner. Brown's article argued that the trial received little public attention because global focus had shifted to Berlin, where the Soviet blockade was underway. The blockade was intended to force the three Western Allies out of West Berlin and is widely regarded as a major turning point in the emerging Cold War confrontation between the United States and the Soviet Union.

The notes that Muench added to his diary during a 1948 meeting with Magee and Becker are telling and disturbing at the same time: "trials without precedent—contrary to all American traditions. Eighty Jews—émigrés—[work for] the prosecution staff. . . . American name [is] blackened in history."[67] Muench's assistant reported in January 1949 that, according to the lawyers, Weizsäcker was likely to be condemned to 10 years in prison, which was needed to keep the reputation of the Nuremberg tribunal intact, reflecting "the influence of certain elements and of certain political currents" over the trial. Considered in context, this cryptic sentence also seems likely to refer to Jews and the political Left.[68] Hellmut Becker, another former Nazi Party member,[69] worked with Magee and the conservative elite to exploit various journalistic and political connections to help Weizsäcker's case.[70] Even as conservative media highlighted the good intentions of the accused, in court, prosecutors laid out a clear case for Weizsäcker's involvement in crimes against peace and humanity, including deportation of Jews. The trial even produced the only existing copy of the top-secret minutes of the so-called Wannsee Conference, held in January 1942, which coordinated and streamlined the Nazis' genocide against Europe's Jews.[71]

ANNULLING NUREMBERG

In early March 1949, Marianne Weizsäcker thanked the Vatican for its efforts thus far and offered the recognition that judgment day was coming.[72] When Weizsäcker was convicted in April 1949, sentenced to seven years in prison,[73] the Vatican just kept fighting. Magee requested that the U.S. High Commissioner in Germany, General Clay, refuse to confirm the sentence,[74] and Weizsäcker's legal team suggested that the Holy See should intervene as well, as evidenced by documentation in the archives. A note that appears to be from Becker proposed, "It is enough to let the government in Washington know that the Holy See is interested in the fate of its former ambassador. . . . In the present case it is noteworthy that one of the three judges (the Catholic), was for the acquittal of Weizsaecker."[75] The Vatican decided to bring out the big U.S. cannons; it asked Cardinal Spellman for help.[76] A telegram, from Montini to Cicognani in Washington, read:

> It is our expressed wish to inform the Cardinal Archbishop of New York [Spellman] that Mr. Weizsaecker, former German Ambassador to the Holy See from July 1943 to the end of the war, was sentenced to several years in prison, despite his advanced age. We would like to get General Clay not to confirm the sentence. See your Excellency how it is most convenient and possible to signal or support this desire.[77]

The pope's top adviser, the future Pope Paul VI, thus openly called for de facto impunity for a convicted Nazi war criminal. It was an incredibly forceful demand, but it did not prompt the expected outcome. Cardinal Spellman largely rejected the request,

> At the present time I know of nothing I can properly do in the present circumstances. The matters suggested in your letter were considered by the Judge at the trial and while there was a wide divergence on the opinion of these judges, the majority voted in favor of his conviction.[78]

So instead, encouraged by both Montini and Muench, Magee wrote Pius XII in May 1949, "I beg of Your Holiness the great privilege of another private audience for the purpose of discussing von Weizsäcker's case and to seek advice of Your Holiness in this matter."[79] Such phrasing implies that Magee viewed the pope somewhat as a co-counsel in Weizsäcker's defense. Marianne Weizsäcker instead appeared to regard him as a personal connection. In her letter, in German, to Pius XII, she declared her astonishment at the harsh seven-year sentence her husband received, complaining that the judges had not recognized her husband's work for peace, which meant that the outcome was a misjudgment (*Fehlurteil*) by the court.[80]

Although some of these documents have only recently come to light, the pope's support for Weizsäcker was well known at the time, and it provided ammunition for the powerful anticlerical press. On May 14, 1949, the main mouthpiece for the Italian Communist Party, *L'Unità*, published a harshly critical but essentially factually correct article with the headline "The criminal Von Weizsaecker blessed by His Holiness. A spokesperson for Hitler in the good graces of Pius XII."[81] The Vatican Secretary of State was, of course, carefully following and dealing with press attacks from around the world; in this case, they sought to coordinate a Catholic response with the editor of the *Osservatore Romano*, Conte Dalla Torre,[82] with the recognition in an internal note that

> L'Unità in an article on the former German ambassador to the Holy See Von Weizsaecker condemned as a "war criminal" reproduces some letters of blessing from His Holiness and a letter from H. E. Mons. Montini and ends by recalling that of the six thousand Jews that Baron von Weizsaecker would have sent from France to Auschv[w]itz "not one has returned".[83]

The Secretary of State strove to find the original letters: "It would be good to intensify the research so that tomorrow we can answer something about that in the *Osservatore Romano*. The two documents found (one in French and the other in German) have been faithfully reproduced by L'Unità," wrote Monsignor Angelo Dell'Acqua.[84] The next day, the Vatican responded with an article in *Osservatore Romano*, asserting that the communist version took things out of context on purpose, because *L'Unità*'s goal was not to print historical facts but rather to spread propaganda.[85] The journalistic duel did not end there; *L'Unità* kept the Vatican busy responding, as notes in the Vatican archives reveal.[86] The Vatican earned a lot of bad press from the Left and others for the aid it offered Nazi war criminals (not only Weizsäcker, but also Hans Frank, Oswald Pohl, Otto Ohlendorf, Arthur Greiser, Albert Forster, and others). Its efforts to respond to such criticisms seemed effective, though, especially when Christian Democrats won the crucial Italian elections of 1948.

Such reassurance may have given the Vatican more confidence to seek new ways to secure clemency for Weizsäcker.[87] It decided that Bishop Muench would be the best representative to approach U.S. High Commissioner John McCloy. As Muench reported to Montini, he personally handed McCloy a letter in favor of Baron von Weizsäcker, which made clear that he was speaking as the pope's messenger: "Herewith I beg leave respectfully to enter this plea in accordance with the instructions received from Pius XII." Then he presented his, and the Vatican's, case:

> In it, as your Excellency will be able to see, after having pointed out the particular reasons that justify the intervention of the Holy See, I thought it well not only to appeal to the traditions of clemency of the Republic of the United States, but also to point out that in the present case serious doubts have been raised by competent persons about the justice of the sentence, which constitutes a presumption in favor of the accused and a reason—in the event that these doubts are not sufficiently eliminated—to annul or at least mitigate the verdict ["*per annullare o almeno mitigare il verdetto*"].

The High Commissioner offered assurances that, before confirming the sentence, he would ask trusted lawyers to look at the court documents again. Muench also reported McCloy's affirmation that he would not approve a verdict that was not based on justice,[88] seemingly in line with his conviction that "our American nation will be honored by the verdict of history when once it has been written for having taken a magnanimous decision in the case."[89] As these documents indicate, Muench appears convinced that history was on his side, and he had no issues exaggerating Weizsäcker's merits.

The request to annul Weizsäcker's court sentence undermined any remaining claims of Vatican neutrality.[90] Weizsäcker's sentence eventually was reduced from seven to five years, and that concession appears due in large part to the pope's interventions. But even then the Holy Father was not satisfied. Word reached the Vatican in February 1950 that McCloy told Cardinal Frings of Cologne, in confidence, that Baron Weizsäcker would be released from Landsberg prison in September that year.[91] Even a day of imprisonment apparently was too much, such that the pope's advisors worked furiously with the legal team to coordinate efforts to petition for early release. The efforts eventually paid off.

Weizsäcker was released from Landsberg prison on October 16, 1950, as part of U.S. High Commissioner McCloy's generous amnesties, designed to strengthen the young alliance between the United States and the newly formed West German government against the Soviets. Press photos show him walking out of the prison gate, right after his wife. A few days later, Weizsäcker thanked the pope for all the help the Vatican provided to ensure his freedom: "Your Holiness's voice reached the United States, both during my trial and after the verdict. I lack eloquence, but not gratitude for all that I owe to Your Holiness and to the Church."[92]

His freedom was short-lived. Weizsäcker died of a stroke at the age of 69 in August 1951, in the comfort of his home in Lindau at Lake Constance. The Lutheran bishop Theophil Wurm, a longtime crusader against Nuremberg justice, delivered the funeral speech. Monsignor Montini sent a telegram with condolences from Pius XII to the widow.[93] Even in death, Weizsäcker and his family could count on the pope's blessing.

THE PROSECUTOR

For many critics of Nuremberg, Weizsäcker's prosecutor Robert Kempner became the personification of the "revengeful Jew," which make his ultimate defense of Pope Pius XII all the more remarkable.[94] Before the war, Kempner had been a prominent Prussian state official. When the Nazis came to power, he fled to the United States as a stateless refugee and made a name for himself in academic and government circles. Once the war was over, he returned from his American exile to occupied Germany to serve as a close aide to Justice Jackson's prosecution team. Then his role became even more prominent in the subsequent Nuremberg trials; he served as the prosecutor in case eleven, "the Ministries case," in which Ernst von Weizsäcker was arguably the most prominent defendant.

Just like many Nuremberg prosecutors, Kempner wanted to establish the guilt of the accused but also the political and moral responsibility of the German elites for the crimes committed under Hitler's regime. Kempner's role, as an émigré with partial Jewish heritage, returning as an American official to judge his fellow Germans, opened him to powerful criticism, as summarized by the historian Dirk Pöppmann:

> Against this background the German public perceived Kempner as a resentful retaliator who had come back to Germany only to take revenge on his former colleagues although as an emigrant he could not know anything about life and times in Nazi Germany. On the other side, Weizsäcker was regarded as an almost impeccable and patriotic character who was about to fall victim to victor's justice.[95]

As should come as no surprise, church leaders repeatedly took aim at Kempner too. In May 1948, the Protestant Bishop Theophil Wurm, a bitter opponent of the Allied war crimes trials, wrote a widely publicized open letter to Kempner, alleging torture and forced confessions and adding, "such methods must shake the legal and moral authority of a judgment, because by such occurrences it is degraded to the level of an act of revenge which is clad in sham forms of law." Wurm stressed, perhaps sarcastically, that it was necessary for the Allies to avoid the "appearance that in Nuremberg merely the victor judges the vanquished."[96] The outspoken bishop also claimed that the need for revisiting of the Dachau and Nuremberg trials represented a question of justice.[97] When Wurm made the heated exchanges between him and Kempner public, he triggered a bitter press controversy,[98] in which some public figures and journalists supported Wurm, others Kempner.[99] The tenor of the critique against Kempner reiterated common motifs, painting him as an arrogant German-Jewish, left-wing émigré who wanted to play educator of Germany, with its collective guilt.[100]

While I was doing research at the United States Holocaust Memorial Museum in Washington, D.C., a helpful archivist pointed me to the Kempner papers conserved there. The documents I unearthed in those archives add an interesting twist to the Kempner story. In 1954, Kempner's wife Ruth converted to Catholicism, became very pious, and grew close to Giovanni Montini (the future Pope Paul VI).[101] After her conversion, she and her husband were received in a private audience by Pope Pius XII and years later by Pope Paul VI. A group photo preserved in the archive shows Kempner and his wife at an audience with Pope Paul VI in 1966 at the Vatican.[102] Under her newly chosen name, "Benedicta" ("Blessed" in Latin) Kempner also developed a friendship with Sister Pascalina Lehnert, Pius XII's housekeeper and confidant. Both before and after the 1963 controversy surrounding Hochhuth's play *The Deputy*, which focused on Pius XII and his alleged public silence on the Holocaust, Benedicta and her husband spoke out in defense of Pius XII.

The couple published letters in the 1950s and 1960s stating that not only had the pope been an opponent of National Socialism and helped Jews but also that the Holy Father had never defended Nazis on trial.[103] In a 1958 journal article, Robert Kempner wrote, "In the interest of historical accuracy [corrected by hand to *truth*] it must be stated, that Pius XII never made a request to spare somebody who had even the smallest part in the crimes against Jews and other minorities, as some people tried to make believe."[104] This stunning claim is particularly remarkable coming from Weizsäcker's prosecutor. The Holy See intervened for many Nuremberg convicts, including some of the worst Holocaust perpetrators, and Kempner knew it. The pope had personally and wholeheartedly come to the defense of Weizsäcker. Yet Benedicta appeared determined to defend the WWII record of Pius XII to the highest echelons of the Church in the face of Hochhuth's accusations.[105] For her efforts in the interest of the Catholic Church, in 1966, Benedicta Kempner was awarded the prestigious Vatican medal "*Pro Ecclesia et Pontifice*" ["For the Church and the Pope"] by Pope Paul VI. The Kempners' efforts to defend Pope Pius XII's record raise questions about Robert Kempner's relationship with the Catholic clergy. He was heavily criticized and attacked by Weizsäcker's defenders during the trial, both in and outside the Vatican. He was also well aware of the constant intervention of Montini, Frings, and Faulhaber in support of Nazi war criminals. And yet, at the same time, he actively worked to establish friendly relations with all of them, or so it seems.[106] Kempner's memoirs contain an anecdote that might shed some light on his reasoning for maintaining such relations. When Cardinal Faulhaber intervened to protect a high-ranking Nazi war criminal in Nuremberg—likely Weizsäcker—Kempner traveled to Munich to see the cardinal. He presented Faulhaber with the evidence against the man, which convinced Faulhaber, who then allegedly stated, "If I had known that, I would never have thought of standing up for this man!"[107] As a result, Kempner concluded, "So, ignorance about the respective individual case must be the reason for the Church's intervention."[108] Contrary to his assessment, though, even if ignorance might have applied in some cases, it certainly cannot explain Vatican support for so many prominent Nazi criminals. Thus, Kempner's connections with the upper ranks of the Catholic hierarchy remain difficult to interpret, and further research will be required to clarify these relationships.

CONCLUSION

As the case of Ernst von Weizsäcker shows, Pope Pius XII directly and personally intervened on behalf of a wanted, ultimately convicted high-ranking Nazi official. Did his actions cross the line? In the Lateran Pacts of 1929, the Vatican committed to remaining neutral in international affairs and refraining from mediating disputes unless asked by the states involved. On the basis of this neutral status, the Vatican territory granted asylum rights to Weizsäcker. Furthermore, during Weizsäcker's trial, the Vatican's involvement might be justified as part of its spiritual mission of love and compassion, which included clemency appeals.

When we consider the pope's request to annul Weizsäcker's sentence, though, the interventions moved far beyond appeals for clemency; it signaled fundamental, active opposition to the trial and, arguably, Nuremberg justice itself. The evidence provided here is clear; Pope Pius XII was not neutral. He clearly took sides. He shielded Weizsäcker from extradition, asked for guarantees of immunity, attempted to stop Weizsäcker's trial, worked closely with his defense lawyers, and requested that his sentence be annulled, all of which indicates that his goal was not clemency but rather impunity for a high-ranking Nazi official. It is remarkable—and requires reemphasis—how much personal interest the pope took in Weizsäcker's case and the protection he promised to Weizsäcker and his family in personal, handwritten letters. In light of this clear evidence, it is essential to recall the role Weizsäcker played for the Nazi regime, as one of its highest-ranking diplomats.

Yet the Vatican was ready and willing to exploit the contentious, complex historical moment to successfully manage to delay Weizsäcker's extradition. By the time he finally stood trial, denazification efforts and war crimes trials had lost their momentum; the Cold War confrontation was heating up, in light of a communist coup in Prague and the Berlin blockade. The international community's efforts at justice were being diverted. Even former

Prime Minister Winston Churchill had begun criticizing the criminal proceedings, referring to them as a "denazification trial" (a twisted terminology) and a "deadly error."[109] Churchill's attitude likely reflected his broader perspective on the benefits of integration of West Germany into an anti-Soviet bloc and his strategic recognition that alienating Germans did not help that aim. Germans now metamorphosed from enemies to Allies, from perpetrators to victims.

PART 2

SAVING GERMANY

5

GERMANS AS VICTIMS

The portrayal of Germans as victims of the Nazis and the war, rather than the perpetrators, emerged as an early, powerful, and deeply controversial narrative, touted by both the Catholic Church in Germany and the pope. Even though the international Nuremberg trial involved only a handful of Nazi leaders, the Vatican still held some reservations. And then, even among those few German leaders that the Vatican acknowledged were guilty of war crimes and atrocities, their embrace of Christianity in Nuremberg prison cells meant that the Vatican would work intensely to save their lives. Along with depicting the Catholic Church in Germany as a martyr that resisted the Nazi regime, the pope perceived ordinary German Catholics as victims, twice over: first seduced and betrayed by the Nazis, then subjected to the Allies' vengeful postwar treatment. The narrative crafted by the Vatican and others was eagerly and rapidly embraced by German leaders and mainstream German society.

This narrative was perhaps no clearer than on February 20, 1946, when Pope Pius XII elevated three new German cardinals in Rome and thus clearly signaled that he was not treating Germans as pariahs. Far from it—the new cardinals believed they had a mandate to defend the German people against the so-called injustices of Nuremberg. A document, allegedly penned in March 1946 by the Bishop of Münster, Clemens August Count von Galen, one of the newly elevated German cardinals, contains what has since become perhaps the most widely cited condemnation of the Nuremberg trials and denazification program. Entitled *Rechtsbewusstsein und Rechtsunsicherheit* (loosely translated as "Legal Awareness and Uncertainty"), this 20-page pamphlet describes the Nuremberg court as a "political show trial" aimed at defaming the German nation and holding it collectively guilty.[1] It represents the opening salvo in a remarkable, hard-fought, and ultimately successful crusade by the Catholic and Protestant churches in West Germany to end the Allied war crimes trials.[2] The Church's early argument—that the overwhelming majority of the German people were not Nazi perpetrators but were themselves victims of the Nazis—remained at the heart of their rejection of widespread purges and trials.

THE OUTSPOKEN LION BISHOP

Bishop Clemens August von Galen, widely admired in Catholic Germany for his speeches against the state-sponsored murder of people with disabilities in the Nazi "euthanasia" program, received the nickname the "Lion of Münster," reflecting his reputation for speaking his mind.[3] After the Nazi regime fell, he spoke out again, this time against real or perceived injustices perpetrated by the Allies. In his first interview with Allied media, published in *The New York Times*, von Galen expressed a sense of depression upon seeing foreign troops on German soil, referring to it as "the terrible doom now breaking over Germany" in an April 1945 article. The article went on to explain, "The cleric appeared piqued that thus far no high-ranking American officer had visited him." When asked why he left Münster, the bishop responded, "Ask the Americans when they bombed me out." He also made it clear that, though he opposed the Nazis, he remained loyal to the Fatherland and therefore "would have to consider the Allies to be enemies." In turn, von Galen seemed less concerned about Nazism than about communism, "expressed great concern at the possibility of communism in Germany," and when asked how to get rid of Nazism claimed, "It will depend on whether you [western Allies] let the Russians into Germany and then we will have communism. It also depends on whether you let the Germans go hungry after the war. Because, if you do, there will be many Communists."[4]

In a sermon a few months later, von Galen went further in his criticisms, arguing that the violent expulsion of millions of Germans not only from

Germany's former eastern provinces but also from neighboring countries represented an assignment of collective guilt. He condemned revenge against German children and women as unchristian. With the claim that only "real justice" would make permanent peace possible, he concluded: "If anyone says that the entire German population and each of us is implicated in the crimes committed in foreign countries and especially in the concentration camps that is an untrue and unjust accusation against many of us."[5]

By October of that year, the Lion Bishop had gone even further: He declared the British sometimes worse than the Nazis, because they locked up political opponents (i.e., former Nazis) in "concentration camps" and would not allow the suspected criminals to receive mail or packages. In complaining, he talked about the "foreign rule of National Socialism" (*Fremdherrschaft des Nationalsozialismus*) that held society hostage and reiterated the accusation that the Allies were treating the Germans as collectively guilty. Speaking with a Swiss journalist, he offered an argument against such treatment by reminding the journalist that the Nazi Party never won an absolute majority in free national elections. He further argued that once Hitler gained power, thousands of anti-Nazi Germans, who included gentiles, communists, socialists, and monarchists, as well as Catholic clergy, ended up in concentration camps or fled the country. Then he recalled the tens of thousands of Germans with disabilities who had been murdered. On the basis of these combined arguments, the bishop asserted that denazification practices could only be regarded as unjust and that they would lead to "nihilism and bolshevism."[6]

As these multiple examples from 1945 illustrate, von Galen's reputation for being outspoken was not exaggerated. But although these interviews and sermons are exceptional in their own right, the pamphlet that has been attributed to him—written before his elevation to cardinal—demands the most attention.[7]

I first came across a copy of this explosive pamphlet in the papers of Cardinal Frings in Cologne. *Rechtsbewusstsein und Rechtsunsicherheit* begins with a reference to a 1937 encyclical of Pope Pius XI, "With Burning Concern" ("*Mit brennender Sorge*"), discussed earlier, which attacked Nazi racism and the violations of the concordat. The pamphlet emphasizes justice as the basis of Catholic community, as expressed in the Latin phrase *Justitia fundamentum regnorum* ("justice is the foundation of power"). It also includes a warning: Anyone who ignores this principle will fall from power. The Nazis ignored this papal advice and undermined the German legal system in their determination to terrorize the population, and look at what happened to them. But the Allies also are disregarding the legal system, the pamphlet continues.

It asserts that the Allies were prolonging the confusing period of legal uncertainty by making assumptions about the German people's "collective guilt" for the horrors of the war. In this way, the Allies were no better than the Nazis, who condemned all Jews collectively. The text calls particular attention to American hypocrisy, detailing the country's history of racism and brutal treatment of Native Americans and Black people. Then it alleges that Austria exported antisemitism to Germany. Yet the author reserves special disgust for the Soviets, whose very presence in Germany discredited any Allied efforts to introduce democracy to the country. According to the author's logic, Soviet practices and crimes, like gulags, inspired Hitler's concentration camp system, which made them worse.

Ultimately, the goal of the pamphlet seems to be to establish equivalence between many Allied policies and Nazi practices. Former Nazi party members lost their livelihoods or were locked up in camps. Just like the Gestapo, Allied military police randomly arrested people and searched their houses without any oversight. Accused Nazi criminals were held under terrible conditions. Allied military war crimes courts stood on thin legal grounds, it claimed.

This anti-Nuremberg pamphlet circulated far beyond a clerical audience. It seemingly offered a concise summary of what many Germans thought but believed they could not say in public. Yet no author signed their name or ever took public credit for this remarkable document. Seeking to determine if the author was a church official—and if not, to learn how it might have ended up in Cardinal Frings's papers, where I found it—I began to search for other copies or references to it. It proved difficult to find a copy of the full text; at the time of its publication, it had not been printed but rather was duplicated each time, manually, by individual typewriters and copyists. Throughout the Munich archives and Munich university library, I came up with nothing. It was only through the assistance of a friendly librarian that I was finally able to locate a copy, housed at a branch of the Munich city library. How it ended up there, I can only guess.

I sat down in the library's reading room with the text and encountered stunning information the moment my eyes landed on the heading: "Speech by Cardinal Graf von Galen in Rome, March 1946: Legal awareness and legal uncertainty."[8] Even on my first reading of the text, it was clear that the pamphlet used the direct, combatively undiplomatic language that von Galen had been known for. For a prominent, German, newly named cardinal to make such an argument publicly in 1946 would have been a remarkable moment in history. Considering its potential significance, I needed to be sure and therefore undertook a deeper analysis.

The author was clearly well-educated and eloquent, and the arguments implied a likely legal background. Of course, the title of the copy in the Munich city library clearly attributed authorship to von Galen. This copy also indicated that it reflected a speech delivered in 1946 at the church of Santa Maria dell'Anima in Rome, part of the Austrian national institute where Bishop Alois Hudal served as rector. Von Galen was in Rome in early 1946, which was when Pope Pius XII elevated him and two other German bishops. Although the Vatican's daily newspaper the *Osservatore* published an article on the "Te Deum" mass in the Anima Church, it made no mention of a speech by von Galen.[9] Furthermore, von Galen died just about a month after becoming a cardinal, so he could not issue any confirmation or denial as the pamphlet began circulating more widely. Because von Galen had been Bishop of Münster, I decided to request some answers from the Münster church archives, and in return, I received an official statement that had been published as early as June 1946. It reads, in full:

> Under the title 'Legal Awareness and Legal Uncertainty' (occasionally with the addition 'Speech of Cardinal von Galen given in the Anima Church in Rome') a document is currently spreading in the area of our diocese and beyond. The document in question is dealing with the current legal status in Germany. We hereby ascertain that the immortalized cardinal did not give such a speech or a similar speech in Rome or elsewhere. Furthermore, we note that the above-mentioned document was neither written by himself nor on his behalf. Apparently, the attribution of authorship to the Cardinal von Galen is intended to give this document increased importance. We ask the most honorable clergy to announce the above facts from the pulpit wherever felt necessary.[10]

This declaration left little space for interpretation. The Church officially denied von Galen's authorship. Its publication also suggests that as of 1946, the Münster diocese felt compelled to distance itself and von Galen from the pamphlet. Rumors were spreading that the Nuremberg defense lawyers sought to use this document to argue against the Allies' denazification program, citing its moral authority as a document authored by von Galen. Evidence shows that the defense for Admiral Erich Raeder received a copy of the speech, but they wanted proof of its authenticity before using it in court.[11] When the vicariate of Münster asserted that the cardinal never gave such a speech, it became worthless in court. Yet it was far from worthless in the court of public opinion, where Germans embraced its rationales to contest and reject the Nuremberg trials.

If the vicariate of Münster told the truth, and von Galen did not author the text, who did? Furthermore, why would the person responsible for the copy that I found in Munich want to attribute it to the deceased cardinal? I can offer at least one answer to the second question: Cardinal von Galen was popular and prominent, both in Germany and with the pope. In the Cologne archive, a single folder includes both a copy of the pamphlet and an exchange of letters, dated December 1945. The correspondence, between Cardinal Josef Frings of Cologne and Archbishop Lorenz Jaeger of Paderborn, reveals that Jaeger's office had been working on an extended memorandum to protest Allied war crimes trials and denazification measures.[12] Jaeger and Frings coordinated their efforts in denouncing the Allies' errors: Jaeger would draft the text, and Frings, in his capacity as head of the Fulda Conference of Bishops, would formally submit it to the Allies. As Frings wrote, "Wouldn't our approach be more uniform and impressive if this path were chosen addressing both the German and Allied authorities?"[13] On December 15, 1945, Jaeger wrote to Frings that he had finished the "expert opinion on legal uncertainty" ("*Gutachten über Rechtsunsicherheit*"); he concluded this letter optimistically, "I wish that Christmas may bring us all true peace."[14]

Does this correspondence imply Jaeger's involvement in the controversial pamphlet? During the Third Reich, he gained a reputation as a staunch anti-communist who was rather Nazi-friendly. His ambivalence did not prevent him from negotiating with the Allies though.[15] Together with von

Galen, Faulhaber, and Frings, among others, he condemned the notion of collective guilt and became a spokesperson for his German flock. The similarities between the "expert opinion on legal uncertainty" that Jaeger drafted and the text incorrectly attributed to Cardinal von Galen suggest a likely connection. Thus, even if we cannot conclusively establish authorship of the pamphlet, many indications point to its having been penned in Jaeger's office or by officials close to him.

Other scholars share this view. A likely candidate is the provost of Paderborn Cathedral, Paul Simon, at least according to Dieter Riesenberger's 1992 biography of him. Simon did not support the Nazis, but he sharply criticized the Allies and equated the Nazis' reign of terror with the British occupation of Germany. He opposed the Nuremberg trials—especially the idea of Soviets prosecuting Germans in the name of humanity. Perhaps most tellingly, drafts of the speech can be found in Simon's papers.[16] Without minimizing the importance of determining authorship, we can establish at least that the pamphlet's text reflects commonly held views across the German Catholic hierarchy, as evidenced by the exchange between Jaeger and Frings.

In line with the "Germans-as-victims" narrative, Archbishop Jaeger also wrote to Pope Pius XII in December 1945. Referring to Pius XII's time as nuncio in Germany and visits to Paderborn, Jaeger emphasized the war's destructive effects. The Paderborn that the pope had known, Jaeger wrote, was destroyed, and millions of German refugees found themselves in misery. He described Germans being buried where they died, along a roadway covered in refugees' tracks. Jaeger also expressed concern about developments in the Soviet occupation zone, including bans on religious education. Not only did Catholic schools there fear for their future existence, but the concordat of 1933 was not being respected by the Soviets, who instead were "aiming at the separation of church and state." Along with these dismal reports, Jaeger offered a source of hope in describing how religion had returned to Germany, where "Millions, who still yesterday bowed their knees to the false gods of the world are looking for new shores on the ocean of life."[17] I read this statement as a clear reference to the Nazis, with Hitler as the false prophet. It indicates that, primarily, the Nazis were heretics who embraced a new (secular) paganism and who needed to be redeemed, not tried.

THE CARDINAL OF THE PEOPLE

Considering their correspondence, we cannot ignore Cardinal Frings. He shared Jaeger's views, and in coordination with the Vatican, he was the key German Catholic campaigner against Nuremberg. For centuries, Cologne, situated on the river Rhine, had been an important Catholic stronghold in Germany. Its archbishop has enjoyed special status since the Middle Ages and was decisive in electing emperors. To this day, a medieval gothic cathedral serves as a visible reminder of the archbishop's power and the enduring faith of the city's Catholic populace. The over-600-year-old cathedral stood as one of the few buildings in the old city center that survived massive Allied bombing raids during the war, though it sustained serious damage. Leveraging this historical might, Cardinal Joseph Frings, who served as Archbishop of Cologne from 1942 until 1969, arguably became the most powerful German Catholic leader in the postwar years.[18]

His power stemmed from more than the history of the office, though. A painting on a column in the cathedral's northern transept portrays Cardinal Frings playing the violin, one of his favorite hobbies. This rather unusual depiction of a cardinal hints at his standing in the community, as a popular and well-liked bishop. Appointed Archbishop of Cologne in 1942 by Pope Pius XII, Frings opposed Nazi authorities to defend the rights of the Church. He also spoke out against the murder of innocents, "an injustice that cries to the heavens"[19]—an important statement, though it excluded any explicit mention or identification of Jews and other victims.

Frings's popularity also grew in the postwar years, reflecting his efforts to relieve the postwar suffering of the local German populace, who confronted insufficient food and heating supplies for the winter. The archbishop reassured the starving and freezing population that stealing coal or food out of sheer need was not a sin. Cologne citizens even coined a new term, "fringsen," to refer to such acts of "self-help." He was also a steadfast enemy of atheistic communism, reflecting an opposition that was not just political but personal. His brother Heinrich, arrested by the Soviets at the war's end, died a miserable death in a communist "concentration camp," as the cardinal bitterly recalled.[20] In showing himself quick to forgive perpetrators, including the worst Holocaust murderers, Cardinal Frings had little interest in the fate of Jewish victims and focused mostly on the postwar fate of German Catholics. When he headed the German Catholic bishops' conference in Fulda, his opposition to the Nuremberg trials and other Allied denazification efforts carried significant weight. After all, as I must reemphasize, he was widely considered the de facto leader of the German Catholic Church in those postwar years.

Perhaps unsurprisingly then, the first meeting between Frings and Allied representatives, in Cologne in July 1945, did not go well. Offended that the British had asked him to travel from his downtown residence to their local headquarters in Cologne—a city within the British occupation zone—Frings protested (according to official transcripts) that "as representatives of a cultured nation, you should have respected my rank and come to see me." He continued his disgruntled complaints: "[B]ased on my position I am equal to the rank of a general." For a citizen of a defeated nation that surrendered unconditionally, the bishop's self-confidence seems remarkably unscathed; it had clearly survived the war. After voicing his complaints, Frings met with two British officers, one a representative of Field Marshal Bernard Law Montgomery and the other a colonel, during which he shifted the discussion to the urgent needs of the German civilian population, including the critical food situation, limited housing, and the arrivals of expellees from Eastern German territories. He described former prisoners of the Nazis—mainly Poles and Russians—roaming the streets, allegedly plundering and committing other crimes. As Frings's complaints made clear, he was disappointed with the new rulers of Germany, as were the Germans in his diocese.

Speaking for his flock, he explained that after the fall of Hitler's government, the German people expected improved economic conditions, but "Instead, everything has become worse," and Frings threatened it could be worse still. He warned Montgomery's emissary that the harsh denazification measures and loss of the agriculturally rich eastern provinces created poverty and chaos, thereby "pushing the people into the arms of communism." The irritated British colonel would not let the claims stand; he replied that British occupation was mild compared with the Nazi occupation of Holland and France. He also emphasized that the church fell under the state's jurisdiction. The archbishop vigorously rejected this notion, exclaiming, "I am subject of the pope!" Even if the Nazi occupation forces might have been responsible for "some harshness," it was up to the Allies to do better, Frings stressed.[21]

Notably absent from the meeting was any discussion of German guilt or responsibility. Frings portrayed Germany as a cultured nation and saw no reason for Germans to abase themselves before the Allied victors. Instead, he echoed the growing claim that most Germans had not been Nazis and were now being treated unjustly by the new authorities.[22]

This interaction sheds meaningful light on the postwar confidence of the Catholic Church in Germany. Both the two major Christian churches, Lutheran and Catholic, found themselves "in a position of unique authority" at the war's end, but it was the Catholic Church that dominated.[23] No government ruled in Berlin anymore; churches were the only German authority left on the national level, and their infrastructure remained mostly intact. According to the historian Frederic Spotts, "Until a German government was reestablished in 1949, the [two] churches constituted the most powerful and articulate voice of the German people."[24] In exploiting this newfound authority, Catholic leaders in Germany, including Frings, counted on the backing of Pius XII. The world may have judged them guilty, but the pope stood with the Germans, showing deep interest in German affairs and the future of the country.

Cardinal Frings found clear reassurance and solid support in Pius XII's address of June 2, 1945. When German Catholic leaders gathered for their first postwar meeting in Fulda, at the grave of Saint Boniface, the apostle of the Germans, the pope's speech offered guidance for the Catholic leadership in Germany. In this programmatic address, the pope reiterated the claim that the Church had been a bulwark of anti-Nazi resistance and argued that the German people should be helped rather than punished. As described by the historian Jacques Kornberg,

> In the pope's view only the hands of the few were stained with blood, while the majority were merely misled, seduced, taken in, or ignorant of what was happening around them. Pius XII's assumption that most Germans were virtually victims of the regime was certainly convenient in a pope who wanted to avoid divisive issues and recriminations after the war, indeed, avoid anything that might shake the church and bring disorder and discord.[25]

A POPULATION OF MARTYRS

As these diverse accounts indicate, German Catholic leaders aligned fully with the pope in mourning their defeated, occupied, and ruined country. Exhibiting bullish resistance to the world's judgment, the German bishops issued a pastoral letter on August 23, 1945, that asserted guilt belonged to individual Catholics, not collectively to the Church. Following the pope's lead, the Catholic Church in Germany described itself as having engaged in principled resistance to the Nazi regime, as evidenced by the many priests who had been persecuted, incarcerated, and even murdered. In two exemplary sentences, the bishops shrugged off any question of the Church's complicity or guilt:

> We profoundly deplore the fact that many Germans, even in our own ranks, allowed themselves to be deceived by the false teachings of National Socialism, remained indifferent to the crimes against human freedom and human dignity; many by their attitude lent support to the crimes, many became criminals themselves. A heavy responsibility falls upon those who, because of their influence, could have prevented such crimes and did not do so but made these crimes possible and in this way associated themselves with the criminals.[26]

Thus, even when acknowledging some German guilt, the bishops watered down any responsibility by implying that most Germans had been seduced by the Nazis and gone along with the regime, not as perpetrators but merely as bystanders. The truly guilty constituted only a minority of the nation. In addition to depicting the German Catholic Church as a church of saints, with only a few black (or rather, brown) sheep, the narrative doubled down on the assertion that the Catholic Church itself had been a victim of the Nazis.

A few weeks later, the Vatican newspaper *Osservatore* featured a prominent article covering the Fulda conference and the pastoral letter. Translated into Italian, the pastoral letter appeared in full, with only a few editorial comments. Thus readers in Vatican City could easily consider the arguments that the Catholic Church in Germany had fought "against the false race theory and against the hatred between nations" and that "Catholics have protected fellow citizens of other bloodlines." Through these efforts, the bishops asserted, they had shown real Christian *caritas* (charity) and empathy with the "innocent persecuted non-Aryans." The letter continues, "Catholic people, we rejoice that you, in large part [*weitem Ausmasse*], have not stained yourself with the idolatrous cult of ugly force. We rejoice that so many of our faithful have never bowed their knees before the God Baal." Italian readers would have received the message that Germans had committed horrible crimes, and that some Catholics had been seduced by the false teachings of National Socialism, but that the responsibility lay with those in office, who knew and could have prevented the terrible crimes. But as the bishops assured these readers, ordinary men and women, including Nazi foot soldiers, did not approve of the regime's actions: "Justice wants that responsibility is always and everywhere examined on a case-by-case basis so that the innocent do not suffer with the guilty. This is why we bishops have made every effort and also for the future we will do the same."[27]

Thus, the Church's repeated message was clear: Germans had committed crimes, but Germans were not collectively guilty. An underlying but still clear theme in the letter also demands special consideration, namely, that the Catholic Church in Germany was a bastion of resistance against the false teachings of Nazism. The reason for such posturing is obvious. The Church urgently needed to resecure its moral authority and project its own victimhood if it was to have any hope of re-Christianizing the German population, especially the youth. At the time, the Church also was working to bring God back to the center of German life and community and to make "state, race or nation" secondary values. Accordingly, the bishops' declaration contained a strong appeal to leave behind secular teachings and return to God:

> A time of worldliness has collapsed and has left us with a tremendous field of ruins. Let us remove these ruins, especially in repentance and return to the Lord our God! Let us go to work and build anew on the firm foundation of faith in the Triune God, in submission to God's holy will![28]

The bishops urged Germans to embrace Christian *caritas* and help others in solidarity, which would offer comfort after the terrible suffering of the war: "Heavenly splendors are open to all, if they died in the peace of Christ, even if in the last moment, they had the grace to reconcile with God."[29]

Reviewing it today, I note that the bishops' self-exculpatory text left out nearly every unpleasant fact about the Church: its nationalism, its Christian antisemitism, and any of the many deals that church leaders had made with fascist regimes to protect itself. More so than any other actor, the pope set the tone with his June 2 message, which he repeated in multiple exchanges with the German bishops. In near-record time, Munich's auxiliary bishop Johannes Neuhäusler wrote his one-sided report, *Cross and Swastika* (*Kreuz und Hakenkreuz*), about the German Catholic Church's victimhood. Published just one year after the end of the war, it was one of the books hailed by Pius XII as an "impressive justification of the clergy."[30] Cardinal Faulhaber penned its foreword. In announcing its publication, the *Osservatore* reported that the book documents "the resistance of the Catholic bishops against the Nazi regime."[31] Neuhäusler himself had been imprisoned by the Nazis in the Dachau concentration camp, which established him as a moral voice in postwar Germany. The influential book is indicative of the Vatican's official views and position regarding the Catholic Church's role during the Nazi regime; it dominated the discourse for decades.[32] Only decades later did German Catholic bishops openly admit the complicity of their predecessors in supporting the war and turning a blind eye to the persecution of Jews.[33]

Neuhäusler's papers also include a letter, dated January 1947, to all Catholic bishops in Bavaria. It summarized a publication issued by Germany's Protestant Church, detailing their victims of the Nazi regime. In response, Catholic leadership in Munich stressed that it "would certainly be valuable, if a more detailed overview of the persecution of the Catholic clergy could soon be published."[34] Also among Neuhäusler's papers, I found a report by a close confidant of Pius XII, sent to U.S. bishops, that refers to the fight by the Catholic Church in Germany against Nazism as "one of the most glorious chapters in church history."[35]

Not all Catholics, clergy included, were on board with this kind of "abuse of the martyrium for the faith for propaganda purposes . . . with the purpose to show the Allies, that not all Germans . . . were Nazis," according to a letter from a fellow Catholic priest in Neuhäusler's papers.[36] Even if we consider such dissent and challenges to Neuhäusler's narrative, though, the Germans-as-victims motif remained the position of many top Catholic officials, at the time and for decades thereafter.[37]

THE POPE'S TEARS

German Catholic leaders came to rely on the pope's support, but in the final throes of the war, their direct communication with the Vatican was interrupted. Both sides worried about the gaps in their communication, so much so that by May 1945, the Vatican was appealing for Allied help in the matter:

> For some time all communications between Vatican City and the Most Reverend Ordinaries in Germany have been interrupted. In order to obtain prompt and exact information concerning religious conditions in Germany, it is the earnest desire of the Holy See that His Eminence Cardinal Michael von Faulhaber, Archbishop of Munich and Freising, be enabled to come to Rome as soon as possible.[38]

German bishops, and especially Faulhaber and Frings, were eager to reconnect with the Holy Father, and in September 1945, Father Ivo Zeiger arrived in Germany to see Frings, on a direct mission from the pope. Zeiger was not just any messenger. Director of the Germanicum Institute in Rome and an intimate advisor to Pius XII, he spoke fluent Italian and had powerful contacts around the world, including in his native Germany. As Ventresca explains in his Pius XII biography, "Father Zeiger was something of an éminence grise in Pacelli's inner circle."[39] Considering his prominence, selecting Zeiger as the emissary to reestablish lines of communication with the German bishops underscores the importance that the pope placed on getting in touch with them.

In seeing Zeiger off to Germany, Pius XII reportedly had "tears in his eyes" and entrusted him with delivering his best wishes to the German bishops, with "*tutto affetto, con tutto cuore*" ("with my deepest sympathies, with all my heart"). In addition to expressing these sincere affections, Pius XII tasked this one-man mission with raising concerns about the disrupted channels of communication, the plight of Catholic education, and the degree to which German youth were infected by the Nazi spirit. Not least of all, Zeiger was to relay the pope's special concern about the fate of German POWs in Italy. Once he arrived in Germany, Zeiger assured the bishops of the pope's "undiminished love and respect . . . despite the wave of hatred which is being directed at the German people from all sides at the present time, the Holy Father wants to help the German people without respect to their confession [not just Catholics]."[40] As the pope had told him to do, Zeiger sought to learn what the Vatican could do to ease the suffering of the German population.

Such willingness to provide aid implied offers of humanitarian relief, but it also strongly indicated the relevance of religious assistance. In highlighting this type of assistance, Zeiger reaffirmed the validity of the 1933 concordat, which protected the rights of the Catholic Church in Germany and required (as Zeiger explicitly reminded them) state assistance in collecting annual membership fees (*Kirchensteuer*), establishing confessional schools (i.e., separate public schools for Catholic and Protestant youth run by federal authorities), and publishing freely and without state censorship. Allied diplomats had confirmed these rights, and thus, the pope believed the Allied forces in Germany should respect them. In turn, Zeiger's visit and the messages he shared "inaugurated a period of direct and explicit papal guidance over the German hierarchy [senior leadership of the Catholic Church] (ending only with the death of Pius XII) and helps explain the bishop's unbending obstinacy in holding to the Reichskonkordat and the demand for confessional schools."[41] Of course, as we will see, Frings and his follow Catholic leaders did not hesitate to act on the pope's instructions.

Zeiger's report about this visit, prepared for the pope, is preserved in the Vatican archives. Zeiger paints a vivid picture of a war-devastated country, explaining that "The journey through the German lands is extremely sad in many respects." Although many villages were left mostly intact, the cities showed "a horrible picture of destruction." Zeiger also described the millions of Eastern German refugees and reported that women and girls feared being raped by the Allies (especially in areas under Soviet control). Noting that the Allies had fired every civil servant from their jobs, whether they had been Nazi party members or not, Zeiger predicted that the policy would prove catastrophic. He shared reports that Russians, Czechs, and Poles were committing large-scale brutalities against German civilians, whereas the good-natured Americans were well liked by the Germans. Sounding a hopeful note, Zeiger ended his report to his friend the pope by listing various signs that religious life would flourish again in a new golden age for the faith. The Germans would come to love the pope more than ever, because

> The Church is seen by friend and foe as the only organized great power that everyone wants to lean on. I have the impression that more is expected of the Church than it is able to achieve with the best will in the world. In any case, a very big hour can strike for the Catholic Church in Germany.[42]

The timing of Zeiger's visit, soon after the Potsdam conference (July 17–August 2, 1945), deserves some attention too. In Potsdam, the "big three" Allied leaders—Stalin, Truman, and Churchill (soon to be replaced by Clement Attlee)—had met and agreed on far-reaching decisions regarding Germany's future. Among these decisions was the transfer of much of the country's eastern territory, de facto awarded to Poland and the Soviet Union, and the rules for the removal of the German population from those areas. The German Catholic bishops condemned the Potsdam decisions as harsh and unfair, then alleged that, in practice, they legitimized ethnic cleansings. The expulsion of Germans and ethnic Germans from Poland and Czechoslovakia was part of one of the largest forced migrations in modern history. It involved an estimated 12 million German expellees and refugees from Eastern and Central Europe, most of them women and children. Exposed to violence, harsh winter conditions, disease, and postwar deprivation, historians estimate that at least 600,000 expellees and refugees lost their lives.[43] Mass rape, beatings, and random killings of Germans were common. In the Czech town of *Přerov* (Prerau), in June 1945, 265 German refugees—men, women, and children—were dragged off a train by Czechoslovakian Army soldiers and shot so that their bodies fell into hastily dug-out trenches. The youngest victim was 8 months old.[44]

It is unsurprising that the German bishops mobilized against these expulsions, but in this effort, they were emboldened by the pope's support and sympathy to put the idea of German suffering center stage. Just three weeks after Potsdam, Frings (acting as spokesperson for the German Catholic bishops) issued a memorandum to the Allied Control Council for General Eisenhower, which provides a summary of the Catholic Church's worries about the collective punishment of German people. The letter starts with a condemnation of the Nazi regime as "guilty of the worst and most inhumane crimes and thereby covering the German name with shame" ["*schlimmster und unmenschlichster Verbrechen schuldig gemacht und dadurch den deutschen Namen mit*

Schmach bedeckten"]. Frings then strategically thanked the Allied leaders at Potsdam for not *collectively* condemning the German people as a "bunch of criminals" and for declaring their intent to punish only truly guilty people. He also expressed gratitude for continued protections of religious freedom, such as the Allies' efforts to allow the bishops to communicate directly with the pope in Rome, "in whom we see the earthly deputy of Christ appointed by God" ("*indem wir den von Gott bestellten irdischen Stellvertreter Christi sehen*"). But on behalf of the bishops, Frings also pleaded with the Allies to reverse their decision to expel all Germans from the East, and he denounced Allied violence, such as the widespread rape of German women and girls. Taking a diplomatic position, Frings concluded with the promise that Christian churches stood ready to contribute to the moral and religious reconstruction of the defeated nation and would help integrate German refugees.[45] But even with these diplomatic efforts and unctuous pleading, the letter offended U.S. officials, who recognized it as an attempt to influence Allied decisions. They neither acknowledged the letter nor forwarded it to Eisenhower.[46]

Although that effort did not succeed, on November 1, 1945, Pius XII wrote to Cardinal Faulhaber of Munich. The letter, designed to be shared publicly, sought to give the German bishops further guidance in their postwar decisions. In expressing his deep care for the German Catholic Church, the pope explained he did everything he could to support it against the attacks of the Nazis and that he knew "very well, and this is here publicly acknowledged to your credit—that in dutiful observance of your office you withstood and resisted with complete conviction the unhealthy teachings and methods of unbridled National Socialism and that you had the better part of your people at your side." Beyond persisting in the narrative of widespread Catholic resistance, the letter called for fair punishment of the few evildoers, with great care taken to avoid punishing the innocent together with the guilty. The pope also referred to the challenges, explaining that reconstruction would be difficult, because so many priests had been imprisoned or killed, and many churches lay in ruins. Finally, in indicating his awareness of what was happening in eastern Germany, thereby alluding to Polish and Czech revenge, the pope expressed the hope that people's common Catholic faith would help end the cycle of revenge and bring about peace. The pope's letter was to be read publicly from all pulpits in Germany.[47] In so doing, local clergy helped reinforce and spread the pope's assertions that the German Catholic Church had engaged in uncompromising opposition to the Third Reich.

Frings also followed up with the pope a few weeks later, thanking him for his positive words of support for German Catholics and German people. In informing the Holy Father that he, Frings, had been elected head of the Fulda Conference of Bishops, which all bishops except those from the Soviet occupation zone would attend, Frings noted that questions about Catholic schools and the validity of the concordat remained unresolved questions with the Allies. The letter goes on to detail the misery caused by the lack of food, clothing, and heating materials, as well as Allied administrative purges that were causing massive disruptions to German society, such that "A lot of suffering also comes to good families as a result of the denazification measures, even those who belonged only formally to the [Nazi] party are removed from their positions as teachers, judges, doctors or in the economy or even taken to political prisoner camps." Offering a remarkable claim about the plight of German refugees expelled from eastern provinces, Frings claimed that "The greatest catastrophe that even this war has seen is taking place there. It is extremely painful for us that Catholic nations are also taking part in this work of extermination." He took encouragement from efforts by French, Swiss, British, and U.S. Catholics to halt the injustices against the German people, as well as from Pius XII: "Giving heartfelt thanks for all that Your Holiness has done and will do for the good of our poor, humiliated people."[48]

VAE VICTIS!

The brutal, mass expulsions of Germans came to take up more of the bishops' attention. In the summer of 1946, Frings and six other bishops from the Fulda Conference wrote to U.S. leaders and included a petition to President Truman, calling for aid for ethnic Germans expelled from Czechoslovakia, Poland, and Hungary: "The lives of ten thousands of starving or dying people are at stake. We think it our duty to ask your Excellency [Truman] for help, as a terrible catastrophe can only be prevented by your initiative and the generosity of the American people."[49] General Lucius Clay, who at that time was deputy military governor for Germany, was unwilling to forward the petition to the president. He believed it both presumptuous and without merit for German bishops to criticize and condemn major Allied decisions, all while pleading for help. Potsdam had been necessary to keep peace in Europe, as was the expulsion of German minorities from Poland and Czechoslovakia. In Clay's view, the Allies were doing their best to transfer people in an "orderly and humane" manner, even if the reality on the ground contests this idealized depiction.[50]

If the U.S. authorities refused to help, then Frings decided that Catholic priests should read, from their pulpits, an explicit condemnation of the expulsions of Germans. Staking a moral claim, Frings wrote, in his role as representative of the German bishops, that they

> can no longer be silent about the horrible fate of more than 10 million East Germans. . . . The expulsions are done with horrible brutality, by ignoring all standards of humanity. . . . The international community is silent on this horrible tragedy. It is like an iron curtain has come down on this part of Europe. We know that it is precisely in those areas that Germans have committed terrible crimes against members of other nations. But since when has it been allowed to take revenge on innocent people and atone for crime through crime? One should hold the really guilty to ruthless accountability. But who wants to be responsible for the mass dying of children, mothers, old people?[51]

Cardinal Frings's statements here arguably express what many Germans thought. For them the brutal expulsion of millions of Germans from their traditional lands was a massive crime, which could not be justified by citing German atrocities committed in Poland and the Soviet Union during the war. Nor could revenge against innocent people ever be justified. During the Nuremberg trials, some defendants also pointed to these events, equating the postwar expulsion of Germans by the Allies to the Nazis' war crimes and systematic extermination of Jews and other "enemies" of the Reich. It was as if to say, "Well sure, war is horrible. All sides commit crimes. Now why don't we all just move on?" The unique and horrific nature of the Shoah was not widely recognized until decades later. In addition to challenging the moral authority of the Allies to sit in judgment of Germany, the Catholic bishops prognosticated that destroying German society represented a threat to the very essence of Western culture.

Although such claims of moral equivalence are pointless and deeply problematic, it is necessary to consider the evidence of Allied violence against civilians, particularly during the forced expulsions. First-hand accounts described how, "Until the end of May [1945] in Berlin reigned the terror!" Looting, deportation, and sexual violence were widespread under the Soviet rule. German women and girls, ranging in age from 10 to 75 years, suffered gang-rapes by Red Army soldiers; not even nuns wearing religious habits were spared. In desperation, many German women in Berlin hid on roofs for weeks, according to one report.[52]

The situation was much better in Western Germany, but violence occurred there too. French and British troops, as well as U.S. GIs, raped German women and girls. The extent of these violations remains disputed; rape by Western Allies was a taboo subject for decades, especially during the Cold War. Only in recent years has this sensitive and important topic gained attention.[53] According to the French historian Marc Hillel, 385 women were raped in Konstanz and 500 in Freudenstadt. But smaller villages and towns were affected too.[54]

The bishops actively sought to make the Vatican aware of these crimes. Cardinal Faulhaber informed Monsignor Walter Carroll, from the Vatican Secretariat of State, that Moroccan troops in the French Army had raped more than 6,000 German women in the Stuttgart area in just one night—numbers that appear to have been exaggerated, such that most sources refer to 1,200 victims. The Vatican reacted with a carefully worded telegram to the papal nuncio in Paris, asking what might be done.[55] Yet the claims by Faulhaber exemplify German Church leaders' willingness to report on events without much fact-checking.[56] The crimes were terrible enough as they were; inflating the numbers seems unjustified. In addition, the bishops appealed to German rape victims to keep any babies that resulted from the violations or give them to foster homes instead of aborting them, offering strong warnings that the destruction of life is never justified. Referring again to the sanctity of life, the bishops condemned the widespread suicides by citizens of the defeated nation: "Only God gives life, and only He can take it."[57]

After receiving such reports, the Vatican sought to intervene. It had no leverage with the Soviets, but Vatican leadership flexed its influence in the United States. In Washington, Archbishop Amleto Giovanni Cicognani repeatedly appealed to the U.S. secretary of state on behalf of the Germans.[58]

Confronted with reports of mass rape against German women, some U.S. officials in Berlin rejected the Vatican's outrage. The Office of Military Government report downplayed the claims forwarded by the Vatican, asserting that the incident "usually becomes less breathtaking" if objective facts are considered. Even if unlawful attacks happened, they were less frequent and violent than implied. The U.S. officials also offered a questionable explanation for the inaccuracies: "German reports are prone to emphasize rape because of its erotic appeal to some Americans and British. As a matter of fact, rape and its less violent sister acts are common. All war is rough. People who dislike being treated rough should not commence wars of aggression."[59] In the view of this U.S. official, the Germans got what they deserved.

The papal initiatives were not limited to such official channels, though. In close coordination with the Catholic Church in the U.S., the pope was able to spread his vision for peace to a broader audience. The U.S. Catholic bishops, represented by Bishop Francis Spellman of New York and Archbishop Samuel Stritch of Chicago, penned "Between War and Peace" as an open letter in November 1945. In claiming, "The war is over but there is no peace in the world," they pointed to Soviet takeovers in eastern and southeastern Europe and expressed their shock at news from Slovakia, Croatia, Slovenia, and other southeastern European countries, where "religious persecution [was] both brutal and cunning." Italy also needed support, because "The fate of Christian culture is at stake in Italy," and the danger of communism was lurking everywhere. Such threats also demanded concern about the future of Germany, Austria, and Hungary, because "to treat [the former Axis nations] in a spirit of vengeance is neither right nor wise." The guilty needed to be punished, but—in a claim that should be familiar to us by now—the idea of collective guilt had to be rejected, as was being imposed through the forced expulsions of ethnic Germans from the east.[60]

The U.S. bishops' letter spread widely. When the *Osservatore* published a translation, with associated commentary, this version was forwarded to the U.S. State Department. The newspaper's commentary starts with an acknowledgment: "The trial against the German war criminals is now being held at Nuremberg. This is a trial which in itself is just and exemplary." But as it goes on, it emphasizes the Soviets' engagement in "the extermination of the

German people," illustrated with a photo of long columns of war-wretched German refugees. Then the article offers a clear indication of the *Osservatore*'s perspective:

> Vindictive reprisal is not justice. The victor who really wished to pacify the vanquished and be worthy of victory must apply the maxim of Roman law: *Parcere subjectis et debellare superbos* ("Have pity upon the vanquished and punish the haughty"). Christian civilization suggests a more enlightened charity which is, after all, wiser and more fruitful. But Moscow has turned down the most noble appeals of the Holy Father branding them as sterile or as commoving false pity. This is not surprising as the American Bishops admonish us: "The world is only one insofar as men live together as brothers under God."

The *Osservatore* article ends with a classical reference: "But those who have declared war against God do not surprise us by showing that they prefer to throw the sword of Brennus on the souls of the vanquished people rather than the sword of justice.[61] The Celtic army leader Brennus, upon defeating the ancient Romans, threw his sword onto the scales and shouted the famous phrase *Vae victis* (Woe the vanquished!). From communists who declare war on religion and God, nothing reasonable or good could be expected, according to the Vatican newspaper.

Bishop Aloisius Muench offered a unique perspective too, as an American of German heritage. In his Lenten Pastoral of 1946, titled "One World in Charity," the influential cleric followed the pattern we see over and over again: He started by decrying the atrocities committed in the worst war of history. But he also and equally condemned the brutalization of the German civilian population, suffering from bombing raids, forced deportations, and the widespread rape of German women, including nuns, by the Soviets. Near the end of his speech, Muench declared that it was time to end the cycle of violence and revenge and called for "Christian charity [to] follow the example of the good Samaritan" by acting with mercy and compassion for anyone suffering. He repeated the condemnation of notions of collective guilt but also went a step further, by depicting Germans as victims of Jewish vengefulness.[62] Although the German translation and distribution of "One World in Charity" in Germany in 1947 was illegal, Muench had no issue with its publication—quite the contrary, as he confided in private. His German victimization narrative relied on anti-Jewish tropes, and it resonated with German audiences who saw themselves as victims, first of Nazi insanity and then of Allied revenge. As Muench's biographer Suzanne Brown-Fleming notes, "*One World* became a sensation in Germany [. . .]."[63]

Such resonance also appears in the expressions contained in the anonymous pamphlet discussed above. Unlike the pamphlet attributed to von Galen, though, Muench's speech was not anonymous. Anonymity might provide plausible deniability for the Church, regarding its embrace of the argument of German victimhood. But Muench made the argument, clearly and in his own name, and then was rewarded for his position by Pius XII. Claims of victimhood thus were welcomed and embraced by German brethren in Christ, who largely asserted that the majority of Germans were not Nazis, even while the Americans asserted that most of them were. There can be little doubt that many Germans, if not the majority, supported the Nazi regime at some point.[64] Furthermore, there can be no doubt that the Church's other argument—that only a tiny group of Nazi leaders were responsible—lacks any factual foundation. Instead, we know that complicity in Nazi war crimes was widespread.

CONCLUSION

The pope's argument that most Germans were not Nazi perpetrators but rather were victims themselves became a central and repeated theme in the Church's opposition to war crimes trials. The narrative became so powerful that Church leaders went so far as to compare Allied violence against German civilians to the crimes of the Nazis. Cardinal von Galen, the Lion of Münster, in a heated moment, referred to Allied crimes as worse than those committed by the Nazis. It might not have gone quite so far formally, but the Vatican argued that the ethnic cleansing that resulted from the expulsion of millions of Germans from their traditional lands was a grave injustice that could not be justified as a response to the atrocities Germans committed in Poland and the Soviet Union. As defendants at the Nuremberg trials echoed these arguments and various religious and media channels promulgated the messages, a widespread belief emerged among Germans, namely, that they had nothing to be ashamed of and bore no responsibility.

In light of such a broad embrace, the comments of Konrad Adenauer, West Germany's first postwar chancellor, are notable. In 1946, writing to one of his friends, a Catholic priest, he asserted that the German people and German churches carry deep guilt for the crimes of the Nazi years. Adenauer had no doubt that the German people and clergy knew about Nazi crimes but remained mostly silent. If Church leaders had spoken out earlier, they could have prevented vast evil.[65] Yet Adenauer also was Catholic, and he never offered any such clear statements in public. Instead, for most Germans "collective guilt was replaced by collective innocence," as Aleida Assmann fittingly put it.[66] In all the Catholic leaders' diverse efforts to intervene, one element remains consistent: They embraced a narrative of victimhood, in which Germans had been victims of the Nazis first and of the Allies later. This widespread distortion of history was rejected in Germany only decades later.

6

VICTORS' JUSTICE

Even as Germans claimed victimhood, and the pope challenged some aspects of Nuremberg, the victorious Allies kept widening the war crimes program. The Vatican and Church leaders in Germany cried foul, accusing the Allies of exacting "victors' justice" and taking barely disguised revenge on the vanquished. It was in this context that Pope Pius XII issued his plea that the world forgive and forget war and genocide. He regarded this as the only way forward and believed ongoing trials and purges would prolong wartime chaos and play into the hands of "godless" communism. In coming to the defense of Germany against this perceived "injustice," like Catholic avengers for "true justice," Catholic clergy even worked to reverse verdicts in war crimes trials. Their concerted actions represented systematic, "conscious support of the perpetrators,"[1] to such an extent that one German scholar labeled clergy "the most effective helpers of National Socialist [war] criminals."[2] This confrontation between the Pope and the Allies over the ongoing Nazi war crimes trials in Germany was manifested in their different ideas of justice.

As we have seen, the pope opposed widespread purges and war crimes trials from the start, with the assertion that the German people were collectively innocent, not collectively guilty. The ongoing trials gave the lie to this assertion, revealing the widespread complicity of German elites.[3] Between 1946 and 1949, the United States organized 12 further Nuremberg military trials, without the other Allies, and indicted 185 defendants.[4] However, the vast majority of Nazi war criminals held in the U.S. zone of Germany were tried not at Nuremberg but rather through the lesser known U.S. Army trials in Dachau. Of the 1,672 accused there, expedited trials resulted in 1,416 convictions and 426 death sentences.[5] Around the same time, the British and French were holding war crimes trials in their respective zones of occupation. Altogether, approximately 5,133 people were prosecuted for war crimes in the western zones of Germany, and 668 were sentenced to death.[6] Thousands of trials of Nazi officials, local collaborators, and fascist leaders occurred all over Europe.

German Catholic clergy spoke out, publicly and frequently, against such efforts, seemingly encouraged by the pope. During the later Nuremberg and Dachau trials, Vatican opposition became increasingly fundamental. The pope took personal interest in many proceedings, throwing the full weight of the Vatican behind the defense of quite a few accused war criminals as in the case of Weizsäcker. Such papal interest and involvement are evident in the newly released papers related to Pius XII in the Vatican archives. Combining these archival records with the German Catholic archives reveals a fascinating picture.

THE DAMNED

Following the initial International Nuremberg Tribunal, the Holy See's intervention in the trials of high-ranking Nazis grew more principled in nature. Perhaps the most remarkable intervention involved the case of the prominent German industrialist Alfried Krupp von Bohlen und Halbach. The Krupp family ruled over an impressive business empire, employing more than 120,000 people in the 1930s. Krupp factories were essential to the Nazi war machine during World War II. The power, intrigues, and questionable choices of the Krupp family during the early years of the Nazi regime were immortalized by Italian filmmaker Luchino Visconti in his 1969 film *The Damned*, which only thinly veils the references to this industrialist dynasty. A popular slogan among the "Hitler Youth" claimed that its members were, "Nimble as greyhounds, tough as leather, hard as Krupp steel!" At war's end, in April 1945, Alfried Krupp was immediately arrested by the Americans. By August 1947, in Nuremberg, 12 officials of the Krupp company, including Alfried, were tried for their involvement in the Nazi regime's war preparation, the company's use of slave labor, and its plunder of raw materials and resources from occupied countries.[7]

Perhaps noting the success achieved by others in similar situations, Alfried's mother Bertha Krupp wrote to the pope, pleading as a "Christian wife and mother" for him to prevent the trial.[8] The letter came to the pope through the Prince-Archbishop of Salzburg, Andreas Rohracher, who had earned a reputation for criticizing the trials. Unsurprisingly, he strongly supported the request and recommended direct intervention with President Truman by turning to the familiar argument that the trials lacked moral justification, "in view of the participation of Russian Judges in the trial, [of a nation] which is responsible for even greater crimes than the German industry, to warmly support Mrs. Krupp von Bohlen's request."[9] The archbishop either did not understand or fudged the facts, namely, that "Russian" judges ruled in the subsequent Nuremberg trials; Moscow had no active role in these proceedings. Regardless of the factual inaccuracy, the letters produced the desired results, prompting the Vatican to get busy intervening with U.K. and U.S. diplomats in the Vatican, by mimicking the language adopted by Baroness Krupp, "to prevent the forthcoming trial, before the international tribunal at Nuremberg."[10] Krupp's defense lawyers also made extensive use of a speech that Cardinal Frings gave in Cologne on March 14, 1948. In criticizing the trials, Frings expressed solidarity with the accused and lauded the Krupp family and its business by name.[11]

After Alfried Krupp received a 12-year prison sentence, and the court ordered that all Krupp properties be confiscated, his mother issued another appeal to the pope, asserting that the sentence had been stamped with "hatred and revenge," and "My heart . . . tells me that this is injustice."[12] In response, Monsignor Giovanni Montini wrote Bertha Krupp in November 1948, stating, "The Holy Father, who has already done much to come to the aid of these gentlemen, has now instructed our office to take new steps to change the sentence passed against them, if possible."[13] Those instructions apparently included directions for the pope's delegate in Germany to enter into talks with U.S. authorities in Germany, such as General Lucius Clay's top advisor Robert D. Murphy, "a good Catholic," as the pope's envoy stressed. Notably, the Americans' case was under review at that precise moment, and Murphy hinted that reduced sentences were in the cards, such that further interventions by the pope might be premature.[14] His predictions proved correct: In January 1951, the Americans released Alfried Krupp and restored most of his fortune.

The Vatican archives reveal that appeals from individual Nazi perpetrators and their families, like Bertha Krupp and others discussed earlier, were frequent and widespread. When I encountered this evidence, I could not help but think about members of other groups who also had pled with the Holy Father for support and help. During and before WWII, the pope received thousands of petitions from Jewish victims of the Nazis, begging for aid. These newly available records are being studied in a project undertaken by the German University of Münster.[15] It will be fascinating to use these insights to establish a telling comparison. When it came to assistance from the Vatican, what could Nazi victims expect versus Nazi perpetrators?

In another case of a Nazi criminal pleading for help, we can consider Erwin von Helmersen, an SS doctor in the notorious death camp of Auschwitz-Birkenau. His assignment to Auschwitz represented an intense indicator of his guilt, and Helmersen was deeply involved in the Nazis' eugenics project. His defense strategy was based on his (dubious) Christian faith. Helmersen's Protestant family were members of the Baltic German nobility and had fled from the Soviets. While Erwin was facing trial in Poland, his father Harald pleaded with the pope for help in letters that also contained affidavits from Catholic and Protestant clergy, stressing the SS officer's Christian credentials ("Erwin is completely in Christ") and claiming that he was incapable, by nature, of the horrible acts of which he was accused. None of those priests had been in Auschwitz with the accused, of course.[16] The Vatican Secretariat of State was not optimistic that this intervention, targeted toward communist Polish authorities, would be successful: "on ne peut rien faire" ("we cannot do anything"), an internal note reads. Yet the Vatican still penned a draft letter, to August Hlond in Warsaw, informing the Polish cardinal that Harald von Helmersen had asked for help with the "liberation" of the SS officer from prison and instructing him to see what could be done, in the name of Christian mercy.[17] Simultaneously, the Vatican reassured Harald that it would do what it could, but that the circumstances (likely, control by Polish communist authorities) "present particular difficulties."[18]

I searched for and found Erwin von Helmersen's SS file in the U.S. National Archives, outside of Washington, D.C. It is 38 pages long and detailed; in combination with other sources, it provides a clear picture of his Nazi career. Born in Bremen, Germany, on November 4, 1914, Helmersen was a committed Nazi from an early age, starting with his time in the Hitler Youth. He joined the Nazi Stormtroopers in 1933 and became an official member of the Nazi Party in 1937. During the 1930s, he worked in the Office for Political Education of the National Socialist Student Association, eventually becoming its director. In January 1940, he joined the SS, while also pursuing doctoral studies at the Kaiser Wilhelm Institute for Anthropology in Berlin.[19] During December 1942, he began working in the Berlin-Lichterfelde hospital with the eugenicist Fritz Lenz. Once he received his degree, he was assigned to Auschwitz as a camp doctor. From August to December 1943, he worked with the infamous Dr. Josef Mengele in the "newly established Zigeunerlager (Gypsy camp)."[20] In 1943, he married; they had a baby boy in January 1944. At the end of World War II, Helmersen was captured and sentenced to death by a Polish court; he was executed on April 12, 1949, in Kraków, Poland.[21]

Although the Vatican's intervention for Helmersen failed to save him, I still wondered what prompted the intervention, and particularly whether Helmersen had Christian convictions. Therefore, I compared his SS file with statements made in his defense, referring to his alleged deep Christian faith. In his personal SS papers, Helmersen claimed that his religion was "*gottgläubig*," Nazi terminology that is difficult to define precisely. It is purposefully vague and could mean deist, atheist, or believer in Nazi-paganism (Germanic gods). Yet embracing this description offers a clear indication that the person had broken with traditional Christian faith and instead had committed fully to the Nazi *Weltanschauung*. Among the many citations Helmersen received from the Nazi regime, the Iron Cross first class (EK1) and neo-pagan Germanic "*Julleuchter*" are notable. According to assessments by his SS superiors: "Commitment to the National Socialist worldview: unconditionally."[22] This evidence indicates that Helmersen's loyalty lay far more with Hitler than with Christ. It also suggests sheer opportunism rather than any sincere convictions on the part of the guilty Nazi officer.

Cases such as these provide exemplary glimpses into the Vatican's strategies for intervening on behalf of the accused. But the Vatican's goals went beyond individual cases, however prominent each of them might have been. What the Vatican wanted, ultimately, was to shift the balance of postwar justice in favor of the defendants. To understand this objective and identify a key moment in the Vatican's crusade against Allied postwar justice, we can turn to the controversies surrounding the Malmedy war crimes trial.

THE MALMEDY CONTROVERSY

In December 1944, during the Battle of the Bulge near the town of Malmedy, 84 U.S. prisoners of war were gunned down and killed by the SS. The crimes created particular horror among the U.S. public, who called for action.[23] The murders at Malmedy powerfully influenced U.S. policy and attitudes toward the war crimes trials, too, arguably providing the push needed to initiate trials against lower-ranking Nazis and concentration camp guards, as were held in Dachau between 1945 and 1947.[24] The SS perpetrators of the Malmedy massacre were put on trial as part of these proceedings; all 73 defendants were convicted, and 43 were sentenced to death.

Over the course of 1948, though, opposition to Nazi war crimes trials grew stronger. The Soviets were blockading Berlin, and communists staged a coup in Czechoslovakia. But beyond the cooling, Cold War political climate, such resistance also stemmed from allegations that some of the convicted SS soldiers had been tortured while in U.S. custody to force their confessions.[25] It seems likely that the prisoners were treated roughly by guards, which could have included slaps, but no evidence supported the specious claims of systematic torture.[26] However, the lack of evidence did not stop the allegations from firing up opposition to the trials.

The accused and convicted soldiers had never accepted their verdicts anyway. Their defense counsel labeled the trial vengeful and based on illegally obtained evidence, while also claiming that U.S. forces had similarly shot surrendered German personnel.[27] Historian Steven P. Remy offers a clear summary of the outcomes of such allegations:

> What followed was a decade-long transatlantic controversy surrounding accusations that American interrogators had tortured the defendants, forcing them to sign false confessions and thus sealing their fates at the trial. A loosely

> interconnected network of Americans and Germans sought to overturn the verdicts and, more broadly, discredit all Allied war crimes trials.[28]

This collaborative effort to reject the war crimes trials indeed involved a diverse coalition, ranging from defense lawyers, right-wing networks, and old Nazis to American politicians and German bishops, together with the Vatican, all coordinating their actions to ultimately undermine the foundations of Nuremberg justice.[29]

When the Malmedy allegations were made public, they energized the Holy See in particular. A detailed petition to the pope came from Leonardo Jenny, general secretary of the little-known private "Swiss League for Human Rights," seeking support for the convicted SS soldiers. The Vatican Aid Commission summarized these concerns in an internal memo, focused particularly on the Malmedy trial:

> It is requested that an intervention by the Holy Father be made to change the methods of the American police and justice system in Germany, which are alleged to be brutal and unjust, and in the majority of trials and investigations seem to lead to results that are essentially false and unjust.[30]

This remarkable statement by a Vatican official condemns not just some but the majority of the trials as unjust. It offers a glimpse into Vatican officials' reasoning.

Although Malmedy gained widespread attention, the Vatican was also closely attuned to happenings in the Mühldorf trials. Mühldorf, a subcamp of Dachau, had been the site of brutal atrocities, especially near the end of the war. Erika Flocken, a female concentration camp doctor in that camp, was sentenced to death for her role in the Nazi mass murder program. As might be expected, her crimes did not prevent the "Swiss League for Human Rights" from asking the Vatican to aid her defense. Seemingly undeterred by her crimes, a petitioner for Flocken wrote to the pope, "May I respectfully ask Your Holiness for your utmost attention to stand up for the Good in this matter as well."[31] Defining "the good" in this context is a task for each reader of this book to undertake.

Summarizing its response to these appeals, the Vatican Secretariat of State wrote the U.S. diplomat Graham Parsons in March 1948 that the

Holy See had been asked for its help to obtain commutations of the death sentences of the 43 SS members that had resulted from the Malmedy trial. It erroneously referred to them as members of the Wehrmacht, the German army, not the *Waffen* SS, to which they actually belonged.[32] The final draft sent to Parsons did not include an already written third paragraph, alleging brutal and unjust methods by the U.S. military and prosecutors. This paragraph seemingly was removed at the last minute, before the letter went to U.S. diplomats at the Vatican. Why? An internal note, apparently written by Montini, provides clues: "The number 3 [the third paragraph] won't be offensive? Please think carefully! Gbm [Giovanni Battista Montini]."[33] The pope's top diplomats knew enough not to offend the Allied diplomats so openly.

Troubled by the accusations and potential blowback in the Malmedy case, U.S. authorities ordered a stay of the executions, and General Lucius Clay, at that point head of U.S. Military Government for Germany, set up an investigation board. The board eventually found that simulated trials likely had taken place and that the treatment of prisoners "at times exceeded the bounds of propriety,"[34] but it noted no evidence of systematic mass torture. Following a review of the reports, in March 1948, 31 of the 43 Malmedy death sentences were commuted to prison terms. For Church leaders, even this concession was not enough. They called for the review of all the Malmedy trials, as well as all the Dachau and Nuremberg proceedings. In support of these calls, the pope made his views on punishment public.

In a crucial document, Pius XII wrote to the German bishops on March 1, 1948, expressing once more his deep connection with the German people and the Catholic Church in Germany. He noted that the war had left Germany devastated and impoverished, and though the pope had tried to help as much as possible, Germany needed international help. In the interest of a better tomorrow, it was up to the rest of the world to forgive and forget the recent horrors:

> We therefore never tire of appealing publicly, and even more so in private consultations, to the reason and conscience of the world and to the leading men, as well as to the brotherhood of the [Catholic] believers, and to make them understand that, as things are today, the fight against the misery in Germany and other hard-hit countries requires sacrifices. It is the common duty of all countries and peoples, which can still provide aid, that they may be broad-minded

> enough to forget the past and, even if the most horrible things happened to them at the hands of Germany during the war in order to give you [Germans] too, as well as Europe and all of humanity hope for a better tomorrow under the sign of love.[35]

Pius XII then claimed neutral humanitarianism for the Church: "the kingdom of God does not know victors and vanquished, but only those in need of help and those willing to help."[36] He mourned in detail the fate of 12 million Germans expelled from eastern provinces and countries.

As we have already seen, *The New York Times* reported on this letter on April 16, 1948, detailing its claims that "the world should forgive and forget Germany's war crimes" and instead help to rebuild the country. The article further indicated that Pope Pius XII was aware of the crimes committed by the Nazis in Russia and Poland, but that he believed revenge was not the answer. All energies instead should be focused on reconstructing Europe.[37] While calling on the rest of the world to "forgive and forget" Nazi crimes, the pope, in early 1948, according to a record in the Vatican archives, sent blessings to Catholic prisoners in Landsberg,[38] a large complex that provided the main U.S. prison for Nazis convicted in the Dachau and Nuremberg trials.[39] The message could not have been clearer: Punishing German perpetrators and their collaborators all over Europe was the wrong policy. With this blessing from the pope, the Catholic Church in Germany initiated a systematic campaign to increasingly discredit the entire program of war crimes trials.[40]

CATHOLIC AVENGERS

Two German bishops were particularly active in this campaign. One was Cardinal Josef Frings of Cologne, who, as we have seen, had been opposed to the war crimes trials from the beginning. A sentence in his memoirs is telling in this regard: "A special activity at that time required the care of the so-called war criminals, soldiers who were charged with any kind of crime."[41] This brief characterization of the Nazis reflects how Frings mocked and questioned the war crimes program overall. On October 6, 1946, in an address to a group of Catholic faithful, Frings talked specifically about the Nuremberg verdict, a passage that is worth citing to show his view:

> After the verdict has been pronounced, the sense of justice [*Rechtsbewusstsein*] of all those who think legally, not only in Germany, demands that crimes that have happened elsewhere [and committed by others] now also find the punishment they deserve. Otherwise the justice that is at work would not, in spite of all objectivity, be that justice with the bandage in front of the eyes, which proceeds without any respect for the person, but would be more like the goddess of victory with the drawn sword who knocks down the enemy.[42]

That is, for Frings, the trials violated basic principles of Western law, namely, that punishment should be based on equal treatment—if those on the victorious side were not charged/put on trial, then German perpetrators should not be. He emphasized, like other bishops, that crimes committed by both sides during the war needed to be punished. In condemning victors' justice and criticizing the Allies for not punishing Allied war crimes, Frings's speech also followed the themes expressed in the anti-Nuremberg pamphlet, often attributed to Cardinal von Galen, that was causing an uproar around the same time. The day after the executions ordered by the International Nuremberg Tribunal took place, Cardinal Frings called for an immediate halt to denazification efforts and war crimes trials. In a high-level meeting with a group of English bishops on October 17, 1946, he demanded that the end of the International Nuremberg Tribunal "must [also] be the end of revenge, and the beginning of reconstruction."[43] Furthermore, he demanded a complete break with denazification efforts that sought out former Nazi party members and participants, arguing that they required too many people to be "excluded from the national life and allowed to rot. Does England really wish to kill 20 million people?"[44] This explosive question refers to administrative removals of former Nazis from positions of power and the civil service, purges that he considered out of proportion and likely to destabilize German society. The Bishop of Chichester George Bell attempted to appease Frings, explaining that no one wanted Germany to fall into chaos. The English bishop also agreed with Frings that continuing the trials could be considered "mere revenge."[45]

Frings found another committed brother-in-arms in Munich's auxiliary bishop, Johannes Neuhäusler. As noted earlier, Neuhäusler, a former Dachau prisoner, seemed beyond reproach in his anti-Nazi credentials. In 1947, Pope Pius XII ordained him titular bishop of Calydon, as well as

Auxiliary Bishop in Munich. He earned papal honorifics for his work, including being named papal chamberlain of honor, and assistant to the papal throne.[46] As we have seen, he readily peddled the rather one-sided narrative that the Germans had been the first victims of the Nazis. He went even further when it came to the war crimes trials. He decried Nuremberg as an injustice; describing his approach to U.S. leaders like New York's Cardinal Francis Spellman, he claimed to be working "in the interest of justice and mercy" and "in order to prevent judicial murders" ["*Justizmorden*"]. Neuhäusler demanded an appellate authority over subsequent Nuremberg and Dachau trials; otherwise, "[h]orrible and never to be repaired wrong would be done." Clearly hinting at the Malmedy controversy, he cited widespread doubts about methods of investigation, dubious witnesses, and harsh sentences. He leveraged his past as a Nazi victim to issue the claim, "As much as I myself was persecuted by the Nazis and had to experience all sorts of injustice in a four-year imprisonment in a concentration camp, I want to do everything to ensure that we ourselves seek and exercise justice."[47] Neuhäusler, Frings, and others tirelessly intervened with General Clay and other officials, all the way up to President Truman, to stop the executions of Nazi war criminals.[48]

With the pope's blessing, Frings and Neuhäusler also felt empowered to take on the Allies' criminal punishment system. At the conclusion of the war crimes tribunals, the bishops' attacks shifted toward Landsberg prison and the executions taking place there. Convicted war criminals in Landsberg had been reaching out to the bishops regularly. Their solicitations indicate that they counted on sympathy and support—and for good reason. One example among many comes from a March 1949 letter, written to Neuhäusler, by the former SS officers Hans Eisele and Willi Witteler, who had been condemned to death. Alleging that the "so called war crime trials" sought revenge and not justice, they ranted about

> a deliberate plan to denounce thousands of Germans as war criminals. . . . Your Excellency, we all know that you are trailblazers when it comes to enforcing the law—also in our case. We can sense the difficulties that arise again and again. We thank you, Your Excellency, from the bottom of our hearts for your assistance so far and ask that you continue to assist us.[49]

They also were eager to take active roles in Neuhäusler's campaign, such as by providing materials to discredit prosecution witnesses, shared through the willing channel offered by the Catholic prison chaplain Karl Morgenschweis.[50] Both Eisele and Witteler had served as concentration camp doctors; they both had reportedly participated in brutal experiments on prisoners. Witteler "requisitioned" people for malaria experiments. His death sentence was commuted and reduced to 20 years in prison. He also received a letter of support from the prominent Pastor Martin Niemöller, stating that he was a "real physician," not some SS doctor.[51] Eisele managed to present himself as a "repentant Christian" and gained release in 1952, after which he fled to Egypt to escape further prosecution.

The Fulda Conference of German Catholic bishops also prepared a memorandum on the prisoners in Landsberg. Writing on their behalf, Frings requested appeals for the convicted Nazis from U.S. General Clay. Frings asserted his concern that innocent people might be executed. The arguments contained in the appeal pertained not just to clemency but also questioned the legal basis of the Nuremberg and Dachau trials and claimed that "During the last few years the confidence in justice was heavily shaken." Therefore, the bishops called for both a stay of all executions and a full review of sentences resulting from the Nuremberg and Dachau trials by an appeal court. The bishops' statement concludes with the promise that such a review "may punish the real guilty ones and give back to the German people and the whole world the conviction that victors and vanquished are subjected to the same law, as they once will stand before the same divine Judge."[52] General Clay likely knew where this was going; the bishops made little attempt to couch their accusation of victors' justice. In response to the memorandum, Clay firmly stated that the Nuremberg and Dachau trials had not been an expression of arbitrary power wielded by victorious nations but instead were based on laws and due process. Clay continued that, considering the overwhelming evidence against the accused, his conscience led him to consider the sentences just and appropriate. Any revision process or appeal was not necessary. As General Clay concluded, "the war crimes tribunals were established in the interests of high justice with the hope that the world would recognize their contribution to peace and that they would be a deterrent to future aggressors."[53]

While Clay maintained his position, back in the United States, the defenses of Nuremberg justice were crumbling. At the end of July 1948, a three-person commission of the Secretary of the Army, headed by Colonel Gordon Simpson, started its assigned task: to look into 139 confirmed but not-yet-executed death sentences from the Dachau trials, 12 of which were Malmedy cases.[54] Just days before, Montini, the Vatican Undersecretary of State, had ordered the papal delegate in Washington, Amleto Giovanni Cicognani, to intervene with U.S. authorities directly, in an effort to achieve the commutation of all death sentences in the Malmedy and Mühldorf cases. Cicognani approached Monsignor Howard Carroll, the Secretary General of the powerful National Catholic Welfare Conference (NCWC), and the Jesuit Reverend Edmund A. Walsh at Georgetown University in Washington. Walsh reported to Cicognani that the sentences already had been reduced, some of the accused had been acquitted, no executions had taken place, and appeals were under way.[55] In their efforts, Frings and Neuhäusler thus found the support of the universal Catholic Church—with its vast financial resources, media, diplomats, and moral authority—priceless.

ALL THE POPE'S MEN

Despite Walsh's assurances, in October 1948, the stay of execution was lifted. Ten of the remaining 139 death-row candidates in Landsberg were executed. A new round of diplomatic wrangling thus began, featuring intervention efforts by Neuhäusler, Frings, and the pope too. Frings lost no time; on October 23, 1948, he sent a telegram, in the name of the German bishops, to the Vatican: "The news of the lifting of the execution stop and of 10 weekly hangings in Landsberg shocked us all. We ask for help for so many whose guilt before God is perhaps only minor."[56] Three days later, Monsignor Montini replied, "The Holy Father, who is not ignorant of the troubled matter and who has already done much to save the lives of the condemned, has now instructed our office to take new steps to change their lot, if possible."[57] Heinrich Wienken, head of the office of the Fulda Conference and later a bishop himself, also pointed out that Pius XII had raised a clemency appeal to the Polish government for the Nazi *Gauleiter* Arthur Greiser. He found this effort justifiable, in that Wienken believed some convicted Nazis were "totally innocent" and that confessions had been forced through "illegal methods."[58]

In parallel, the Catholic Church in the U.S. announced its support for the German bishops' appeals to General Clay to stay the executions, and German Church leaders insisted that evidence that led to the convictions had been obtained improperly. The Bishop of Augsburg Joseph Kumpfmüller showed solidarity with Nazi prisoners by holding a mass in Landsberg prison and distributing the Holy Communion to 150 Catholic prisoners—a detail that did not escape the Catholic press.[59] Meanwhile, the Vatican Secretariat of State expressed support for the pleas of Cardinal Frings and the German bishops to halt the executions and commute the sentences to less severe punishment.[60] When U.S. diplomats in the Vatican received such pleas, they sought advice from the U.S. political adviser for Germany regarding how to respond. Internal notes reveal that they decided to quote from Clay's letter to Cardinal Frings: "In every case where an execution has been ordered I have been satisfied on the evidence that the accused was guilty of the crime which he was charged and that his conduct called for the penalty imposed. Where clemency was indicated it has been granted."[61] Neither the German bishops nor the Vatican seemed convinced.

Bishop Neuhäusler appealed once again to General Clay, warning him of the danger of executing innocent people. The letter opened by reaffirming his moral authority as a former concentration camp prisoner before arguing that the United States had nothing to lose by re-examining the verdicts and reviewing the evidence against those sentenced to death. Neuhäusler thanked Clay for the renewed stays of execution but called for a formal investigation. Warning that worldly authority must prove everything before using "the sword, which was given to it by God," he alleged serious flaws in the judicial process. He cited the respected Landsberg prison chaplain, Fr. Karl Morgenschweis, who believed that many of those executed were innocent. Although Neuhäusler acknowledged that he could not judge their guilt himself, he urged that Morgenschweis's assessment not be dismissed lightly. Other documents in the same file alleged unreliable witnesses, including possible impostors, and argued that, under German and international law, the already executed Kiwitt and Hellenbroich would have been acquitted. A telegram requesting papal intervention failed to reach Pius XII because of a nationwide strike by Italian postal workers. Once carried out, the executions could not be undone—a point also Neuhäusler repeatedly emphasized.[62]

The next day, the tireless Neuhäusler thanked Frings for permission to publish the Fulda bishops' memorandum about the right to an appeal, as well as for the telegram he had sent to Clay. After asking for advice about how church newspapers should counter Clay's arguments about the legal basis of the war crimes trials, the bishop rather cynically complained that Clay rejected the notion that these laws were created by the victors and only applied to the Germans, "as if there were no war criminals elsewhere."[63] The Catholic Christian press matched the rhetoric of Frings and Neuhäusler, reiterating that the Nazi prisoners might not be totally without guilt, but mercy should apply to all.[64] Neuhäusler also came up with the idea of putting the term "war criminals" in quotation marks, a punctuation choice soon adopted by other clerics and defenders of convicted Nazi criminals, including the pope's right-hand men, like Montini.[65] Language matters. In the campaign against Allied war crimes trials, "Nazis hardly appeared as perpetrators, but more and more as victims of a merciless 'victor's justice.'"[66]

The Vatican Secretariat of State relied on Aloisius Muench, the Vatican envoy to Germany, to put the pope's wishes into practice. As discussed previously, Bishop Muench was an American with German heritage, making him a logical go-between for connecting the Vatican and U.S. authorities. On October 29, 1948, Monsignor Montini instructed Muench to intervene with U.S. authorities in Germany on behalf of the convicted Nazis:

> Your Excellency, The Secretariat of State of His Holiness, lending its support to the appeals of the German hierarchy [Frings speaking for German bishops] for commutation of the sentences of capital punishment passed on persons allegedly guilty of war crimes, would request your good offices in referring these appeals to the competent American authorities. Reports emanating from Washington, indicate that the Department which treats war criminals has been deluged with letters of protest, principally from Polish and Jewish elements,

> complaining of the miscarriage of justice evident in the recent amnesties granted in Germany, especially in the [Ilse] Koch case. . . . The Secretariat of State of His Holiness would be deeply grateful to you if you could find it possible to transmit these pleas to General Clay, indicating, if you believe it opportune, the feeling of horror that ran through the German people following the ten hangings that took place recently in Landsberg prison.[67]

Through her actions, Ilse Koch had earned her reputation as a notorious sadist and her nickname, "the witch of Buchenwald." Her husband had been *Kommandant* of the concentration camp. Yet as this letter makes clear, the Vatican had apparently little interest in or sympathy for protests raised by Jewish and Polish people against "amnesty" for war criminals. Muench kept Montini appraised of developments in Germany, including ongoing interventions by Neuhäusler, whom his staff called an "illustrious prelate."[68] Materials from Neuhäusler and Frings held in the Vatican archives, including letters, appeals, newspaper articles, and defense statements, provide evidence that the Vatican was well-informed by German bishops and coordinated with them on almost every step.[69]

With clear agitation, Neuhäusler also informed Frings about new reports of forced confessions by Landsberg prisoners: "What I was told in the last few days by 'clerks' of the Dachau trials is deeply troubling. Now I understand that an appeal could hardly be allowed. This would unearth too many unpleasant things. I will keep your Eminence informed about any new developments."[70] General Clay wanted to go through with the executions as soon as possible, and he did not react well to the Vatican's demands for clemency without exception for all German war criminals,[71] expressing instead that "I regret that I do not believe that a blanket clemency action is justified in view of the nature of the crimes."[72] In response to the memorandum drafted by the pope's representative Amleto Giovanni Cicognani, the U.S. government rejected charges of impropriety and labeled them products of German propaganda. Military authorities would carry out further executions, though only in the most severe cases.[73]

Although Montini appeared inclined to support almost any and every move by the German bishops, Muench might have understand the mood of the U.S. authorities better than those bishops or the bishop of Rome. He advised the Vatican to step carefully, writing to Montini in November 1948:

> Only yesterday morning I telephoned one of the special advisers of General Clay in Berlin, Captain Peter Flanagan, a lawyer and a good Catholic, in the matter, and he informed me that only such were being executed whose guilt has been established beyond all doubt. . . . Not all the accused are guiltless; some have committed crimes, and now seek the help of the Church unjustifiedly.[74]

UNIFIED FRONT

For many Church leaders, it had now become a matter of principle: The Nuremberg system was wrong and needed to be stopped. Cardinal Frings and other anti-Nuremberg hawks refused to back down. By late November 1948, even the powerful Cardinal Samuel Stritch, archbishop of Chicago, came around to this view, noting that

> Many are concerned about the lack of a solid legal basis for the trials of accused war criminals. It seemed to me that if these defendants had been tried under German law, the desired result would have been achieved. Your advocacy of the right to appeal is fully consistent with our legal tradition and practice.[75]

Such support from an American cardinal was priceless; Frings and Neuhäusler publicized the letter widely.

The Nazis' defense lawyers and the Catholic bishops increasingly coordinated their efforts, too. Neuhäusler was the driving force behind the "Church Committee for Prisoners Aid" (*Komitee für kirchliche Gefangenenhilfe*), designed to help Nazi war criminals. Seeking support for all Landsberg prisoners, Neuhäusler collaborated with Dr. Rudolf Aschenauer, a young Catholic lawyer and former Nazi, who became both his legal advisor and close confident.[76] Aschenauer was a confidant of Frings too, according to their correspondence, included in the cardinal's papers.[77] The "Church Committee for Prisoners Aid" was funded by both Catholic and Protestant churches and provided assistance free of charge to war criminals held in Landsberg.[78] This cross-church cooperation was unusual in Germany, where the divide sparked centuries before by Martin Luther's Reformation still ran deep. But their common national goal brought them together in a tactical alliance to overwhelm and defeat Nuremberg justice. Such close cooperation, foreshadowing further ecumenical dialogue, would have been unthinkable before the war.

As noted earlier, the Protestant equivalent of Neuhäusler and Frings was Theophil Wurm, *Landesbischof* in Württemberg and a nationwide leader of the Protestant Church in Germany (*Evangelische Kirche Deutschlands*). Wurm's papers, consisting of thousands of documents, reveal how much time, energy, and money the churches invested in opposing Nuremberg justice.

In response to an appeal in support of the war criminals, authored by Wurm and other Lutheran leaders of Germany, including Pastor Martin Niemöller, General Clay indicated his regret "that an effort is now being made to discredit a court which with high intent is endeavouring to establish precedents in international law, which may serve to prevent again a world being plunged into chaos."[79] Having received similar responses from Clay, Neuhäusler and Wurm coordinated their continued campaigns; Neuhäusler described their "loyal brotherhood in arms" ("*treue Waffenbrüderschaft*") that bound the two fierce church representatives.[80] Their crusade also was joined by Helene, Princess of Isenburg, a strict Catholic. She created the association "Silent Help for POWs and the Interned" to intervene for Nazi war criminals; she also was often accused of being close to extreme right-wing circles. Nicknamed "the mother of the Landsbergers," the princess was insistent in her repeated appeals to Pius XII for support for her crusade.[81]

By 1949, in both the United States and England, political will for being tough on the Germans had eroded. West Germany became a largely sovereign nation, under chancellor Konrad Adenauer, and its new democratic constitution ("basic law") abolished the death penalty.[82] In addition, lobbying by political and church authorities was producing results. In January, Senator William Langer of North Dakota described the Dachau trials as a disgrace to the United States on the Senate floor.[83] By March, a Senate subcommittee started looking into the allegations of mistreatment of German prisoners in U.S. custody, mostly in reference to the trials held in Dachau (including the Malmedy case). The irony of this development is hard to ignore. As historian Hilary Earl put it,

> it was the Malmédy massacre that initially inspired Americans to conduct war crimes trials in post-war Germany to begin with, and now it was the trial of those involved in the massacre that would lead to the disrepute of the American war crimes trial program and ultimately bring the entire judicial process down.[84]

As witnesses, the subcommittee called both defendants and their lawyers.[85] The infamous Senator Joseph McCarthy, a Cold War hawk, blew the same horn, such that the bishops regarded him as an ally.[86] The publicity surrounding the congressional inquiry substantially discredited the Nuremberg system in the United States. Yet when the Senate subcommittee presented its report on October 14, 1949, it concluded that, even if mock trials took place in some isolated cases, no evidence of systematic torture emerged. The detailed report offers fascinating insights into the Dachau trials against the backdrop of the changing political climates in the United States and Germany. In particular, the authors sought to understand efforts to undermine the Dachau trials. In a subchapter titled "Motivation behind the current agitation concerning war crimes in general and the Malmedy case in particular," they dedicated significant attention to the role of Christian churches in Germany, whose

> activities are not confined to the Malmedy case alone, but have been aimed at the entire scope of war crimes and the administration of prisons throughout Germany where war criminals are confined. Your subcommittee believes that there is danger that these sincere Christian efforts of these well-intended clergy may be used by others to further causes which are foreign to the fundamental sentiment [Christian charity] which motivated the clergy to interest themselves in such cases.[87]

However, there is little in the report about the involvement of the Vatican or Pope Pius XII, nor any criticism of the role of prominent German clergy. Instead, the intelligence analysts seeking to understand the churches' bitter opposition to war crimes trials alleged Soviet influences and "national Bolshevism" as the driving force. These insinuations were patently absurd, but the country's focus on communism prevented most U.S. observers from seeing the bigger picture.[88] At the dawn of the Cold War, the Senate worried about the potential for war between the United States and Soviet Russia. The subcommittee worried that campaigns seeking to undermine the trials would discredit the United States in Germany and potentially allow for increased Soviet influence. Yet committee members also had little illusion about the long-term goals of critics: "In the event of the withdrawal of the American occupation forces, it is quite probable that there would be efforts made to have a general amnesty program to release these former Nazis and SS officers."[89]

Following all these debates, in November 1949, the U.S. Army created a war crimes modification board to handle Dachau convicts; soon thereafter, the U.S. High Commissioner for Germany set up a similar board, to review clemency requests by later Nuremberg convicts.[90] In the end, the United States might not have retreated from Germany, but the outcome was the same: de facto amnesty for most Nazi war criminals.[91] In the Malmedy case specifically, none of the Nazi soldiers who had been sentenced to death were executed. By the late 1950s, most of them were free again—an extraordinary triumph for the Christian churches that had spearheaded the campaign against so-called "victors' justice."

CONCLUSION

Following the International Nuremberg Tribunal, the pope increasingly lost patience with any Allied efforts at criminal justice, as he advocated a "forgive and forget" approach and urged society to move past the very recent atrocities and focus on the future. German bishops, Pope Pius XII, and his closest advisors all strongly criticized Allied war crimes trials, including the Nuremberg trials and the Dachau trials. The Church successfully sought clemency and amnesties, leading to the release of convicted Nazi criminals. As early as 1946, Catholic Church leaders were condemning denazification efforts and war crimes trials. In October of that year, Cardinal Joseph Frings asserted that the conclusion of the first Nuremberg trial should mark "the end of revenge." Together with Bishop Neuhäusler, Frings rallied against Allied postwar justice, supported by both their Holy Father and the Protestant Church in Germany.

Such cooperation between Catholic and Protestant leaders was notable, given their historical tensions. It seems remarkable that the protection of

Nazi criminals was the nationalistic cause that united them. But all these religious forces aligned in their claims that the trials were expressions of "victors' justice," as well as their allegations that the Allies had committed equally atrocious war crimes, for which they should be held accountable. As noted previously, they cited Soviet forces' mass rapes of German women and other brutalities, carpet bombing of German cities, the Soviet attack on Poland, and the violent expulsion of millions of ethnic Germans from their homes in Poland and Czechoslovakia, equating these acts with those committed by Nazi Germany. In this view, the primary moral difference between the Germans and the Allies was that Germany lost.

In making this case, Church leaders repeatedly cited the dangers of communism and warned U.S. and British representatives that their denazification measures and continued war crimes trials would destabilize German society and lead to the rise of "godless" communism. These concerns resonated increasingly with Western Allies. As the Cold War escalated, pragmatism began to take precedence, and denazification became less of a priority. (West) Germany and its people could offer a crucial bulwark to defend the West from communism. Noting such trends, Pius XII felt increasingly empowered and convinced that ongoing war crimes trials were the wrong policy.

7

THE HARVEST OF SOULS

Pope Pius XII's closest advisor sent a telegram, dated February 21, 1951, to Landsberg, the notorious prison for Nazi war criminals: "Holy Father in fatherly love gives Oswald Pohl on his sick bed as sign of rich heavenly consolations the requested apostolic blessing. Montini."[1] The massive backlash to this promise, signed by the pope's deputy secretary of state, required the Vatican's top diplomats to find a solution. They first denied the telegram, then downplayed its significance. But those claims were difficult to make. Oswald Pohl was not just an "everyday" Nazi—he was one of the leaders of the Third Reich. SS *Obergruppenführer* Pohl oversaw the slave labor universe of the concentration camps, exploited prisoners' labor, and disposed of prisoners' belongings, including the gold teeth of murdered victims.[2] How could the Vatican defend its support for such a mass murderer?

Pohl converted to the Catholic faith while in prison, and the Vatican tried to save his life. These motives appear to have been so strong that the Vatican was willing to risk damaging the Church's reputation. Whether the subject was Pohl, who oversaw the Third Reich's slave labor system, or Hans Frank, the general governor of Nazi-occupied Poland and a major Holocaust perpetrator, conversion remained a consistent goal of the Catholic Church. Some Catholic clergy even likened Oswald Pohl to saints, presenting his conversion as a modern parallel to those of St. Paul or St. Augustine. As this chapter shows, the Vatican and German bishops went to great lengths to protect Nazis, underscoring the deep connection between the Vatican's "re-Christianization" program and its increasing resistance to Allied denazification efforts.

Pohl was by no means the only Nazi mass murderer whose soul the Vatican wanted to save, but certainly one of the most notorious. According to the American High Commissioner, John J. McCloy, "a human torturer of his magnitude . . . has probably never existed before in history."[3] During Pohl's trial, in a subsequent Nuremberg proceeding, overwhelming evidence of his crimes led to a death sentence for war crimes, crimes against humanity, and membership in a criminal organization.[4] Despite all that evidence, Pohl repeatedly claimed, "I was not involved in the murder of the Jews."[5] He portrayed himself as a victim of the circumstances and downplayed his own role in the concentration camp system.[6] His strategy was reinforced by numerous petitioners.

THE APOSTLE OF THE NAZIS

Many of these petitions came from Catholic clergy, including the Vatican. The Vatican and Catholic clergy offered a narrative of forgiveness and sought to save the war criminal Oswald Pohl from the gallows. Church advocates for Pohl went so far as to portray the mass murderer as an apostle, leading, it was hoped, other Nazis back to the Church. This goal was worth much effort. Consider, for example, a January 8, 1950, letter from Karl Morgenschweis, the Catholic chaplain at Landsberg prison, addressed to the office of the bishop of Augsburg, "Concerning the admission of the former SS General Oswald Pohl into the [Catholic] Church":

> Dear Excellency *Herr* Bishop: The former SS General Oswald Pohl as the highest-ranking supervisor of all concentration camps was sentenced to death at the Nuremberg trial and, while waiting for the decision [on his appeal of his death sentence], wants to become Catholic.

According to the chaplain, Pohl had such a desire to become Catholic that he would not rest until he achieved it. He attended church services, studied Catholic teachings, and wanted to convert to the Catholic faith "not out of fear of nearing death, but out of deepest inner conviction." Morgenschweis went on to make a remarkable comparison, asserting that "with the same enthusiasm, which he once served a phantom [Hitler], he now wants to dedicate his life to the Catholic religion and as an apostle wants to lead many back to the Church."[7]

The chaplain credited this mass murderer for his "enthusiasm," even if for a wrong cause, and then went so far as to idealize him as a sort of new apostle. In the tradition of Saint Paul, Oswald Pohl could bring modern heathens back to the true faith. Here, those modern heathens are Nazis. The claim follows a now-familiar theme, prioritizing the re-Christianization of a secular (nazified) society. Morgenschweis argued that high-ranking Nazi leaders could convince their followers to follow them again, into the new faith. As a sign of his seriousness, Morgenschweis added, Pohl wished to officially convert only after receiving a pardon. Pohl was aware of the potential for attacks from his former Nazi comrades, who would disapprove of his conversion. He also wanted his wife and children to become Catholic; his youngest had yet to be baptized.

Morgenschweis admitted some possible barriers to Pohl's role as a new apostle, though none of those obstacles had to do with Pohl's past as a Nazi leader and mass murderer. Rather, the challenges were due to Church rules, as defined by the code of canon law: Pohl had been baptized Lutheran as a child, officially renounced the Lutheran Church in 1937, and had been married twice. The second marriage, in 1942, was not celebrated in a Christian Church but rather took place in a civil ceremony. Therefore, the Church did not consider the second wedding valid. Before he could convert, his relationship with his current wife had to be formalized. Noting the extraordinary circumstances—the likelihood of his execution and his current imprisonment, which prevented any sexual relations with his wife, then or in the near future—the priest asked for an exemption. He requested further that Pohl be admitted to the Catholic Church right away and receive the holy sacraments.

Another concern Morgenschweis raised was whether Pohl's Christian baptism needed to be repeated "conditionally." This notion deserves some explanation. His first baptism was well documented, but it took place in a Lutheran church, and deep mistrust of Lutherans existed among Catholics (and vice versa). Catholics would worry that the baptism had not been done correctly and that, for example, holy water had not touched the body of baby Pohl. In dubious cases, baptisms could be repeated, just to be safe; such

Christian baptisms were repeated conditionally (*sub conditione*). In normal times, such baptisms were unusual, though they became somewhat more common in the postwar years. Finally, Morgenschweis asked for the bishops' mandate to free Pohl from his current state of excommunication, to admit him to the Catholic Church.[8]

A week later, the office of the bishop of Augsburg answered, imposing a few conditions for Pohl's conversion. He had to be re-baptized, *sub conditione,* and promise a Catholic marriage with his second wife as soon as possible, as well as the baptism of his five-year-old child.[9] Assuming these conditions were met, the bishops' office granted Morgenschweis permission to admit SS General Oswald Pohl into the Catholic Church. This admission would be communicated to the civil registry by the prison chaplain's office.[10] In other words, Morgenschweis received an order *expressis verbis* (!) from the bishop's office to baptize Pohl and register it according to extant regulations. As far as I can determine, Morgenschweis baptized and converted Pohl on February 12, 1950, then confirmed him on May 24, 1951.[11] On February 12, 1951, the anniversary of Pohl's' conversion, Cardinal Frings of Cologne intervened in his favor with the U.S. High Commissioner in Germany, with the claim of serious errors in his case.[12] Both Auxiliary Bishop Neuhäusler of Munich and Protestant Bishop Theophil Wurm also intervened to save Pohl's life.[13]

Pohl's wife Eleonore kept in close contact with Morgenschweis, who helped the family in many ways. In a letter to Cardinal Faulhaber, Morgenschweis asked for financial help for Eleonore Pohl, noting that she and her children were being forced to live in miserable circumstances. To initiate the request, Morgenschweis stressed that Oswald Pohl was to be converted, by him personally, in a week's time. He also stressed that Eleonore wanted to be Catholic and guarantee a Catholic education for their children.[14] Some records in the archives challenge these claims, though. Another Catholic Church official described Eleonore Pohl as a hardcore Nazi who hoped for the resurgence of Hitler's party, likely possessed hidden Nazi loot, and even alleged that she literally climbed over dead bodies to satisfy her needs. A letter from the Catholic Caritas organization denied that the woman deserved the help of the church, because she showed no sign of religious interest and never went to mass.[15] Morgenschweis stayed his course. He was determined to look after both husband and wife, together with a Benedictine monk from the St. Ottilien monastery near Landsberg.[16]

Pohl is not the only Nazi leader who had good reason to be grateful for the support of Christian churches after his conversion, but he discussed his conversion more publicly than other prominent Nazis in Landesberg.[17] With the active help of Father Morgenschweis and with the permission of the Church authorities, the conversion of this "former General of the Waffen SS" was celebrated. The cover of a 1950 booklet titled *Credo: My Road to God* officially authored by Pohl, features a blurb that reads, "Pohl shows that salvation from the current moral degradation of the whole humanity can only come through unconditional commitment to the holy Trinity as the absolute standard of all moral values."[18] The content of the booklet itself indicates that Pohl's inner voice is what led him back to God. It does not contain any expressions of compassion for the Nazis' victims, any admission of guilt or responsibility, or any solicitation of forgiveness from victims. Rather, Pohl used *Credo* to indicate that his belief that Nazism was based on false teachings and that Christianity was the true faith, for his and the world's ultimate salvation.

Even if Pohl's soul really was saved, his life was not. In June 1951, Pohl was executed, together with six other Nazi war criminals, in what became the last executions performed in West Germany. By that time, resistance against war crimes trials and executions had spread well beyond the Church and its influence. To integrate West Germany into U.S.-led alliances, German elites were needed again, and the past had to be laid to rest, and quickly.

In the Landsberg death register, Morgenschweis listed what he seemingly believed was most relevant about Pohl's background: "General of the Waffen SS" and "author of the work 'Credo: My Road to God.'"[19] *Credo* likely was written largely by Morgenschweis, based on the tone it features and the theological knowledge it demonstrates. Furthermore, Morgenschweis apparently regarded Pohl's very public conversion as a triumph: He had saved a Nazi soul for Christ.

Although the effort to keep Pohl alive failed, Morgenschweis cited the exemplary case, even after his execution. He had a powerful interest in documenting everything that had to do with Pohl and his return to Christ, and a carefully drafted narrative of Pohl's miraculous conversion gained substantial traction after his death. Dated June 26, 1951, a letter from

Morgenschweis to Pohl's daughter explained, "you know that your father died on June 7 early in the morning. . . . He really went his way to God until the completion. . . . After his last confession, holy communion and blessing he was completely in God filled with inner joy." Whether filled with joy or not, in the last moments of his life, Pohl was not filled with any sense of responsibility; he denied any personal culpability for the crimes of the regime he had served so enthusiastically.

According to Morgenschweis, the SS general's last words on the gallows were, "I have served my Fatherland faithfully for more than 30 years. It is impossible to find proof for any order or command given by me during this whole time, to kill, torture, beat or abuse anybody, also no Jew. . . . Praised be Jesus Christ—For ever and ever. Amen!" These reported last words likely were to provide material for potential future pious stories about Pohl. Morgenschweis further assured Pohl's daughter that he and others had decorated her father's graveside with flowers. It is worth noting a recognition that is missing from Morgenschweis's account: Few, if any, of Pohl's victims received flowers, a funeral, or proper gravesites.[20] At the end of the letter, Morgenschweis promised, "We want to save the honor of your father in the public, and therefore a presentation of the truth will be published. Defense Lawyer Wiehl will work on that, while I will write the final words to the 'Credo' booklet."[21] In response to criticisms of his consistent, repeated defense of the SS general, Morgenschweis persisted with the same narrative, asserting,

> We do not worship Pohl as a martyr, because in a certain way like all the leading members of the [Nazi] party he shares a certain guilt; but two facts are certain: First, he did not commit the crimes, he was accused of in Nuremberg, something which even [U.S. High Commissioner] McCloy had to admit himself. Second, Pohl completely converted and dedicated himself to God, something I would wish for every good Christian and Catholic.[22]

Beyond just documenting Pohl's case, on June 19, 1951, he celebrated a festive requiem mass for Pohl in a church not far from Brüningsau, Pohl's estate. Although Morgenschweis sought to have Pohl buried there, in accordance with Pohl's wife's wishes, "I would have thought it would be nice at the time if my husband had found his final resting place near me,"[23] he instead was buried in the Landsberg prison cemetery. His grave sits under number 250, next to SS *Brigadeführer* Erich Naumann, convicted for the mass murder of Jews, Sinti, and Roma, among other Nazi victims.[24]

Notably, a 1950 article in the Augsburg diocese's newspaper describes those who would be denied Christian funerals: people who had left the Church, who lived in a "wild marriage" (i.e., unmarried or not married in a Church), who intended to cremate their dead bodies, or who had committed suicide. In explaining the reasons for denying funeral masses to these people, the article indicates that the Church wanted to reward its faithful children, not disobedient ones.[25] Many of the listed reasons for exclusion (leaving the church, wild marriage, planned cremation) arguably applied to Pohl, and yet even in this seemingly clear-cut case, Morgenschweis worked to gain an exception to protect the man he himself described as the "highest-ranking supervisor of all concentration camps." He knew he could count on the Vatican's blessing for his work to save souls. With its tacit rejection of Protestantism, Pohl's conversion to Catholicism symbolized another victory for the pope.[26]

PAPAL BLESSING FOR A NAZI BUTCHER

The files available from the formerly secret Vatican archives detail the involvement of the Holy See in Pohl's case. The papal nuncio in Germany, Aloisius Muench, informed Monsignor Montini in April 1951 (two months before Pohl's execution) that the German media was making a big fuss about allegations of a papal blessing for Pohl.[27] How the blessing came about is a topic of much debate and confusion, but its authenticity was clear. Even when the Vatican's Secretariat of State claimed initially that the telegram was fake, the Vatican admitted, in an internal note, that an official denial was too much: "The denial is really phrased in very harsh terms."[28] It thus retracted the denial and instead pled ignorance: The Vatican (in other words, Montini) claimed it did not know who Oswald Pohl was. This questionable claim became the official Vatican version. Muench informed Montini that Munich's Catholic media had printed a statement, issued by the prison chaplain Morgenschweis, that the telegram about the papal benediction for Pohl was not meant to be public but instead was "a purely private matter, it is not a diplomatic step or a Vatican stance, as the fact was interpreted."[29]

The story continued (according to Morgenschweis), indicating that a German monk in Rome, at the urging of a fellow Franciscan brother—a former SS soldier (!)—had asked the Vatican for Pohl's blessing.[30] Montini answered Pohl's lawyer, reasserting the claim that Catholic officials did not know that the request for a papal blessing was intended for the SS General Pohl, and not an ordinary Catholic by the name Pohl; the target had not been made clear in the request.[31] Given the prominence of Pohl's case and the processes adopted by the Vatican Secretariat of State, it is unlikely Montini was unfamiliar with Oswald Pohl's identity. Pohl's lawyer also disputed the Vatican version and noted that he had requested the papal blessing explicitly for his client in a telegram to the Vatican.[32]

Having established that the Vatican was involved, the defense lawyers worked to make good use of the papal blessing and publicized it in the press, hoping that a telegram from the pope would cast doubt on their client's guilt. One newspaper featured the headline, "The Pope telegraphs to man on death row—Is Oswald Pohl innocent?"[33] The defense also produced a flyer, showing a facsimile of the Vatican telegram, together with a photo of Pius XII praying, and posing the controversial question, "Is Oswald Pohl a German Dreyfus?" This comparison refers to a famous French Jewish army officer, Alfred Dreyfus, who was falsely accused and ultimately fell victim to an antisemitic conspiracy against him.[34] Pohl's New York–based lawyer Frederick Wiehl sent additional copies of the telegram to the press and obtained some internal correspondence from the priests involved.[35] Stressing Pohl's innocence, the lawyer also compared him to Jesus:

> We Catholics know that our Lord Jesus was brought before the judge of the Roman occupying power in Jerusalem, Pilate, under the false accusation that he was "King of the Jews" and was sentenced to death. Although this verdict has never been legally overturned, we all still believe in his innocence today.[36]

These outrageous comparisons, together with other press coverage of the Pohl case and papal entanglements, caused a stir in the Vatican. But a few weeks later, Muench forwarded Pohl's conversion booklet *Credo* to Montini and, while acknowledging the press controversy surrounding the papal blessing, also explained, somewhat apologetically,

> The Rev. Karl Morgenschweis, chaplain of those prisons, who was able to closely follow the radical change of Pohl, in the preface to said booklet, asserts that the motive for the conversion of the infamous general, was not in the personal interest, nor other human intentions; but it only took place under the beneficial influence of God's grace. It is, therefore, the sincere return to the Lord of a misguided soul. In fact, the prisoner spends the whole day reading religious books, meditating and praying more deeply.[37]

Thus, the papal nuncio embraced Morgenschweis's narrative that the conversion of the mass murderer was nothing short of a miracle. Even though Pohl, while on trial or in his allegedly self-written booklet, never admitted any personal guilt or apologized to the victims, Muench, Morgenschweis, and German bishops still tried to reassure the Vatican that the blessing was appropriate, despite the backlash sparked by the leak of the telegram to the press.

On multiple occasions, Morgenschweis wrote Montini directly about the Pohl saga, retelling over and over the events from his point of view. Morgenschweis insisted he had done nothing wrong and blamed the leak on Pohl's lawyer: "But I didn't know anything about any of this. . . . I had kept it secret, including from Pohl's fellow prisoners and, above all, from the public, because I suspected that the enemies of our Church and the Vatican would exploit the matter politically."[38] He also again reminded his audience that, ultimately, it was he who had brought Pohl back to Christ. In response, Monsignor Montini, the future pope, thanked Morgenschweis for his work, assured him that he was highly esteemed, and concluded, "I wish from the bottom of my heart God's constant protection for you and your self-sacrificing, soul-zealous work."[39] Thus, the takeaway from the archival record must be that the Vatican was upset the telegram had been leaked and caused some damage (including press attacks published in communist East Germany). It did not, however, appear upset about or regretful for the conversion or interventions on behalf of Pohl. After all, the salvation of souls was worth almost every sacrifice.

This interpretation earns support from the realization that the Vatican's support for Pohl was not an isolated case. Records in the Augsburg Church archives provide unique insights into the re-Christianization efforts of the Catholic Church in the postwar years, beyond Pohl's prominent case. The

Augsburg diocesan archives, located northwest of Munich, contain records from Landsberg prison, where hundreds of war criminals from the Nuremberg and Dachau trials were held, and Protestant and Catholic prison chaplains competed for their souls.[40] I was granted rare access to these records, which was no small achievement. The Vatican archives maintain a reputation for being difficult to access; Catholic Church archives in various countries can be equally challenging to review. If granted at all, such access requires overcoming multiple hurdles and restrictions. The papers in Augsburg include expansive records related to high-ranking Nazi officials, including concentration camp commanders, district leaders, and mayors. By reviewing this rich documentation, I gained unique insights into the postwar praxis of proselytizing Nazis in detention and prison camps. The picture that emerges is fascinating.

The records reveal just how many accused Nazi war criminals sought conversion to the Catholic Church throughout the postwar judicial process. Ernst Kaltenbrunner, Heinrich Himmler's right-hand man in the SS, embraced the Catholic faith while on the docks in Nuremberg.[41] Rudolf Höss, the notorious commandant of Auschwitz, called for a Catholic priest, took holy communion, and confessed days before his execution in 1947.[42] The wife and children of Martin Bormann, the powerful head of Hitler's chancery, were all converted and baptized Catholics after the war.[43] The pope took great interest in all these situations, but even more confounding are cases in which the direct involvement by Vatican representatives is manifestly evident. Even Otto Ohlendorf, the leader of a killing squad murdering Jews in the Soviet Union, could count on Catholic clergy pleading for him.[44] According to Ohlendorf's former pastor, in a letter to papal nuncio Aloysius Muench, his protégé was only responsible for the murder of 90,000 Jews in a purely legal sense. He should be saved from the gallows because he was about to convert to the Catholic faith. His next assertion shows just how influential the Pohl case was: The priest suggested that Ohlendorf's conversion would transform him into an apostle of the Christian faith and draw many former Nazis to the Church.[45]

The list of conversions by prominent and lesser-known Nazis and fascists is extensive, and could fill many books. Though it is impossible to detail them all here, we can usefully engage with some new case studies that became clear only through my efforts to access and understand previously restricted Church archives.

RE-CHRISTIANIZING NAZIS

Years before the Pohl case, Father Morgenschweis made sure to keep Pius XII personally informed of his work and the unique opportunity the Landsberg prisoners represented for the Church. In a 1948 petition, Morgenschweis indicated that of the 926 Nazi criminals in jail, 347 were Catholic. He appealed, in the name of these prisoners, to Pius XII:

> We also ask for kind intercession so that the shackles can soon be loosened through grace where justice cannot loosen them, so that this also makes a contribution to the pacification of the world. So we send your Holiness greetings from the walls of the prison in which so many good and noble people have to suffer because of the error into which they were led.[46]

An elegant, printed version of this petition appears in the archival files, alongside pleas from Catholic prisoners in Landsberg, self-described as "children of the Holy Father," who declared that they had lost faith in earthly justice and hoped for the pope's support and true justice.[47] The pope responded in kind, sending rosaries and images of saints to the Nazi prisoners, for which Morgenschweis expressed his gratitude, calling out particularly the Holy Father's honest interest in the fate of the "so-called 'war criminals.'" This phrasing and punctuation, as adopted by Morgenschweis, signals his rejection of the description of the Nazi prisoners. In addition to using ironic quotes to question the categorization of the war criminals, Morgenschweis argued that the Nazis were either innocent or being punished too harshly. In another example of the power of language, he staked a moral position: "I want to do everything that is possible to win for Christ and our Holy Church and to strengthen these people, who are really often misled, in a true, Catholic life of faith in the living community of the Church." The document was signed: "Karl Morgenschweis Catholic Priest War Criminal Prison Landsberg."[48]

Who were these poor, "misled" people? Let's take a closer look at some of them.

Figure 1. Pope Pius XII sitting on a throne, 1950. Credit: Courtesy of CSU Archives / Everett Collection—History / Alamy.

Figure 2. View into the courtroom during the Nuremberg Trials at the Palace of Justice. Top Nazi leaders, including Hermann Göring, are on the defendants' bench. Credit: Donor: Robert Jackson. Photographer: Charles Alexander. U.S. Chief of Counsel for the Prosecution of Axis Criminality. NARA 72–879. Public Domain.

Figure 3. Justice Robert H. Jackson at the International Nuremberg Trial, August 1946. Credit: NARA, 111-SC-252946_001. Public Domain.

Figure 4. Satirical cover of the Munich magazine *Der Simpl* (July 1946), depicting Cardinal Michael Faulhaber as a hen. Caption translates as: "And she spread her wings protectively over them." Credit: Max Radler, Die treusorgende Glucke, Der Simpl 1 (1946) Heft 8, Frontpage. Universitätsbibliothek Heidelberg.

Figure 5. Caricature from *Der Simpl* (June 1946), showing brown Nazi sheep marching toward a "denazification" machine. They emerge from beneath as white, innocent sheep and are blessed by a Catholic cleric. The banner, which translates as "There is more joy over one repentant sinner than over ten righteous ones," is a reference to Luke 15:7. Credit: Max Radler, Schwarz wird weiss oder mechanische Entnazifizierung, Der Simpl 1 (1946), Heft 6, p. 63. Universitätsbibliothek Heidelberg.

Figure 6. Bishop Johannes Neuhäusler, right, with Cardinal Francis Spellman, center, in Munich, walking alongside Father Aubrey J. O'Reilly (Chief of Chaplains, Southern Area Command), left. October 1953. Credit: AEMF, NL Neuhäusler 433.

Figure 7. The cover of the booklet Credo–My Road to God, officially authored by the Nazi criminal Oswald Pohl and edited by the Catholic prison chaplain Karl Morgenschweis, features a graphic illustration of rays of light shining through prison bars, symbolizing Pohl's conversion during his imprisonment. The cover identifies him as a General of the Waffen-SS. Credit: Front cover of Oswald Pohl, Credo: Mein Weg zu Gott (Girnth Verlag, 1950). Photograph by Gerald Steinacher.

Figure 8. Photo (L–R): Bishop Aloisius Muench, Cardinal Joseph Frings, and Archbishop Lorenz Jaeger, with an unidentified fourth man, chatting with each other at the opening of the 73rd German Catholic Day in Bochum on September 1, 1949. The image captures a moment of informal interaction among three influential Catholic churchmen in postwar Germany. Credit: dpa picture alliance / Alamy, Image ID: T4BFN9.

Figure 9. Ernst von Weizsäcker, one of Hitler's top diplomats, during his sentencing. Credit: Department of Defense. NARA 238-OMT-XI-D-082_001. Public Domain.

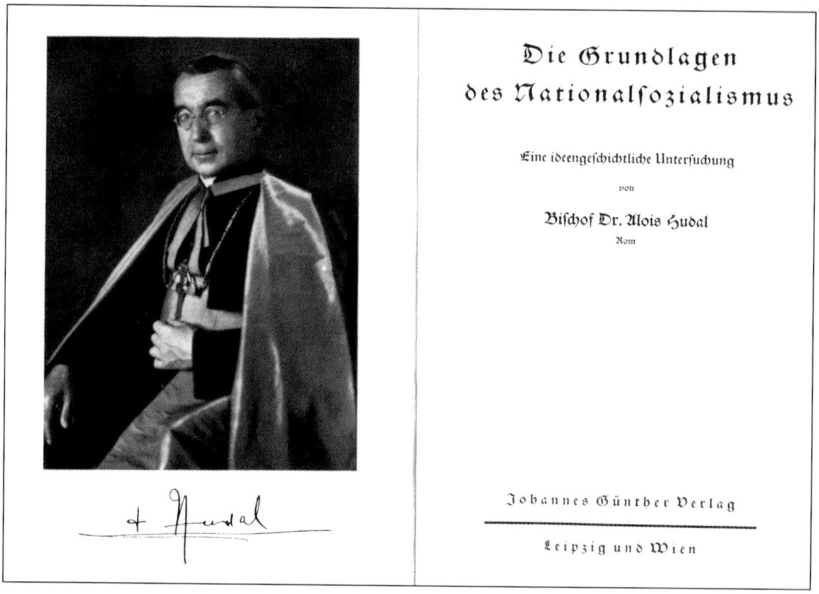

Figure 10. Cover photo of Bishop Alois Hudal in his book *The Foundations of National Socialism* (1937). After 1945, Hudal became one of the most outspoken Catholic dignitaries to assist Nazis in escaping postwar justice. Credit: Book front page. Photo by Steinacher.

Figure 11. The American Monsignor Andrew Landi of the National Catholic Welfare Committee, at the Fraschette camp in Italy, September 3, 1947. Landi worked closely with the Pontificia Commissione di Assistenza (PCA). To a large extent, the Catholic Church in the United States financed the Vatican's refugee and relief efforts in the immediate postwar years. Credit: Roman Catholic Diocese of Brooklyn Archives.

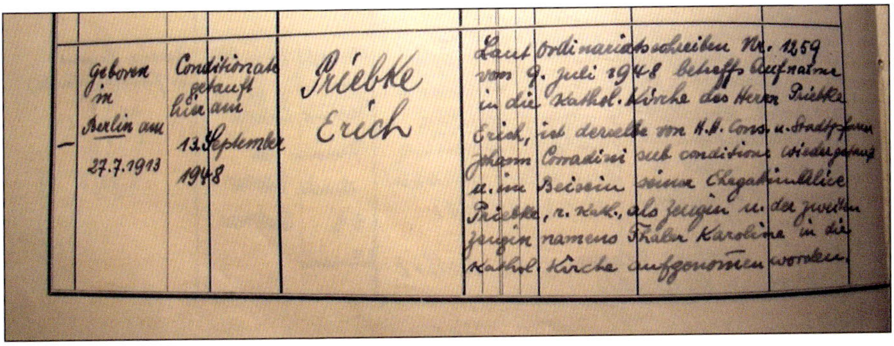

Geboren in Berlin am 27.7.1913

Conditionate getauft hier am 13. September 1948

Priebke Erich

Laut Ordinariatsschreiben Nr. 1259 vom 9. Juli 1948 betreffs Aufnahme in die kathol. Kirche des Herrn Priebke Erich, ist derselbe von H.H. Coop. u. Stadtpfarrer Johann Corradini sub conditione wiedergetauft u. im Beisein seiner Ehegattin Alice Priebke, r. kath., als Zeugin u. der zweiten Zeugin namens Thaler Karoline in die kathol. Kirche aufgenommen worden.

Figure 12. Catholic baptism record for Nazi criminal Erich Priebke, dated September 13, 1948, performed by parish priest Johann Corradini of Sterzing (Vipiteno), northern Italy. The entry notes that permission to "re-baptize" the former Protestant was granted by the local Italian bishop. At the same time, Bishop Alois Hudal and the baptizing priest assisted Priebke in obtaining falsified papers under the alias "Otto Pape" to help him escape justice. Credit: Steinacher, Church Archives of Vipiteno/Sterzing.

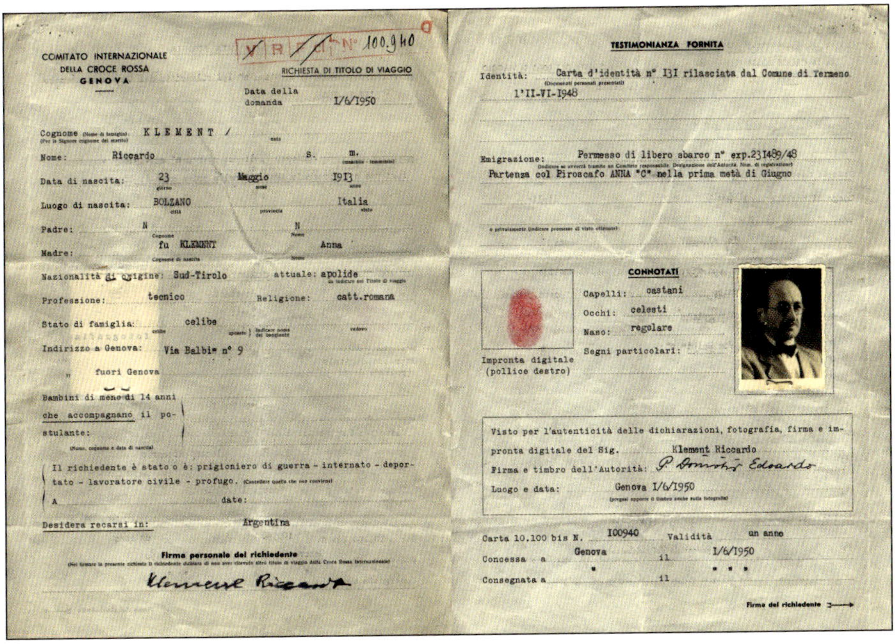

COMITATO INTERNAZIONALE DELLA CROCE ROSSA GENOVA

V R N° 100.940

RICHIESTA DI TITOLO DI VIAGGIO

Data della domanda 1/6/1950

Cognome: KLEMENT

Nome: Riccardo s. m.

Data di nascita: 23 Maggio 1913

Luogo di nascita: BOLZANO Italia

Padre: N N

Madre: fu KLEMENT Anna

Nazionalità di origine: Sud-Tirolo attuale: apolide

Professione: tecnico Religione: catt.romana

Stato di famiglia: celibe

Indirizzo a Genova: Via Balbi n° 9

" fuori Genova

Bambini di meno di 14 anni che accompagnano il postulante:

Il richiedente è stato o è: prigioniero di guerra - internato - deportato - lavoratore civile - profugo.

A date:

Desidera recarsi in: Argentina

Firma personale del richiedente

Klement Riccardo

TESTIMONIANZA FORNITA

Identità: Carta d'identità n° 131 rilasciata dal Comune di Termeno l'11-VI-1948

Emigrazione: Permesso di libero sbarco n° exp.231489/48

Partenza col Piroscafo ANNA "C" nella prima metà di Giugno

CONNOTATI

Capelli: castani

Occhi: celesti

Naso: regolare

Segni particolari:

Impronta digitale (pollice destro)

Visto per l'autenticità delle dichiarazioni, fotografia, firma e impronta digitale del Sig. Klement Riccardo

Firma e timbro dell'Autorità: P. Dömöter Edoardo

Luogo e data: Genova 1/6/1950

Carta 10.100 bis N. 100940 Validità un anno

Concessa a Genova il 1/6/1950

Consegnata a il

Firma del richiedente

Figure 13. Application form for an International Red Cross travel document for Adolf Eichmann, submitted under the alias Riccardo Klement. The document stated that he was a Roman Catholic from the Italian town of Bolzano (Bozen). The document is signed and was vouched for by Father Eduardo Dömöter, who worked with the Papal Aid Commission. The resulting travel document facilitated Eichmann's escape to Argentina in 1950. Credit: ICRC Archives, Geneva, ACICR_CTV_100940_KLEMENT Riccardo.

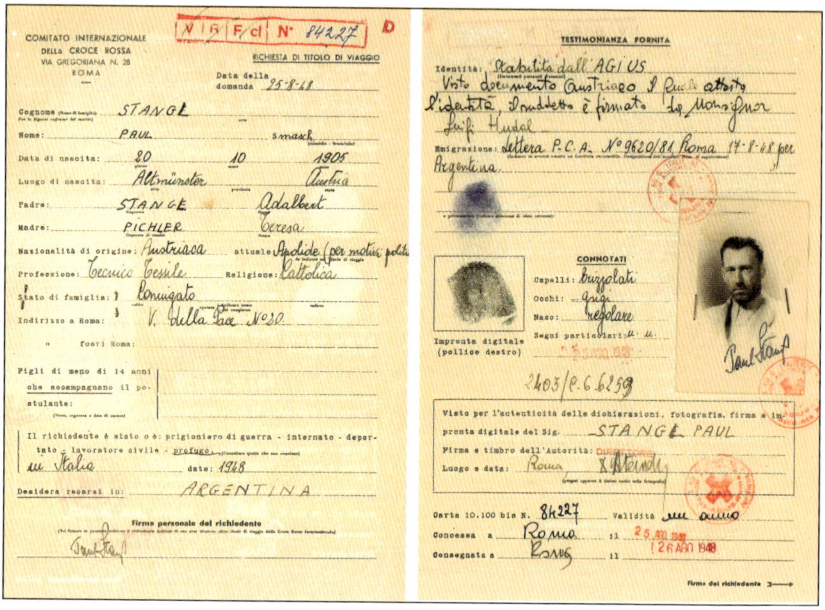

COMITATO INTERNAZIONALE
DELLA CROCE ROSSA
VIA GREGORIANA N. 28
ROMA

N | R | F/cl | N° 84227 D

RICHIESTA DI TITOLO DI VIAGGIO

Data della domanda 25-8-48

Cognome: STANGL
Nome: PAUL s.masch.
Data di nascita: 20 10 1905
Luogo di nascita: Altmünster Austria
Padre: STANGE Adalbert
Madre: PICHLER Teresa
Nazionalità di origine: Austriaca attuale Apolide (per motivi politici)
Professione: Tecnico Tessile Religione: Cattolica
Stato di famiglia: Coniugato
Indirizzo a Roma: V. della Pace N°20
fuori Roma:
Figli di meno di 14 anni che accompagnano il postulante:
Il richiedente è stato o è: prigioniero di guerra - internato - deportato - lavoratore civile - profugo in Italia date: 1948
Desidera recarsi in: ARGENTINA
Firma personale del richiedente
Paul Stangl

TESTIMONIANZA FORNITA

Identità: Stabilita dall'AGIUS Visto documento Austriaco il quale attesta l'identità, Suddetto è firmato da Monsignor Luigi Hudal
Emigrazione: lettera P.C.A. N° 9620/81 Roma 17-8-48 per Argentina

CONNOTATI
Capelli: brizzolati
Occhi: grigi
Naso: regolare
Segni particolari: = =

Impronta digitale (pollice destro)

2403/P.C.6259

Visto per l'autenticità delle dichiarazioni, fotografia, firma e impronta digitale del Sig. STANGL PAUL
Firma e timbro dell'Autorità:
Luogo e data: Roma

Carta 10.100 bis N. 84227 Validità un anno
Concessa a Roma il 25 AGO 1948
Consegnata a Roma il 26 AGO 1948

Paul Stangl

Firma del richiedente →

Figure 14. Application for a Red Cross travel document for Nazi criminal Franz Stangl, 1948. Holocaust perpetrator Stangl applied under the name "Paul Stangl" for travel papers from the International Committee of the Red Cross at its delegation in Rome, claiming to be stateless "for political reasons" and identifying as Catholic. His address in Rome was listed as Via della Pace 20—Bishop Hudal's residence. Monsignor Hudal vouched for his identity, as handwritten notes on the document show. Credit: ICRC Archives, Geneva, ACICR_CTV_84227_STANGL Paul.

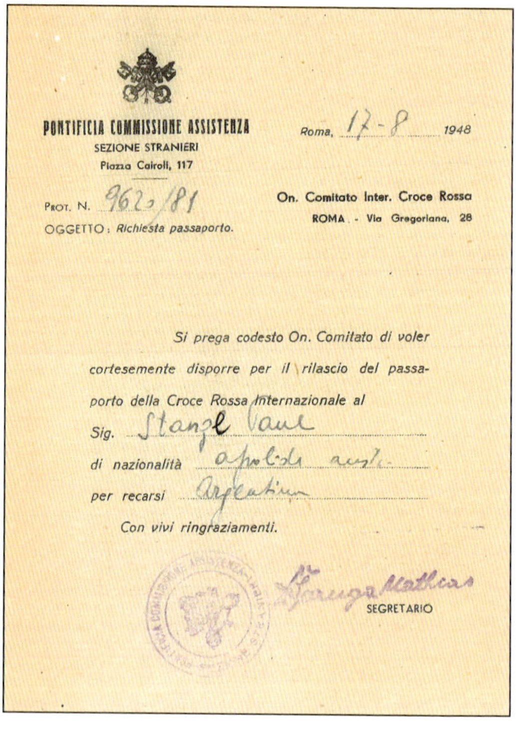

PONTIFICIA COMMISSIONE ASSISTENZA
SEZIONE STRANIERI
Piazza Cairoli, 117

Roma, 17-8 1948

PROT. N. 9620/81

OGGETTO: Richiesta passaporto.

On. Comitato Inter. Croce Rossa
ROMA - Via Gregoriana, 28

Si prega codesto On. Comitato di voler cortesemente disporre per il rilascio del passaporto della Croce Rossa Internazionale al

Sig. Stangl Paul

di nazionalità apolide austr.

per recarsi Argentina

Con vivi ringraziamenti.

SEGRETARIO

Figure 15. Franz Stangl, ex-commandant of the Treblinka extermination camp, also obtained a recommendation letter from the Papal Aid Commission in Rome, in 1948. The document was addressed to the delegation of the International Committee of the Red Cross in Rome, requesting the issuance of travel papers for the "stateless" Stangl for immigration to Argentina. Credit: ICRC Archives, Geneva, ACICR_CTV_84227_STANGL Paul.

In January 1946, Morgenschweis identified 12 convicted war criminals he had readmitted to the Catholic Church, when asking the office (Ordinariate) of the bishop of Augsburg retroactively to allow such readmission. He indicated that all of them had declared their decision in writing and were willing to have their children be baptized and themselves (re-)married according to Catholic rites.[49] Furthermore, he sought to save the souls of even executed Nazis. The former *Kreisleiter* (Nazi district leader) Franz Strasser had left the Catholic Church in 1938 and, according to available records, lived as a convinced Nazi. After the war, a U.S. military court tried and sentenced him to death for shooting unarmed, surrendered U.S. airmen, in a clear violation of international laws and standards of warfare. A photo from January 1946 shows the war criminal on the gallows and Morgenschweis praying for him.[50] One month later, Morgenschweis asked his bishop to formally allow Strasser's readmission into the Catholic Church.[51]

Retroactive sanctioning of such admissions was not uncommon. On the evening before the execution of Martin Gottfried Weiss and Leonhard Eichberger, in May 1946, Morgenschweis admitted them to the Church, after receiving oral permission from his superiors over the phone. A month later, he asked for formal written permission. The commander of multiple concentration and death camps, SS *Obersturmbannführer* Weiss had a long career of murder. When he was arrested in April 1945, he was still serving as the commandant of the Dachau concentration camp near Munich.[52] Eichberger was his subordinate at Dachau; he admitted to shooting prisoners and other atrocities. Morgenschweis reported to his bishop that both men died with inner calm, similar to other inmates at Landsberg who had returned to Catholicism. With regard to Weiss, Morgenschweis felt compelled to point out that he was "especially happy because he would die in the faith of his youth." The priest did not spare even a single word for Weiss's murderous career or his victims.[53]

Another telling case, indicative of Morgenschweis's views, involved the readmission of three SS officials who committed atrocities at the Mauthausen concentration camp. They were convicted and sentenced to death, yet Morgenschweis carefully referred to them as "military prisoners" or "prisoners," not war criminals. To demonstrate that they "regretted" having left the Catholic Church, the chaplain noted that they regularly attended Sunday services. He never mentioned any demonstrations or expressions of remorse for the crimes they perpetrated in the concentration camp. Over and over again, Morgenschweis (and others) showed little concern for the victims and concentrated solely on the perpetrators' well-being and religious life.[54]

One of the SS officers at Landsberg was Dr. Willy Jobst, "the notoriously cruel chief physician" of Ebensee, a subcamp of Mauthausen, and one of 61 camp personnel from Mauthausen on trial at Dachau. As historian Tomaz Jardim described him, "Jobst and [his assistant] had turned the hospital at [the sub-camp] Ebensee into a site of mass killing through lethal injection, as well as deliberate starvation and exposure."[55] Jobst also had served in many concentration camps before being ordered to Mauthausen.[56] Due to Morgenschweis's efforts, Jobst died as a Catholic when he was hanged at Landsberg in 1947.

He was not the only war criminal with medical experience. The planners of the later Nuremberg trials purposefully sought to hold the elite members of the Nazi state accountable, which included the medical doctors working in or supervising the camps, as well as those who had murdered disabled prisoners. The Nuremberg "Doctors' Trials" exposed the complicity and cruelty of these Nazi physicians, who violated their ethical codes, oaths, and basic humanity. Nazi camp doctors often were particularly brutal, a tendency that did not deter Morgenschweis from defending these educated, privileged men who committed truly heinous acts.

Professor Wilhelm Beiglböck, a medical doctor from Vienna, was sentenced to 15 years in prison at Nuremberg for conducting gruesome experiments on prisoners in the Dachau concentration camp.[57] *Herr Doktor* found favor with Morgenschweis, though. The Austrian-born physician was a member of the Nazi party and the Nazi Stormtroopers (SA); he left the Catholic Church in 1938. Soon before his early release from prison in late 1951, he had asked Morgenschweis for readmission to the Church, and he appears to have gained Morgenschweis's sympathy. As the chaplain wrote, after his release, Beiglböck had no place to go. His wife had left him, and he could not return to Austria. To make matters even worse for the Nazi doctor, Beiglböck was on a list of people wanted by the Russians. Morgenschweis readmitted the Nazi doctor into the Church and then retroactively asked for permission, noting that "For him it has been a big calming for the soul, to know, that he is a member of the Catholic Church again." In this case, the request again was granted, indicated by a handwritten note on the document that reads, "will be approved after the fact" ["*wird nachtraeglich genehmigt*"].[58]

Beiglböck was not the only SS doctor readmitted by Morgenschweis, as the files in the Church archives of Augsburg show. In another case, Morgenschweis argued that he had not waited for the bishop's permission because the man in question, a former Nazi, had "such a strong desire for receiving the holy communion" ["*grosses Verlangen nach dem Empfang der hl. Sakrament zeigte*"].[59] This man was no other than SS *Sturmbannführer* Fritz Hintermayer, head Nazi doctor in Dachau, who supervised medical experiments on prisoners. He had a distinct reputation for being corrupt, as well as a murderer.[60]

Re-Christianization went beyond readmitting former Catholics, though. As Oswald Pohl's case revealed, the Church also actively encouraged the conversion of former Lutherans to the Catholic faith. Morgenschweis's activities in Landsberg aligned with this broader goal, as further demonstrated with the prominent example of Dr. Waldemar Hoven. He was sentenced to death during the Nuremberg Doctors' Trials. In 1948, while on death row, he requested admission to the Catholic Church. He had been born and raised a Lutheran and had left that Church in the 1920s. His wife and children were Catholic, though, and he wanted to be remarried with Catholic rites. This war criminal had personal support from the archbishop of Freiburg,[61] where Hoven was from, which could explain why the archbishop was invested in his case. Such support for a Nazi war criminal on trial, fighting for his life, contrasts with the seriousness of his crimes. Hoven was a member of the SS and a physician at the Buchenwald concentration camp, where he had conducted medical experiments on prisoners. He was also involved in the Nazi euthanasia programs, designed to murder people with disabilities. His trial resulted in convictions for crimes against humanity, war crimes, and membership in a criminal organization.[62] None of those facts appeared in Morgenschweis's correspondence about Hoven. His victims seemed all but forgotten.

Competition between Catholic and Lutheran clergymen for the souls of former Nazis also appears to have been a relevant factor; in any case, it is a prominent theme in Morgenschweis's correspondence. Again, relations between these two mainstream Christian dominations in Germany were still tense. This can be seen in the case of the *Kreisleiter* Richard Drauz of

Heilbronn, who was executed in December 1946. A Lutheran pastor had had Drauz's children baptized; according to Morgenschweis, Drauz's Catholic widow was being hassled by the Lutheran pastor to convert as well. Such complications triggered an unpleasant confrontation between the two Christian prison chaplains,[63] perhaps provoked by Drauz. Right up to his violent death, Drauz continued to be courted by both Morgenschweis and his Lutheran competitor, and the man might have been playing them against each other. Whatever the case, Drauz had joined the Nazi Party as early as 1928. A fanatic, he continued sending people to their deaths up until the very last days of the war.[64] But he was eager to save his own skin. After the German surrender, Drauz and his family fled to the Rhineland region and allegedly found refuge in a Catholic monastery near the West German town of Montabaur, where the U.S. Counterintelligence Corps eventually tracked him down and arrested him for the murder of American POWs.[65]

The German clergy, including Frings, Faulhaber, and Neuhäusler, constantly updated the Vatican about the fate of the war criminals in Landsberg prison, largely based on information received from Morgenschweis. While leading a group of pilgrims to Rome in 1954, the chaplain reached out to Montini once again, reminded him of their exchanges in the Pohl case, and asked for an audience with the pope. He hoped to submit, personally, a memorandum about the remaining Nazi war criminals imprisoned in Landsberg. Neuhäusler offered full support for this request, according to Morgenschweis,[66] but Montini indicated that no such special audience could be granted, though the Holy Father sent Morgenschweis his apostolic blessing for his soulful work.[67]

As such blessings indicate, Morgenschweis's efforts were not isolated. They represented part of the wider effort to re-Christianize all of Europe's increasingly secular societies, of which the secular Nazi ideology was just one example. Communism, liberalism, and freemasonry were also on the list. In the hope of turning the tide in its favor, the Church focused many of its efforts on former Nazis locked up in prisons and POW camps. Priests sent reports to their local bishops, updated with their the latest "soul counts."

A notable priest making such efforts was Father Leonhard (Korbinian) Roth, himself a former Nazi prisoner, locked up in Dachau during the war. When Dachau concentration camp was liberated by the Americans, Roth stayed behind and worked as a prison chaplain; the camp had been converted into a holding facility for suspected Nazi war criminals. Roth had a particularly strong connection to Neuhäusler, and they likely knew each other from their time as prisoners in the concentration camp. In December 1945, he thanked Neuhäusler for his material and spiritual support for the Nazi prisoners and reported that they believed the Catholic Church was the only entity that cared about them: "With this love that you [Neuhäusler] demonstrated, you became a pioneer for Christ in these men."[68] With a stylistic choice similar to Morgenschweis's, Roth's monthly reports to Neuhäusler included the mention that the prison compound for SS men comprised about 10,000 "so-called war criminals." Those he referred to as "so-called war criminals" included former concentration camp commanders, camp guards, Gestapo, and SS officers. Roth defined his mission in three categories: (1) re-entry to the Church of Nazis who were once Catholic, (2) conversion of former Protestants, and (3) conversion combined with (re-)baptism in special cases. As he noted to his superiors, Roth was pretty successful in his religious efforts among rank-and-file Nazi soldiers but not as much with SS officers.[69]

At the Vatican, Monsignor Ferdinando Baldelli, head of the Papal Aid Commission in Rome, submitted a detailed report to the Vatican Secretariat of State in July 1947 describing the spiritual assistance offered to the more than 500,000 German POWs in Italy. Written by Monsignor Karl Bayer, a German confidant of the pope, the report detailed all the help that the Holy Father had given to the German prisoners—food, cigarettes, books, calendars, and Christmas trees. In a report for the pope that was forwarded to Bishop Aloisius Muench in Germany too (to keep the German clergy in the picture), Bayer proudly reported,

> Thousands of prisoners returned to the practical and active life of the faith and hundreds of non-Catholics embraced the faith of our Holy Church by seeing the example and tireless work of the prison chaplains. . . . On Sunday . . . 153 prisoners (most of whom were converted) received the sacrament of Holy Confirmation in the Rimini [POW] camp.[70]

Such enthusiasm for the prospect of a religious renewal of society shown by Morgenschweis, Roth, Baldelli, and many other priests in the immediate postwar years soon ebbed. By the early 1950s, priests in Germany, Italy, Austria, and elsewhere in Europe became disillusioned when the hoped-for re-Christianization of societies failed to materialize. In a 1953 letter from Morgenschweis to his superiors, he laments that though he worked hard at Landsberg prison, the results had been limited. The prison had been turned into "a real stone quarry," and "despite all the efforts only a few little plants of Catholic life are flourishing," which Morgenschweis blamed on "the increase of anti-Catholic and Communist elements and the general desperation of the remaining prisoners."[71] This report seems less than accurate, though. Among the former Nazis in Landsberg, there were hardly any communists (Nazis and communists were deadly enemies). But re-Christianization work was not limited to former Nazis; Morgenschweis also oversaw and celebrated the return and conversion of a few communists. Still, his hopes of saving the souls of the Nazi neo-pagans under his care were dashed.

Operating in Dachau, Roth took a different view. He certainly was disappointed that the Christian renewal had not taken place, but for this former victim of the Nazis, something else also bothered him even more. As noted in his 1958 speech for Nazi victims, given on the grounds of the former concentration camp, Roth hit a nerve when he said,

> Unfortunately, in Germany, it is the case that former Nazis are once again in high and top positions of authority, playing a decisive role in the new Germany. One should not persecute them as they persecuted us; however, it is not appropriate that these Nazis, who upheld the Hitler regime and led it to victory, are now in prominent positions in the offices.[72]

Church authorities reprimanded him for publicly raising this uncomfortable truth.[73] Thorough denazification had failed, in part due to resistance by Christian churches.

A forgive-and-forget mentality, a pressing desire for the re-Christianization of Europe, and criticisms of Allied justice all drove the tireless Catholic harvesters of Nazi souls. But in identifying such motives, we cannot ignore the evidence of personal ambition, German national pride, and a refusal to accept responsibility for the Church's complicity with fascism. Morgenschweis outspokenly denounced the Allies' war crimes trials and, as late as 1966, reassured a right-wing group of Germans that

> No matter how deeply we regret what happened, we need not be ashamed. If the French are not ashamed—you know French history with its events, including what happened to Germans—and if the Russians do not need to be ashamed, etcetera, why should we be ashamed? We are not a nation of criminals! And yet today we are treated like that—abroad.[74]

The difference in the Church's response to Roth's position and its response to Morgenschweis's correspondence is instructive. Morgenschweis did not raise such strong criticisms or concerns, and he was rewarded by his superiors. In 1950, the bishop of Augsburg named him a counselor. In 1952, he received the German government's medal of service, *Bundesverdienstkreuz*. In 1959, Pope John XXIII appointed him a Chaplain of His Holiness, which carries with it the title monsignor. The Bavarian Red Cross lauded Morgenschweis for his commitment to advocating for war criminals—now being referred to as "prisoners of war."[75]

When Bishop Joseph Freundorfer of Augsburg visited Landsberg prison on April 2, 1950, Morgenschweis's direct superior held a festive mass for the Triduum (the end of Lenten season) to prepare for Easter. Two weeks later, the city's Catholic newspaper pointed out how unusual such a festive mass was in a prison. The article acknowledged that the Landsberg prisoners felt like victims of the Nazi regime and the "unlucky outcome of the war," and it advanced the narrative that they had been infected by the Nazi spirit, which led them to leave the church. Thus, the bishop's visit was a welcome success, as was his message: "God is still present and the love of God judges differently than the worldly judges." The bishop added that the Nazi prisoners were being judged by the public, regardless of their guilt or the extent to which they had been seduced by a blindness that made them follow Hitler, just like so many others in Germany and abroad.[76] The bishop's suggestion that Nazi operatives had been seduced by Hitler closely resembles the way Morgenschweis described Oswald Pohl to him. Freundorfer offered absolution and forgiveness. The Church would not judge Nazi criminals; it would defend them against worldly judges and public opinion.

This tone was not novel; it had been set weeks earlier in the same Catholic newspaper. With the title "The Seven Words of Jesus on the Cross," it condemned revenge against or denouncing of former Nazis. The author of the article acknowledged that for many German victims, it would be difficult to forgive past injustice suffered, but doing so was a necessary precondition for reconciliation. Therefore, in the author's estimation, the German people had to stick together and be united.[77]

During this period, baptism and the salvation of souls ranked among the Church's highest priorities. The drive for conversion extended not only to former Nazis and communists but also to Jews—a central concern of the papacy for centuries. A prominent example is the conversion of Israel Zolli (Zoller), the Austrian-born Chief Rabbi of Rome. His baptism, together with that of his wife, took place on February 17, 1945, at the Basilica of Saint Mary of the Angels in Rome, underscoring that such missionary efforts continued even amid the Holocaust. The news of their baptism caused a stir, with the Jewish community in Rome mourning Zolli as dead, but also "denounced him as a meshummad (apostate, one struck by God) and excommunicated him."[78] The Vatican newspaper *Osservatore Romano* instead reported the conversion proudly, "In a few days the newborns [*neonati*] will receive confirmation and communion." It indicated Israel Zolli would assume the new Christian name "Eugenio" to honor Eugenio Pacelli (Pope Pius XII) and the help that Catholics had extended to the persecuted Jews of Rome.[79] A year later, the *Osservatore Romano* rejected racial antisemitism and quoted the ex-chief-rabbi of Rome—Zolli—while reporting about his conversion: "There is no Semitic race."[80]

Shunned by his former community, Zolli worked as a scholar for the Vatican. The power of the sacraments and baptism is also evident in the famous controversy surrounding Jewish children who were hidden in Catholic monasteries and homes during the Holocaust. Some were baptized, and Catholic clergy went to great lengths to prevent their return to Jewish families after the war. Some children were even kidnapped by Church officials. Since their baptism made them part of the Catholic family, Church teachings at the time taught that returning them to their Jewish relatives would potentially threaten their Catholic upbringing. Pope Pius XII was informed about such cases and supported the reasoning that canon law in such cases was to override all other considerations.[81]

CONCLUSION

The "re-Christianization" of secular societies in Europe was a crucial goal in postwar Europe, pushing Catholic leaders to work to save as many souls as possible by bringing former Nazis back. As one Jesuit scholar concluded, "The conversion of the Nazis was regarded as a cornerstone of postwar re-Christianized Germany and Europe."[82] The danger was communicated clearly: To avoid allowing Germany to succumb to paganism or communism, it had to be re-Christianized and forgiven. These views aligned with the Vatican's, which saw conversion and forgiveness as central to both its political and religious mission. It also needs to be noted that Christian teaching tends to focus more on the sinner than the victim for theological reasons. The sinner's soul is believed to be in danger and in need of salvation, while the victim's soul is seen as intact and not at risk.

It seems safe to assume that the Nazi perpetrators were not always truthful about their religious awakenings. The support—moral, financial, religious, and legal—they could gain clearly was another driving factor. The accused in the dock often had no one else to turn to, and certainly not the German state, which no longer existed. The Nazi Party and its once-powerful organizations were gone, disgraced, dispersed, and banned. Their former leaders were dead, on trial, or in hiding. Rank-and-file Nazis, fending for themselves and their families in war-devastated Germany, recognized Christian churches as an attractive alternative that could meet their need for protection. The Catholic Church, with its universal connections, was particularly appealing, and it showed itself willing to forgive Nazi perpetrators without even requiring them to meet minimum standards of Catholic forgiveness: admitting personal guilt, repenting, and asking for forgiveness.[83] The case of Rudolf Höss, the commandant of Auschwitz, provides the rare exception that demonstrates the rule. His admission of personal guilt and request for forgiveness was widely noticed. Yet he asked the Polish people for forgiveness and referred to his victims as the "Polish nation," rather than acknowledging the Jews from all over Europe whom he murdered in Auschwitz.[84] This case also raises the thorny question of whether forgiveness is or should be available to perpetrators of genocide. Forgiveness offered by victims was not required for Catholic absolution. Instead, the victims were mostly forgotten during this Catholic campaign of "cheap forgiveness."[85]

The Church embraced, as its main mission, saving souls and spreading the gospel of Jesus, tied to charitable work (*caritas*). According to one of the pope's closest confidants, though, "Despite all acts of charity, concern for the salvation of souls remained Pius XII's main concern."[86] To the Church, the Nazis were heretics who had adopted a new (secular) paganism and worshipped false (secular) gods, so they needed to be redeemed. In a 1943 speech to the College of Cardinals, Pius XII explained, "We have never intended to draw up a bill of indictment, but rather to bring men back to the paths of truth and redemption."[87] Saving souls was the goal, and ultimately, it did not matter whose souls. Pius XII celebrated the conversion of a group of American GIs (apparently all Protestants) in St. Peter's Cathedral in Rome by proclaiming, "This harvest of souls is worth every sacrifice!!"[88] These religious motives must be addressed and accounted for when considering the Vatican's decision-making in regard to Nazi war criminals.

PART 3

HOLY WAR

8

GODLESS COMMUNISM

On March 8, 1948, Pope Pius XII granted an interview to Anne O'Hare McCormick, a devout Catholic, respected journalist, and editorial board member of *The New York Times*. With the Republic of Italy's first parliamentary elections just weeks away, both felt the gravity of the moment. A communist victory on April 18 posed a serious threat—not just to Italy, but to the Vatican, given Catholicism's central role in the country. The withdrawal of Allied troops in December 1947 and Italy's full return to sovereignty on January 1, 1948, had only heightened fears. In the escalating logic of the Cold War, a communist win in Catholic Europe's heartland was seen as a worst-case scenario. Over the course of about 35 minutes, the pope offered his pessimistic predictions, prompting the journalist to ask Pius XII about his intentions, if the worst came to pass. His forceful response signaled his attitude, namely, that "if the Communists win and Italy is taken over, he will remain at his post in Vatican City, come what may, death or anything else."[1] In other words, he was prepared to die a martyr's death, opposing "godless" communism until his last breath. But until that moment came, the pope planned to fight with all the means at his disposal to prevent communism from taking over.

As we have seen, Pope Pius XII's anti-communism can be traced back to the turmoil following World War I, as the collapse of the Russian, Austrian, and Ottoman Empires destabilized Europe. During the 1917 Bolshevik Revolution, the Red Army frequently targeted clergy and churches, reflecting Karl Marx's famous claim that "religion is the opium of the people." Fearing the spread of communism, Church leaders—among them the future pope—opposed the 1919 Treaty of Versailles, warning that a weakened Germany would only fuel unrest and empower leftist revolutionaries. While serving as nuncio in Bavaria, the future Pius XII saw his predictions come true and witnessed the turmoil personally, when communist revolutionaries stormed his Munich residence. From these events, the pope drew a clear lesson: Europe needed a strong Christian Germany to counter the spread of communism.

MODERN-DAY CRUSADE AGAINST COMMUNISM

As pope, Pius XII maintained these negative views of communism before, during, and after WWII. As has been documented here, he sought to change the Allies' formula for Germany's unconditional surrender while also expressing his concerns about the growing Soviet communist influence in Europe,[2] reflecting his belief, as one historian stated, "that unconditional surrender would harden resistance in Germany, prolong the war, and advance communist domination in Europe. The ultimatum [of unconditional surrender] was no inducement to the Germans to overthrow Hitler, and make peace."[3] In turn, he also opposed U.S. material support for Stalin's Soviet Union, which he feared would give communism the upper hand against Nazi Germany. As explained by Harold Tittmann, the trusted aide of the U.S. diplomat Myron C. Taylor,

> At the beginning of the Second World War, communist militant atheism was still regarded in the Vatican as more obnoxious than modern paganism in Germany. There was always the chance that the Nazis confronted with the power of the Catholic Church in Germany, might change their policy of persecution [against the Church], while in Russia, where the cult had disappeared altogether, there was little hope or no hope for improvement.[4]

As the Soviets advanced, following a number of major German defeats, Pius XII increasingly embraced the ideal of Christian Germany as a bulwark against Soviet communism.[5]

Anti-communism and re-Christianization were two sides of the same coin for Pius XII. To achieve the goal of the re-Christianization of Europe—a spiritual reawakening—in a society that had grown more and more secular since the Enlightenment, he would need to return to his days of diplomacy and engage with modern politics.[6] Only by taking such a modern approach could he achieve his goal of a return to a more Christian past.

Once Germany had surrendered unconditionally, and the Soviets were standing in Berlin, Budapest, Warsaw, and Vienna, U.S. Catholic leaders raised their voices as well. In April 1945, the U.S. bishops, organized through the National Catholic Welfare Conference (NCWC), expressed strong disagreement with the outcomes of the Yalta Conference, which had placed Poland and the Baltic countries de facto under Soviet control. They condemned the lack of civil and religious liberty in communist countries with a metaphor: "The bulwark of democracy is religion and justice is its password."[7] As the U.S. envoy to the pope, Myron C. Taylor saw what was happening and did not mince words when describing "Moscow's anti-Vatican propaganda and the possible reaction of the Soviets to this latest 'broadside of the American Catholic Episcopate' against the principles of Communism and the policy of the Soviet Government."[8]

By April 1945, it was quite clear to all involved that the Soviets and the Vatican were engaged in a war—at least one of words. Soviet press and radio attacks on the Vatican intensified that summer, leading a U.S. diplomat in the Vatican to inform Washington, "Whatever the purpose of the Soviet attacks may be, it is evident that the Holy See is not remaining insensible to them."[9] Evident indeed; in a critical speech on June 2, 1945, Pius XII referred to the peril of a new tyranny emerging from Europe's chaos. In thinly veiled language, he rejected Soviet communist dominance over Eastern Europe as contrary to the wishes of the local population. Furthermore, Pius XII highlighted atrocities, including the murders of priests and deportation of civilians in communist Yugoslavia.[10]

On another front, the Vatican newspaper *Osservatore Romano* simultaneously engaged in a press war with the Soviets. Moscow referred to the Vatican as a helper of fascists, citing its silence during the war and its appeals for clemency for war criminals: "when Mussolini and Hitler tortured millions of people the Pope was silent, but now that the liberated people demand that the bandits answer for their crimes, the Pope asks for clemency."[11] To rebut such charges launched by Soviet newspapers, the Vatican noted,

"There is not a single Soviet newspaper which has not been attacking us" as "reactionary" and "anti-Soviet," and yet, "Opposition to a single party . . . and the desire to insure freedom of the press and respect for religion do not mean that one is reactionary."[12]

While fighting these propaganda battles, the Vatican closely followed persecutions of the Church by communists. Reports of such activities came from various countries, including Ukraine, Croatia, Yugoslavia, and Hungary. By examining some exemplary events in each of those nations, we can get a sense of how the Vatican dealt with these attacks.

The pope appears to have taken a particular interest in the situation facing the Catholic Church in Soviet-controlled Ukraine. Describing an encyclical letter "L'enciclica 'Orientales omnes' issued on the occasion of the 350th anniversary of the union of the Ruthenians [Western Ukrainians] with the Apostolic See," the *Osservatore Romano* explained in a January 20, 1946, full-page article, that "The Holy Father, recalling the reasons and benefits of this historic event, invites pastors and peoples to say special prayers for the necessary comfort of the persecuted brothers due to their centuries-old loyalty to the Catholic Church."[13] The Ukrainian Archbishop Ivan Bucko, whom the pope assigned the task of caring for Ukrainians stranded in Western Europe, appealed for protection against the forced repatriation of Ukrainians to their homelands, now under Soviet control.[14] In the encyclical letter, the pope included the claim that "All the Eastern Churches, as history proves, have ever been the object of the deep affection of the Roman pontiffs."[15] Therefore, the forced union of the Ukrainian Greek Catholic Church with the Orthodox Church, which was controlled by communist Moscow, was, according to *Osservatore Romano*, an "act of violence imposed by the Bolshevik regime" and against the will of Catholic Ukrainians.[16]

The newspaper was not the only one making allegations. As it reported in October 1946, Soviet leaders publicly accused the Ukrainian Catholic bishops and clergy of collaborating with the Germans during the war. Specifically, the Soviets alleged that Catholic bishops, in coordination with SS *Gruppenführer* Otto Wächter, had helped create the *Waffen* SS division *Galizien*, which was composed mostly of Catholic Ukrainians.[17] Although there was no shortage of Ukrainian Nazi collaborators, the majority of Ukrainians fought with the Soviets and against the Third Reich. Yet the kernel of truth within the propagandistic, blanket accusation of collusion with the SS was enough for the Soviets to sentence Ukrainian Catholic clergy to horrible gulags—in line with their broader, long-standing patterns of anti-religious policies. In response, large waves of Ukrainians, including hundreds of priests, fled and became stranded in the West. The Vatican's ongoing efforts to help these uprooted émigrés were repeatedly reported on by the *Osservatore*.[18]

The newspaper also made frequent mention of Croatia as a traditional bulwark of Catholic Christianity and the West. In January 1945, it cited the work of the Pontifical Croatian Institute of Saint Jerome (Pontificio Collegio Croato di San Girolamo), located in Rome, under the leadership of rector Monsignor Juraj Magjerec, and its ongoing dedication to hosting Croatian residents, pilgrims, and refugees. The published report stressed the ancient mission of the Croat nation, as a shield of Christianity against Islam. It also highlighted the great admiration and appreciation that popes had expressed over the years, for all the sacrifices Croats made in the "defense of the Catholic West."[19]

Despite the *Osservatore* report's consistently positive view of the Croatian state and its role in Catholicism, the country's fascist regime in WWII, under Ante Pavelić, committed countless atrocities against Serbs, Jews, and Roma. It engaged in concerted efforts to establish a homogenous Catholic nation, using criminal tactics such as ethnic cleansing and forced conversions of Orthodox Christians. The leadership of the Croatian Catholic Church, seeking Croatian independence, initially welcomed the Pavelić fascists (known as Ustaša), seeing them as the fulfillment of century-old national aspirations. The fascist dictator Pavelić was even granted private audiences by the pope on two occasions, and many Catholic clergy offered their support to the fascist regime, some going so far as to participate actively in the atrocities. Clergy members were listed as camp commanders, notably in the horrific camp Jasenovac, where unspeakable brutality occurred. Yet these crimes were only briefly mentioned in the *Osservatore*, mainly in relation to later communist accusations against those Catholic clergy working in support of the Pavelić regime.[20]

Regarding Croatia, we find that few events were covered so widely and frequently in the 1946 issues of *Osservatore* as the trial of Aloysius Stepinac, the archbishop of Zagreb, who ranked formally as the highest Catholic dignitary in his nation. Although not a hardcore supporter of Pavelić, the archbishop was a Croatian nationalist and anti-communist. He had navigated his Church through the war, a fascist Croatian state, and the immediate postwar chaos. He also stood accused, together with 18 "collaborators of the invaders," in the words of the Yugoslavian court, of "forced conversions of Serbs to the Catholic faith."[21] From the very day the trial started, October 2, 1946, nearly every issue of *Osservatore* provided coverage or comments, expressing disapproval of forced conversions but also claiming that those under Stepinac were voluntary. The coverage the *Osservatore* dedicated to these trial proceedings was massive in its sheer volume. The "trial in Zagreb" could not be missed by regular readers of the Vatican newspaper, for whom Stepinac was portrayed as a martyr for the faith.[22] Following the brief trial, the *Osservatore* also printed the guilty verdict and the resulting sentence: 16 years of hard labor for "archbishop Stepinac, Primate of Yugoslavia."[23]

Once that verdict arrived, the Vatican extended its reactions to repeated, full-out condemnations.[24] The pope even drew on his most powerful weapon: The Vatican excommunicated all Catholics who had participated in the prosecution, an action directed mainly at the Yugoslav communist leader and baptized Catholic, Marshal Josip Broz, nicknamed "Tito." It was the first excommunication of a head of state since Emperor Napoleon some 140 years earlier. The speedy, uncompromising nature of this excommunication has led some scholars to raise the question of why a similar measure never was taken against Hitler, who was born, baptized, and died a Catholic.[25] In any case, while Tito and his communists were being condemned, the narrative of Stepinac as a religiously persecuted martyr was firmly established. Pius XII made him a cardinal in 1953, while Stepinac was still under house arrest, and a few years before he passed away. In 1998, Pope John Paul II beatified Stepinac as a martyr of the faith.

Stepinac was not the only martyr; the Catholic clergy of Croatia as a whole received praise as witnesses of the faith. Stories of religious persecution in communist Yugoslavia also extended beyond the trial.[26] The October 10, 1946, edition of the *Osservatore* reported on "the death of a heroic Yugoslav bishop," Monsignor Giovanni Simrak, who had died as a result of the abuses to which he was subjected in a communist prison.[27] About a week later, the newspaper also reported that Yugoslavian authorities planned to initiate proceedings against Monsignor Ivan Šarić, archbishop of Sarajevo.[28] He had gained a reputation for supporting Pavelić's regime and making antisemitic statements;[29] he fled to Austria at war's end and successfully avoided extradition to Yugoslavia. Another escapee to Austria was Bishop Gregorij Rožman of Ljubljana, the German-friendly, hardcore anti-communist who had blessed the Nazi forces fighting the leftist partisans during the war—all good reasons for him to hide from Yugoslavian authorities. Apparently worried that Tito's agents would kidnap the clerics from their temporary Austrian refuge, the Vatican Secretariat of State intervened for both Archbishop Šarić and Bishop Rožman in 1946, asking the British for their "removal from the immediate proximity of the Jugoslav frontier" out of "concern for the safety of their Excellencies."[30] Ultimately, Šarić lived out the remainder of his days in Franco's Spain, while Bishop Rožman reached safety in Salzburg, in the American zone of Austria, where Archbishop Andreas Rohracher took him under his wing.[31]

Reporting on the Stepinac case had barely died down when new events, this time in Hungary, caught the attention of the *Osservatore*. It was increasingly falling under Soviet influence. By March 1947, the Americans were protesting against increased Soviet influence over Hungarian affairs as well.[32] Over the course of the gradual, Soviet-led, communist takeover of Hungary, relations with the Catholic Church deteriorated. Thus the "sacrilegious" arrest of the prominent Cardinal József Mindszenty, primate of Hungary and the highest-ranking Catholic clergy of the country, received substantial coverage in January 1949, as did the international protests that it sparked.[33] As an outspoken, undiplomatic opponent of the new communist masters, Mindszenty represented a clear target, as well as a clear force that the Catholic world wanted to protect.[34] In reporting on the "painful echo after the arrest of Mindszenty," the *Osservatore* included a telegram from the American Jewish League Against Communism to the powerful Cardinal Francis Spellman from New York: "The message referenced the words of Cardinal Spellman, who has called the action of the Hungarian government an attack against God himself and on the nations, who believe in Him."[35] Eventually, Mindszenty was sentenced to life in prison for charges that appeared largely politically motivated, such as treason and currency violations. The Vatican insisted on his "morally and civilly" innocent status. Just as was the case in the Stepinac trial, people involved in the proceedings against Mindszenty were reportedly formally excommunicated.

The Catholic Church found itself in an undeclared war with the Soviet bloc and communism everywhere. In Poland and Czechoslovakia, too, new communist rule and attacks against the Catholic Church were noted with great concern.[36] Pius XII's anti-communist orientation dictated much of his decision-making.[37] In the words of a biographer of Paul VI,

> When the war in Europe ended in May, 1945, Nazism and Fascism were obliterated, but Pope Pius and his staff knew that one great enemy of the Church remained. All the forces and wiles of Vatican diplomacy were marshaled to counter the advance of communism. . . . Perhaps the greatest danger the Holy See faced was a communist takeover in Italy itself.[38]

Italy, the heartland of Catholicism, became a battlefield, and in his December 1946 speech, Pius XII drew clear lines in the sand for the combatants: "For Christ or against Christ, for His Church or against His Church."[39]

THE ITALIAN ELECTION

The 1948 Italian elections, scheduled for Sunday, April 18, marked a pivotal moment for both the country and the pope. The Catholic community harbored deep concerns about the possibility of a communist takeover, given the strength of the Italian Communist Party, with its more than 2 million members and many more supporters—making it the strongest representation of communist power in Western Europe. The notion that communists, in alliance with the socialists, could emerge victorious in the 1948 elections and seize power through the ballot box was a nightmare scenario for the Vatican. The prospect of the tiny Vatican state, with the pope at its helm, being surrounded by a communist Italy, felt like the promise of a terrible siege.[40]

It was at this crucial moment that Anne O'Hare McCormick sat down with the pope for their conversation. She shared her insights from the meeting with U.S. diplomats, who were particularly worried about the pope's assertion that he would remain in Rome, even if it came under communist rule.[41] The U.S. diplomats in the Vatican explained (apparently not for the first time) to the State Department, "This coincides with the impression I wrote you before Christmas. Many Catholics abroad, of course, will take the line that he will have no right to remain as a prisoner of the Communists."[42] The British Minister to the Holy See had told his U.S. counterparts in March 1948 that Monsignor Tardini, the Vatican Undersecretary of State, had warned, "It would be impossible to administer the Universal Church from inside the Iron Curtain,"[43] implying that the pope would leave Rome and go into exile. But McCormick insisted that the pope had told her, in strict confidence during her March 8 audience, that he would stay.[44] Summarizing the options, a U.S. diplomat in Rome acknowledged,

> This subject has been increasingly discussed of late and there has been considerable local opinion to the effect that Portugal might be an emergency refuge for the Holy See. On one occasion some time ago I received an impression in conversation with the Portuguese Ambassador that he had been rather actively interested in this possibility. Brazil has also been mentioned.[45]

Monsignor Montini inquired about what the Americans could do to ensure the protection of the pope, a topic that also was raised in the U.S. Congress.[46]

While others were discussing what to do with him if the communists won, the pope was mobilizing Catholics against those communists.[47] The Catholic Church of the United States had a crucial role, serving as an intermediary and conveying the pope's concerns about the future of Italy. As early as November 1945, U.S. church leaders sought to highlight the risk of communist agitation by citing the example of Soviet takeovers in Eastern and Southeastern Europe, often forced on the nations in question. Citing news from Slovakia, Croatia, Slovenia, and other Central and Eastern European countries, they described "religious persecution which is both brutal and cunning."[48] However, these appeals emerged in the immediate postwar months; they appeared to have prompted little response among Washington diplomats engaged in war crimes trials.

As head of the universal Catholic Church, though, the pope was determined to be heard. Pascalina Lehnert, the pope's confidant, recalled decades later in her memoirs that the pope's fears of a communist victory were so great that the challenges of the fight seemed reasonable:

> Who does not remember the elections of 1948! After a lost war, during destruction, poverty, misery, and hardship everywhere, when passion and hatred divided people's minds, it was easy for the enemies of God and the Church to influence the masses. To sow discord and disunity and to further incite a populace already in turmoil. What did the Holy Father pray, sacrifice, dare, work for, what did he conceive and prepare! Little of it has emerged into the public eye.[49]

In this sense, Pius XII arguably fought as "one of the first cold-war warriors,"[50] undertaking a "lonely cold war"[51] for years before the Americans joined him.

The American's entry into the Cold War was far more gradual, and it was marked by the Truman Doctrine. In March 1947, President Harry S. Truman offered a programmatic speech that pledged U.S. support for free nations threatened by Soviet communist influence. But even as the United States sought to push back against communist influence worldwide, 1948 saw the communist takeover in Czechoslovakia, the Berlin blockade, and the division of Germany. As global tensions rose, the Italian election of 1948 represented a significant potential threat to the United States, too. If the communists won, Moscow's reach would extend to most of Western Europe and into the Mediterranean. The outcome also raised the prospect of an Italian civil war, similar to the situation in Greece in the immediate postwar years.

Cardinal Spellman's leading role in trying to rally U.S. support for the pope in the anti-communist fight preceded these events.[52] Although perhaps not an obvious source for its reporting, the *Osservatore* quoted a long piece that Spellman initially published in *Cosmopolitan Magazine* in late 1946, under the headline "Do we want a Soviet peace?" In it, this close confidant of Pius XII could clearly spell out what the pope could not: "It is not in defense of my faith that I condemn atheistic Communism, but as an American, I defend my country, for while Communism is an enemy of Catholicism, it is also a challenge to *all* men who believe in America and in God."[53]

In Washington, though, the papal envoy Archbishop Cicognani provided a formal channel between the pope and the U.S. government, and his correspondence with U.S. Catholic Church officials made their strategic plan for collaboration clear:

> It has been brought to the attention of the Chairman of the Executive Board of the National Catholic Welfare Conference that in Italy serious dangers are seen in the agitations inspired by the communists. In these critical times the Italian people must be aware of the dangers. It is pointed out that letters written by persons of Italian descent in the United States to their relatives and friends in Italy, warning about the dangers of communism, have been well received and have proved very efficacious.[54]

If such solutions failed, the risk was the "enslavement" of the Italian Catholics, such that "Atheistic Communism will make a police state of Italy if it gains victory. Atheistic Communism will consider the subjugation of Italy as its greatest achievement. It aims at the destruction of Catholicity in Italy in order to limit and to nullify the world influence of the Catholic Church."[55]

As long as the interests of the Catholic Church and the U.S. government aligned, they worked together to achieve an end they both believed would justify the means. The pope's support, insights, and advice on how to beat the communists was of great interest and helped to define how the U.S. government, the embassy, the Central Intelligence Agency, and the U.S. Catholic Church fought communist forces in the Italian election.[56] The Vatican was eager to form a closer alliance with the United States and to support its programs aimed at strengthening Western Europe. U.S. diplomats in Rome stressed that Montini welcomed the Marshall Plan for the economic recovery of Europe, referring to when he "spoke also of the need for the Marshall Plan to pass Congress before then saying, almost with humor, that it must pass 'Now, I mean sooner than now.'"[57] The Vatican appreciated the support the U.S. government offered. It hailed Myron Taylor, the president's representative with the pope, as "the great and sincere friend and benefactor of the Italian people," and frequently mentioned him in *Osservatore* articles regarding U.S. support. The Vatican clearly was striving to establish good relations with this new superpower, the only viable international counterbalance to the Soviets.[58] These new allies thus joined a worldwide fight against communism, and as the historian Guiliana Chamedes recognizes, "When, with the launching of the Cold War, anticommunism and anti-Sovietism started to become central features of American foreign policy, the papacy and European Christian Democratic Parties rejoiced."[59]

THE POPE'S SECRET WEAPON

In the course of their alliance, both the Vatican and the U.S. government strongly supported the Italian Christian Democrats (*Democrazia Cristiana*) in the 1948 national election. The Americans provided direct financial support, and people close to the Vatican frequently asked for more "cash for the Christian Democrats."[60] Prior to the election, the Irish ambassador in Rome pleaded with his U.S. counterparts to support the "militant Catholics that are really organizing and fighting this election campaign."[61] The plea referred to the Catholic Action [*Azione Cattolica*] movement, an organization of lay Catholics defending the faith, which had come to the forefront during the election. In response, a U.S. report predicted that "if Italy does not go Communist it will be thanks to them. [The Irish diplomat] therefore urges that we do all possible to assist them."[62]

The Lateran Pacts restricted the Vatican's engagement in politics, but Catholic voters still had to be mobilized. Therefore, the Church took part in the election campaign by working through the Catholic Action's "Civic Committees" [*Comitati Civici*], which represented the propaganda arms of the Christian Democrats' campaigns against the communists.[63] The Civic Committees could circumvent "Vatican neutrality."[64] Organized by Dr. Luigi Gedda, president of the Italian Catholic Action Men's Union, these Civic Committees undertook frequent propaganda, organized mass rallies all over Italy, and, through its members, remained "busily engaged in pre-election work."[65] It regularly informed U.S. diplomats about all such activities—correspondence that remained classified as secret by the U.S. State Department for years. State Department officials knew precisely what the operations entailed; they described Civic Committees as "the Vatican-inspired anti-communist political action weapon in Italy."[66] Even though "The Committees were not actually the idea of the Pope himself, . . . good authority has it that His Holiness enthusiastically espoused the idea when it was submitted to him."[67] Thus, rather than remaining unpolitical, the Vatican actively worked to convince the United States to finance anti-communist forces in Italy. Gedda and Montini repeatedly alleged that the Italian Left was receiving funds from communist governments through routes moving through Poland and Switzerland.[68] The Civic Committees also proved quite effective. Launched only in February to influence the April 18 election and led by both Gedda and his ecclesiastical associate Monsignor Fiorenzo Angelini, they made a real difference, according to the U.S. State Department.[69]

Even if the Vatican influence through the Civic Committees was somewhat clandestine, the powerful tensions in Italy in the weeks leading up to the elections were evident in the pope's traditional Easter address. Weeks in advance of the celebration at St. Peter's Square, public posters called for people to show up in large numbers. The *Osservatore Romano* announced the event repeatedly and issued a challenge to the faithful in stressing that the current "grave hour of anxieties and dangers traces the path of salvation for humanity."[70] Among the 400,000 Roman citizens assembled in St. Peter's Square and beyond that Easter, many were members of Catholic Action who arrived in organized groups carrying—as suggested by the *Osservatore Romano*—flags and large signs asking for peace and "calling on the faithful to give proof of their militant Christianity." Their signs were reinforced by handbills, dropped by plane among the crowds in St. Peter's Square and produced by the Catholic Action's Civic Committees, that called for citizens to vote (without explicitly mentioning any party). In the resulting scene, with its "heightened . . . dramatic and emotional quality of the occasion,"[71] the pope began to pray through loudspeakers for the victims of war and other suffering people, as he nearly always did.

As was his tradition in every year before, the pontiff also gave the Easter blessing "*Urbi et Orbi*" ("for the city and the globe") in multiple languages. But beyond those points of similarity, the pope's 1948 address was unusual in its directness and political tone. He described a clear choice for the future and fate of Italy, Catholic Christianity, and the pope himself, proclaiming that

> The great hour of the Christian conscience has struck. . . . May this conscience of Christianity be awakened to a full, virile appreciation of its mission of help and salvation for a human race wavering in its spiritual framework. . . . Should this conscience only half arouse itself, should it not give itself courageously to Christ, then His verdict, His terrible verdict is no less formal: "He that is not with me is against me." . . . You, Beloved Sons and Daughters, know full well what the alternative signifies and involves for Rome, Italy and the world.[72]

For his listeners, the pope established the coming election as a crossroads for Italy: Choose to be with Christ or with the godless. To any undecided voters or communist sympathizers, Pius XII made it clear that they could not have it both ways.

In addition to the crossroads for Italy, he offered another one for voters, who could not follow Christ and Stalin as two masters simultaneously:

> Your conscience knows that the actuation of social justice and of peace amongst nations can never be affected and assured if men close their eyes to the Light of Christ and open their ears instead to the false words of the agitators who lay the cornerstone of their work in the denial of Christ and God.[73]

Although the speech never included the term "communism," the formulation of "agitators" as working for the "denial of Christ and God" was likely clear enough for the Catholic faithful. Thus, the pope powerfully reminded the audience of the problem with communists: They are godless, deny the existence of God, and persecute Christian churches wherever they are in power. Reporting on the speech, U.S. diplomats noted "the Pope's outspoken condemnations of Communism."[74]

However we want to assign the credit, the outcomes of the 1948 Italian Parliamentary elections represented a great victory for the pope, because the Christian Democratic coalition won 48 percent of the vote, relative to just 31 percent for the left-wing coalition of socialist and communist forces.[75] The pope's demeanor was one of relief and gratitude for "the 'healthy reawakening' of the Christian conscience (a reference to the success of the Italian elections)," in the words of a U.S. diplomat.[76] Later, in a June radio broadcast, Pius XII also defended the work of Catholic activists [*Comitati Civici*] "outside the purely religious field [that] foreshadowed an extension thereof," to include social reform. Despite reflecting his "constant preoccupation with the worldwide struggle between Christian morality and Atheist Communism," the radio address featured a less dark tone and apparent relief about the election outcomes. Yet as a U.S. foreign service official in the Vatican also recognized with regard to the radio message, "its militant character is evident from the two mottoes he gave, the first being that which was said of an ancient Pope, 'He feared nothing on earth!' and the second 'Vigilante! Watch!'"[77]

Pope Pius XII's willingness to fight to prevent a communist victory in Italy reflected his beliefs about the intensity of the threat. The work performed by the "Vicar of Christ" in that arena was not limited to religious affairs; it featured active participation, by himself and his Church, in mobilizing the Catholic vote for the anti-communist, pro-Catholic Christian Democratic Party. Although such politicization of Catholic action is notable, it does not represent the pope's most dramatic move against communism. That tactic, still to come, involved leveraging the innate power of religion.

EXCOMMUNICATING COMMUNISTS

On July 1, 1949, the Congregation for the Doctrine of the Faith (once, and better, known as the Catholic Inquisition) issued a decree, excommunicating all members and supporters of the Communist Party. Historian Peter Kent fittingly described the move as a "significant counter-offensive by the Holy See in the religious cold war with the Communist bloc."[78] What did the decree say exactly, and why was it timed as it was? It appears that Pius XII was willing to hurl God's anathema against the communists only after the Italian elections were over and won by the Christian Democrats.

In Italy, many Catholics were members of the Communist Party, despite repeated reminders from the pope and Catholic clergy that such a duality was unacceptable. Posters appeared during the 1948 elections, warning voters, "God sees you in the voting booth!" They could not claim to be good Catholics in public while secretly voting for the communists; they might be able to deceive society, but not God. The pope reiterated his point by quoting Jesus, "He that is not with me is against me," and categorizing Catholics voting for communism as against him.[79] In these actions, the Church defined communists openly, but not formally, as opponents. Yet even after his Easter speech, the pope still sought to retain his neutral, diplomatic image when it came to influencing elections.

Therefore, it was up to other high-ranking Catholic dignitaries to make the case that communists faced the ultimate sanction of excommunication, which would exclude them from salvation and threaten them with eternal condemnation. In March 1948, Cardinal Eugène Tisserant, a powerful player inside the Vatican, reportedly ordered readings of the following instructions for the faithful of his Diocese:

> All Catholics favoring or propagating the principles of "Marxist Social-Communism" expose themselves to perversion and loss of the Faith; they cooperate in the diffusion of false doctrines, they deny religious truths, they cooperate in the struggle against God and His Church. . . . [T]hey are in strident and open contradiction with their own consciences, and in the same conditions in which a Jew, a Muslim, a pagan would be, who while refusing to give up his religion would at the same time claim to be a Catholic.[80]

A communist-voting Catholic was committing "a serious sin" and could not receive the Holy Sacraments or obtain the ritual blessings of the Church. The Cardinal went on to say, "After death, they may not have Christian burial or be buried in holy ground beneath the sign of the Cross."[81] Catholic supporters of communism were thus warned that, just like Jews, Muslims, and pagans, they would be excluded from the blessings of the Church.

Such actions were closely monitored and recorded by U.S. diplomats in Rome. For example, they noted the responses to a claim by the communist leader Palmiro Togliatti that Italians could be communists and still be good Catholics. It was the powerful cardinal from Milan, Ildefonso Schuster, who refuted this idea. Schuster had a long record of outspoken anti-communism and involvement in matters beyond strictly ecclesiastical affairs. Shortly before the end of World War II, Schuster had negotiated with Nazi forces in Italy to shorten the combat and also to prevent a takeover by communist partisans in Northern Italy. Following his historical pattern of direct action, Schuster made clear that Catholic faithful would be committing an offense against the Church and its teachings if they voted for candidates who attacked the Church and violated religious principles. This thinly veiled reference to the communists came, as U.S. diplomats noted carefully, just shortly after Schuster had an audience with the pope.[82]

Still, the Church was careful to avoid actually excommunicating any Communist Party members before the election. Once it was over, and the Christian Democrats emerged victorious, such restraints fell to the wayside. The pope excommunicated communists, and the international community reacted with astonishment. "Catholic Communists to be excommunicated" trumpeted the Australian newspaper *Advocate*, adding "Pope Pius has ordered the excommunication of Catholics who are militant Communists." The accompanying article cited recent estimates of 300,000,000 Catholics worldwide but had no estimates of how many of those also professed communism. The newspaper regarded the excommunication order as unprecedented in the 2,000-year history of the Church.[83] In the United States, which never had a Catholic majority, the pope's actions still generated substantial interest. Even though contemporary newspaper articles that covered the decree implied that its practical impact might not be substantial, a prevalent theme highlighted the battle of a religious (i.e., Christian) West versus an atheist (communist) East. *The New York Times* also noted consequences of the excommunication decree for the development of East Germany, whose own Christian Democratic Party, feeling empowered by the decree, pushed harder against communist pressure to fall in line. It was the summer of 1949, and the Soviets still showed some restraint in their occupation zone of Germany. A few months later, the East German communist state was officially founded, and the division of Germany was formalized.

Another story in *The New York Times* reported on meetings by Cardinal Konrad von Preysing, the bishop of Berlin, with Catholic Church leaders, seeking to understand the practical consequences of the excommunications. When Preysing gave a press conference in July 1949 with Myron C. Taylor—whom Monsignor Montini had personally informed of the excommunication of the communists[84]—it perhaps unsurprisingly drew attacks from East Germany's communist press.[85] But such events suggest that the clergy struggled to understand the real meaning and impact of the excommunication order. Papers in the archives of Cardinal Frings in Cologne reveal how he told it to his flock, using a question-and-answer style: "Is it allowed to join the communist parties as a member or to support them?" "No, communism is materialistic and anti-Christian." The communist leaders were "bitter enemies of God, the true religion, and the Church of Christ."[86] Frings guidelines also ultimately concluded that, for Christians, it was forbidden to read books with communist ideas. They had to stay away from everything communist, and in turn, no communists could take part in the sacraments.[87]

Despite such struggles, the Vatican consistently made its position clear, once the decree had been issued: It was against any compromise with the regimes of the anti-Christ. I appreciate the way the historian Peter Kent puts it:

> The religious cold war was now joined in earnest, since the Vatican had brandished its weapon of excommunication to challenge the strategies of the east European Communists for subverting Catholic communities which had been forced to live under communism. The specific conflicts and persecutions in eastern Europe and elsewhere had now been universalized into aspects of a holy war against unrighteousness [. . . .] The Holy Office decree forced some east European churchmen to choose between loyalty to their [state-controlled] church and loyalty to the Holy See.[88]

Despite his unwavering commitment, though, it ultimately was a losing battle for the pope. Many communist countries arrested resident priests, closed the churches, and nationalized church property, such as hospitals and orphanages.[89] Bishops and local church authorities in communist Eastern Europe were forced to accept their new reality if they wanted to continue operating and maintaining a Catholic life. The limitations of the pope's power were clear in Eastern Europe, but even in Italy, the excommunication of communists was rarely enforced, such that there were few practical consequences.[90] Communism and Catholicism found a way to coexist in a very Italian way, as immortalized in the satiric, iconic 1950s movie series *Don Camillo*, in which the communist little town mayor Peppone (a Stalin look-alike) and the Catholic priest Don Camillo are bitter enemies who also share a sense of humanity and decency that invariably prevails when a crisis (e.g., flood) threatens their community.

Even if it lacked many real-world consequences, the excommunication order remains remarkable, for several reasons. First, the pope never condemned the Nazis or fascists in such a way. This is not to say that the Vatican never spoke out; the pope condemned the false teachings of Nazism, and particularly its racism and racial antisemitism. The Vatican also protested against violations of the concordat of 1933 and the persecution of the Church. Yet it never took the ultimate step of issuing a blanket excommunication of members of the Nazi regime. Second, the excommunication targeted people on the basis of their membership in a political party. All communist Catholics, en masse, received a blanket excommunication, a consequence that Catholic Nazi Party members never faced.[91] It was absolutely possible to be both a Nazi *and* a Catholic. Many of Hitler's followers stayed within the Church and never left, even if a few declared themselves *gottgläubig*, meaning they embraced Nazi paganism. Even Adolf Hitler himself remained a Catholic, at least on paper, and he was never excommunicated. According to Church historian Hubert Wolf,

> There is no trace in the Vatican archives of any effort to initiate excommunication proceedings against Adolf Hitler. Pronouncing a Reich chancellor and head of state anathema was simply out of the question. Hitler remained a member of the Catholic Church until the day he died. Like the pope, even the devil could be Catholic.[92]

CONCLUSION

It was his anti-communist dedication and determination to defend the interests of the Church that largely drove the actions of Pius XII. He watched the expansion of Stalin's communist empire and its worldwide influence with deep concern. Early Church attempts to come to a *modus vivendi* with the communists were unfruitful. At the end of the war, communism was stronger than ever, and everywhere it gained power, it openly rejected and repressed religion. At this point, the Vatican sought to forge new or renewed alliances with the United States, Great Britain, and Italian conservatives to fend off their common enemy.

As communists and Christian Democrats in Italy fought their bitter campaign, which some scholars have justifiably labeled a "religious war,"[93] the Vatican came to the realization that it could not limit itself to spiritual–religious dimensions, because those dimensions were so closely intertwined with the political world. Re-Christianization would be needed to mobilize the "Christian conscience" and create a strong anti-communist "militant Christianity." In this effort, religion and the rebirth of the Church had to take priority, as a way to deal with the devastation and darkness brought by the war. As detailed in a 1944 *Osservatore* article, even if scholars might attempt to relegate religion to books, it would reemerge in people's lives. Therefore, religion should become the soul of nations and inform politics: "Yes, absolutely, also into politics: Because man does not live on bread alone, but also from belief. As long as religion will not come back into the lives of the people, there will be no welfare and no peace for mankind."[94]

In the spirit of such "militant Christianity," called for to fight the new enemy of communism in Italy and elsewhere, the Vatican was willing to support anti-communists of all kinds, including former Nazis and fascists. For Nazis and fascists hiding in Italy, this willingness, combined with the shift in Allied priorities away from the prosecution of Nazi war criminals and toward fighting the new enemy, produced an ideal environment. Nazis on the run had less to fear, and their anti-communist credentials proved priceless. In this shadowy, secret war era, many novel opportunities arose, including those for escaping any postwar prosecution. Italy and the Vatican would again take a central role, as the next chapter shows. Eastern European clergy in Rome got dragged into the fight, especially when the pope threw the mantle of protection over thousands of Catholic fascists and Nazi collaborators from Eastern Europe. Under the label of charity and neutral humanitarianism, these actions culminated in substantial aid to fascists and Nazis, including Holocaust perpetrators, through what is known today as the Ratline.

9

PAPAL HUMANITARIANISM

One crucial and frequently disputed question in the context of the Vatican and postwar justice is the extent of Pope Pius XII's direct involvement in helping Nazis escape accountability by fleeing overseas. For years, researchers have worked to document the role of Catholic priests and bishops who, all too often knowingly and willingly, aided Nazis—facilitating their emigration to South America and elsewhere. In my 2011 book *Nazis on the Run,* I dedicated a chapter to the Catholic Church's role in the Italian Ratline and documented the involvement of individual clergy, including Bishop Hudal, as well as Papal aid organizations. During my research for that book, I concluded that it was unlikely the pope could have been unaware. Catholic assistance to Nazis, fascists, and war criminals was institutional, systematic, and not secret at the time. Now privy to new evidence drawn from recently released Vatican documents, I am able to reaffirm that assessment and provide new support for this claim, showing that the pope directly participated in operations to shield accused fascists from postwar retribution.

Pope Pius XII knew of and authorized the channeling of alleged Fascists and Nazi collaborators to South America. With his approval, senior Vatican officials played a central role in helping thousands of these people emigrate overseas—arguably contradicting Allied agreements, which called for the extradition of war criminals and Nazi collaborators to the countries where they had committed their crimes. According to these agreements, if they had fled abroad, they should be extradited to stand trial. The Vatican opposed these policies with all its might, organizing a coalition of the willing. I am now able to tell the story of this discreet papal operation for the first time, supported by the newly unearthed documents from the formerly secret Vatican archives. The documentation I have gathered is voluminous and rich; many of the details it contains will necessarily be subject to further research. Here, I prioritize a clear understanding of the main takeaways and turning points in the papal project to establish an overseas escape route for Nazis and quislings, which ultimately profited also wanted war criminals.

THE PAPAL AID COMMISSION

Some fundamental Vatican disagreements surrounding the Allied treatment of defeated nations, which included questions of refugee aid and postwar justice, are effectively summarized in the institutional operation of a key Catholic organization, the Papal Aid Commission (*Pontificia Commissione Assistenza*; reflecting the original Italian, I abbreviate it PCA hereafter). Under the supervision of the Vatican Secretariat of State, the PCA was involved in facilitating the escape of Fascists and Nazi collaborators to overseas destinations that did not subject them to extradition. These operations were closely tied to the Vatican's broader conception of neutral humanitarianism and to its political priorities in the postwar period.

In 1944, Pope Pius XII called for the creation of an ad hoc organization, named the Papal Aid Commission for Refugees,[1] and he assigned its supervision to the Vatican Secretariat of State, an office that was then run by the Undersecretaries of State Giovanni Montini and Domenico Tardini. They reported directly to the pope. The Pope gave them the task of addressing the plight of the many Catholic and other refugees in the postwar years, especially the millions stranded in Italy, Austria, and Germany. These refugees represented a diverse group: Holocaust survivors, anti-communists, forced laborers, ethnic Germans, and former POWs, among others.

The PCA was designed to help alleviate their suffering through religious, legal, and financial support for war victims. The Vatican also particularly focused on Catholic refugees from Central and Eastern Europe, whose affiliation with Axis powers often meant that they were denied

Allied support or even threatened with forced repatriation or extradition to their now-communist home countries. In turn, emigration assistance quickly became a crucial element of the PCA's mission, particularly because Italy offered the easiest route out of Europe. From Austria and southern Germany, Italian international ports (e.g., Genoa) were close, and the Austrian–Italian mountain border was relatively easy to cross. Unlike Germany and Austria, Italy hosted few Allied check points or controls after 1946, and Italian authorities seemed interested mainly in shipping off the undesired foreigners as soon as possible. As a result, Italy saw a constant influx of refugees and other uprooted people, and in turn became a hot spot for Vatican relief.[2]

For Pope Pius XII, the creation of the PCA exemplified his ideal of *caritas* and charitable work, and he expressed great interest in its efforts. On January 22, 1945, during a private audience with the president of the PCA, Monsignor Ferdinando Baldelli, Pius XII made decisions about its final design details, including the name.[3] Writing about the creation of the PCA, the pope's longtime confidante Sister Pascalina Lehnert stated, "How enthusiastic Pius XII was when Monsignor Baldelli asked him to be allowed to call the 'Pontificia Commissione di Assistenza' into existence. How interested the Holy Father was in this! It was his ideal because the modest beginning corresponded with his inclination to do good in secret."[4] Archival records in the Vatican show that the PCA's creation and continued efforts also were supervised and coordinated by Montini, who in turn informed the pope of its activities. The PCA was to operate "*sotto gli auspici della S. Sede*" ["under the auspices of the Holy See"], as Baldelli wrote to Montini.[5] In its mission statement, the PCA cites the ideals of neutral humanitarianism and *caritas*, in the tradition of the Good Samaritan who helps anyone who asks for help. Another aspect of the PCA mission was to spread the gospel of Jesus Christ, without actively proselytizing, such that its mission statement reads:

> That is, the more we maintain absolute apoliticality in the exercise of the ministry of Charity, putting oneself above any consideration of a political nature, we are confident that the spirit of Faith and Truth will slowly but deeply affect the souls of those we are assisting. "Not doing politics is good politics; by not proselytizing, we are nevertheless carrying out a work of religious penetration."[6]

In theory then, the humanitarian relief offered by the PCA could be tied to preaching and soul saving, but restraint was advised.

Theory does not always translate into practice, though, and bias cannot be simply decreed away. The recorded minutes from an early meeting of the PCA, chaired by Montini, provide evidence of the anti-communist character of the organization from its very inception: "Monsignor Baldelli insists on the need for this body to be international to oppose other internationals: 'it is necessary for the People today to hear another international being sung, the international of charity.'"[7] This was a clear reference to the "Internationale," the anthem of all communist and socialist movements. It calls for the overthrow of the capitalist economic order, the international solidarity of workers, and the creation of a just, classless, and democratic society.

The PCA's first headquarters were the Villa Bonaparte at Via Piave 23 in Rome, the former German embassy to the Holy See. As we saw earlier, when the German Ambassador Ernst von Weizsäcker and his closest staff vacated those premises in July 1944, they went straight to the Vatican for refuge. The Vatican maintained the German embassy and even kept some of the German household staff.[8] This was now turned into and used as the main headquarters of the Vatican aid organization.

Although officially neutral and humanitarian, the PCA primarily focused its efforts on aiding Catholics, including baptized Jews. While it did not formally exclude Jews, Vatican records indicate a bias: Helping Jews and communists was not a priority. Anti-Jewish attitudes were common within the Church, often reflected in language and views. A striking document in the Vatican archives is a note from Monsignor Angelo Dell'Acqua, a close advisor of the pope and later cardinal. On April 11, 1946—just a year after the liberation of Auschwitz, we might note—he commented on a hunger strike by Jewish refugees stranded in the Italian port of La Spezia, displaying an utter lack of understanding for or empathy with the victims: "It is not the habit of Jews to suffer long and patiently: on the contrary, they like to live, and to live well."[9]

It is one thing for a top Vatican official to express such an absolute lack of compassion for Jewish victims and their postwar plight. But in addition, as Jewish refugees were flooding into Italy in search of safe passage, the Vatican officials actively opposed the emigration of Holocaust survivors to Palestine for a number of reasons. The question of the future status of Jerusalem was one of them. As Dell'Acqua stated, "It is not appropriate for the Holy See to support the emigration of Jews to Palestine."[10] Regardless of its claimed mission, the PCA's willingness to help Jewish Holocaust survivors was apparently limited. But chaos reigned, and there was no shortage of work to support desperate Catholic and other war victims.

Millions of people were uprooted or expelled from their former homelands in Croatia, Romania, Hungary, and elsewhere in the aftermath of World War II. Many of these—often formerly stateless—migrants sought to start anew in other countries. However, many were ineligible for refugee aid from the Allies. Some were former Axis nationals; others had collaborated with the Nazis in their homelands. Instead, they turned to nongovernmental and religious organizations—primarily Catholic relief institutions in Italy. To assist with emigration, the PCA helped refugees obtain travel documents from the International Committee of the Red Cross (ICRC). The Red Cross, maintaining a stance of neutral humanitarianism similar to the Vatican's, provided aid to all war victims, regardless of whether they had been citizens of Allied or Axis nations.

The Red Cross travel papers they procured functioned as "substitute passports," recognized by many countries, including Argentina, Syria, and Egypt. The issuing process was relatively simple: The PCA would issue official reference letters to delegations of the ICRC in Rome or Genoa, de facto vouching for the applicant. Once the papal officials had established these credentials of the petitioner, Red Cross delegates in Italy would issue travel documents. Neither the Red Cross nor the PCA conducted any real background checks; they possessed neither the resources nor clear guidelines for such a vetting process. Furthermore, even the basic requirements, such as statelessness, were repeatedly ignored by ICRC officials. In this chaotic issuing process, abuses of the travel paper service were widespread, and deserving refugees and war victims were joined by fascists and Nazi criminals in their emigration to the Americas, the Near East, or elsewhere. Unsurprisingly, therefore, the PCA soon became known as a reliable escape vehicle for Axis war criminals and Nazi collaborators from all over Europe.[11] The Red Cross, often in close cooperation with the PCA, issued approximately 120,000 travel documents during those postwar years. As we will see, the number of war criminals, fascists, and Nazi collaborators who used the system to flee Europe likely reached the thousands.[12]

AN EMBARRASSING FIASCO

Vatican involvement in overseas migration began around the end of 1946, when the Argentine government sent a mission to Italy to facilitate immigration. In December 1946, the papal nuncio in Buenos Aires recommended a Catholic monk named Father Clemente Silva to Monsignor Giovanni Montini. He was sent as an Argentine emissary to coordinate immigration from Europe. The new Argentine government, under the leadership of the military officer and Mussolini admirer President Juan Perón, was eager to modernize, and it believed that recruiting European labor and talent, including German experts, would serve that goal. Ferdinando Baldelli was, from the beginning, keen to participate in resettlement projects.[13] A memorandum of the PCA, obviously prepared for the Argentine diplomats, introduces its emigration office for foreign refugees, located at Via Piave 39 in Rome, as follows: "It deals exclusively with political refugees, who are estimated to currently be about 200,000 in Italy, belonging to 25 different nationalities. These are individuals who are in disagreement with the governments of their nations."[14] This description and the language it uses are curious; it refers to political refugees, though at the time, it was widely known that thousands of fascists and Nazis, originally from countries that had more recently turned to communism, were hiding out in Italy. The Argentinians seemed unbothered. Soon thereafter, a delegation from the PCA visited Argentina to discuss emigration possibilities, as well as what aid the Vatican could offer the Argentinian government.[15]

Baldelli wrote to the papal nuncio Giuseppe Fietta in Buenos Aires, detailing the great success of the PCA mission and the friendly welcome received in Argentina. His confidence in the outcome of the meeting matched his sense of how the news would be received at the Vatican, as he indicated when writing,

> The Holy Father, in the extended audience granted on the 11th of this current month to the P.C.A. Mission, wanted to be informed of everything. He was very pleased with the members of the Mission, showed great appreciation for the work of those who assisted in fulfilling its delicate duties, and imparted his august encouragements along with the Apostolic Blessing.[16]

Thus, if Baldelli is to be believed, Pius XII gave his blessing to the project from its very inception. But we do not need to rely on Baldelli's perceptions; the Vatican apostolic archive offers other evidence of the pope's early endorsement.

It was not long before hundreds of refugees left Genoa, under the auspices of the PCA, headed for Argentina, Brazil, and Paraguay.[17] The PCA aid and migration operations were financed to a large extent by the Catholic Church in the U.S. through the National Catholic Welfare Conference (NCWC). The steamship that carried this first wave of refugees from Italy to South America was called the *Andrea Gritti*.[18] The Vatican archive reveals that it was one of the first transports of foreign "refugees" managed under the supervision of the PCA. The archives also reveal that it went terribly wrong. It was improvised and full of flaws. For example, in January 1947 Baldelli asked for Montini's last-minute help in procuring assistance from the papal nuncio in Argentina, who agreed only after the ship was already well on its way.[19] But the urgent telegrams from Baldelli and Monsignor Andrew Landi (the NCWC representative) to their South American contacts were not sufficient to save the project.[20]

The many issues that arose are summarized in a long report by the NCWC representative in Rio de Janeiro to his superior in Washington, D.C., which in turn was shared with the Vatican Secretariat of State. The critique was devastating. Everything had been badly organized and overly improvised; lists were inaccurate; people did not show up; documentation was faulty; authorities were not fully informed; and any information that did arrive came too late. Monsignor Landi from the NCWC in Rome was criticized for not informing Church authorities ahead of time. The Brazilian government felt disrespected and misinformed, and as a consequence, it stopped issuing visas. Brazil also wanted only certain groups of immigrants—mostly, experts in specific fields—to colonize its countryside, not masses of displaced persons who would be stranded in Brazilian cities. Furthermore, Brazil rejected any Jews among the refugees on the *Andrea Gritti*, allegedly because they were not settling in the countryside. The Brazilian police also discovered eight undesirable emigrants with international records that tagged them as "anarchists." The travel documents were called into question as well, such that "An investigation is underway to determine who issued the visas and who procured all those International Red Cross booklets that many used as passports." The NCWC official sought to make the problems perfectly clear to his Washington-based superiors: "I feel very much concerned, also, because the fact that the whole program is seriously jeopardized. Other countries may take the same position as Brazil and chances for new homes for thousands of displaced persons will become more and more remote."[21] Indeed, the refugees were almost sent back to Europe.

That the transport co-sponsored by the Vatican was a mess was also the perception of Sir Herbert Emerson, director of the Intergovernmental Committee on Refugees (IGCR). The IGCR was created, with an initiative by the United States in 1938, to deal with the many Jewish refugees fleeing Nazi-dominated Europe in the pre-war period. The postwar refugee crisis was no less dramatic, but the IGCR was phased out in 1947, before it was resolved. Emerson referred to the *Andrea Gritti* incident as a "fiasco" and said that responsibility should be shared among the IGCR, the PCA, and the NCWC in Rome. Beyond assigning blame, he asserted that addressing the situation of Yugoslavian refugees in Italy was critical. Emerson categorized them into three groups: war criminals ("blacks") who would be repatriated; suspected Nazi collaborators and quislings ("greys"), whom he regarded as the real problem; and the "whites," ordinary refugees who deserved help. The memorandum also proposed some creative solutions. He instructed the "Screening Commission" to be "most lenient" in interpreting the categories and to "place as many 'greys' amongst the 'whites' as possible," because extraditing these "greys" to communist Yugoslavia would result in their certain death. Emerson further suggested that the Holy See should actively relocate these refugees and proposed that Spain's fascist government might welcome them. The report ended with Emerson noting his plans to come to Rome to discuss the matter further with the pope and Monsignors Tardini and Montini to find a solution.[22]

Emerson thus appeared eager to resolve the postwar problem of refugees and displaced persons, including Nazi collaborators and fascists. Distinctions between different categories, such as war criminal versus collaborator, were being softened, especially because these "political refugees" could all be categorized as tough anti-communists. Soon many "Blacks" were categorized as "Greys, " and "Greys" became "white" refugees. In other words, many Nazi perpetrators and Quislings were soon officially classified as "war victims."

These determinations reveal how the emerging Cold War was overshadowing the refugee crisis, as well as efforts for postwar justice. But let's take a closer look at how that worked.

Documents from the Vatican archives outline the uproar that the *Andrea Gritti* incident caused among papal policy makers. But perhaps even more important, they indicate the lessons the Vatican took from it. To avoid further fiascos, the Vatican professionalized its discreet emigration operations, as indicated in a note on Vatican Secretariat of State letterhead from mid-March 1947. It indicates that its General Affairs section had discussed the issue of Yugoslavian refugees, who were a concern of the PCA. The PCA wanted to continue shipping them overseas, but noting the many grievances with the first trip (obviously a reference to the *Andrea Gritti*), caution was necessary to avoid sabotaging future emigration efforts. The open question was how to improve them. A handwritten note, in pencil, on the memo add: "The Holy Father has already given His venerable opinion on the matter."[23]

In response to Baldelli's detailed report to Montini about the problems with the *Andrea Gritti* transport,[24] Landi was asked to report personally to the Vatican and explain how they could avoid another debacle. He reassured the Vatican leaders of their plausible deniability:

> Monsignor Landi summarized the phases of the first Gritti expedition: he then stated that this time precautions were taken in the selection of the emigrants and that in any case, no responsibility would be attributed to the Holy See, because it would have been a matter of only filling out the form of the Collegio San Girolamo and having it endorsed by the P.C.A.[25]

Landi also seemed to imply that, going forward, there would be no Jews or "anarchists" on the ships, something the Brazilian government had complained about. In response, the Vatican requested that Landi provide a written project description, detailing how to relaunch the migration scheme. The work of supervising these transports remained the responsibility of the PCA.[26]

The Vatican sent Monsignor Walter Carroll to Washington to negotiate directly with relevant refugee organizations, who used the *Andrea Gritti* incident as a justification of the need for collaboration. The Holy See made it clear that it wanted to be part of this "humanitarian mission." Around the same time, the Vatican also created its own Migration Bureau in Geneva, which was a geographic hub for humanitarian organizations at the time.[27] In Washington, Carroll met with NCWC leaders, officials from refugee organizations, and U.S. government representatives.[28] Reporting back to his Vatican superiors, Carroll mentioned excellent talks he had with Patrick O'Boyle and Edward Swanstrom of the NCWC, which led to the NCWC offering its full support to the Vatican Migration Bureau, reflecting its desire to avoid another *Gritti* incident. For now, though, it would help with the next transport of refugees, planned for departure soon on the steamship *Filippo*.[29] In April 1947, O'Boyle wrote Montini to assure him of the NCWC's full support for the Vatican project.[30] Thus, American money would help finance the operations.

Moving forward in the coordination efforts, the Vatican raised particular attention to the fates of Eastern European Nazi collaborators, whom the Allies had labeled "greys."[31] Despite not being classified explicitly as war criminals, they remained excluded from aid by Allied refugee organizations. Furthermore, the Italian peace treaty, which was set to go into effect in September 1947, would soon demand their forced repatriation to their now-communist home countries. Time was therefore of the essence. This urgency was emphasized in a memorandum recounting a private audience that Pius XII held with an Allied officer in March 1947. During the meeting, the official expressed concern that Russians, Ukrainians, and Poles might be forced back to their homelands following the peace treaty. An urgent solution was needed, especially for the many Yugoslavs. Yet, because of its mandate, the International Refugee Organization (successor to the IGCR) could not assist them, because—according to the memo—"The reason being that while fighting for the independence of their own country they had joined forces with the Germans. This particularly applies to some 2,000 of the Croats in the Allied Commission Camps. His Holiness expressed great sympathy and inquired if anything more could be done to help." The Allied official then went on to state that "In view of His Holiness' interest in these Croats [. . .] , it might be practicable to devote some Vatican funds to transporting them to South America or elsewhere, where visas can be obtained."[32] The Pope's interest in these Croatian Nazi collaborators translated into concrete actions and substantial efforts to assist them.

HIS HOLINESS'S RESCUE OPERATION

A newspaper article published around the same time caught the Vatican's attention. It announced that the British were urging the U.S. government to grant 30,000 Chetniks (Serbian nationalists), currently residing in Italy, displaced persons status. In a letter to Montini reporting on this article, an American priest suggested a similar tactic for the Croatian Ustaša (fascists) and suggested sharing the idea with Monsignor Carroll.[33] Montini then instructed the papal delegate in Washington to ask Carroll to raise the Ustaša issue with U.S. authorities and to emphasize that, if the Ustaša were not accepted as displaced persons, there would be serious consequences not only for them but also for the host countries.[34] Notably, Montini used the term "Ustaša" in the correspondence, referring directly to the Ustaša rather than employing broader or more abstract terms such as "Croats." Internal Vatican memos recognized the sensitive nature of the mission to benefit the Ustaša, given that the Yugoslavian and Western governments considered them "dangerous," "hardcore fascists."[35] In April 1947, the Washington delegate, Cicognani, reported to Montini on Carroll's discussions with U.S. officials regarding British and American promises to hand over Ustaša leaders labeled as war criminals to Communist Yugoslavia. In practice, however, the individuals in question had become difficult to locate. "It seems that the Anglo-Americans are making little effort to find them," Cicognani wrote sarcastically to Montini. And it was Cicognani who put the term "war criminals" in quotation marks in his letter to Montini. According to Carroll, there were 800 Yugoslavs in "grave danger," and the U.S. Department of State wanted the Holy See to take on the issue, find a host country, and discuss it with the Argentine government.[36]

The actual detailed memorandum of Carroll's meeting with the State Department on April 2, 1947, are worth a closer look. He met with Major General John Hilldring, Assistant Secretary of State, and George Warren, Director of Immigration for the U.S. State Department. They informed him that the British were confidentially sending Chetniks to Germany and Ukrainians to England. With regard to the 800 Yugoslav "Greys" who needed to be moved before Allied troops left Italy, the minutes of the meeting indicate that

> General Hilldring and Mr. Warren stated that, in view of the urgency of this matter, there is probably no way in which the Holy See and its Migration Bureau could, at this time, render greater service to the general resettlement program than through an immediate and forceful interest in this project. They suggest that the Holy See might urge Argentina and the Argentine Immigration representatives now in Italy . . . to grant to these 800 DPs the first Argentine quota assignments. . . .[37]

Hilldring and Warren also assured Carroll that any action taken by the Holy See for the resettlement of this group would be appreciated by the U.S. and British governments, but any further details could be hammered out among the International Refugee Organization (IRO), the PCA, and representatives of national Catholic agencies in Rome. Noting strong Congressional opposition to accepting 400,000 displaced persons into the United States, Hilldring claimed the rejection was based on the "misconception that these people are all Communists, Jews and ne'er-do-wells."[38] This summary of the meeting minutes is a remarkable document; its shows that a U.S. assistant secretary of state worked with the Vatican to assist suspected Nazi collaborators. The U.S. State Department even appeared to have been taking the lead in this particular instance. The Vatican received a "go-ahead" for its special mission and was promised support. However, rescuing Nazi collaborators from likely punishment by resettling them overseas was not official Allied policy and therefore needed to be done quietly. A note in the Vatican archives, next to the Carroll memorandum and apparently resulting from an audience with the pope, offers a reminder: "We must proceed with great caution. . . . One must say clearly that the Holy See is not in a position to provide information or assurances about these individuals."[39]

In the next few months, the Vatican continued to negotiate with refugee organizations, the Argentinians, Allied authorities, and the NCWC to move thousands of émigrés. The documentation is nearly as vast as the transport operations. I summarize the negotiations briefly here. Many of these discussions centered on the IRO, established in 1947 by the Western Allies to resettle the one million displaced persons remaining in Europe. For the Vatican, the IRO was a natural partner. However, its founding mandate expressly excluded former Axis nationals, war criminals, and Nazi collaborators. The

Vatican therefore had to persuade IRO leadership to amend its policy and reconsider the blanket refusal of aid to former Axis collaborators. All of this was intertwined with the broader struggle against communism in Italy itself and also in neighboring Yugoslavia, whose government the Vatican vehemently opposed due to their harsh persecution of the Catholic clergy.

In September 1947, an IRO official reported to the U.S. ambassador in Rome, James C. Dunn, in a "strictly confidential" memo about a recent meeting, that "I had a very interesting talk with the Pope, and later with Msgrs. Tardini and Montini, as well as Msgr. Carroll of the Vatican Secretariat of State." The official explained that Tardini had indicated to him, also in confidence, that the Vatican opposed the extradition of Nazi collaborators to Yugoslavia and that it was worried that the Italian government appeared to be acquiescing to the demands of the neighboring communist country. Alarmed by the imminent withdrawal of Allied troops from Italy, the Vatican feared that Italy would become "another Greece," the site of a bloody civil war between pro-Western and communist forces.[40] The Vatican's Allied counterparts were becoming increasingly receptive to these concerns, reflecting their own worry about communist takeovers. Among many Allied organizations and leaders, this looming communist threat shifted the fault lines of the international ideological conflict. From this shifted perspective, Nazi collaborators were "political refugees," as well as, even more importantly, "anti-communists." The Vatican insisted that the anti-communist fellow-travelers deserved help; after all, they were Catholics. The urgency of the situation was not lost on IRO leadership, and its director in Geneva assured the Vatican of its support in finding a solution for Yugoslavian quislings.[41] The IRO officials took charge of defining what was practically possible when transporting the "refugees," given the urgency of the situation in Italy.

When Carroll and Landi met with IRO officials in Italy to discuss the "greys," they learned that the British were planning to move 900 refugees to Germany to avoid their forced repatriation to Yugoslavia. The authorities were willing to delay this move, however, if there was reasonable hope that some entity could facilitate their transport to South America within two or three months. During this period, 200 people and their families would be reconsidered for reclassification as "whites"; IRO officers responsible for screening refugees agreed to this status review. There were 25,000 pounds sterling available for the transportation of "greys," but the recommendation was that they be transported along with a similar number of "whites" to ensure that they remained unobtrusive. Leftover funds from the IGCR also were mentioned as still accessible.

In the next step, the Vatican began negotiations with the Argentine government to secure a ship. Reportedly, the Argentine government offered a 50% reduction in shipping costs; rations would be provided by the Allied authorities until the transport was concluded. The Catholic Croat Committee in Rome was asked to raise funds from its international network of Croats.[42] The next day, Baldelli followed up with a letter to Montini, updating him about the talks. This letter offered the reassurance that there would be no more Allied screenings for war criminals, except for the IRO screening for eligibility. However, anyone who lived under assumed names in the camps would need to undergo additional screening. The situation remained delicate, considering the persistent uncertainty about the possibility for extradition.[43] Meanwhile, the Argentine government agreed to admit a limited number of Croats and Slovenes if Italy agreed to pay half of the cost of their transportation.

The IRO also imposed a limitation: Its money could be used only for those who, after screening, were deemed eligible for IRO assistance.[44] The wives and children of Nazi collaborators could travel on IRO funding, but the men themselves could not. Therefore, for the Vatican, the best solution was to reclassify "greys" as "whites," frame them as victims of war rather than perpetrators or collaborators, and thus ensure that everyone was being transported and fed on the IRO's dime.

In Vatican memos, the situation of refugees in Italy was portrayed as dire, due to threats from Soviet Russia, Poland, and Yugoslavia. The Soviet government had presented Italy with lists of war criminals, referring to about 500 people, and demanded their surrender, under Article 45 of the Peace Treaty with Italy. Neither the IRO nor the Anglo-American authorities recognized these lists; they insisted their "screening" had cleared these people of war crimes. Yugoslavia and Poland submitted their own lists of refugees that they defined as war criminals. The Vatican memo mentioned that it knew the Italian government did not want to extradite these refugees, but it faced a difficult political risk, and little chance of success, if it tried to resist Russian, Polish, and Yugoslavian pressure. According to the Vatican, most of the names on the lists qualified as "whites," eligible for IRO care and transportation overseas. Some of them already had been granted visas for Argentina, Peru, and other countries, and in addition, "the Argentine Emigration Delegation . . . at Rome has had full authority to visa the 'greys' and their dependents and has done so with the greatest secrecy and prudence." This remarkable opportunity became available to 500 suspected Nazi collaborators and fascists ("greys"), which greatly increased the chances of saving them from punishment, while also offering a solution in which the Italian government would be incidentally "relieved of much embarrassment."[45]

THE QUISLINGS

In these pursuits, the Vatican relied ever more on its Croatian expert: Father Krunoslav Draganović. Draganović fanatically supported the Croatian Ustaša fascists and their central mission: a Catholic, ethnically pure, independent Croatian state. During its brief wartime existence—established under the patronage of Hitler and Mussolini—the Ustaša regime murdered hundreds of thousands of Jews, Serbs, Roma, and political opponents in a wave of brutality that even horrified their Nazi overlords. After the war, many Ustaša leaders tried to escape into Austria or Italy to evade Tito's communist partisans' often ruthless reprisals.[46] At war's end, Draganović was stationed in Rome working under the umbrella of the PCA, giving him an excellent position from which to help his Croatian compatriots and others on the run.

Facilitating and intensifying secretive operations to channel hardcore fascists to safety was right in his wheelhouse. To the Vatican, he and his superior stressed the urgency of intervention, claiming that the British were continuing their "terrible work" of extraditing "*presuntivi criminali di guerra croati*" ("alleged Croatian war criminals").[47] While acknowledging that real war criminals must be punished, he claimed that what Yugoslavia was accusing the Croatian nationalists of were only "political crimes." The argument adopts a political and linguistic framing—portraying Croatians as fighting for national independence in line with the principle of self-determination—rather than offering a genuine assessment of criminal responsibility of the Ustaša regime.

Therefore, the Croat priest recommended that the extradition of all these so-called war criminals had to be halted, until rule of law could be established in Yugoslavia. Draganović also offered an alternative, namely, that they be sent to an Allied or international court that could deliver a just decision.[48] Over time, Draganović became ever more involved in the practical coordination of shipping hundreds of Croats, including many Ustaša, to South America, with the consistent help of the Vatican Secretariat of State, especially Montini, along with IRO officials, Argentinian government representatives in Italy, and the PCA.[49]

Vatican documents show a close collaboration between Montini and Draganović. At the request of Draganović, Montini sent a telegram with instructions for the papal nuncio in Buenos Aires,

> The Croatian Catholic Committee for Emigration requests that the government urgently communicate to the Argentine Consulate in Rome a list of 2,500 approved Croatians for immigration, authorizing the same consulate to issue visas. Please send a telegram confirming the outcome of this intervention and verify the abolition by the Argentine government of consular fees for refugees and immigrants, as announced in the local newspapers but unknown to the Argentine Consulate in Rome.[50]

In a way, Montini and Draganović seem to have reversed roles at times, with Montini working for Draganović instead of the other way around.

Argentine visas and transport ships were crucial for the operations, but the refugees and fugitives also needed to be fed while waiting weeks or months before they could leave. Here, too, the Vatican collaborated closely with Draganović and the Croatian Confraternity at San Girolamo, Draganović's homebase, as well as the PCA, whose president, Ferdinando Baldelli, wrote to Montini on October 4, 1947, to apprise him of the latest developments and conditions of the many Croat and Slovene "refugees" in Italy. The PCA had established national committees for Croats and Slovenians, as it had for every other national community of refugees. For the Croats, it operated under the aegis of the Pontifical Croatian Institute San Girolamo in Rome and its rector, Monsignor Giorgio (Juraj) Magjerec. The PCA's monthly allocations were 170,000 lire for the Croat national committee and 70,000 lire for the Slovenian committee. The beneficiaries also received clothing donations and other assistance from the NCWC. As Baldelli proudly concluded, "Finally, everyone, without distinction, was assisted with advice regarding emigration, recommendations for the issuance of passports [from the Red Cross], visas, residence permits, etc."[51] As the collected documentation makes clear, some donated money apparently benefitted not only the women and children of former fascists and Nazi collaborators, but the "greys" themselves.

When the Vatican sought to inform British ambassadors about the latest developments and concerns related to "displaced persons," it noted the favorable reply it had received from the Argentine government regarding its humanitarian appeal. Specifically, Argentina had granted the visas and transportation resources necessary for refugees' resettlement in Argentina; some IGCR funds apparently were available for those purposes too. A list of 3,000 names had been airmailed to the Argentine consuls in Italy, authorizing them to grant visas and facilitate those cases. A handwritten note, "visto dal SP [Santo Padre] 8 October 1947," indicates that the pope had seen and approved the memo.[52]

Still, questions remained about who would pay for the transport of thousands of refugees, and who would take charge of housing and feeding them while they waited their turn. These questions were the main topic of discussion in an audience with the pope on October 12, 1947, including whether Monsignor Landi from the NCWC or the Italian government might provide some funding. Notes from this audience reveal the Vatican's hesitancy about paying for their support, as well as the recognition of the complications that such funding would create:

> Keep in mind that if the Holy See provided the money, it would become known, and therefore the Holy See might face new and possibly greater difficulties from the Yugoslav government. It would be wise to consult Monsignor Undersecretary: if he deems it appropriate for the Holy See to transfer the sum, the matter must be brought up again in an audience.[53]

Another note, dated the same day, states that the undersecretary (likely Montini) had no new information for the pope, so the next step was to proceed with the "execution of the orders given by the Holy Father himself, which contain the wisest decision for the case."[54] Accordingly, the Italian government was contacted, as was Monsignor Landi, with the request that the NCWC organize $20,000 to pay for one month of food and housing for the Croat "greys" in Italian camps. It was a papal request, but Landi indicated that he had to check with his superiors in the Catholic Church in Washington before making any such commitment. All these actors hoped that the "greys" could be shipped to Argentina through Genoa, and soon.[55] Internal notes again indicate that the pope was continually kept informed about new developments, the money from the NCWC, and the exchanges with the Italian ambassador.[56]

At that point, things started developing more rapidly. The British and U.S. authorities wanted to move the Croat quislings from Italy to their respective occupation zones in Germany, where they would be safe and could avoid repatriation or extradition from Italy when the peace treaty came into effect. But the Croats seemingly did not trust the assurances of these Allies, such that hundreds of them fled the Italian camps to avoid being forced to move to the U.S. or British zones in Germany. Some "greys" fled to France; others allegedly hid in the mountains of Yugoslavia, intending to fight Tito. A large number, however, arrived at San Girolamo in Rome, prompting Rector Magjerec and Draganović to report to the Vatican that the Pontifical Croatian College was completely overwhelmed and lacked the resources to support so many people. Moreover, such a large concentration of fugitives risked attracting the attention of the Italian police and could lead to intervention. In seeking help from the pope, Magjerec and Draganović suggested that the PCA might be able to find a solution. They also raised a related concern: when the time came for embarkation, many of those on the run would not possess proper documents, which could create further difficulties. For this reason, they argued that a small office should be established to deal with these unfortunate people and help them obtain visas for travel to Argentina. Otherwise, there was a risk that when the ships on which they were to embark arrived, they would not have their papers in order. Such an office, they suggested, should be located somewhere that would not arouse suspicion—for example, within the premises of the PCA. A handwritten note in the margin of the memorandum shows that the pope was informed of the situation but decided this time not to allow the premises of the PCA to be used for this purpose.[57]

Faced with the pope's apparent caution, Draganović and Magjerec pressed for more rapid transport of Croats out of Italy and to Argentina. An audience held two days later laid out the numbers. The pope's staff revealed the vast amount of money given to Croats, totaling 2,063,100 lire, and Slovenian refugees, equal to 1,159,839 lire—much more than was being granted to any other foreigners in Italy.[58] Citing these numbers, the pope let Draganović know that he was greatly concerned about the fate of the Croats and reminded him of how much help already had been provided. The PCA would continue to support the Croats and send 170,000 lire per month for the work of the Croatian Confraternity at San Girolamo. The Croatian Confraternity also would receive repeated, large payments from the NCWC (US$10,000 per year, facilitated by Cardinal Stritch of Chicago); the Swiss Caritas would chip in, too, according to the pope's spokesperson. The memorandum concluded by stating that the problem was not limited to Italy: Croat refugees were living not only in Italy but also in Austria and Germany, numbering some 25,000 people.[59]

Giving proof to its reminders of the support it was offering, the Vatican Secretariat of State worked to establish agreements with the Argentine government. Internal memos to Montini indicate that, in October 1947, during the Marian Congress of Buenos Aires, an appeal authorized by the pope reached President Perón, on behalf of 749 refugees in camps in Italy. Their dependents were eligible and often already had been transported by the IRO, but the heads of these families (likely a reference to their past as Nazi collaborators) remained ineligible. Even so, due to the charity shown by the Holy Father, many people were now happily established in Argentina, having been transported via the Argentine Dodero shipping line. The papal nuncio in Argentina facilitated further negotiations on this "matter which was always maintained as an affair of great secrecy."[60] According to internal notes, the Vatican Secretariat of State struggled with the best terminology to use. A handwritten note asks, "SA M—Is it appropriate for the Holy See to use this term 'greys'? Can we not simply refer to them as refugees?"[61] In the final letter to the papal nuncio in Argentina, in which Montini urgently requested visas, the term "grey" refugees was penciled out.[62]

By late October 1947, the Vatican had finalized its transport program and its agreement with the Argentine government. It would transport 150 persons on each ship, starting in November. Financial transactions would be executed through the Banca Centrale in Buenos Aires. Ongoing practical problems would be addressed with the Argentine Emigration Commission in Rome and Genoa. But the devil lies in the details. Therefore, the highest levels on each side—Perón's government and the Vatican—received detailed briefings about the operations to which they had given their blessing. Vatican emissaries held regular meetings with President Perón to resolve the problem of the "greys," and the pope was updated about the "nitty gritty" of the negotiations, like the contingencies for "greys" on Argentine shipping lines.[63]

Such information seemingly was necessary to help the pope make the ultimate decisions about how the Vatican would contribute and where the money would go. During an audience with one of his staff, Pius XII determined that the PCA would pay to house and feed the "greys," whereas the Vatican Secretariat of State would be responsible only for negotiations with the government, without getting involved in the daily operations.[64] Thus, the transport of 150 "greys" was planned. It would leave Genoa for Argentina on November 7, 1947. After yet another appeal from Draganović for cash, the Vatican ordered Baldelli to provide additional funds for the room and board of Croats waiting embarkment in Genoa.[65] A memo for Monsignor Montini demonstrates that, at that point, Draganović had been put in charge by the Vatican and granted an additional 100,000 lire to help arrange the emigration. Draganović had become the unofficial emigration handler for the Holy See, smuggling suspected Croatian fascists out of Europe.[66]

THE PROTECTOR OF ALL

The Vatican also looked after Croat "greys" in Germany, whose movement the U.K. and U.S. military authorities had codenamed "Operation Boston." Upon leaving Germany, these suspected Nazi collaborators were supposed to find a new home in South America, and in October 1947, an American monsignor reported to Montini that 381 "greys," not counting their family members, would quietly leave from Hamburg, heading to Buenos Aires, soon. The Argentinian Delegation for Immigration in Europe had been given the green light from its government, so it would provide visas, transportation, and money for their ship tickets.[67] Operation Boston had the full support of Montini, who instructed the papal nuncio to approach the Argentine authorities with a request for help with the emigration of the greys from Hamburg. He suggested they could be transported by the Argentine Dodero Shipping

Company on its regular trips from Hamburg to Buenos Aires, "to avoid inconvenient situations, which would provoke their forced return to Italy."[68]

Despite these detailed plans, things almost went terribly wrong. A confidential report by a British official in charge of Operation Boston, shared with the Vatican Secretariat of State, describes a visit by an Argentine immigration delegation to the U.S. and British zones in Germany, during which they offered anyone who wanted it the opportunity to emigrate to Argentina. The delegation conducted health tests of the prospective migrants, took photos, and completed the necessary paperwork for them to be transported by the Dodero Shipping Company. But someone forgot to tell Dodero; its officials knew nothing about the mission. Only through the creativity and determination of the Argentine official Franz Ruffinengo and Father Draganović was the mission saved, according to the report. The paperwork got completed at the last minute, thanks to the "sausage machine" devised by Ruffinengo to process it in the camps. Draganović and Ruffinengo also smoothed things over with the shipping agencies, despite having been involved in a vehicle crash from which they suffered minor injuries. Through their efforts, Ruffinengo, an agent of the Argentinians, and Draganović, the special unofficial envoy of the Holy See, had saved the day, the report concluded.[69] A memo preserved in the Vatican archives suggested, perhaps as a reward, that Draganović's crucial role should be recognized, though it also advised caution:

> From the attached report and the self-sacrificing labor of Prof. Draganović in the transportation to Argentina of the refugees ineligible for IRO assistance, it is evident that he has worked hard and ably on behalf of these unfortunate people. The information in possession of the Holy See will perhaps make it impossible that he should have a position of official responsibility, but his experience is such that it might well be opportune to make a prudent use of this expertise.[70]

Draganović was clearly valued by the Church, but his problematic reputation also dogged him. In his own view, Draganović saw Operation Boston as a success. His concluding report to his superiors details how well the system worked, due to the coordination of this coalition of the willing:

> The great gratitude of the 'grey' refugees benefited and saved in an extraordinary way goes first and foremost to the Holy Father, Protector of all sufferers, and to the Most Excellent President of the Argentine Republic with their closest collaborators. Furthermore, it should be noted the worthy work of the Argentine Delegation in Italy with its humble leaders, then of the Rev. Monsignor Landi and Monsignor Baldelli who helped with financial means to continue the work, and finally the Auxilium in Genoa with the very present Archbishop of Genoa S.E. Siri who with paternal benevolence welcomed and protected these unfortunate refugees in his city. On the side of the I.R.O. I showed Col. Findlay the utmost concern and very human feelings.[71]

The references to the "Auxilium" and Archbishop Siri in Genoa require further consideration, related to the roles they played.[72] In 2017, I researched Church archives in Genoa, a key postwar port for refugee departures. Some archives were inaccessible or missing, but valuable information about the "Auxilium" operations emerged from a binder of Catholic Caritas archives, which completes the picture provided by the Vatican documents. These records show that, over the years, Baldelli transferred money directly from the PCA to Genoa's Archbishop Giuseppe Siri and his local PCA branch in Genoa, called the "Auxilium." For example, on February 26, 1948, Baldelli sent a check for 268,812 lire with the note, "Reimbursement of expenses incurred by this Section for the assistance to Croatian emigrants during their stay in Genoa."[73] Other documents at the Vatican reveal the additional forms that the close collaboration among San Girolamo, the Auxilium, the PCA, and the Vatican top leadership took. On December 15, 1947, Baldelli wrote to Montini, under the letterhead of the PCA's Office for Foreigners, noting that Monsignor Magjerec requested payments for Croat fugitives.[74] Two days later, Baldelli and the secretary of the PCA foreign section Francesco Eccharri sent a check to Monsignor Giuseppe Cicali of the PCA in Genoa, explaining:

> Attached herewith, I am pleased to enclose to you a cheque from the Bank of America and Italy no. 008130 for 164,576 lire in reimbursement of the expenses incurred for the assistance provided to the group of approximately 150 Croatian refugees, bound for Argentina, during their six-day stay in your city. Please kindly acknowledge receipt at your earliest convenience.[75]

On February 5, 1948, Archbishop Siri wrote to Montini to thank the pope for his generous support, in the amount of 200,000 lire, "which the Holy Father has kindly made available to the office of Genoa for emigration to Argentina." The Vatican State Secretariat also felt compelled to hand out blessed images of the Holy Father to emigrants as they left Genoa.[76]

In 1947, the Auxilium in Genoa reported, to the PCA Roma at Via Cairoli 117, about the lodging of "Croatians directed to Argentina" who had left for South America just weeks earlier:

> the moral and spiritual assistance, provided in addition to Professor Stefano [Krunoslav Stjepan] Draganović, their escort, was completed by our Chaplain in charge of Emigration, Reverend Don Timossi. These emigrants depart satisfied with the treatment received and have words of gratitude for the Papal Aid Commission, which has done so much for them.[77]

Later in November, another letter from Genoa to the PCA in Rome described a group of 150 Croatian refugees to Argentina, who had been lodged and cared for by local priests in the refectory at the Principe train station in Genoa: "as per your instructions, this [Catholic] refectory has provided for their assistance during the days of their stay in this city, . . . there remained 19 people, mostly women and children, awaiting instructions from the Rome Committee [PCA], through Prof. Draganović."[78] I note here that Draganović was being referred to as the logistical head of this operation.[79] In December 1947, the Auxilium confirmed the arrival of another large group of Croats, who stayed in Genoa for three days before leaving for Argentina on December 6 aboard the ship *Tucuman*. It attached a bill for the "expenses incurred by us, for food, luggage transport, and other." One of its passengers was Dinko Šakić, the commandant of the notorious Jasenovac concentration camp.[80]

Although these few remaining files in the archives in Genoa focus primarily on Croats, quislings of other nationalities received help too, as the Vatican kept widening its operations in support of European fugitives and refugees. In May 1949, Draganović provided a summary report to his superiors:

> In the autumn of 1947, I was asked to collaborate with the Migration Office of the Secretary of State of His Holiness to address the issues of European

> refugees who were declared "ineligible" by the IRO. The problem consisted of organizing groups of refugees and presenting them to the Argentine immigration commissions and their sponsorship for Argentina. This task required a lot of work and several trips to Italy, Austria, and Germany.[81]

He went on to highlight that refugees from Soviet-occupied Europe continued to struggle. He had recently spent five months in Argentina, where he established top-level contacts, whom he recommended to serve as members of a new Argentine Immigration Delegation, which already was on its way to Italy. Argentina accepts everyone, all immigrants, he assured the Vatican officials, except for communists. The conspiratorial priest also emphasized the importance of Red Cross travel papers, especially for German refugees from the East ("*Volksdeutsche*") and "greys" not recognized by the IRO. Draganović signed the report personally, but someone else, in handwriting, added where to find Draganović at the moment: Via Oslavia 28, telephone number 20.284. Draganović might have been very cautious about revealing his whereabouts, as communist agents were after him, but Vatican leadership knew how to contact him.[82]

CONCLUSION

As part of its humanitarian mission, the Holy See took great interest in the fate of the millions of refugees displaced by the war, providing them with housing, food, and spiritual and legal assistance, including help with emigration. Victims of war were helped, but so were many perpetrators. Pope Pius XII's Vatican was directly involved in channeling suspected Nazi collaborators from Eastern Europe to overseas. By the fall of 1946, the Vatican had negotiated with Allied refugee organizations and the Argentinians to facilitate the emigration of refugees and fugitives who were not recognized or being aided by the Allies. Of particular concern were East European fascists and Nazi quislings, categorized as "greys" by the Allies—that is, ex-enemies who were neither war victims ("whites") nor war criminals ("blacks"), but whose collaboration with Axis forces made them ineligible for Allied migration help.

Initially, sending Nazi collaborators to Latin America was done discreetly, and arguably in violation of international wartime agreements. But as the Cold War heated up, the Vatican found more leeway and more support from

Washington, London, and Rome. And the Argentine Perón government was eager to take in anti-communist, mostly Catholic immigrants. Monsignor Montini repeatedly thanked President Perón for his vital support. The Catholic Church and other Christian churches lobbied for their Eastern European coreligionists and anti-communists fleeing Stalin. But in so doing, they blurred what seemingly should be a clear distinction between Nazi victims and Nazi perpetrators. In 1948, a Jewish-American journalist challenged the Vatican's assistance to Nazi collaborators, an allegation that the Catholic magazine *America* rejected as "anti-Christianism quite comparable to . . . anti-semitism."[83] Tensions between groups lobbying for Jewish and Catholic refugees grew intense, as described by historian Peter Novick: "The DP [displaced persons] program had been started to aid survivors of the Holocaust; but by the early 1950s it was the displaced victims of Stalin, not of Hitler, who were fashionable, and the Holocaust figured hardly at all in discussions of DPs."[84] The Vatican and Washington thus found themselves mostly on the same page. With the blessing of Pope Pius XII, Vatican emigration offices negotiated with the Allies and host countries such as Argentina to discreetly resettle uprooted Christian Central and Eastern Europeans, among them Catholic Nazi collaborators and fascists, who were leaving Europe and their past behind for good.

10

THE VATICAN RATLINE

On June 14, 1950, PCA president Baldelli wrote to the office of Archbishop Siri in Genoa that the "assistance for Croatian refugees in Genoa is now concluded." He listed a few open bills from years back still requested by the Auxilium, which the PCA had become hesitant to pay.[1] However, in a sense, 1950 marks an endpoint of the operations; by then, most Nazi perpetrators had left Europe or were about to start new careers in Western Europe. In a strange coincidence of history, the former SS *Obersturmbannführer* Eichmann boarded a ship in Genoa bound for Argentina on June 14, 1950, the very same day Baldelli wrote that the delicate papal operation had been concluded. Like so many others, Eichmann too received help from the Papal Aid Commission. He was issued Red Cross travel papers, facilitated by a Hungarian priest working within the Vatican's relief network. Assisting suspected or confirmed Nazi collaborators to avoid extradition to communist homelands—where they might face indiscriminate revenge—can be understood, to a degree, as part of the Vatican's rationale. These individuals were often Catholics, staunch anti-communists, and now stranded members of defeated fascist forces in Western Europe. They had sided with the Axis, but not all of them were war criminals.

But aiding Eichmann—a principal architect of the Holocaust—is a different matter. He could have stood trial in Germany, judged by Allied courts, and afforded due process. So how did the Papal Aid Commission become involved in helping Eichmann and other unquestionable Nazi perpetrators? The Papal Aid Commission played a key role in the so-called Italian Ratline.

When confronted with evidence of its involvement, the Vatican consistently denied any role. While those denials may be understandable from an institutional standpoint, they are unconvincing. To understand how it worked and how the Papal Aid Commission was involved, let's unravel it step by step, beginning with a character we are already well familiar with: Krunoslav Draganović.

THE VATICAN AND THE GOLDEN PRIEST

Draganović certainly worked closely with the Vatican Secretariat of State in its efforts to avoid the extradition of Eastern European Nazi collaborators and prominent war criminals to their now-communist home countries. A few examples of this cooperation will suffice. In March 1946, the Brotherhood at the Pontifical Croatian Institute in Rome—that is, Draganović's homebase—successfully sought help from the Vatican Secretariat of State to prevent the extradition of various alleged war criminals and quislings.[2] In April 1946, the nuncio in Belgrade wrote to Monsignor Tardini that the Yugoslav government was complaining that the Pontifical Croatian Institute of San Girolamo had become a "center of anti-Yugoslav political intrigue. . . . It was stated that a meeting in honor of [Ante] Pavelić, the former chief of the Independent Croat State, had been held in the College."[3] In April 1947, the Vatican Secretariat of State made an appeal to the British, asking them not to extradite 15 alleged fascist criminals and Nazi collaborators wanted by Yugoslav authorities and currently being held in Italy, including high-ranking members of the fascist Ustaša regime, such as Vladimir Kren.[4] These moves marked the beginning of a wider confrontation between the Vatican and communist Yugoslavia.

Given this broader context, perhaps we should not be surprised that actors like Draganović enjoyed such steady support from the Vatican's top leadership, unswayed by protests over Draganović's operations. Apparently, the British Foreign Office had identified Draganović as early as January 1947 as a "notorious friend of the [Croatian fascist] Ustashi" and one of the key resources for Axis war criminals finding escape routes, with the help of the PCA. An internal note in the British Foreign Office indicates that it shared such information with the Vatican.[5] My access to the newly opened Vatican archives enabled me to find additional proof that Vatican leadership—Monsignors Montini and Tardini, the pope's closest aides—worked with Draganović, who would eventually be known under the nickname the "golden priest."

Some examples are particularly illustrative of how Vatican officials actively covered up Draganović's activities, as well as their involvement in those activities. In his May 1949 request to the Vatican for help in fighting extraditions, Draganović listed Croatians wanted by the communist Yugoslav authorities, including Jakov G., an accused war criminal who was interned at the Italian camp of Lipari and wanted to emigrate to Argentina,[6] along with Zvonimir Linić and Josip Ličen. Despite Yugoslavian protests, the Vatican helped Jakov G. depart the internment camp and channeled him to Argentina, where his wife and children were allegedly already living. According to Draganović, both Ličen and Linić had been condemned to death in their homeland "for political reasons," but escaped prison while awaiting execution, in the course of which escape they had killed a prison guard. Draganović asked the Vatican to approach Italian authorities on their behalf, with the argument that they should be treated as political refugees "from behind the iron curtain," not as common criminals.[7] Records indicate that the Vatican intervened with the Italian government, though too late: Both had been handed over to the Yugoslavian authorities already. The Italian Ministry of the Interior also explained to the Vatican that Ličen and Linić had been convicted by a Yugoslav court in 1947 for double homicide and two robberies, so when authorities formally asked the Italian government to extradite them, Italy agreed.[8]

Draganović's letter to the Vatican was attached to the pleas that the Holy See made to the Italian authorities.[9] Yet the Vatican seemingly hesitated to update Draganović that it would be doing just as he asked. A draft letter to Draganović from the Secretariat of State, promising help in these cases (which is present in the archives in an addressed envelope), was never sent. The records reveal why: The Vatican wanted nothing in writing that could be used as evidence of its complicity. Such secrecy proved wise, because working with the Croatian priest was politically dangerous. Vatican documents repeatedly depict the Pontifical Croatian Institute San Girolamo in Rome, a staunchly anti-communist entity, as nonetheless riddled with Yugoslav spies. Furthermore, the Vatican State Secretariat had received word from the Italian police that Draganović should go into hiding or else leave Italy, "because Slavic agents are determined to eliminate him."[10] But a note, likely from Monsignor Giulio Barbetta, also advised caution when dealing with Draganović: "Isn't it dangerous to give a letter from the Secretariat of State, which could give reason to rumors that the Holy See is engaged in relations between the exiles and the Italian Ministry of the Interior?"[11] In other words, actors within the Vatican knew full well that written documentation, describing how the Vatican and the Italian government were conspiring to shield suspected war criminals, could damage the Holy See. Thus internal notes concur regarding the need for secrecy:

> It seems to me that Mons. Barbetta's opinion should be followed. Draganović is wanted, it is said, by Tito's agents. He does not live in S. Girolamo degli Illirici but lives at an unspecified address. The priests of the college of S. Girolamo, however, are in contact with him. Through them I warned him of the danger that hangs over him. Perhaps it is more prudent to have one of the priests of the college come to the Secretariat and put the note (or notes) on the question on neutral paper without letterhead so that the Holy See does not appear.[12]

A handwritten note at the bottom of this document adds, "Ex Aud. S.S. in die IV-VIII-49," which indicates that this was discussed with the pope in an audience, and then continues: "If done, then only verbally, but nothing in writing."[13] The Vatican Secretariat of State proceeded accordingly. It informed the rector of the Pontifical Croatian Institute to change communication methods and provided a short summary of the Vatican's actions, on neutral paper rather than Vatican letterhead, for Draganović.

Even as the Vatican worked, intentionally and carefully, to cover up its collaboration with Draganović, it apparently continued to support both his anti-Yugoslavian and anti-communist activities and his tactics for enabling the escape of wanted war criminals. On September 21, 1949, the papal nuncio in Italy, Cardinal Francesco Borgongini Duca, wrote to Monsignor Tardini in the Secretariat of State, noting that an official from the Italian Ministry of the Interior had visited him with an urgent case—so urgent, indeed, that the Italian Minister of the Interior Mario Scelba was waiting for an answer from the Vatican.[14] The crisis had to do with Jure Bujanović, a Croatian priest, described in the correspondence as an Ustaša who was wanted for war crimes in his homeland.[15] Bujanović appears to have been a key member of the Ustaša community in Rome, who also had strong connections with the Croatian exile community in the United States.[16] The detailed memorandum explained that Bujanović, "The priest in question was, as reported by police, a direct collaborator of Drago Jilek; and Jilek, as we know, was not only a former Ustasha chief, but an originator of terrorist groups that acted, more or less effectively, in Tito's Yugoslavia."[17] Jilek had been recently kidnapped, presumably by Tito's agents, from his Roman hideout. Bujanović had been hiding illegally in Italy for four years, living in the monastery of the Franciscan Missionary Sisters of Mary in Grottaferrata near Rome. Italian authorities recommended that Bujanović flee to South America soon, because his Italian police protection was costly and his continued stay could cause political complications or worse.[18] The Vatican agreed, and an official put his thoughts on paper:

> It would certainly not be bad if Bujanović left Italy. However, I allow myself to point out that, in my humble opinion, it is not convenient for the Holy See to take any initiative: secrecy is absolutely not guaranteed, an interest could lend itself to interpretation harmful to the cause of the Church in Yugoslavia.[19]

On February 3, 1950, the Italian Ministry of the Interior sent the Vatican a long and "strictly confidential" ["*riservatissima*"] update. Despite Bujanović's illegal status in the country, he was still being protected by Italian security forces in his monastery hideout, but it would be good to send him overseas soon.[20] Draganović's superior, Rector Juraj Magjerec, suggested Bujanović leave for Australia, where many Croatians were living without spiritual assistance from their own Catholic priests. The Vatican State Secretariat agreed and pushed Bujanović to leave Europe.[21]

Bujanović was tightly linked to Draganović; the Vatican discussed helping both of them escape with new papers, for reasons outlined in a memorandum I found in the Vatican archives:

> The activity of the priest Don Krunoslav Draganović, his movements, having been named in sensational political trials, have given his person a prominence

> that does not seem useful to the welfare mission entrusted to him among the Yugoslav emigrants. One gets the impression that the talents of the aforementioned priest could be better used in another country and that a less conspicuous person would be in better conditions to carry out the aforementioned assistance activity.[22]

The terminology chosen for this memo—"welfare mission" especially—is notably euphemistic, given Draganović's actual behaviors. The "sensational political trials" likely refer to a case in Yugoslavia, during which Croatian saboteurs revealed that Draganović had played a role in sending them there.[23] Magjerec, the rector of the Pontifical Croatian Institute, received another reminder that Draganović should leave Italy, due to the danger he faced. Draganović held an old refugee passport, courtesy of the Italian government,[24] and now he was being offered a "certificate of statelessness," so he could "go wherever he wants." Recall that statelessness was a precondition for a travel document from the ICRC, to which Draganović had easy access, because the PCA worked so closely with the Red Cross in arranging such papers. A message from Italian police authorities, dated February 22, 1950, described Draganović as highly valued but also "too much known and exposed."[25] In a document on the letterhead of the Vatican Secretariat of State and signed by Giovanni Battista Montini, the future Pope Paul VI inquired about the state of affairs for Bujanović and Draganović, about "whom the Italian authorities had made certain suggestions."[26] A handwritten note at the bottom of this letter indicates that Monsignor Magjerec had been instructed to deal with them and was "now waiting for response."[27] In all these efforts, the Vatican, especially Montini, coordinated with and informed Italian authorities, such as in one report that explains the care Draganović took, such as changing his residence regularly, never moving around alone, and never going out in the evenings. He was aware of the threats from the Yugoslavian legation in Rome, who "without doubt had condemned him to death," but, according to the report, Draganović did not want to leave Italy, because of his dedication to working with Catholic Croatian refugees in Rome. Maintaining this version of the story, Vatican authorities assured the Italian police that the priest "does not engage in politics in any way."[28] He stayed in Rome.

Thus, the Vatican Secretariat of State, and Montini in particular, was apparently fully aware of Draganović's actions and aided him officially, and then also lent discreet assistance for his political activities. The aid that Draganović offered former Croatian Ustaša fascists, many of whom had been accused of atrocious crimes against Serbs and Jews, was problematic for the Italian government, but less so for the Vatican, it seems. In 1948, when Italy became fully sovereign again, the Allies left it up to the new government to deal with extradition requests. In the Cold War, Italy came down firmly on the American side, and in 1949, it became a founding member state of NATO. Perhaps as an unintended result of the international partnership, it stopped handing over alleged Nazi collaborators and fascists to Yugoslavia and other communist countries. The collaboration between the Vatican, Italian authorities, and the U.S. government in combating communism at times arguably amounted to an obstruction of justice—to the great benefit of some of the worst war criminals and Holocaust perpetrators. Draganović was a willing participant in the larger battle of the Cold War, in which Nuremberg trials and Ratline anti-communist tactics represented skirmishes. The Vatican's primary motivation in this context was opposition to communism, which in some cases led to complicated and not entirely antagonistic relationships with former Nazis.

NAZIS ON THE RUN

In March 1948, lobbying for more help for Nazi collaborators in Italy, Draganović proposed that the operation should not be limited to Croatians and Slovenes, because other groups, like Albanians, Russians, Ukrainians, Polish "greys," and "ethnic Germans" (*Volksdeutsche*) also had been labeled ineligible by the International Refugee Organization. Draganović began advocating for these larger groups as well. Most of them initially had been categorized by the Allies as ex-enemies or Nazi collaborators, such that they were not allowed to emigrate. The problem could be overcome, though, if the PCA would help these Catholics. Draganović added that Argentina could cover most of the expenses for the "greys," with the understanding that they would repay the costs within two to three years.[29] To smooth things over further, Draganović even traveled to Argentina for a stint. Montini was kept informed. The fact that he was there and even approached the papal nuncio shows his self-confidence at this point, which must have raised eyebrows among the Vatican leadership.[30] Before long, German and Austrian Nazis prominently featured among Draganović's clients. Let's look at some examples of Nazi war criminals escaping with Catholic help.

Franz Stangl was commander of the Treblinka extermination camp, where the Nazis murdered almost 1 million Jews and unknown numbers of Poles, Roma, and Soviet prisoners of war. In 1948, Stangl escaped from Allied detention with his accomplice Gustav Wagner. They fled to Italy, where they received assistance from Bishop Alois Hudal, who headed the Austrian committee of the PCA. Hudal moved them into a hideout in a Catholic institution and arranged Red Cross travel documents for their emigration, along with letters of recommendation from the PCA.[31]

We have encountered Hudal before. A Christian antisemite, anticommunist, and pan-German nationalist, he served as rector of the Austrian–German national college, the Santa Maria dell'Anima, in Rome, only a stone's throw from the iconic Piazza Navona.[32] In that role, he had strongly advocated for a Catholic compromise with the Nazi regime. Following the concordat with Hitler's Germany in 1933, Hudal was named titular bishop of Ela, during a ceremony presided over by Eugenio Pacelli (the later Pope Pius XII). A marble plaque in the Anima Church reminds visitors of that moment to this day. Driven by an impressive energy, Hudal was involved in many ventures, including the publication of his 1937 book, *The Basic Foundations of National Socialism,* which made the case for the coexistence of Nazis and the Church.[33] In contrast with many Church figures who allowed evidence to sway them, Hudal never wavered from his position. By joining the PCA, he gained a perfect position from which to help his Nazi allies after their defeat.

The list of Nazis whom the bishop helped is long. It includes the Gestapo officer Erich Priebke, co-responsible for the March 1944 murder of 335 Italians (many of them Jewish) in the Ardeatine Caves Massacre in Rome. As Italian authorities intensified their search for Priebke after the war, his lodging with a helpful priest grew too risky. So Hudal, in collaboration with two priests from the Italian South Tyrol region, helped Priebke procure travel documents from the Red Cross under the assumed name "Otto Pape."[34] Priebke could feel safe under the mantle of the church. A note in Hudal's paper reveals his hideout: "Can be reached through Father Dr. Fr[anz] Pobitzer, Bolzano, Franciscan monastery."[35] Before Priebke left for Argentina, the former Lutheran converted to the Catholic faith and was (re-)baptized *sub conditione* by one of his priestly escape assistants. The baptism of Erich Priebke took place under his real name, performed by the very same priest who helped procure him Red Cross travel papers with the alias Otto Pape.[36] In other words, there can be little doubt that they knew whom they were providing with a false identity. The correspondence between these priests and Hudal speaks volumes; it offers a textbook case of a conspiracy to obstruct justice in the context of the Ratline.

Returning to the case of Stangl and Wagner, the conspiracy is nearly as evident. Gustav Wagner, Stangl's second-in-command, was mostly truthful when applying for Red Cross papers in 1948, using his real name and birth date. By that time, perhaps he felt safe enough under the protection of the Church. But Hudal proposed making some alterations to Stangl's file, to avoid drawing undesired attention to the internationally wanted killer. Stangl allegedly protested when the bishop changed his first name, from Franz to "Paul," on the application form for the Red Cross papers. Hudal pacified the mass murderer under his protection, suggesting "Let's let sleeping dogs lie."[37]

Some applicants for assistance with their travel papers from the PCA and Red Cross were open in disclosing their Nazi background. When the Austrian Catholic Walther Ottowitz decided to emigrate to Argentina in 1948, he laid out his mid-level career in the Nazi Party in a short biography attached to the application.[38] Rather than disqualifying him from help, Hudal took this personal history in stride and then recommended Ottowitz to the Vatican emigration office, to obtain further support for his emigration to Argentina.[39] This recommendation appears inside a file that also contains documentation of the requests of Albanian refugees for assistance in emigrating to Argentina. On November 29, 1948, Monsignor Montini sent a letter to Giuseppe Fietta, the papal nuncio in Argentina, asking him to help some people of Albanian, Austrian, and Yugoslavian nationality who wanted to emigrate but needed help obtaining the necessary permits and visas from Argentina. A handwritten note on the letter indicates this request was not just business as usual: "The subject is certainly complex and delicate, and it is understandable how there might be some difficulties." But Montini regarded such efforts as justified, because all these émigrés had been vouched for by clergymen and the PCA. Among those worthy candidates, Montini referred by name to an

"Austrian Mr. Attowitz" [*sic*].[40] That very same folder contains a letter from Ottowitz, in which he describes himself as a "political refugee" from Austria. He acknowledged having been staying illegally in Italy, and hiding from Italian authorities, during which time he worked as a gardener for Catholic nuns from Yugoslavia. "My desire [is] to emigrate to Argentine," the man stated, and Hudal and Montini made sure that the Nazi's wishes came true.[41]

The Austrian office of the PCA, which Hudal ran, was one of 16 initial national aid committees formed to help foreign refugees and POWs. The Holy See provided significant sums to support the work of these national committees, which were treated as integral to the Vatican relief infrastructure.[42] Much of this funding came, directly or indirectly, through the Vatican and from American Catholics through the NCWC. For example, in December 1948, Hudal received a check directly from Monsignor Andrew Landi from the NCWC for 27,000 lira.[43] On April 4, 1949, Montini sent Hudal good news: The "Holy Father" was granting him 30,000 lira to benefit needy Austrians, as well as blessings for Hudal and his staff at the Anima Institute.[44]

Hudal's papers at the Anima, as well as the records in the Vatican archives, help map his vast network and repeated interactions with the Vatican Secretariat of State, especially Montini. Much of the content of these records relates to PCA refugees, which often meant interventions for fascists and Nazi officials, including war criminals. To defend Nazi war criminals on trial or in prison, Hudal joined in concerted efforts with the likes of Montini, Tardini, Frings, Faulhaber, and Andreas Rohracher. But he also intervened personally in certain cases, not just for Weizsäcker but also for Konstantin von Neurath, Herbert Kappler, and Walter Reder. In this regard, Hudal doesn't stand out; he matches the bigger picture.[45]

Hudal was working tirelessly to fulfill his perceived mission aiding Nazis. Thus, it made sense that he would be the recipient of a letter from Dominik Moroder, a former SS officer and wanted war criminal, writing from a mountain hideout. Moroder described openly that he had been hidden from authorities in a Franciscan monastery in Italy for two years after the war, protected by Father Prof. Franz Pobitzer, a Franciscan monk and high school teacher in Bolzano. Moroder explained that he was still in hiding, keeping himself busy with wood-cutting Virgin Mary figurines.[46] As Italian authorities continued actively searching for him, Moroder eventually managed to escape to Argentina,[47] possibly with the aid of his helpful monk. And helpful, Pobitzer was. It was Pobitzer, in cooperation with Hudal, who had already helped the war criminal Priebke escape justice with a new identity.

The Bolzano region (Bozen in German), located in close proximity to the Italian–Austrian border and its mountain crossings, provided a perfect location for Nazis and notorious Holocaust perpetrators to enter Italy.[48] In March 1950, Father Pobitzer recommended two new men to Hudal, "sent to me by trustworthy contacts." He added his best wishes for the Easter holidays and asked for the bishop's blessings. A note on the document, in Hudal's handwriting, provides the detail "Franz Noelke . . .—Prof. Draganović 29/III/50."[49] Having received the request from Pobitzer, Bishop Hudal lost no time warmly recommending, to various Italian and Argentinian authorities, the "refugee" Francisco (Franz) Noelke who "is leaving for Argentina in few days." Hudal stated that he knew Noelke very well and described him as a man who had lost all his papers while fleeing from the Russians.[50] In September 1950, Noelke successfully applied in Genoa for travel papers to Argentina, claiming to be a stateless ethnic German from the town of Termeno (Tramin), just south of Bolzano.[51] As it turns out, neither of these conflicting stories was true. "Francisco Noelke" was a completely invented identity. His real name was Erich Müller, a close collaborator of Nazi minister of propaganda Joseph Goebbels. He also was just one of a group of top Nazi criminals fleeing to Argentina under various assumed names.

Another name included in the group was Riccardo Klement. In his applications, he claimed to be an ethnic German born in Bolzano, in 1913, out of wedlock, to Anna Klement. Asserting his statelessness, Klement sought Red Cross documents for traveling overseas, in an application signed by a Franciscan priest, Father Edoardo Dömöter of the Hungarian office of the PCA.[52] Dömöter worked closely with Hudal to assist Germans who deserved help[53]—and those who did not. It turns out that "Ricardo Klement" was none other than Adolf Eichmann, one of the key organizers of the Holocaust. Nuremberg prosecutors had sought Eichmann after the war; he laid low in Germany, under a different assumed name, chopping wood and raising chickens. But inspired by the examples of many other Nazis, by May 1950 he decided to make his way to Italy. Eichmann proudly recalled the assistance he received from a helpful Catholic priest when crossing from Austria, over the mountains, into Italy:

> For years [the priest] had helped all kinds of refugees. Once it had been Jews, now it was—Eichmann! I was most grateful to receive my suitcase from this excellent, cycling priest about a kilometer and a half behind the Italian border, and allowed myself the now traditional swig of alcohol to celebrate my success. This time it was a red, South Tyrolean wine! The priest directed me to a taxi-driver, who first took me to his flat. Here I left my Tyrolean costume and put on less conspicuous street clothes.[54]

The obscenity and ruthlessness of this linguistic juxtaposition—once Jews, now Eichmann—which appeared in his own notes made during his 1961 trial in Israel, bears no further comment.

The continued support that he and other Nazis received deserves closer examination. Local helpers provided Eichmann with new papers under his fictional "Riccardo Klement" identity, locating his origins in the town of Termeno. They hosted him in monasteries. Once he reached Genoa—a half-day train journey from Bolzano—the former SS *Obersturmbannführer* was taken under the wing of Father Dömöter. Eichmann finally departed for Argentina from Genoa in June 1950.[55]

Joseph Mengele used the same system to acquire identity papers, allegedly also from Termeno, to escape Allied justice. The angel of death of Auschwitz, who "selected" prisoners for the gas chambers, was known for his brutal experiments, including those on twin children. With the help of Nazi networks, he managed to get Red Cross papers for his escape to South America in 1949.[56] Unlike several other Nazi fugitives, however, no documentary evidence to date identifies a Catholic priest as having formally vouched for his identity. Josef Mengele came from a well-off family and did not depend on the support of Church circles, such as temporary refuge in monasteries or subsisting on monastic charity. Many of his fellow Nazis on the run, however, relied on the assistance of Catholic clergy and papal charitable networks. So did a certain Teodoro Kremhart, who submitted an application for a Red Cross passport in Genoa on October 31, 1949. His identity was attested by Father Dömöter, and the document carries the round stamp of the Hungarian Section of the PCA, indicating formal ecclesiastical involvement in the process.[57]

One central question is whether the helpful priests knew who they were aiding. While we cannot establish this in every single case, there are certainly examples where we have ample evidence that the priests were aware they were involved in illegal activities. We have already discussed cases such as Stangl and Priebke. The case of "Teodoro Kremhart," mentioned above, will further illustrate this point:

Hudal's papers in the Anima College in Rome are like a vast puzzle, requiring skill, knowledge, and experience to piece together. One letter in the Hudal archives, addressed to a certain "Comrade Greil," details how the necessary documents for overseas emigration were obtained. It includes a request and precise instructions to produce papers in the name of "Teodoro Kremhart," born in 1906 in Termeno (Tramin), South Tyrol, along with his wife Anna, both listed as residents of Termeno. The letter emphasizes: "This agenda is of high importance and for an old comrade (Bubi von Alvensleben)."

The writer notes that the attached 500 lire should be forwarded to Father Franz Pobitzer to cover any additional expenses. The completed documents for "Kremhart" were to be sent to Father Eduard Dömöter at the Monastery of S. Antonio in Genoa. The letter concludes with thanks for the comradery and assistance and is signed by Hans Aichinger—at least as far as I could decipher the signature.[58]

Hans Aichinger, the apparent author, was an Austrian Nazi fugitive. The recipient, "Johannes Greil," was apparently another Austrian Nazi; his real name was likely Johann Feil, a wanted Nazi and SS *Oberführer*. While in Rome, Feil received assistance from Bishop Hudal, including Red Cross papers for emigration to Argentina.[59] A handwritten note, likely by Hudal himself, reads: "recommended to P. Doemoeter Genova 30/X/49."

This letter is remarkable. It offers further insight into how Hudal, Dömöter, and Pobitzer collaborated to obtain false identities for Nazi criminals. Notably, it reveals that "Kremhart" was a cover name for the prominent SS officer Ludolf von Alvensleben—nicknamed "Bubi"—a member of Himmler's inner circle. Alvensleben was responsible for mass executions in Nazi-occupied Poland in 1939/40 and later served as SS and Police Leader in southern Russia, where he oversaw further brutal repression and killings. In 1946 he escaped from an internment camp in Germany, fled via Italy, and ultimately avoided prosecution by fleeing to Argentina.[60] Alvensleben's case is further strong evidence that the priests who provided help knew exactly what they were doing—and for whom.

Many details of the application process also strongly point to a network at work—a system in place for mass murderers like Alvensleben, Eichmann, Mengele, and others. As proof of their identities, this group of fellow Nazis on the run submitted identification cards to the Red Cross that were allegedly issued by the municipality of Termeno. The dates of issue should have raised some questions: Mengele's was dated April 1948, Alvensleben's and Mueller's May 1948, and Eichmann's June 1948. The choice of location, the dates, and methods used point to the existence of a single, orchestrated effort by Hudal, Dömöter, Pobitzer and Draganović all operating under the roof of the PCA.

Nazi networks, too, played crucial roles, especially in South Tyrol, the overwhelmingly German-speaking Italian region that borders Austria. Much evidence details the many occasions in which local Tyrolean Nazis helped their German and Austrian comrades make their next moves once they had crossed the border into Italy, including procuring new identities and Italian papers.[61] But without Catholic support, those networks would not have gotten so far, as acknowledged by Eichmann and other Nazis on the run. The prominent Nazi fighter pilot Hans-Ulrich Rudel recalled the extent of the help he had received from Catholic priests in Italy with gratitude:

> There were some who had hiked through the Alps from monastery to monastery in monks' habits. One can take whatever position one likes about Catholicism, but the significant number of our people that were saved, often from certain death, by the Church during those years, above all by individuals of towering humanity inside the Church, should certainly never be forgotten![62]

Although the efforts by Hudal, Draganović, Pobitzer, and Dömöter are remarkable and documented, they were by no means the only Catholic "individuals of towering humanity" rescuing wanted war criminals. On the contrary, the PCA's help was systemic.

During research conducted in the Vatican archives in 2021, I uncovered a report by Monsignor Bardelli listing the PCA national committees and their members. Many of the names, like Hudal's and Dömöter's, were familiar; these clergy were known to have helped war criminals escape Allied justice. But other names surprised me. I had not realized they functioned as heads of other PCA national committees.[63] The PCA committee for Ukrainians was headed by Bishop Ivan Buchko, whom you might recall the pope had appointed as Apostolic Visitator to the Ukrainian (Ruthenian) Catholic refugees stranded in Germany. In numerous interventions, supported by the Vatican Secretariat of State, Buchko asked Western Allies not to hand Ukrainians who fought with the Germans over to forced repatriation by the Soviets.[64] Buchko pleaded with the pope to save the around 8,000 Ukrainian men of the *Waffen* SS Division *Galizien* being held in an Allied POW camp in Northern Italy. These "blossoms of the Ukrainian nation," as Buchko called them, never were handed over to Stalin but were instead allowed to emigrate to Great Britain and Canada.[65]

In May 1947, Italian security forces inquired about Buchko, his committee staff, and the assistance they were receiving from the Vatican. The security forces decided to keep Buchko and his staff under strict surveillance. Although the reason for this decision is not clear from the remaining files, we might reason that Buchko's origins in now-communist Eastern Europe had something to do with it. In a message to Montini, confirming that Buchko's committee had been part of the PCA's structure since May 1945, Archbishop Antonino Arata from the Oriental Church explained that most Ukrainian Nazi soldiers in the POW camp at Rimini had left for Great Britain or the United States, so the committee would likely be wrapped up soon. The authorities need not worry.[66] Arata's estimation proved incorrect, however, and 18 months later, in August 1948, Monsignor Buchko appealed directly to the pope and Montini to facilitate the overseas emigration of 120,000 Ukrainians stranded in Germany. He raised the alarm that Protestant "sects" were very active in emigration matters, "not to speak from the Jewish ones," whereas the Catholic institutions were lagging behind.[67]

The list of sponsors of passengers on the cruiser *S. Cruz*, sailing in March 1948 from Genoa to Argentina and Brazil, depicts just how far the circle of aid had widened. The organizers included the IRO, Monsignor Landi (identified as being "for Mons. Carroll" from the Vatican), the Argentine Consulate, the Croatian Confraternity's "Division of Emigration" at Via Tomacelli 132 (at the Pontifical Croatian Institute, also known as Draganović's headquarters), the Slovene Welfare Society, the Serbian Welfare Committee, and the Polish Emigration Office.[68] The various documentation surrounding these transports shows that, along with Croats and Hungarians, growing numbers of Ukrainians, Poles, Romanians, Russians, and Baltic peoples made ready use of the system devised by the Vatican and the Argentine authorities—with the discreet support of some Allied authorities, too.[69]

The *S. Cruz* papers include a name that draws particular attention. At the address Via della Pace 20 in Rome, which was Bishop Hudal's residence, the document lists a Dr. Ferenc Vajta.[70] Ferenc Vajta (also spelled Vatja or Vajda) was a Hungarian Nazi collaborator and intelligence peddler, working in the shadows of the early Cold War, not unlike Draganović.[71] When World War II ended, Vajta fled to the Vatican and found safe haven there, but he constantly feared potential extradition to Hungary. In 1947, he emigrated to the United States, which soon deported him to Italy, once his Nazi past was revealed. During this interlude in Italy, the devout Catholic became "head of the Hungarian Emigration Committee" and a guest under Hudal's roof—a case of being the right person at the right place and time. His efforts on behalf of Hungarian war criminals, including militants from the Arrow Cross (Hungarian Nazi party), ensured that they would escape punishment for their involvement in the Holocaust in Budapest. Ferenc Vajta made it to South America for a new start, too.

The list of PCA national committees and staff that I found in the Vatican archives also includes another name—one I promised that we would return to discuss. Draganović, just like Hudal, attained this position because of his proximity to other Catholic authorities and functionaries that coordinated the work of the PCA; neither of them could have successfully performed their efforts on behalf of fleeing war criminals on his own.

The twisted benefits of their collaborative approach are clear in the case of Oswald Menghin, a prominent Nazi wanted by Austrian authorities. In 1948, Menghin's escape was coordinated by Hudal and Draganović, as well as facilitated by other dignitaries, including Archbishop Andreas Rohracher of Salzburg and Augustin Bea, who held the position of pope's confessor at that time and later became a prominent cardinal. With their combined assistance, Menghin, a fervent Catholic, managed to emigrate to Argentina and continue his academic career there.[72] Draganović coordinated Red Cross papers for him under the name "Menghin Ambrosio" and housed him in a Church institution in Genoa.[73] While making these moves, Draganović presented himself as the Vatican's emigration expert, brought in for special clients. Furthermore, Draganović's documented cooperation with high-ranking Church officials shows that he was not acting alone.

THE *ANDREA GRITTI* INCIDENT

Despite its efforts to keep such collaborations quiet, the flight of war criminals did not escape the attention of the press, which accused the Vatican Secretariat of State of aiding, through the PCA and the Pontifical Croatian Institute, criminals escaping justice. In January 1947, the Yugoslav newspaper *Borba* alleged that the ocean liner *Andrea Gritti*, departing from Genoa and Naples in December 1946, carried dozens of Croatian and Serbian war criminals who had received visas and financial assistance from the PCA, as well as travel documents provided to them by the "Brotherhood of St. Jerome" at the Pontifical Croatian Institute, with tickets paid for by the Allied Intergovernmental Committee of Refugees (IGCR).[73] *Borba* published other accusations, too. It claimed the Vatican was conspiring with Draganović to hide former Ustaša officials and followers of Pavelić in Catholic monasteries in Rome. It identified Cardinal Eugenio Tisserant as a liaison between the exiles and the pope, transmitting petitions to save the life of Serbian Nazi collaborator Milan Nedic (though Nedic subsequently was handed over to the Allies).

The Associated Press publicized the *Borba* stories; Italian newspapers like *Il Quotidiano* also picked them up, though the pro-Catholic newspaper rejected accusations that the Holy See was protecting war criminals: "The Church protects all the persecuted who turn to her for help, without asking for anything, not even a feeling of gratitude."[75] The stories spread further by coverage in *L'Unità*, the preeminent communist Italian newspaper, which repeated the accusation that the PCA was helping Nazi war criminals flee overseas. Italy's daily newspapers also reported, during January and February 1947, on a group of "refugees" under the protection of the PCA and housed in a Catholic workers' dormitory who had been arrested in Genoa. As it soon turned out, the men were French *Waffen* SS members who wanted to evade extradition to France by fleeing to South America or Spain. These Nazi collaborators held travel documents from the Red Cross and letters of recommendation from the Vatican. The title of a front-page article in *L'Unità* on January 31, 1947, cut to the chase: "It is easy for the war criminals to emigrate: Letter 1241 of the Papal Aid Commission." The newspaper stated that hundreds, if not thousands, of Nazis and fascists hiding in Italy had obtained Red Cross passports, organized by the Papal Aid Commission.[76] Conservative Italian newspapers responded by reprinting the defense that the Church would never serve Tito's revenge and instead helps everyone in need, without asking anything in return. The Church had helped *perseguitati* (persecuted people) in the past, so why should now be any different?[77]

Italian diplomats followed these accusations closely, too.[78] The Associated Press reported on February 1, 1947, that the Yugoslavian government had presented two written notes to the Vatican Secretariat of State regarding the aid it allegedly was providing to war criminals. The AP report cited an Italian Foreign Office report, and revealed that one of the notes pertained to five war criminals, reportedly hiding in Vatican territory. The Yugoslavs, in turn, cited the British Foreign Ministry as a source of this information. The other note referred to the role of the PCA in providing, according to the Yugoslavians, "war criminals" with money and passports so that they could reach South America. It further specified that the exiles left the port of Genoa at the end of December 1946 on the *Andrea Gritti*.[79] Another Italian Foreign Office report offers a summary of what happened when the Yugoslavian chief diplomat to the Vatican, a Mr. Gabricevic, confronted Monsignor Tardini with these accusations in a note protesting wanted war criminals being given safe haven by the Church, as revealed by the press. In response,

> Monsignor Tardini denied that in the Vatican or extraterritorial buildings there were people wanted as war criminals. . . . As for the activity of the Papal Aid Commission, Monsignor Tardini could assure that, as its very name indicated, it dealt only with assistance, a very noble task which it carried out with feelings of Christian charity in favor of refugees without distinction of race, language or religion. . . . If certain foreigners had managed to leave Italy using apocryphal documents that they had been able to obtain fraudulently, no charges could therefore be addressed to the Vatican and Mr. Gabricevic should have directed his research and his complaints in other directions.[80]

The Vatican sought input from the PCA President Baldelli soon after the press attacks against his office were published. Writing to Monsignor Tardini, Baldelli rejected PCA responsibility for the *Andrea Gritti* carrying war criminals to safety. Rather than reflecting on any shortcomings on his side, Baldelli pointed the finger at the Red Cross, the Argentine Consulate, and the IGCR. Specifically, Baldelli argued that it was the IGCR that controlled the passenger lists and checked backgrounds, with the help of the interallied command in Caserta. The Confraternity of San Girolamo only issued recommendation letters, he protested, not official documents, and the PCA had no way of knowing who was considered a Nazi war criminal by the Yugoslavian government. He briefly addressed four individuals, named by the Yugoslavs as war criminals, by dismissing the claims. According to Baldelli, the men were known to either the Allies or the PCA, putting them beyond suspicion.[81]

Of course, this blanket rebuttal is highly implausible. The PCA in many cases knew full well whom the Yugoslavian government considered a Nazi (or Ustaša) war criminal. As we have seen, the Vatican frequently received information about Ustaša on the run who were wanted as war criminals by Yugoslavia. That information largely drove the efforts to protect them. The Vatican (and Draganović) usually rejected the "war criminal" label and sought to rebrand all these escapees as "victims" of communism.

The British Foreign Office appeared to find the press reports credible, enough so that it took a closer look and confronted the Vatican with the widely reported accusations:[82]

> I think that there may be some truth in this report as a Monsignor Dragonović [sic!] of the Brotherhood of St. Hieronymus, Rome, is a notorious friend of the Ustachi and is in constant correspondence with Fr. [Branimir 'Branko'?] Jelić's Committee here. Furthermore, we know . . . that a shipload of some 300 refugees left Genoa for Latin American some time ago under Vatican auspices.[83]

Official steps followed. A British Foreign Office report from January 1947 took the title "Exodus of Yugoslav War Criminals to S. America." In it, the British envoy Sir D'Arcy Osborne detailed the institutions and actors involved, including Monsignor Walter Carroll, the only American in the Vatican Secretariat of State and a PCA staff member. Carroll did not deny the possibility that one or two war criminals may have escaped on the *Andrea Gritti*, because, he claimed, it was impossible to verify the identity of all the refugees.[84] Carroll failed to mention that PCA officials often vouched for applicants for Red Cross papers. The voucher process did not include any effective background checks, as far as I can determine. In a revealing point, Monsignor Carroll also asked Osborne to forward lists of wanted war criminals to the PCA. Soon thereafter, Carroll wrote to Montini, warning him of potential attacks against the Vatican that could be based in the PCA's involvement in dubious migration schemes.[85] The Vatican Undersecretary of State did not appear particularly concerned, despite this warning, and did little to censure the PCA's activities.

In February 1947, Osborne took the next step and met in person with Monsignor Tardini to confront him with the allegations.[86] The Vatican was cornered, but it found a solution, by claiming that the five Yugoslavs located by Tito's agents had left Vatican premises for an unknown destination.[87] Regarding the PCA's involvement in facilitating the escape of Nazi war criminals, Tardini offered Osborne a clear untruth, claiming that the Vatican State Secretariat had nothing to do with the PCA. This assertion pushed plausible deniability a bit too far, and the British diplomat offered a strong and straightforward rejection of it, calling the PCA a "Vatican organisation and the instrument of Papal charity and consequently responsibility for it could not be disavowed."[88] The frustration of the British diplomats is clear in another internal note:

> I am afraid the Vatican has not been helpful. . . . The main fact is that the R[oman]. C[atholic]. Church apparently has no wish to come to terms with Tito and is willing to support his enemies. But if Pope Pius XII wishes to assume the mantle of Gregory VII [an eleventh-century saint and one of the greatest Roman pontiffs] he can do it better than by harbouring Ustashi.[89]

Allied intelligence services and diplomats continued to investigate underground escape networks in Italy on their own, too.[90] A report by Vincent La Vista, senior official at the U.S. Embassy in Rome, dated May 15, 1947, and declassified in 1984, has been quoted frequently. In strict confidence to the State Department in Washington, La Vista wrote:

> The Vatican of course is the largest single organization involved in the illegal movement of emigrants. . . . The justification of the Vatican for its participation in this illegal traffic is simply the propagation of the Faith. It is the Vatican's desire to assist any person, regardless of nationality or political beliefs, as long as that person can prove himself to be a Catholic. This of course from the practical point of view is a dangerous practice. The Vatican further justifies its participation by its desire to infiltrate, not only European countries but Latin-American countries as well, with people of all political beliefs as long as they are anti-Communist and pro-Catholic Church.[91]

La Vista's report also details the role of the PCA, and Bishop Hudal in particular. An American diplomat at the Vatican, Graham Parsons, discussed La Vista's report with Monsignor Carroll. Written instructions from the State Department told Parsons to stress that criminal elements and spies were taking advantage of the humanitarian aid that allowed them to "secure documentation for travel." He seemingly did so; an undated U.S. memo that I found in the Vatican archives offers a summary of the Allied concerns: "Mr. Parsons then said that information reaching the United States Government indicated that unscrupulous persons, often engaged in illicit and clandestine activities, had been able increasingly to secure documentation for travel through the unwitting assistance of charitable organizations and governments and institutions cooperating therewith." Furthermore, Parsons had been instructed to tell the Holy See to take precautions to avoid being compromised,[92] though what form those precautions should take remained unspecified. In Parsons's own reports, he records Carroll as saying that the aid agencies were not connected with the Vatican—a claim that fundamentally contradicts clear evidence pertaining to the Papal Aid Commission.[93]

Deniability and discretion were themes when it comes to the Vatican's involvement in the Ratline operations. Hudal on the other hand was never particularly discreet when engaging in his "charitable work" for Nazis and Holocaust perpetrators, which ultimately led to his downfall. In 1949–50, he published a series of political articles in German, Austrian, and South American outlets, condemning Nuremberg justice, depicting Germans as victims, and embracing Pan-Germanism (the ideology that all German-speakers are German and should live in one nation). In response, communist newspapers attacked Hudal as a "Nazi bishop" dreaming of a Greater German Reich.[94] Cardinal Muench in turn informed the Vatican that Hudal was publishing articles in a newspaper, "with a distinctly Nazi tone, and . . . articles like the one in question, especially its first part, can prejudice the already difficult issue of emigration,"[95] likely warning his superiors of the risk the Vatican already faced due to its own efforts to transport fascists and accused Nazi collaborators to South America. In the article, Hudal indeed proudly bragged about channeling many Germans, through Italy, to Argentina.[96] By this point, the Vatican was troubled by "Inopportune articles by Monsignor Hudal," especially as he continued to cause problems.[97]

When Hudal's help for the Nazi criminal SS *Gruppenführer* Otto Wächter, governor of Galicia, became public knowledge, Hudal turned into more than just an inconvenience for the Vatican.[98] In September 1949, Italian newspapers repeatedly accused Hudal of helping Wächter and other top Nazis hide in Rome.[99] This included a newspaper cartoon showing Hudal pushing Hitler in a hospital bed into a Roman hospital, titled "After the Wächter Case." Hudal says, "This is Adolf Hitler. He has liver pain." The hospital counter clerk replies, "Go ahead."[100] This satirical depiction of Hudal's activities in favor of Nazis (albeit not Hitler) is a strong indication of Hudal's notoriety in Italy at this point. By 1949, Hudal's function as a Nazi escape enabler had grown notorious in the German press too. German newspapers in December 1949 described the Nazi escape routes from Germany via Austria to Italy in detail, asserting that "In church circles Hudal is considered the brown [Nazi] bishop."[101] Reflecting his belief in the righteousness of his actions, however, Hudal kept talking publicly about the Wächter case; in February 1950, in a long interview with an Italian newspaper, he justified himself with the assertion, "I am a priest, not a policeman. I helped him."[102] Such continued press attacks, and Hudal's refusal to help matters, pushed the Vatican to act. By 1952, Hudal had stepped down as the rector of the Anima College and retreated with bitterness to his estate outside of Rome.

At the time the La Vista report was finalized in May 1947, the political climate was shifting rapidly. The Cold War confrontation between East and West—between the Americans and the Soviets—was intensifying. Priorities changed: fighting the new communist enemy increasingly took precedence, while the prosecution of Nazi criminals became less of a priority. La Vista and other sources provided ample evidence of how the Italian Ratline operated and who was running it. The U.S. military and intelligence agencies could have easily shut it down then and there—but they did not. In March 1947, just two months before La Vista submitted his report, President Truman delivered his anti-communist speech, laying out what is known today as the Truman Doctrine, and in September 1947, the Central Intelligence Agency was established to fight worldwide communism. Rather than being dismantled, the Ratline in Italy was repurposed for U.S. Cold War objectives. As Cold War tensions escalated, the Allies soon lost interest in punishing Nazi war criminals. Many Nazis and Axis war criminals were co-opted by the Allies to fight a common enemy: communism.

This shift is best illustrated by the case of Klaus Barbie. As Gestapo chief in the French city of Lyon under Nazi occupation, Barbie had a brutal reputation: he was responsible for the torture of prisoners, the persecution of Jews in hiding, and the suppression of the French Resistance. At the end of the war, he was arrested by American forces and was urgently wanted by French authorities for his many crimes. But Barbie convinced his U.S. captors that he could be useful. He claimed to possess valuable intelligence on communists and offered access to agents who were still active in Europe. His captors agreed. Rather than handing him over for prosecution, U.S. intelligence recruited Barbie as an anticommunist asset, viewing his knowledge as more valuable than justice.

Once the French learned of his whereabouts, Barbie needed to be removed from the scene. U.S. intelligence turned to Krunoslav Draganović for help. Barbie was brought to Italy, sheltered by Draganović in monasteries, and provided with a Red Cross travel document under the alias "Klaus Altmann." In 1951, he was channeled out of Europe to Bolivia. Draganović continued his crusade, but became a nuisance for the Vatican when its relations with communist Yugoslavia improved in the 1960s. Draganović eventually retreated to anonymity and died in 1983.

When Barbie was extradited from Bolivia to France in 1983, his longstanding ties to U.S. intelligence became public, sparking an international scandal. Soon thereafter, the La Vista report, detailing the escape of Nazi perpetrators in the early postwar period, was declassified and garnered international media attention, prompting calls for U.S. authorities, the

International Committee of the Red Cross, and the Vatican to account for their actions. Vatican spokespersons again continued to deny any involvement and dismissed the claims as "nothing but air!"[103] The U.S. government, on the other hand, apologized for its role in the obstruction of justice. Eighty years after the end of World War II, the Vatican still appears to be struggling to come to terms with this history, including its involvement in helping Nazi perpetrators evade postwar punishment. However, the opening of the Vatican archives by Pope Francis offered a powerful sign that the Church is willing to confront difficult aspects of its past, and in 2023, I spoke at a conference at the Pontifical Gregorian University in Rome about the involvement of the Papal Aid Commission and the Vatican Secretariat of State in enabling Nazis to escape punishment. But old habits die hard. As recently as 2001, in an official *Festschrift* celebrating the centenary of the Pontifical Croatian Institute in Rome, Father Krunoslav Draganović was portrayed as a hero for his fight against communism and his assistance to Croatian refugees.[104] Despite the many facets of Krunoslav Draganović's life and activities, his central role in facilitating the postwar escape of Nazi perpetrators and collaborators remains an essential and inescapable part of his historical record—one that cannot be ignored.

As another example of the ongoing contrasts, during my visit in 2022 to the Teutonic College in Rome, I found a plaque dedicated to the Irish priest Hugh O'Flaherty, whose rescue operations for Allied POWs, anti-fascists, and Jews during the Nazi years were located there. The inscription reads, "Monsignor Hugh O'Flaherty, born in Ireland . . . Founder of the Rome Escape Line. Tireless defender of the weak and oppressed. Resided in this College 1938–1960 where he saved over 6000 lives from the National Socialists." This prominent plaque proudly and clearly commemorates his heroic aid to the victims of the Nazis. In the cemetery of the very same Teutonic College is the grave of Bishop Hudal, who helped so many Holocaust perpetrators escape justice after the war. No plaque or any other commemoration mentions this Roman escape route for Nazis and fascists, run by Catholic clergy and supervised, financed, and ultimately sanctioned by the Holy See. The opening of the Vatican archives, however, indicates a new willingness to confront the past more openly, which might encourage a more balanced view of its own actions during those postwar years. But only time will tell.

CONCLUSION

The history of the PCA provides evidence of Vatican involvement in helping Nazis and fascists—including accused war criminals—flee overseas. The work of the PCA was initiated by the Vatican, and it was supervised and financed (directly and indirectly) by the Holy See. The pope took great interest in the PCA's humanitarian work, and the Vatican Secretariat of State received regular reports about its activities. The PCA was embedded deeply in the Vatican's charitable network, as well as its work saving souls. Its involvement with Nazi war criminals was not a secret, as documented by diplomatic and intelligence reports, as well as popular press articles published at the time. Both U.S. and British diplomats approached the Vatican Secretariat of State with the allegations, to little effect. There is also no denying that the PCA was an instrument of the Holy See. In the words of Prince Carlo Pacelli, a nephew of Pius XII and legal adviser to the Vatican state administration, "In conclusion, the Papal Aid Commission must constitute a valid and agile instrument of the Supreme Pontiff for the implementation of all the charitable purposes that the everlasting motherhood of the Church suggests."[105]

The proof that this agile instrument was used to also aid Axis war criminals must be understood in the context of the Vatican's postwar policies and priorities. Saving the souls of former Nazis and re-Christianizing society, promoting *caritas* and forgiveness for the vanquished nations, and fighting the imminent threat of atheistic communism—these were the primary goals and motivations underlying the Vatican's activities.[106] Even if notorious figures like Bishop Hudal and Draganović were not formally "the Vatican," they were not operating in a vacuum. Bishop Hudal followed the lead of his superiors when he defended his aid for "the former members of the Nazi party and of fascism, especially [for] the so-called 'war criminals'" by describing it as Christian "charity work." And Hudal went on: "To help [people] here, to save a few, to work selflessly and determinedly without thinking of the consequences, is naturally what should have been a demand of true Christianity, which does not believe in the hatred taught by the Talmud [Jewish law], but in [Christian] love, mercy, and forgiveness [...]"[107] One driving motivation behind the Vatican's assistance to Nazis—and even more so to the numerous collaborators, the so-called "greys"—in facilitating their emigration overseas and helping them avoid repatriation was arguably the conviction that the innocent should not be punished alongside the guilty. Church officials appear to have reasoned that if protecting the many required tolerating the escape of some who were culpable, this was a morally defensible compromise. In their view, it was preferable that some guilty individuals evade punishment if, in the process, a larger number of innocents could be spared forced return and possible imprisonment or worse.

Among those who sought Vatican assistance were indeed minor functionaries—"small fry"—men who had occupied lower ranks and now faced uncertain or harsh futures if repatriated. Yet the same channels that offered relief to such marginal figures also facilitated the escape of individuals who had played central roles in mass murder.

EPILOGUE

TO FORGIVE AND TO FORGET?

In May 1949, Bishop Hudal wrote to Monsignor Montini about a troubling situation, namely, that people were still imprisoned "solely for political reasons" ["*unicamente per motivi politici*"], years after the war's end. He argued that the situation was unsustainable, causing grave harm to their families and to Christianity itself. Therefore, he reasoned, it was time to ask all governments for a day of pardon, "in which the past becomes liquidated with a generous and proper Christian act, ending the still pending trials once and for all [!] in a fraternal embrace in the spirit of Saint Francis of Assisi." Hudal continued:

> It is a shame that, also in Countries with Governments that so often talk about humanism, if perhaps not directly about Christianity, or in which several members are practicing Catholics, still today are imprisoned in the jails people that have committed no offense or crime but "that one": that in politics they defended ideas or beliefs that are today denied, while a few years ago, until the tragedy of the lost war, they were confessed by millions [a barely hidden reference to Nazis and Fascists]. The great Wisdom of the Holy See will find the manner and the methods for the proposal of a wide amnesty. Such an action will certainly have a profound and sympathetic echo even among non-Catholics, despite the fact that some Governments will not take action.[1]

Hudal's letter to Montini cannot be taken as anything other than an appeal for forgiveness and forgetting, and the occasion was strategically chosen.

Pope Pius XII had declared 1950 a Holy Year, with special events and high expectations of religious renewal. The Holy Year has been celebrated since the year 1300. Initially, it was to be repeated every 100 years, then every 50 years, and now every 25 years. The intent in 1950 was to draw a clear line between the new era and the recent past. For Bishop Hudal, it provided a priceless opportunity to further his own visions for postwar "justice." Without mentioning Nazis or fascists by name, the references in the letter are pretty obvious and leave little room for alternative interpretations. The Nazis' guilt, according to Hudal, was limited to their political views and convictions, and now, facing "the tragedy of the lost war," they remained imprisoned without having committed a crime. In other words, Nazis (and by extension, all Germans) were being subjected to victors' justice and revenge, solely because they had lost the war.

Hudal's strategy was clever, and effective. A few days later, Monsignor Montini, the pope's close advisor, responded personally to Hudal:

> With Your esteemed letter, dated the 5th of this current month, Your Most Reverend Excellence expressed, in occasion of the Holy Year, his desire for a day of general pardon and wide amnesty. In complete reserve and confidentiality, I am pleased to inform You that this Secretariat of State, on initiative of the Central Committee for the Holy Year, has already taken, in this specific regard, many steps with a number of Governments. Let us hope, with God's help and the good will of the people, something concrete may be achieved. I take the occasion to kiss Your Holy Ring and confirm my deepest devotion.[2]

Hudal headed the Austrian committee for the Holy Year, and he knew that, for the pope, celebrating forgiveness on this auspicious occasion could take the form of generous amnesty. Hudal's request found a welcome reception among Montini and the Holy See, or so it seems.

Even before the Holy Year, the pope had begun openly calling for an end of the war crimes trials and denazification, under the motto "Forgive and Forget." But the Vatican's push for amnesty reached a peak in the Holy Year, an occasion traditionally packed with special events involving the Vatican. Indulgences to reduce punishments for sins were granted, pilgrimages to Rome from all over the world were organized, and the Holy Door of St. Peter's

Basilica in Rome was ceremonially opened. Cardinal Francis Spellman of New York led a large group of American pilgrims to Rome, joined by groups led by the German bishops.[3] Furthermore, the Holy Year provided Pius XII a perfect platform for his "Reconciliation and peace" message, aimed particularly at Catholic nations torn apart by war and political strife. He specified four goals for this Holy Year:

> 1. Sanctification of souls through prayer and penance and unshakable fidelity to Christ and to the Church. 2. Action for peace, and protection of the Holy Places. 3. Defense of the Church against the renewed attacks of her enemies and pleading for the true faith for the errant, the infidels and the godless. 4. Implementation of social justice and works of assistance in favor of the humble and the needy.[4]

Calling for "a new crusade for the great return [to Christ] and the great pardon," Pius XII sought nothing less than a new evangelization of Europe and beyond.[5] For the holy city, the seat of the pope, the Holy Year was a huge event. Tourists in Rome can still admire vast inscriptions commemorating it, such as in the Via Conciliazione leading to St. Peter's Square: "*A IUBILAEI MCML.*" In addition to the four goals for the year, the theological highlight arguably was the pope's announcement of the dogma of the Virgin Mary's bodily ascension to heaven.

The *Osservatore Romano*, the Vatican's newspaper, covered the Holy Year over several months, announcing events and educating readers about the ambitious goals. For the Vatican, it seems, the Holy Year provided a golden opportunity to close the chapter on war and heal the wounds that remained. Vatican diplomats worked tirelessly to implement the pope's wishes for generous amnesty. The Vatican Secretariat of State, under the direction of the pope himself and with the assistance of both Montini and Tardini, negotiated with U.S. representatives—for example, when Monsignor Montini wrote to a non-Catholic U.S. diplomat in October 1949:

> His Holiness already envisages with paternal satisfaction and lively hope, the humanitarian and benevolent acts which will enhance in the eyes of the people the motives of compassion and pardon which are appropriate to the Jubilee

> Year. These sentiments of His Holiness are to be considered jointly with the religious ceremonies, so rich in spiritual values, and the pilgrimages from all over the world.[6]

He went on to refer to the Brazilian government's amnesty initiative for Holy Year 1950:

> You are aware, in this connection, that Brazil, through its Minister of Justice, has already announced an amnesty on the occasion of the Holy Year. This decision, which is at once so humanitarian and so Christian, cannot but have a repercussion on mankind, the value of which cannot be overestimated under prevailing conditions.[7]

Having cited an example to follow, Montini asked if the U.S. government could enact a similar initiative, in line with the pope's desire to "promote the benefits of reconciliation and peace" through "this high gesture of civic and social significance on the eve of the Jubilee."[8] Yet this proposed parallel ignores some key differences. In particular, Catholicism shaped Brazil's religious landscape, whereas the United States historically had embraced diverse Protestant denominations. The election of the Catholic president John F. Kennedy 10 years later was a novelty. Thus, perhaps unsurprisingly, the U.S. State Department was not particularly enthusiastic about adopting the recommendations of the Catholic Church. Even if Washington might have shared Montini's sentiment, its legal traditions also differed from those in continental Europe. Specifically, the United States had frameworks for pardoning individual persons convicted of crimes, but it did not offer general amnesties for groups of major offenders. It also codified the separation of church and state in its Constitution.[9]

A cool response from the United States did not discourage Pius XII, though. He repeated his assertions that forgiving and forgetting were the best guarantees for peace, and that those outcomes could be achieved through amnesties. The text of an editorial in Catholic Action's weekly magazine *Ecclesia*, dated January 22, 1949, outlines the pope's exhortation to the Spanish ambassador to the Vatican, that hatreds resulting from the Spanish Civil War (1936–1939) had to be extinguished. He praised the state for providing "broad" amnesty but added that the fight against hatred remained on the Church's agenda and would continue to be waged by its bishops. He condemned revenge and called on Spaniards to forget their own Civil War.[10] Montini promoted this wider initiative actively, sending letters to various embassies at the Vatican to call for extensive amnesty and clemency efforts by all Catholic nations during the Holy Year. Hudal's letter to Montini clearly reflects his acceptance of these attitudes and motives.[11]

Such papal calls for generous amnesties resonated perhaps most powerfully in Germany, amidst heated debates about the fate of convicted Nazi war criminals. In the papers of Cardinal Frings of Cologne, I found a translation of the pope's Christmas message, referring to the opening of the holy door, which would be done to celebrate the beginning of the Holy Year 1950. On December 23, 1949, the pope warned that "our present age even very recently has been an epoch of apostasy [renunciation of God] and guilt." The Holy Year gave sinners the chance to come back to God, to Christ. He suggested victims and perpetrators should meet in Rome, as pilgrims, who could include "those who were commanded to deal out death and those who suffered its terrible effects, the invader and the conquered; the keeper of the barbed-wire prison-camp and the prisoner who endured its cruel confinement." In addition to encouraging sinners to admit their wrongdoing, cautioning that "Although the Lord is ready to forgive, He does not dispense the sinner from the necessity of sincere repentance and due expiation," Pope Pius XII appealed to all Catholics to bury the past with honest remorse and forgive as one human to another. He also condemned, in clear terms, all forms of revenge:

> When, in recent times, taking their rise from an unfortunate war or political upheavals, waves of reprisals were unleashed, unequalled in history at least for the number of their victims, our heart was pierced with bitter grief—not only because of the misfortune that bred other misfortunes and hurled into the fray thousands of families who were often innocent, but because with utter sadness we saw here the tragic evidence of apostasy from the spirit of Christ. Whoever would be a sincere Christian must know how to forgive.

In a further, dramatic appeal to world leaders, the pope reiterated:

> Hence, in the name of Jesus Christ, who has given to men an example by offering Himself in sacrifice even for His executioners, we implore governments—especially Christian governments—to exercise generously their right of pardon, and to put into effect, on an occasion so solemn and propitious as the Holy Year, that mitigation of punitive justice provided for in the laws of all countries.[12]

The papacy's moral claims and call for forgiveness in the Holy Year had powerful repercussions for German war criminals. The Holy See urged generous amnesty for them, because the "spirit of vindictiveness . . . is not good for peace and prosperity."

It fell to the pope's spokesperson in Germany, nuncio Aloisius Muench, to share these views with the U.S. High Commissioner John McCloy. In December 1949, he wrote, somewhat cryptically,

> [. . .] it is to be regretted that . . . certain organizations are writing you to reject proposals for an amnesty. Such an attitude will keep alive a spirit of vindictiveness that is not good for peace and prosperity. It will reawaken racial resentments that in the interest of these very organizations should be weakened and done to death as quickly as possible.[13]

The papal delegate contended that, on the eve of the Holy Year, "conciliation and peace" was needed, instead of revenge. Along with this assertion, Muench appeared to blame the rise in antisemitism on Jewish people and their alleged vengefulness. With such strong language, Muench not only relied on antisemitic tropes of Jewish vindictiveness but also challenged the U.S. program of accountability. In response, McCloy noted, "with regard to an amnesty for prisoners under the jurisdiction of the Occupying Powers. I assume that you refer particularly to prisoners convicted of war crimes." He then explained that he had "been somewhat disturbed, however, in examining these petitions, by what appears to be a persistent tendency to question the legal basis for the prosecutions and the judicial soundness of the judgments." McCloy made his opinion clear: It was unconscionable that anyone could "reasonably doubt the enormity of the crimes of which the war crimes prisoners have been convicted or the fundamental principles of international justice pursuant to which they were tried." In addition to emphasizing the unprecedented scope of the crimes and the clear legality of the Allied prosecutions, McCloy addressed the idea of amnesty:

> In that connection, I think that the term "amnesty" is perhaps unfortunate. I do not believe that world opinion generally is prepared to accept the proposition that those crimes have yet been sufficiently atoned for or that the German people should now be allowed to forget them. Anything approaching a general amnesty would, I fear, be taken as an abandonment of the principles established in the trials of the perpetrators of those crimes.[14]

McCloy ended by acknowledging that, in individual cases, arguments for clemency might exist, but a general amnesty was out of the question.

These conflicting views of guilt and forgiveness played out around the world. The numbers of Nuremberg critics expanded. Conservative politicians and policy makers, former Nazis, and Christian churches formed an odd but increasingly powerful lobby for war criminals, with the common goal of closing the book on the recent past.[15] Calling for the end of postwar retributive justice became more mainstream, and German leaders readily joined the flow. The German Chancellor Konrad Adenauer, a devout Catholic, by 1951 appealed to the pope for renewed interventions to put an immediate halt to the remaining trials against Nazi war criminals in Germany and Western Europe, particularly in France. Along with their chancellor, the German public was increasingly speaking out against ongoing punishment efforts, trials, and administrative measures.[16] Bishop Hudal thus likely expected to find support when he wrote to Chancellor Adenauer requesting assistance for imprisoned Nazi criminals.[17] It is noteworthy that Vatican officials, including Montini and Muench, stylized the term "war criminals" in quotation marks or avoided it completely, by referring to convicted Nazi leaders as "prisoners of war" or "political prisoners."[18]

In the early 1950s, West Germany would become a sovereign nation and strong Western ally. Germany and the Germans were needed in the fight against the common communist enemy. Chancellor Adenauer leveraged this position of power to inform U.S. authorities that there would be no German military contribution as long as German officers were on trial. The message was clear, and soon afterward, the world experienced the "German-American Grace Fever" [*"Deutsch-amerikanische Gnadenfieber"*], as the German historian Annette Weinke aptly labeled it.[19] Generous amnesty laws passed by the German government in the early 1950s allowed hundreds of thousands of Germans to leave their Nazi pasts behind them: They could no longer be held responsible for crimes committed during World War II.[20] By 1955, Germany had a new army and joined NATO. With very few exceptions, almost all convicted Nazi war criminals in Germany were free men by the end of 1958.[21] According to the historian Norbert Frei, rather than establishing clear norms for injustice and punishment, the amnesty policies totally obscured moral standards and thereby created new confusion about right and wrong.[22] Churches, in their tireless opposition to war crimes trials, helped create a climate in which convicted Nazis came to be seen as martyrs of revenge-driven victors' justice.[23]

In the Soviet-controlled zone of East Germany, forgiveness and "letting bygones be bygones" also became the norm. An East German movie, with the telling title *The Murderers Are Among Us* (1946), depicted a former concentration camp inmate who realizes that German civilians too suffered from the war and dictatorship. The audience walked away with the sense that revenge is not the answer, and that the focus should be on building a better future. Set in the ruins of Berlin, the film contains anti-capitalist, anti-militarist, and antifascist messaging, in line with Soviet communist ideology.[24]

The German philosopher Karl Jaspers, an anti-Nazi, captured the mood in the country when he wrote in 1945, "People simply want to stop suffering; they want to escape misery, to live, but not to think."[25] But Jaspers did not leave it at that. He also reflected on German guilt in the ruins of the Third Reich, famously categorizing four types: "criminal guilt," "political guilt," "moral guilt," and "metaphysical guilt." Criminal guilt applies to those who commit crimes under the law; political guilt is the responsibility people have regarding how they are governed; moral guilt refers to a person's individual actions; and metaphysical guilt implies that the person is co-responsible for the wrongdoing and injustice that occurs in the world, such that "If I do not do what I can to prevent it, then I am complicit."[26] With this reasoning, Jaspers holds every German guilty, according to at least one of these categories.[27] Yet Jaspers also rejected the idea of the collective criminal guilt of all German people.

Church authorities, up to and including the pope, repeatedly made clear that, ultimately, forgiveness had priority over criminal punishment. Even if we accept the Church's preference to focus on saving souls, its demand for unlimited forgiveness and generous amnesty remains surprising. The perpetrators hardly ever met the minimum Catholic standards for forgiveness: They rarely confessed personal guilt, expressed regret, or asked for forgiveness. We also must acknowledge that the surviving victims of the Nazis and their families were not asked their opinion on the Catholic Church's forgiveness campaign.[28]

The Lutheran pastor Martin Niemöller, who survived Nazi concentration camps, offered a nuanced assessment of forgiveness. In his 1947 book *Of Guilt and Hope*, he offered a unique view on guilt, punishment, and forgiveness: "The guilt [of the German people] exists, there is no doubt about it. Even if there were no other guilt than that of the six million clay urns, containing the ashes of burnt Jews from all over Europe."[29] This brilliant observer also aptly described the status of Germany's postwar society: The world blamed the Germans, the Germans blamed the Nazis, and the Nazis pointed to Hitler, who was conveniently dead.[30] Therefore, as a starting point for reconciliation, Niemöller called for confessions of guilt by the perpetrators, to those who suffered.[31] In an interview with a U.S. Army chaplain, he acknowledged that "The German people have already been punished by God; their young men and the old ones died at the front and at home; their cities and villages, and everything that was in them has been destroyed." But he added the insistence that "Goering and the other war criminals must be punished." Asked about the possibilities that the world would forgive the Germans, Niemöller replied carefully: "'The world' will not be able to say: 'We forgive you,' but the Christians all over the world should say that, and they should start all over again with us. Measures of punishment against the people will not help."[32] Unlike some of his Catholic contemporaries, he insisted that leading Nazis must face punishment, while at the same time, as a pastor and theologian, he fervently upheld the Christian principle of unlimited forgiveness.

The records show that many prominent Catholic and Protestant German bishops and clergy dispensed absolution with striking generosity, extending forgiveness and moral rehabilitation in ways that often minimized personal and institutional responsibility for past crimes. More critical views have gained increasing traction in recent decades. Having examined these moral and institutional entanglements in meticulous detail, the German historian Ernst Klee arrived at a stark conclusion in 1992:

> It is often argued, Christian mercy should also be applied to Nazi perpetrators. There is nothing wrong with this idea, but the argument is misleading: The Nazi murderers never regretted anything. They just did their duty, so they said. The forgiving of their guilt weighs even heavier than the silence of the Churches on Nazi crimes and the Holocaust during the Third Reich. The victims were betrayed for a second time. This time, the Churches were under no coercion; they did it of their own free will. That could only mean they did it with conviction.[33]

Klee was no theologian, but his critical view of these men of God and their actions resonates with current theological views, especially during the recent papacy of Pope Francis, which featured more critical reflection on the Church's past behaviors. Catholic theologians of the early twenty-first century have offered increasingly critical assessments of the actions taken by clergy in the Nazi era.[34] In 2024, for example, the Israeli Jesuit priest David Neuhaus raised issues with the forgiveness offered to Rudolf Höss, the commandant of Auschwitz, by clarifying that "This religious act, however, does not constitute a juridical act. The responsibility of the penitent for his or her acts remains in force. Indeed, confessing to God as a penitent involves taking responsibility for the consequences of sin. God does not forgive in place of the victims."[35] We can all agree that some form of forgiveness is essential to any society. Forgetting, however, is something very different. As Italian novelist Umberto Eco wrote in 1995,

> If reconciliation means compassion and respect for all those who fought their own war in good faith, to forgive does not mean to forget. I can even admit that Eichmann sincerely believed in his mission, but I cannot say, "OK, come back and do it again." We are here to remember what happened and solemnly say that "They" must not do it again.[36]

Even in the face of the compelling arguments offered at the time by the philosopher Karl Jaspers and Pastor Martin Niemöller, as well as survivors like Simon Wiesenthal, the Church persistently rejected considerations of widespread guilt and responsibility. After 1945, the rejection of punishment, rather than demands for it, became a rallying cry. While the Church was forcefully opposing the prosecution of Nazis, and just as forcefully preaching forgiveness for the war criminals, it was also encouraging the world to move on by forgiving and forgetting. Perpetrators were to be forgiven; victims were quickly forgotten. As the scholar Aleida Assmann puts it, "within [West German] society, largely excluding the Jewish experience, the strategy of forgiveness and forgetting was practiced as an effective means of social integration."[37]

As a justification for this approach, many Christian clergy accused Jews of being vengeful and portrayed postwar justice as motivated by Jewish revenge. But how common was violent Jewish revenge really? And how did Jews view the Nuremberg justice efforts?

Wartime documents show that revenge fantasies were common among victims, and both victims and perpetrators expressed their anticipation of postwar retribution. In reality, though, acts of violent Jewish revenge were rare in Germany.[38] A plan by a group of Jewish Holocaust survivors, under the leadership of Abba Kovner, to poison the water supply in some German cities, so as to kill 6 million Germans, remained only a plan.[39]

The Soviet-Yiddish poet Abraham Sutzkever was one of the few Jewish people to share testimony at Nuremberg. In his memoirs, he recounted his thoughts of bringing a gun to the courtroom and shooting Hermann Göring; a friend persuaded him that doing so was not in the Soviets' best interests. The choice stayed with him. On the last page of his memoirs, Sutzkever laments, in a disgruntled tone, "I did not bring the revolver and the six bullets with me to the Nuremberg Trial. A Yiddish poet taking revenge on a German supreme commander was not to be."[40]

Thus, despite fantasies or plans for revenge among survivors, violent revenge was rather rare. Although some Jewish victims killed Jewish Nazi collaborators in ghettos and concentration camps during the war and at its end, most survivors instead sought justice through the courts.[41] This historical evidence is not intended to deny selected examples of revenge and violence. Rather, it helps establish that the conspiratorial, antisemitic notions of Jewish vengefulness were vastly overblown. Most Jews were focused on legitimate, difficult questions of justice, rather than revenge, during the postwar trials.

Even during the war, questions about guilt and punishment had plagued Jewish communities in Europe, the Americas, and Palestine/Israel. In 1944, the World Jewish Congress (WJC), which served as an international federation of Jewish organizations, published a "Statement and Resolution on the Punishment of War Criminals," which issued a powerful warning: "if those who are guilty of monstrous crimes against the Jewish people are allowed to escape punishment, it cannot but have the effect of encouraging adventurers in the post-war world to use anti-Semitism as a means of obtaining power and thereafter as an instrument of aggression."[42] Citing the destruction of European Jews as the most monstrous Nazi crime, the WJC argued for postwar retribution and demanded that national and international tribunals prosecute "war crimes," not in a narrow sense, but in a way that would include "all forms of persecution of racial, religious, and political minorities" since 1933.[43]

Once the Nuremberg proceedings were underway, Jews in Germany and around the world followed them closely, as evidenced by the close reporting in Jewish newspapers.[44] The expectations among survivors were high; they wanted Nuremberg to offer a full vindication of Jewish suffering. As Laura Jockusch describes the situation, "Many Jewish observers deemed the mere fact that key figures of the Nazi regime stood trial at Nuremberg to be a triumph over Nazism and to indicate some measure of historical justice."[45] Yet rather than dealing primarily with the Holocaust (a term rarely used then), the international Nuremberg trials prosecuted the war of aggression and crimes against Allied civilians. They thus left some observers deeply disappointed, especially because the court did not fully recognize the specific and terrible fate of the Jews. Instead, their persecution was grouped together with atrocities committed against other victims, usually under the label "crimes against humanity." Furthermore, as noted previously, Jewish victims were given little space to testify.[46]

The subsequent Nuremberg military trials addressed some of these shortcomings. Telford Taylor, U.S. Chief of Counsel for War Crimes, assured longtime WJC President Stephen Wise that he shared the view that "the crimes committed by the Third Reich against the Jewish people must not be condoned, and therefore those guilty of these crimes must be brought to justice," and he stressed that "crimes against the Jewish people have formed a very important part of the charges" brought against Nazi elites in the 12 trials. Yet he also cautioned that it was "quite impossible for the Nuremberg Tribunals to try all Germans against whom there are serious charges of war crimes and crimes against humanity" and emphasized the practical challenges, such that the "number of charges which can be heard and determined at Nuremberg is necessarily limited by available funds and personnel, the size of court rooms, and other similar factors."[47]

Yet for Jewish survivors—traumatized, displaced, homeless, and often penniless—punishing a few Nazi leaders was inadequate and incommensurate with their crimes. They pleaded for a moral condemnation of the German nation as a whole.[48] That is, they often embraced notions of German collective responsibility and guilt (moral and otherwise), which the Catholic Church so vehemently rejected. This ethical stance still stressed a sense of "justice," be it criminal, moral, or reparative. The Austrian Holocaust survivor Simon Wiesenthal famously made "justice not revenge" his credo. Liberated from the Mauthausen concentration camp, he worked with U.S. forces to bring Nazi perpetrators to justice.[49] But his initial optimism that Allied criminal justice would produce punishment and recognition of the victims' sufferings was replaced by deep disillusionment when the Cold War pushed the war crimes trials to the sidelines.

A focus on crimes by Germans and their collaborators during the Holocaust came to be viewed as simply unhelpful in a new reality, in which (West) Germany represented a necessary ally for the United States, while the Soviets simultaneously emerged as a new enemy.[50] In seeking to promote such a transformation in alliances, "it became clear that the American government was laying the groundwork for the rearmament of Germany, and that sweeping the Nazi past into the dustbin of history was the price German elites were extracting for their cooperation in the anti-Soviet crusade," as historian Peter Novick put it.[51] In November 1947, an embittered Wiesenthal offered an accurate prediction about Nuremberg justice:

> The thought will arise in everyone who hears about this issue, whether anything can be done in a time of humanity's petrified conscience, in an era where the powerful of this world consider it appropriate to propagate a cloak of

> silence and a cloth of forgetfulness and to put it into practice. We are faced with the fact that the world wants to settle the account for millions of victims by punishing a few hundred.[52]

Living in mostly Catholic Austria, Wiesenthal constantly confronted the forgive-and-forget mentality of that gentile society. According to a common definition, "forgiveness is the foregoing of one's right to retributive justice, in some way and some degree."[53] But giving up retributive justice, after the horrors and suffering of the Holocaust, was a lot to ask.

Such excessive demands led Wiesenthal to reflect carefully on the complexities of forgiveness, drawing from his experiences during the Holocaust. In *The Sunflower*, first published in 1969, he tells the story of a German soldier, on his deathbed, who asked Wiesenthal for forgiveness for killing Jews and also requested that Wiesenthal pass on a final message to his mother. Wiesenthal listened quietly and respectfully but could not forgive. After the war, Wiesenthal visits the SS man's mother; out of respect for her grief, he withholds the truth about her son's crimes. Thus, Wiesenthal ultimately chooses silence. For the hundreds of students who have taken my annual class on the history of the Holocaust, *The Sunflower* is by far the most resonant and thought-provoking book, as their feedback makes overwhelmingly clear. It helps them to think about justice, revenge, compassion, evil, and, ultimately, the nature of humanity. It also helps them to realize that simple answers remain elusive.

In the second part of the book, Wiesenthal asks prominent religious, community, and political leaders, theologians, and Holocaust survivors what they would have done in his position. The different concepts of forgiveness in Judaism and Christianity become patently clear in these responses. The prominent Catholic Cardinal of Vienna, Franz König, answers that he would have fulfilled the last wish of the Nazi soldier, because "For Christians, the binding answer is in the Gospels [from the New Testament]. The question of whether there is a limit to forgiveness has been emphatically answered by Christ in the negative."[54] This Catholic tradition allows for the possibility of forgiving the Nazi soldier, even by someone other than the victim. Religious Judaism instead requires that the victims who have been wronged must be consulted before forgiveness can take place, or as the prominent U.S. Rabbi Abraham

Joshua Heschel put it, "No one can forgive crimes committed against other people."[55] In actively seeking to do just that, Catholic Church leaders openly contradicted Jewish traditions of forgiveness.

An episode involving the Pope hints at a troubling indifference to the gravity of the Holocaust and a lack of understanding of Jewish suffering. During an audience in the spring of 1957, Pope Pius XII told Archbishop Muench what he considered a humorous anecdote: "Hitler died and somehow got into heaven." In the story, Hitler met the Old Testament prophet Moses and apologized for his treatment of the Jews, only to be told that such things were "forgiven and forgotten here in heaven." Relieved, Hitler then asked Moses a question he had long wondered about: "Did Moses set fire to the burning bush?" The reference to the burning bush was likely a reference to the burning of the German parliament (Reichstag), an event the Nazis were often suspected of starting because it benefited them. Muench later told a fellow Catholic clergyman in Chicago that "Our Holy Father told me the story with a big laugh."[56] It is quite disturbing that both Muench and the Pope apparently did not realize how inappropriate this "joke" was.[57]

Germans too showed little understanding for Jewish and other Nazi victims. A widespread belief grew among Germans that they had nothing to be ashamed of and bore no responsibility. Instead, they embraced their own victimhood—first of the Nazis, and later of the Allies. This distortion of history was only rejected officially by Germany decades later. Today, German society generally acknowledges its role as the perpetrator of the Holocaust and other Nazi crimes, and it has made this acknowledgment central to its official memory of World War II. Germans today are, of course, not guilty of the crimes committed by their ancestors, but there is a strong sense of responsibility to learn from the past, defend human rights and democracy, and honor the victims. In this sense, today's democratic, liberal Germany offers a meaningful model for how societies can confront guilt and accept responsibility for the dark chapters of their history.[58] But as the German scholar Aleida Assmann remarks, this example is especially notable because of how rare it is: "The adoption of the victim's perspective by the perpetrators or victors is an absolute novelty in history. Within this new culture of remembrance, marked by human rights, an ethical imperative is playing an increasingly significant role. The commandment 'You shall remember!'"[59] It remains to be seen if such recognition and remembrance will persist in Germany and spread as a global norm or if, instead, we will turn back the clock and choose to repress past crimes and injustices.

The latter choice is not impossible, as exemplified by the views of Pope Pius XII and many Germans in the postwar years. Catholic clergy continued to defend their help for Holocaust perpetrators and fascists, using arguments about Christian charity and the postulate imperative of forgiving and forgetting. As Bishop Hudal proudly and unapologetically wrote in his memoirs, posthumously published in 1976,

> All of these experiences finally prompted me, after 1945, to dedicate all of my charitable work primarily to former members of NS [National Socialism] and fascism, especially the so-called "war criminals" who were persecuted by Communists and "Christian" democrats. . . . I thank the Lord that He opened my eyes and also granted me the undeserved gift to visit and comfort many victims of the post-war period [Nazis included] in prisons and concentration camps, and to have rescued not a few from their tormentors by providing them with false identification papers for escape to happier countries.[60]

Still, Hudal's help was not limited solely to Nazis. During the war, he aided some Allied POWs and Catholics of Jewish ancestry (so-called "Non-Aryan" Catholics).[61] As was true of all priests working for the PCA, he was expected to embody Good Samaritanism and help everyone who needed help. Whether and how much his well-documented anti-Jewish, anti-communist, and pan-German bias got in the way of assistance to vulnerable populations remains an open question. Reviewing Hudal's papers certainly left me with the impression that aiding Jews, socialists, and communists was not a priority for him. Hudal's charity work focused on Catholics foremost, including those of Jewish ancestry. Hudal's help for some Nazi victims could not diminish the implications of Hudal's deep and willing complicity in facilitating Nazi perpetrators' evasion of punishment. Nothing can make up for his obstruction of postwar justice. Nor should assistance offered to Nazi perpetrators ever be equated with the aid provided to Nazi victims.

And yet, some Catholic clergy continue to defend the Church's efforts to enable Nazi criminals to escape following the war, framing the people who embraced such actions as neutral Christian humanitarians and highlighting the moments in which they also aided Jews.[62] As a historian, I have confronted these recurring themes repeatedly and for many years. On the basis of this extensive experience, I offer a clear assessment that echoes the findings of other scholars: the strong postwar support the Church extended to fascists, Nazis, and their collaborators has no parallel in its support for Nazi victims, Holocaust survivors, or displaced Jewish persons after 1945.[63]

As this book has demonstrated, Pope Pius XII's critical stance toward and eventual opposition to the Nuremberg trials were motivated by his fear of communism, which he identified as the Church's primary enemy before, during, and after World War II. Vatican officials worried that ongoing purges in defeated nations would create chaos and misery, to the benefit of Stalin and his agents. The pope's call to "forget the past and give the Germans the hope of a better future in the sign of love," as reported by *The New York Times*, can be understood in this light up to a point.[64] But it cannot be accepted fully or without recognition of its major shortcomings. This forgive-and-forget mentality, often religiously motivated, ignored and excluded the (Jewish) survivors, an omission that many victims find particularly offensive. Catholic humanitarian aid was also heavily politicized and driven by anti-communist sentiment, which sometimes was wrapped in antisemitic language. Such factors must be considered when evaluating the pope's actions in favor of Nazis and their collaborators across Europe.

In the end, of course, there are no easy answers. No one—the Allies, German society, the pope—had ideal solutions for moving forward after the unprecedented horrors of the war and the Holocaust. As in all human endeavors, especially those undertaken in the face of war, genocide, and dictatorship, the situation reflects what the U.S. Ambassador Stuart Eizenstat, describing the options for dealing with Nazi-era assets in Swiss banks, termed "imperfect justice."[65] Although even well-meaning actors—such as Justice Robert H. Jackson and others involved in legal or moral reckonings—worked diligently to address past crimes, they ultimately could not restore what was lost or make people feel that justice had been fully achieved. At the same time, simplistic appeals to "forgive and forget" overlook the profound wounds left by war and genocide and can be deeply insensitive to the experiences of victims. Forgiveness can never be imposed on victims, and the pursuit of accountability should not be mistaken for vindictiveness. As Umberto Eco warned, remembering—not forgetting—is the best safeguard against repeating atrocities. "Never again!" only holds meaning if we know and remember what happened.

NOTES

Epigraph

1 Neuhäusler was referring to the controversies surrounding the historical record of Pope Pius XII. Johannes Neuhäusler to Deans of the Archdiocese of Munich and Freising, 2 December 1964, Archiv des Erzbistums München und Freising (AEMF), NL Neuhäusler 520.

Preface

1 I grew up in the Austrian Tyrol and lived much of my adult life in the Italian Tyrol (South Tyrol), before emigrating to the United States.

Introduction

1 Adolf Eichmann, "Meine Flucht: Bericht aus der Zelle in Jerusalem," World Exclusive in *The People*, London, NARA, RG 263 (CIA), War Crimes, CIA name files, IWG, box 14, Eichmann, Adolf, vol. 1.

2 "Forgive Germany, Pope Urges World," *The New York Times*, April 16, 1948, 10; and letter from Pius XII to the German bishops, March 1, 1948, published in *Kirchlicher Anzeiger für die Erzdiözese Köln*, 88. Jahrgang, May 1, 1948, 97–105. Addressed by name in this letter were Bishops Faulhaber, Frings, and Preysing.

3 See United Nations, "The rule of law and transitional justice in conflict and post-conflict societies: Report of the Secretary-General" S/2004/616, August 23, 2004, 4. https://docs.un.org/en/S/2004/616.

4 Ruti Teitel, *Transitional Justice* (Oxford University Press, 2000), 27; Ruti Teitel, "Transitional Justice: Postwar Legacies," *Cardozo Law Review* 27, no. 4 (2005–2006): 1615–31.

5 Nina Valbousquet, "L'ouverture des archives du Vatican pour le pontificat de Pie XII (1939–1958): controverses mémorielles, apports historiographiques et usages de l'archive," in *Revue d'histoire moderne & contemporaine* 691, no. 1 (2022): 56–70; Nina Valbousquet, *Les âmes tièdes: Le Vatican face à la Shoah* (La Découverte, 2024); John Cornwell, *Hitler's*

Pope: The Secret History of Pius XII (Viking, 1999); Matteo Luigi Napolitano, *Pio XII tra Guerra e Pace: Profezia e diplomazia di un papa (1939–1945)* (Città Nuova, 2002).

6 Philip Pullella, "Church 'not afraid of history': Pope Francis to open secret Pius XII archives," Reuters, March 14, 2019, https://www.reuters.com/article/us-pope-archives-idUSKCN1QL11Q.

7 Frederic Spotts, *The Churches and Politics in Germany* (Wesleyan University Press, 1973).

8 Suzanne Brown-Fleming, *The Holocaust and Catholic Conscience: Cardinal Aloisius Muench and the Guilt Question in Germany* (University of Notre Dame Press, 2006).

9 Katharina von Kellenbach, *Mark of Cain: Guilt and Denial in the Post-War Lives of Nazi Perpetrators* (Oxford University Press, 2013); Rainer Bendel, ed., *Kirche der Sünder–Sündige Kirche? Beispiele für den Umgang mit Schuld nach 1945* (LIT, 2002).

10 Uki Goñi, *The Real Odessa: How Perón Brought the Nazi War Criminals to Argentina* (Granta Books, 2002). Goñi's groundbreaking book sparked many further studies, including individual biographies of Nazis who evaded Allied justice. To list a few of these contributions: Guy Walters, *Hunting Evil: The Nazi War Criminals Who Escaped and the Quest to Bring Them to Justice* (Broadway Books, 2009); Bettina Stangneth, *Eichmann Before Jerusalem: The Unexamined Life of a Mass Murderer* (Knopf, 2014); Peter Hammerschmidt, *Deckname Adler: Klaus Barbie und die westlichen Geheimdienste* (S. Fischer, 2014); Philippe Sands, *Ratline: Love, Lies and Justice on the Trail of a Nazi Fugitive* (Weidenfeld & Nicolson, 2020).

11 Gerald Steinacher, *Nazis on the Run: How Hitler's Henchmen Fled Justice* (Oxford University Press, 2011).

12 Michael Phayer, *Pius XII, the Holocaust, and the Cold War* (Indiana University Press, 2007).

Chapter 1. Judgment Day

1 Adolf Eichmann, "Meine Flucht: Bericht aus der Zelle in Jerusalem," World Exclusive in *The People*, London, NARA, RG 263 (CIA), War Crimes, CIA name files, IWG, box 14, Eichmann, Adolf, vol. 1; Steinacher, *Nazis on the Run*, 21–22.

2 Dwight D. Eisenhower, *Crusade in Europe* (Doubleday, 1948), 408–9.

3 Moscow Declaration, November 1, 1943; see Bradley F. Smith, *The American Road to Nuremberg: The Documentary Record 1944–1945* (Hoover Institution Press, 1982), 13–14.

4 Patricia M. Wald, "Running the Trial of the Century: The Nuremberg Legacy," *Cardozo Law Review* 27 (2006): 1559, 1574.

5 Atlantic Charter, August 14, 1941, Yale Law School, The Avalon Project, accessed October 30, 2021, https://avalon.law.yale.edu/wwii/atlantic.asp.

6 After the war, the old town was not rebuilt on the same site. A new town, also called Lidice, arose nearby.

7 Betsy Reed, "Churchill proposed 'three for one' bombing of German villages in retaliation for massacre of Czech civilians," *The Guardian*, January 1, 2006, https://www.theguardian.com/uk/2006/jan/02/secondworldwar.conservatives.

8 Richard Breitman, *Official Secrets: What the Nazis Planned, What the British and Americans Knew* (Hill & Wang, 1998), 172ff.

9 See Gerald Steinacher, *Humanitarians at War: The Red Cross in the Shadow of the Holocaust* (Oxford University Press, 2017); David P. Forsythe, *The Humanitarians: The International Committee of the Red Cross* (Cambridge University Press, 2005).

10 See Geoffrey Best, *War and Law since 1945* (Oxford University Press, 1994); and Steinacher, *Humanitarians at War.*

11 Moscow Declaration, November 1, 1943; see Smith, *The American Road to Nuremberg*, 13–14.

12 "The Tehran Conference, Proceedings of the Conference," November 29, 1943, 8:30 p.m., Bohlen Minutes, Foreign Relations of the United States: Diplomatic Papers, The Conferences at Cairo and Tehran, 1943, Bohlen Collection, accessed May 30, 2021, https://history.state.gov/historicaldocuments/frus1943CairoTehran/d368. See also Francine Hirsch, *Soviet Judgment at Nuremberg: A New History of the International Military Tribunal after World War II* (Oxford University Press, 2020), 32; Gary Jonathan Bass, *Stay the Hand of Vengeance: The Politics of War Crimes Tribunals* (Princeton University Press, 2000), 186.

13 On Soviet contributions, see Hirsch, *Soviet Judgment at Nuremberg.*

14 An earlier trial against Soviet Nazi collaborators was held in July 1943 in Krasnodar. See Arieh J. Kochavi, *Prelude to Nuremberg: Allied War Crimes Policy and the Question of Punishment* (University of North Carolina Press, 1998), 64, 68.

15 Kochavi, *Prelude to Nuremberg*, 66–73.

16 Christopher Simpson, *The Splendid Blond Beast: Money, Law, and Genocide in the Twentieth Century* (Common Courage Press, 2002), 246.

17 Christmas message by Franklin D. Roosevelt, December 24, 1943, Recorded Speeches and Utterances of Franklin D. Roosevelt, 1920–1945, FDR Library, accessed November 30, 2021, https://www.fdrlibrary.org/utterancesfdr.

18 Statement of President Roosevelt, March 24, 1944, Library of Congress, Jackson papers box 95, reel 1, Nuremberg war crimes file.

19 Bass, *Stay the Hand of Vengeance*, 10.

20 Michael Burleigh, *Moral Combat: Good and Evil in World War II* (Harper Collins, 2011), 544.

21 Simpson, *The Splendid Blond Beast*, 171. On the WRB, see Rebecca Erbelding, *Rescue Board: The Untold Story of America's Efforts to Save the Jews of Europe* (Anchor Books, 2018).

22 Bass, *Stay the Hand of Vengeance*, 157–69.

23 Cited in Michael Marrus, *The Nuremberg War Crimes Trial 1945–46: A Brief History with Documents*, 2nd ed. (Macmillan, 2018), 11.

24 Marrus, *Nuremberg War Crimes Trial*, 11.

25 John Simon, British Lord Chancellor, "Major war criminals," September 4, 1944, in Smith, *The American Road to Nuremberg*, 33.

26 Simon, "Major war criminals," in Smith, *The American Road to Nuremberg*, 33.

27 War Department Handbook of Military Government for Germany, "Table 'D'—Nazi police, party, para-military and governmental officers to be interned," September 1, 1944, reproduced in Smith, *The American Road to Nuremberg*, 15–16.

28 Elizabeth Borgwardt, *A New Deal for the World: America's Vision for Human Rights* (Belknap Press of Harvard University Press, 2005), 221.

29 Martin Gilbert, *Winston S. Churchill, Vol. 7: Road to Victory, 1941–1945* (Heinemann, 1986), 1201–2.

30 Taylor, *Anatomy*, 42.

31 Bass, *Stay the Hand of Vengeance*, 6.

32 Hirsch, *Soviet Judgment*, 45.

33 Just a few days earlier, April 26, 1945, Judge Samuel Rosenman had asked Jackson if he would be willing to run such a trial against major Nazi war criminals. Memorandum by Jackson after his phone call with Rosenman, April 27, 1945, Library of Congress, Jackson papers box 95, reel 1, Nuremberg war crimes file.

34 Marrus, *Nuremberg War Crimes Trial*, 14.

35 Robert H. Jackson, Report to the President, June 6, 1945, quoted in Marrus, *Nuremberg War Crimes Trial*, 14; for the whole report, see 106ff.

36 Durwood "Derry" Riedel, "The U.S. War Crimes Tribunals at the Former Dachau Concentration Camp: Lessons for Today?" *Berkeley Journal of International Law* 24, no. 2 (2006): 554–609, 554.

37 Annette Weinke, *Die Nürnberger Prozesse* (C. H. Beck, 2006), 20–21.

38 Telford Taylor, *Anatomy of the Nuremberg Trials, a Personal Memoir* (Knopf, 1992), 123–24.

39 See John Horne and Alan Kramer, *German Atrocities, 1914: A History of Denial* (Yale University Press, 2001); Larry Zuckerman, *The Rape of Belgium: The Untold Story of World War I* (New York University Press, 2004).

40 Jürgen Matthäus, "The Lessons of Leipzig: Punishing German War Criminals after the First World War," in *Atrocities on Trial: Historical Perspectives on the Politics of Prosecuting War Crimes*, ed. Patricia Heberer and Jürgen Matthäus (University of Nebraska Press, 2008), 15–16; Gerd Hankel, *Die Leipziger Prozesse: Deutsche Kriegsverbrechen und ihre strafrechtliche Verfolgung nach dem Ersten Weltkrieg* (Hamburger Edition, 2003).

41 Weinke, *Die Nürnberger Prozesse*, 22; Document 59, "Agreement and Charter, August 8, 1945," in Smith, *The American Road to Nuremberg*, 212–20.

42 Geoffrey Best, *War and Law since 1945* (Oxford University Press, 1994), 64.

43 Document 59, "Agreement and Charter, August 8, 1945," in Smith, *The American Road to Nuremberg*, 215.

44 Philippe Sands, *East West Street: On the Origins of "Genocide" and "Crimes Against Humanity"* (Vintage Books, 2017).

45 John Q. Barrett, "Raphael Lemkin and 'Genocide' at Nuremberg, 1945–1946," in The Genocide Convention Sixty Years after Its Adoption, ed. Christoph Safferling and Eckart Conze (T. M. C. Asser Press, 2010), 35–54.

46 "Convention on the Prevention and Punishment of the Crime of Genocide adopted by the General Assembly of the United Nations on 9 December 1948," The United Nations Treaty Collection, accessed August 29, 2024, https://treaties.un.org/doc/publication/unts/volume%2078/volume-78-i-1021-english.pdf.

47 Ian Buruma, *Year Zero: A History of 1945* (The Penguin Press, 2013), 234.

48 Bundesverfasungsgericht, Judgement Nr 2 BvR 1851/94, 24/10/1996, https://www.bundesverfassungsgericht.de/ (accessed October 14, 2024). I thank Dr. Stefan Schulte for directing me to this information.

49 Elizabeth Borgwardt, *A New Deal for the World: America's Vision for Human Rights* (Belknap Press, 2005), 197.

50 Borgwardt, *A New Deal for the World*, 197.

51 Kim Christian Priemel, *The Betrayal: The Nuremberg Trials and German Divergence* (Oxford University Press 2016), 6.

52 Weinke, *Die Nürnberger Prozesse*, 36.

53 Anna M. Cienciala, Natalia S. Lebedeva, and Wojciech Materski, eds., *Katyn: A Crime without Punishment* (Yale University Press, 2007), 1ff.

54 Weinke, *Die Nürnberger Prozesse*, 57; Borgwardt, *A New Deal for the World*, 217. For reactions, see also James Le Sueur, *Uncivil War: Intellectuals and Identity Politics during the Decolonization of Algeria* (University of Nebraska Press, 2006), 104–6.

55 Power, *A Problem from Hell*, 49; Weinke, *Die Nürnberger Prozesse*, 54.

56 For more on the mass suicides at the end of the war, see Christian Goeschel, *Suicide in Nazi Germany* (Oxford University Press, 2009).

57 There are many examples. Allen Dulles, later director of the CIA, shielded the SS *Obergruppenführer* Karl Wolff, the highest-ranking SS leader to survive. See Kerstin von Lingen, *Allen Dulles, the OSS, and Nazi War Criminals: The Dynamics of Selective Prosecution* (Cambridge University Press, 2013). See also Michael Salter, *Nazi War Crimes, US Intelligence and Selective Prosecution at Nuremberg: Controversies Regarding the Role of the Office of Strategic Services* (Routledge–Cavendish, 2007).

58 Memorandum entitled "List of Major War Criminals", August 29, 1945, Harry S. Truman Library, Collection: The War Crimes Trials at Nuremberg, Series: War Crimes File, accessed November 28, 2021, https://www.trumanlibrary.gov/library/research-files/memorandum-entitled-list-major-war-criminals.

59 Martha Minow, *Between Vengeance and Forgiveness: Facing History after Genocide and Mass Violence* (Beacon Press, 1998), 41.

60 Susanne Karstedt, "The Lives and Times of Sentenced Nazi War Criminals: Renegotiating Guilt and Innocence in Post-Nuremberg Germany 1950–1975," in *Transitional Justice: Images and Memories*, ed. Chrisje Brants, et al. (Routledge, 2013), 37.

61 Hans-Christian Jasch and Wolf Kaiser, *Der Holocaust vor deutschen Gerichten: Amnestieren, Verdrängen, Bestrafen* (Reclam, 2017), 17.

62 In contrast with the U.S. prosecution approach, the French prosecution explicitly referred to the guilt of the whole German nation and alleged the country's tendency toward barbarism.

63 Taylor, *Anatomy of the Nuremberg Trials*, 167–68.

64 Taylor, *Anatomy of the Nuremberg Trials*, 167.

65 "Closing Statement by Robert H. Jackson," Robert H. Jackson Center, accessed July 12, 2022, https://www.roberthjackson.org/nuremberg-event/closing-statement-by-robert-h-jackson/.

66 Thomas J. Dodd to Mary Grace Murphy Dodd, June 1, 1946, in Christopher J. Dodd, ed., *Letters from Nuremberg: My Father's Narrative of a Quest for Justice* (Crown Publishers, 2007), 313.

67 Conducted in four languages (German, English, Russian, and French), the proceedings also were published in 42 volumes, each containing thousands of pages of material from the tribunal. The whole series is available from many major archives and national

libraries, as well as accessible online at https://www.loc.gov/rr/frd/Military_Law/NT_major-war-criminals.html.

68 Marrus, *Nuremberg War Crimes Trial*, v.

69 AAV Segr stato Comm Soccorsi 284, fasc. 1034, photo f. 136r.

70 Laura Jockusch, "Justice at Nuremberg? Jewish Responses to Nazi War-Crime Trials in Allied-Occupied Germany," *Jewish Social Studies: History, Culture, Society* 19, no. 1 (Fall 2012): 110.

71 Cornelia Brink, *Ikonen der Vernichtung: Öffentlicher Gebrauch von Fotografien aus nationalsozialistischen Konzentrationslagern nach 1945* (Akademie Verlag, 1998), 103ff.; Weinke, *Die Nürnberger Prozesse*, 46.

72 Richard J. Evans, *Rituals of Retribution: Capital Punishment in Germany, 1600–1987* (Oxford University Press, 1996), 743.

73 See Priemel, *The Betrayal.*

74 Priemel, *The Betrayal*, 3.

75 See Gerald Reitlinger, *The SS: Alibi of a Nation, 1922–45* (Viking Press, 1957).

76 Marrus, *Nuremberg*, 19; Truman Presidential Museum and Library, The War Crimes Trials at Nuremberg, letter from Jacobson to Robert H. Jackson, July 27, 1945, accessed July 12, 2022, https://www.trumanlibrary.gov/library/research-files/letter-jacob-robinson-robert-h-jackson. See also Stangneth, *Eichmann before Jerusalem*, 59–69.

77 Weinke, *Die Nürnberger Prozesse*, 43.

78 Robert H. Jackson, "Closing Statement at Nuremberg."

79 Hitler's architect, Albert Speer, former minister of armaments, uniquely offered some self-critique and remorse, though the honesty of his assertions remains debatable.

80 Quoted in Roger Manvell, Heinrich Fraenkel, *Goering: The Rise and Fall of the Notorious Nazi Leader* (Skyhorse Publishing, 2011), 390.

81 "La conclusione dei giudici al processo di Norimberga," *Osservatore Romano*, October 2, 1946, 1.

82 "Il verdetto di condanna al processo di Norimberga," *Osservatore Romano*, October 3, 1946, 1.

83 "Goering Suicide, 10 Nazis Hang," *Daily News*, October 16, 1946, 3. "Final Scenes at Nuremberg: Unsolved Problem of How Göring Got His Poison," *Manchester Guardian*, October 17, 1946, 5.

84 Bass, *Stay the Hand of Vengeance*, 203–5. See also Kevin Jon Heller, *The Nuremberg Military Tribunals and the Origins of International Criminal Law* (Oxford University Press, 2011).

85 Otto Kirchheimer, *Political Justice: The Use of Legal Procedure for Political Ends* (Princeton University Press, 1961), 340.

86 Bass, *Stay the Hand of Vengeance*, 6; Weinke, *Die Nürnberger Prozesse*, 121.

87 Jeffrey Herf, *Divided Memory. The Nazi Past in the Two Germanies* (Harvard University Press, 1997), 69.

Chapter 2. The Vicar of Christ

1 Robert A. Ventresca, *Soldier of Christ: The Life of Pope Pius XII* (The Belknap Press of Harvard University Press, 2013), 4.

2 Among his friends was Guido Mendes, who had a Jewish family background. Later, Pacelli would help the Mendes family emigrate to Switzerland to escape Italian racial laws. See Ventresca, *Soldier of Christ*, 26.

3 Ventresca, *Soldier of Christ*, 39.

4 John F. Pollard, "The Holy See and Neutrality: Vatican Diplomacy 1870–1929," in *The Vatican and Permanent Neutrality*, eds. Marshall J. Breger and Herbert R. Reginbogin (Lexington Books, 2022), 5.

5 Pollard, "The Holy See and Neutrality," 10.

6 Ventresca, *Soldier of Christ*, 48.

7 Ventresca, *Soldier of Christ*, 26–27.

8 Ventresca, *Soldier of Christ*, 52–54; John Cornwell, *Hitler's Pope: The Secret History of Pius XII* (Viking, 1999), 72–79.

9 See Michael Brenner, *In Hitler's Munich: Jews, the Revolution, and the Rise of Nazism* (Princeton University Press, 2022), 119–128.

10 Ventresca, *Soldier of Christ*, 54–55.

11 Ventresca, *Soldier of Christ*, 57; Phayer, *Pius XII, the Holocaust, and the Cold War*, 259–68.

12 Richard J. Evans, *The Coming of the Third Reich* (Penguin Press, 2003), 72.

13 Segretaria di Stato di Sua Santità al Monsignor Eugenio Pacelli, Nunzio Apostolico, München, Dal Vaticano, 13 May 1924, N. 30542, AAV, Nunz. Berlino 30, fasc. 2, f. 003r-006r.

14 Apostolische Nuntiatur Bayern, München, den 31. März 1924 (Nicht für die Öffentlichkeit!) [Pacelli] "An die Hochwürdigsten Herren Erzbischöfe, Bischöfe und Obere der Orden und Kongregationen in Deutschland", AAV, Archivio della Nunziatura di Berlino (Pacelli), Box 31, Fasc. 4, 005r-006v.

15 Reichskanzler [Wilhelm] Marx, [to Pacelli], 16. Mai 1927, N. 37444, AAV, Nunz. Berlino (Pacelli), 30, Fasc. 3, f. 153r.

16 See also Hubert Wolf, *Pope and Devil: The Vatican's Archives and the Third Reich* (The Belknap Press of Harvard University Press, 2010), 9; Giovanni Miccoli, *I dilemmi e i silenzi di Pio XII: Vaticano, seconda guerra mondiale e Shoah* (Bur Storia, 2000), 213–53.

17 Fürstbischof von Breslau Bertram to Pacelli, 30 September 1924, AAV, Archivio della Nunziatura di Berlino (Pacelli), 91, Fasc. 6, f. 11.

18 Fürstbischof von Breslau Bertram to Pacelli, 30 September 1924, AAV, Archivio della Nunziatura di Berlino (Pacelli), 91, Fasc. 6, f. 11.

19 Ventresca, *Solder of Christ*, 65. See also Frank J. Coppa, *The Life and Pontificate of Pius XII: Between History and Controversy* (The Catholic University of America Press, 2013), 74–100.

20 Maria d'Arienzo, "The Lateran Treaty and the Hermeneutics of the Holy See Neutrality: The Final Defeat of the Papal State and the Roman Question," in *The Vatican and Permanent Neutrality*, eds. Marshall J. Breger and Herbert R. Reginbogin (Lexington Books, 2022), 45.

21 Cited in Dennis A. Castillo, *Papal Diplomacy from 1914 to 1989: The Seventy-Five Years War* (Lexington Books, 2020), 81.

22 See *The Vatican and Permanent Neutrality*, xv. For this book, I use the term "Vatican" to refer broadly to the Pope, his closest advisors and staff, and the institutions under the Holy See's jurisdiction.

23 David Kertzer, *The Pope and Mussolini: The Secret History of Pius XI and the Rise of Fascism in Europe* (Random House, 2014), 98ff.

24 Wolf, *Pope and Devil*, 143.

25 Kevin P. Spicer, "German Catholicism's Lost Opportunity to Confront Antisemitism Before the Machtergreifung," in *Religion, Ethnonationalism, and Antisemitism in the Era of the Two World Wars*, eds. Kevin P. Spicer and Rebecca Carter-Chand (McGill-Queen's University Press, 2022), 128.

26 Anton Pelinka, *Faschismus? Zur Beliebigkeit eines politischen Begriffs* (Boehlau Verlag Wien Koeln, 2022), 55.

27 Mark Riebling, *Church of Spies: The Pope's Secret War Against Hitler* (Basic Books, 2015), 25.

28 Ventresca, *Soldier of Christ*, 107.

29 Emilio Gentile, *Contro Cesare: Cristianesimo e totalitarismo nell'epoca dei fascismi* (Feltrinelli, 2010), 13.

30 John Connelly, *From Enemy to Brother: The Revolution in Catholic Teaching on the Jews 1933–1965* (Harvard University Press, 2012).

31 At the time of Hitler's *Machtergreifung* in 1933, only around 550,000 Jews lived in the German Reich. Given census data indicating a German population of approximately 65 million men, Jews accounted for about 0.8 percent of the population. Zentrum gegen Vertreibungen, Ausstellung "Juden in Deutschland ab 1933," accessed October 18, 2024, https://www.statistik-des-holocaust.de/stat_ger_pop.html; https://www.ausstellung-erzwungenewege.de/juden-in-deutschland-ab-1933.

32 George Mosse, *Toward the Final Solution: A History of European Racism* (University of Wisconsin, 2020); Robert S. Wistrich, *Antisemitism: The Longest Hatred* (Thames Methuen, 1991).

33 Kevin P. Spicer, ed., *Antisemitism, Christian Ambivalence, and the Holocaust* (Indiana University Press, 2007).

34 Lucia Ceci, *The Vatican and Mussolini's Italy* (Brill, 2017), 235.

35 Alfred Rosenberg, *Der Mythus des 20. Jahrhunderts: Eine Wertung der seelisch-geistigen Gestaltenkämpfe unserer Zeit* (Hoheneichen Verlag, 1930). On Rosenberg, see Jürgen Matthäus and Frank Bajohr, *The Political Diary of Alfred Rosenberg and the Onset of the Holocaust* (Rowman & Littlefield, 2015).

36 On the papacy of Pius XII and its views on Jews, see also Nina Valbousquet, *Les âmes tièdes: Le Vatican face à la Shoah* (La Découverte, 2024).

37 Wolf, *Pope and Devil*, 266.

38 Wolf, *Pope and Devil*, 207–8; Lucia Ceci, *The Vatican and Mussolini's Italy* (Brill, 2017), 229–30.

39 Kertzer, *The Pope and Mussolini*, 354–69. Georges Passelecq and Bernhard Suchecky, *The Hidden Encyclical of Pius XI*, trans. Steven Rendell (Harcourt Brace, 1997).

40 Jacques Kornberg, *The Pope's Dilemma: Pius XII Faces Atrocities and Genocide in the Second World War* (University of Toronto Press, 2015), 245.

41 Pascalina Lehnert, *Ich durfte Ihm dienen: Erinnerungen an Papst Pius XII* (Verlag Johann Wilhelm Naumann, 1982), 101.

42 Doris Bergen, *Between God and Hitler: Military Chaplains in Nazi Germany* (Cambridge University Press, 2023), 229.

43 Long forgotten or ostracized in postwar Austria, Jägerstätter was finally rehabilitated, beatified, and declared a martyr by the Church in 2007. The 2019 film *A Hidden Life* by writer-director Terrence Malick brought the story to a wider international audience.

44 See Ventresca, *Soldier of Christ*, 176–88; David Kertzer, *The Pope at War: The Secret History of Pius XII, Mussolini, and Hitler* (Random House, 2022), 224ff.

45 Klaus Kühlwein, *Pius XII und die Deportation der Juden Roms* (Peter Lang, 2019), 46; Kertzer, *The Pope at War*, 216, 224–25.

46 Phayer, *Pius XII, the Holocaust, and the Cold War*, 47.

47 Susan Zuccotti, *Under His Very Windows: The Vatican and the Holocaust in Italy* (Yale University Press, 2000), 1; Kertzer, *The Pope at War*, 260.

48 Zuccotti, *Under His Very Windows*, 162; Kertzer, *The Pope at War*, 359–72.

49 Kühlwein, *Pius XII und die Deportation der Juden Roms*, 257ff.

50 Kertzer, *The Pope at War*, 367.

51 Kühlwein, *Pius XII und die Deportation der Juden Roms*, 286.

52 Brian Fleming, *The Vatican Pimpernel: The Wartime Exploits of Monsignor Hugh O'Flaherty* (Collins Press, 2008). For an overview, see David Bankier, Dan Michman, Iael Nidam-Orvieto, eds., *Pius XII and the Holocaust: Current State of Research* (Yad Vashem, 2012), 115–44.

53 Myron C. Taylor, Vatican City, to the Secretary of State, March 26, 1945 "Subject: Asylum given to Jews by the Catholic Clergy during the German occupation of Rome." NARA, RG 59, Entry 1068, Box 9, Vatican City.

54 Claims that the pope's actions during the Holocaust saved over 800,000 Jews from death lacks substance. For such claims, see Pinchas E. Lapide, *Three Popes and the Jews* (Hawthorn Books, 1967), 214.

55 James Mace Ward, *Priest, Politician, Collaborator: Jozef Tiso and the Making of Fascist Slovakia* (Cornell University Press, 2013).

56 Robert B. McCormick, *Croatia Under Ante Pavelić: America, the Ustaše and Croatian Genocide in World War II* (I.B. Tauris, 2014).

57 See Kevin P. Spicer, *Hitler's Priests: Catholic Clergy and National Socialism* (Northern Illinois University Press, 2008).

58 Yehuda Bauer, *A History of the Holocaust* (Franklin Watts, 2001), 345–46. See also Randolph L. Braham, *The Politics of Genocide: The Holocaust in Hungary*, condensed edition (Wayne State University Press, 2000), 240–43.

59 Kertzer, *The Pope at War*, 445–46; Miccoli, *I dilemmi e i silenzi di Pio XII*, 241–53.

60 Cardinal Domenico Tardini, *Memories of Pius XII* (The Newman Press, 1961), 170.

61 Sacra Congregazione degli Affari Ecclesiastici Straordinari to Myron Taylor, September 20, 1944, NARA, RG 59, Myron Taylor File, Entry 1068, Box 8, Decimal File 1944–45, 800 Germany—fate after hostilities cease.

62 Sacra Congregazione degli Affari Ecclesiastici Straordinari to Myron Taylor, September 20, 1944, NARA, RG 59, Myron Taylor File, Entry 1068, Box 8, Decimal File 1944–45, 800 Germany—fate after hostilities cease.

63 Ventresca, *Soldier of Christ*, 87.

64 Kertzer, *The Pope at War*, 336.

65 Giuliana Chamedes, *A Twentieth-Century Crusade: The Vatican's Battle to Remake Christian Europe* (Harvard University Press, 2019), 235.

66 Radiomessaggio di Sua Santità Pio XII ai popoli del mondo intero, Sunday December 24, 1944, Discorsi e Radiomessaggi di Sua Santità Pio XII, VI, Quinto anno di Pontificato, 2 marzo 1944—1 marzo 1945, 235–251; Tipografia Poliglotta Vaticana, accessed June 5, 2021, https://www.vatican.va/content/pius-xii/it/speeches/1944/documents/hf_p-xii_spe_19441224_natale.html

67 Mark W. Clark, *Calculated Risk* (Harper & Brothers Publishers, 1950), 374.

68 Chamedes, *A Twentieth-Century Crusade*, 271.

69 "Era Atomica" (commentary), "Siamo ad un' era nuova?" *Osservatore Romano*, August 10, 1945, 1; "Una seconda bomba atomica sul Giappone," *Osservatore Romano*, August 10, 1945, 1.

70 "Missione materna," *Osservatore Romano*, June 4, 1944, 1.

71 "Churchill talks with Pope on peace," *The New York Times*, August 26, 1944, 7. See also "Pope on punishing War Criminals, Statement of Pope Pius XII to Winston Churchill," Press Release, Independent Jewish Press Service, August 28, 1944, Truman Library, The War Crimes Trials at Nuremberg Collection, C107-10-54.

72 Tardini, *Memories of Pius XII*, 170.

73 Hans Woller, *Die Abrechnung mit dem Faschismus in Italien 1943 bis 1948* (Oldenbourg Wissenschaftsverlag, 1996), 264–81, 279.

74 James Holland, *Italy's Sorrow: A Year of War, 1944–45* (St. Martin's Press, 2008); Claudio Pavone, *A Civil War: A History of the Italian Resistance* (Verso Books, 2014); Carlo Gentile, *I crimini di guerra tedeschi in Italia: 1943–1945* (Enaudi Editore, 2022).

75 See Roy Domenico, *Italian Fascists on Trial, 1943–1948* (University of North Carolina Press, 1991).

76 Romano Canosa, *Le sanzioni contro il fascismo. Processi ed epurazioni a Milano negli anni 1945–47* (Gabriele Mazzotta editore, 1978), 66; Andrea Casazza, *La fuga dei Nazisti: Mengelke, Eichmann, Priebke, Pavelic da Genova all'impunità* (il melangolo, 2007).

77 Phayer, *Pius XII, the Holocaust, and the Cold War*, 161.

78 Canosa, *Le sanzioni contro il fascismo*, 7. See also Paolo Caroli, *Transitional Justice in Italy and the Crimes of Fascism and Nazism* (Routledge, 2022).

79 Thomas Schlemmer, "Kein Nürnberg in Rom. Italien, die Alliierten und die Kriegsverbrecherfrage," in *Im Schatten von Nürnberg. Transnationale Ahndung von NS-Verbrechen*, eds. Enrico Heitzer et al. (Metropol, 2019), 188–206.

80 Robert Jackson Diary entry Monday August 27, 1945 Robert Houghwout Jackson Papers, Box 95 (Reel 1), Library of Congress.

Chapter 3. The Pope and Nuremberg

1 "Allocuzione di Sua Santità al Sacro Collegio [dei cardinali presenti a Roma] in risposta agli auguri per il Suo onomastico. Il Sommo Pontefice, delineata la natura e i caratteri del sistema nazionalsocialista e le sue persecuzioni contro la Chiesa Cattolica, indica

all'umanità la via sicura per eliminare ogni violenza brutale e traccia per i reggitori dei popoli le note essenziali di una vera pace," in *L'Osservatore Romano*, June 3, 1945, 1; "Text of Pope Pius XII's Address to the Sacred College of Cardinals," *The New York Times*, June 3, 1945, accessed June 3, 2021, https://www.nytimes.com/1945/06/03/archives/text-of-pope-pius-xiis-address-to-the-sacred-college-of-cardinals-i.html. On its importance for Catholic postwar apologetics, see Mark Edward Ruff, *The Battle for the Catholic Past in Germany, 1945–1980* (Cambridge University Press, 2017), 21.

2 "Allocuzione di Sua Santità al Sacro Collegio."

3 Ventresca, *Soldier of Christ*, 220.

4 Tardini, *Memories of Pius XII*, 170.

5 "For the ambassador, June 4, 1945," Harold H. Tittmann, *Inside the Vatican of Pius XII: The Memoir of an American Diplomat during World War II* (Doubleday, 2004), 213.

6 Chamedes, *A Twentieth-Century Crusade*, 239.

7 Claire Hulme and Michael Salter, "The Nazi's Persecution of Religion as a War Crime: The OSS's Response Within the Nuremberg Trials Process," *Rutgers Journal of Law and Religion* 3, no. 2 (2001), https://sites.camden.rutgers.edu/wp-content/uploads/sites/4/2017/03/Nazi-Persecution-HulmeSalter.pdf (misplaced apostrophe in "Nazi's" appears in source).

8 Oral history transcript, "The Reminiscences of Robert H. Jackson," based on interviews by Harlan B. Phillips, 1955, "Part VIII Nuremberg–Operation Justice," 1311, Robert Houghwout Jackson Papers, Library of Congress, Box 259, Folder 3. Special thanks to Lewis Wyman, Reference Librarian at the Library of Congress, for pointing me to this important source.

9 Jackson, "The Reminiscences of Robert H. Jackson," 1311.

10 John Q. Barrett, "With Francis at the Vatican (1928 & 1946)," accessed May 18, 2021, https://thejacksonlist.com/wp-content/uploads/2014/02/20130317-Jackson-List-Francis-Vatican.pdf; Jackson, "The Reminiscences of Robert H. Jackson," 1311.

11 Diary entry August 28, 1945, Robert Houghwout Jackson Papers, Box 95 (Reel 1), Library of Congress.

12 Hirsch, *Soviet Judgment at Nuremberg*, 53.

13 Diary entry August 28, 1945, Robert Houghwout Jackson Papers, Box 95 (Reel 1), Library of Congress.

14 Diary entry August 28, 1945, Robert Houghwout Jackson Papers, Box 95 (Reel 1), Library of Congress.

15 Diary entry August 28, 1945, Robert Houghwout Jackson Papers, Box 95 (Reel 1), Library of Congress.

16 Diary entry August 28, 1945, Robert Houghwout Jackson Papers, Box 95 (Reel 1), Library of Congress.

17 John Q. Barrett in his introduction to Robert H. Jackson, "The Faith of My Fathers," *University of Pennsylvania Law Review* 168, no. 1 (2019): 4.

18 Diary entry, August 28, 1945, Robert Houghwout Jackson Papers, Box 95 (Reel 1), Library of Congress.

19 Jackson, "The Reminiscences of Robert H. Jackson," 1314.

20 Jackson, "The Reminiscences of Robert H. Jackson," 1314.
21 Jackson, "The Reminiscences of Robert H. Jackson," 1315.
22 Taylor, *The Anatomy of the Nuremberg Trials*, 94.
23 Phayer, *The Catholic Church and the Holocaust, 1930–1965* (Indiana University Press, 2001), 138–9.
24 "La sede del Tribunale militare internazionale," *Osservatore Romano*, August 10, 1945, 1.
25 See Jonathan D. Huener, *The Polish Catholic Church Under German Occupation, 1939–1945* (Indiana University Press, 2021).
26 International Military Tribunal Nuremberg (ed.), *Trial of the Major War Criminals by the International Military Tribunal, Nuremberg 14 November 1945 to 1 October 1946* vol. 32, (Nuremberg, Germany, 1948), 84ff.
27 Jackson, "The Reminiscences of Robert H. Jackson," 1315–16.
28 "Allocution of his Holiness Pope Pius XII to the Sacred College June 2nd, 1945," in International Military Tribunal Nuremberg (ed.), *Trial of the Major War Criminals by the International Military Tribunal, Nuremberg 14 November 1945 to 1 October 1946* vol. 32, (Nuremberg, Germany, 1948), 112. Axel Fischer from the "Memorium Nuremberg Trials" helped me locate this and some other sources from the Nuremberg trials.
29 "Allocution of his Holiness Pope Pius XII to the Sacred College June 2nd, 1945," 112.
30 Harold Tittmann on December 3, 1945, forwards to Washington a translation of an article from *Osservatore Romano della Domenica*, December 2, 1945, commenting on the statement "Between War and Peace," by U.S. Bishops, dated November 18, 1945, NARA, RG 59, Entry 1068, Box 9.
31 "Atti del processo di Martin Bormann e notizie sui 'criminali di guerra'", AAV, Segr. Stato Comm. Soccorsi 284, fasc. 1034, here f. 103a.
32 "Atti del processo di Martin Bormann e notizie sui 'criminali di guerra'", AAV, Segr. Stato Comm. Soccorsi 284, fasc. 1034, f. 139r–140r, 151r–152v, 152ar. The internal inquiries date from 1972 and refer to older press articles about Bormann and the Church, published in 1948.
33 For the Vatican's views on "good" and "bad" Germans and the case of ambassador Ernst von Weizsäcker, see David I. Kertzer, *Un Papa in Guerra: La storia segreta di Mussolini, Hitler e Pio XII* (Garzanti, 2022).
34 Frau Martha von Papen to Pope Pius XII, 21 August 1945; Vatican internal summary by Zabkar, AAV, Segr. Stato, Titoli, anno 1950, Stati 735/3, "Processo di Norimberga 1947 Interessamento della S. Sede in favore del Barone Franz von Papen," f. 003r and 002r.
35 Justice Jackson, telegram to Tittmann, contained in a letter from Tittmann to Montini, 28 November 1945, AAV, Segr. Stato, Titoli, anno 1950, Stati 735/3, "Processo di Norimberga 1947 Interessamento della S. Sede in favore del Barone Franz von Papen," f. 009r.
36 Letter Martha von Papen to the Vatican, 15 May 1948, AAV, Segr. Stato, Titoli, anno 1950, Stati 735/3, "Processo di Norimberga 1947 Interessamento della S. Sede in favore del Barone Franz von Papen," f. 014r-015v.
37 Muench's office Visitator Apostolicus to Vatican Secretariat of State, 10 December 1948, AAV, Segr. Stato, Titoli, anno 1950, Stati 735/3, "Processo di Norimberga 1947 Interessamento della S. Sede in favore del Barone Franz von Papen," f. 024r, 024v.

38 Office Muench [Rossi] Visitator Apostolicus to Montini, 29 January 1949, Archivio Apostolico Vatican (AAV), Arch. Nunz. Berlino 159, fasc. 42, Fasc. Kriegsgefangene 1950–1959 II—A—C—15, 025r, 025v.

39 Marie von Neurath to Pope Pius XII, 15 August 1945, AAV, Segr. Stato, Titoli (1936–2005), Anno 1950, Stati 735_1, f. 037r, 039r.

40 Montini to Marie von Neurath, 4 October 1946, AAV, Segr. Stato, Titoli (1936–2005), Anno 1950, Stati 735_1, f. 042r.

41 Marie von Neurath to Pope Pius XII, 18 June 1948, and report of daughter about visit in Spandau, AAV, Segr. Stato, Titoli (1936–2005), Anno 1950, Stati 735_1, f. 052r. 045r-047r.

42 Muench to Montini, 31 July 1948, AAV, Segr. Stato, Titoli (1936–2005), Anno 1950, Stati 735_1, f. 052r.

43 Gabriel N. Finder and Alexander V. Prusin, *Justice Behind the Iron Curtain: Nazis on Trial in Communist Poland* (Toronto: University of Toronto Press, 2018); on Hans Frank, see 79ff.

44 "Reichsminister Dr. Hans Frank, Minister im Regime des Nationalsozialismus", short summary of his background, no date, Archiv des Erzbistums München und Freising (AEMF), NL Faulhaber, Signatur 8504 (Entnazifizierung—Dr. Hans Frank, Bekehrungen von Kriegsverbrechern). See also Niklas Frank, *Meine deutsche Mutter*, 2nd ed. (C. Bertelsmann Verlag, 2005), 378. Frank had been baptized *Alt-Katholik* as a child: Taufregister, Alt-Katholische Gemeinde Karlsruhe, Eintrag Hans Michael Frank, born on May 23, 1900, and baptized on June 4, 1900. Copy in possession of author. Special thanks to Vicar Christoph Lichdi, Alt-Katholische Pfarrei Karlsruhe. See also "Taufschein ausgestellt für Reichsminister Dr. Hans Frank, 22. August 1936," signed Pfarrverweser. Archiv Alt-Katholische Gemeinde Karlsruhe. The "old Catholics" broke away from the pope in the 1800s.

45 Jackson, "The Reminiscences of Robert H. Jackson," 1315.

46 Frank repeatedly denied the events when writing to Church authorities. A note in Cardinal Faulhaber's papers that reported about the Nuremberg incident in detail underlined, somewhat ironically, that Frank would not have left the Church but rather left it again, after having been admitted into the Catholic Church only recently. AEMF, NL Faulhaber, Signatur 8504 (Entnazifizierung—Dr. Hans Frank, Bekehrungen von Kriegsverbrechern), Aufzeichnung.

47 Hans Frank, *Im Angesicht des Galgens: Deutung Hitlers und seiner Zeit auf Grund eigener Erlebnisse und Erkenntnisse, geschrieben im Nürnberger Justizgefängnis* (Friedrich Alfred Beck Verlag Munich—Gräfelfing, 1953), 457–59, here especially 458–59.

48 Regarding Faulhaber and Frank, see Gerald J. Steinacher, "Vergeben und Vergessen? Kardinal Faulhaber, der Vatikan und die Prozesse gegen NS-Kriegsverbrecher," in *Katholizismus im Umbruch? Michael Kardinal von Faulhaber und die katholische „Ordnung" in der ersten Hälfte des 20. Jahrhunderts*, ed. Matthias Daufratshofer, Peer Volkmann, and Moritz Fischer, Münchner Kunsthistorische Studien (Kohlhammer, 2025), 221–42.

49 Telegram-Entwurf (draft), 4 October 1946, AEMF, NL Faulhaber, (Entnazifizierung—Dr. Hans Frank (1943–1951)), Signatur: 8504.

50 Secretariat of State of the Holy See, 8 October 1946, regarding telegram from Berne, signed Bertoli, AAV, Segr. Stato, Commissione Soccorsi 259, Tedeschi Civili Germania fasc. 366, f. 003r, Circa la condanna del Gauleiter Frank.

51 Notes dated 10 October and 11 October 1946, AAV, Segr. Stato, Commissione Soccorsi 259, Tedeschi Civili Germania fasc. 366, f. 002r, Circa la condanna del Gauleiter Frank. The diplomats in receipt of the messages were Gowen (United States), Osborne (Great Britain), and Bourdeillette (France).

52 Typewritten text with handwritten notes, dated October 10, 1946, AAV, Segr. Stato, Commissione Soccorsi 259, Tedeschi Civili Germania fasc. 366, f. 004r, Circa la condanna del Gauleiter Frank.

53 Montini to Faulhaber, dated 4 October 1946 (with original signature by Montini), AEMF, NL Faulhaber, Signatur 8504 (Entnazifizierung—Dr. Hans Frank, Bekehrungen von Kriegsverbrechern). The date of the letter implies that Montini wrote Faulhaber immediately after his first steps, though this date is not completely in line with the timing of events based on the Vatican documents. A handwritten note suggests the letter was received by Faulhaber only as late as December 1946.

54 See „Erklärung Kardinal Faulhabers," in *Neue Zürcher Zeitung*, 22 Oktober 1946, Abendausgabe, Blatt 6, [2]. "Gnadengesuch von Kardinal Faulhaber für Frank, in Neue Zürcher Nachrichten von ca. 20. Oktober 1946" AEMF, NL Faulhaber, (Entnazifizierung—Dr. Hans Frank), Signatur: 8504. See also notes regarding a telephone inquiry by a journalist named Tomaszetwska, from the Polish Catholic press, October 6, 1946, noon. The records show that Faulhaber's office was hesitant to answer any of the journalist's questions about Frank. Faulhaber's staff eventually released a two-sentence statement: "The Cardinal has not submitted a clemency appeal on his own initiative. The Cardinal has stated personal reasons to the Holy Father, which speak in favor of an appeal for Frank." Records in his papers indicate that Faulhaber tried to wriggle himself and the Vatican out of an uncomfortable situation of his own making.

55 See the noted newspaper article, "Anche Fritsche è stato arrestato. I morituri corretti e depressi," *Giornale della Sera*, October 11, 1946, page 1, AAV, Comm. Soccorsi 259, fasc. 366, Frank, f. 009r. For the Vatican's response, see also „Alle Gnadengesuche abgelehnt" in Vaterland, 11. Oktober 1946, Entnazifizierung—Dr. Hans Frank, AEMF, NL Faulhaber, (Entnazifizierung—Dr. Hans Frank), Signatur: 8504.

56 Report by Father Sixtus O'Connor about the execution of Hans Frank, 21 October 1946, AEMF, NL Faulhaber, Signatur 8504 (Entnazifizierung—Dr. Hans Frank). See also Tim Townsend, *Mission at Nuremberg: An American Army Chaplain and the Trial of the Nazis* (William Morrow, 2014), 274.

57 Frank, *Der Vater: Eine Abrechnung*, 10.

58 Pater Sixtus O'Connor to Frank's son Norman, 21 October 1946, AEMF, NL Faulhaber, Signatur 8504 [Dr. Hans Frank (1943–1951)].

59 Lawyer Dr. Gustav Steinbauer to Faulhaber, 5 October 1946, AEMF, NL Faulhaber, Signatur: 8503 (Kriegsverbrecherprozesse in Nürnberg Dr. Hans Frank, Rudolf Heß, Seyss-Inquart u.a.).

60 For instance, in the case of the Nazi mayor of the town of Penzberg, Bavaria. See Steinacher, "Vergeben und vergessen? Kardinal Faulhaber, der Vatikan und die Prozesse gegen NS-Kriegsverbrecher."

61 Frank M. Buscher, Michael Phayer, "German Catholic Bishops and the Holocaust 1940–1952," *German Studies Review* 11, no. 3 (1988): 463–85, 478.

62 Note Dell' Acqua, 7 June 1946, AAV, Segr. Stato, Titoli (1936–2005), Anno 1950, Stati 735_2: 1946, f. 002r.

63 On Faulhaber, see Steinacher, "Vergeben und vergessen? Kardinal Faulhaber, der Vatikan und die Prozesse gegen NS-Kriegsverbrecher"; Thomas Forster, *„Zweiter Kirchenkampf oder Stellvertreterdiskurs? Katholischer Konservatismus und die Interpretation des Katholizismus im Nationalsozialismus nach 1945,"* in *Zwischen Revolutionsschock und Schulddebatte: Münchner Katholizismus und Protestantismus im 20. Jahrhundert,* Theologie geschichte Beiheft 7, ed. Antonia Leugers (Universaar, 2013).

64 Max Radler, „Die treusorgende Glucke," *Der Simpl,* July 1946, cover page. See also Antonia Leugers, „Introduction: Zwischen Revolutionsschock und Schulddebatte," in Leugers (ed.), *Zwischen Revolutionsschock und Schulddebatte,* 8.

65 Max Radler, „Schwarz wird weiss oder mechanische Entnazifizierung," *Der Simpl,* June 1946, 63.

66 Faulhaber to Holy Father [through Father Leiber?], dated October 17, 1946, „In der Schweiz", AEMF, NL Faulhaber, Signatur: 8504 (Entnazifizierung—Dr. Hans Frank). Also quoted in Niklas Frank, *Meine deutsche Mutter,* 385. After Frank's death, the Cardinal personally secured the well-being of Brigitte Frank and her children for years to come. Note without date, about „Mitigation of the denazification tribunal's ruling so that Mrs. Frank and her children could be granted some relief." AEMF, NL Faulhaber, Signatur 8504 (Entnazifizierung—Dr. Hans Frank). See also Niklas Frank, *Meine deutsche Mutter,* 379.

67 Faulhaber to Holy Father, October 17, 1946, „In der Schweiz", AEMF, NL Faulhaber, Signatur: 8504 (Entnazifizierung—Dr. Hans Frank). See also Niklas Frank, *Meine deutsche Mutter,* 385.

68 "Die letzten Äußerungen des hingerichteten Dr. Frank haben Wir mit Ergriffenheit zur Kenntnis genommen. Wir können nur wünschen, dass solcher Gesinnungswandel in den Kreisen derer, die früher in den gleichen Irrtümern befangen waren, bekannt werde und zu Nachdenken und Nachahmung Anlass biete," dated March 1, 1947; also cited in Frank, *Meine deutsche Mutter,* 390.

69 Considering their last words, or lack thereof, I assume the two holdouts were Alfred Rosenberg and Julius Streicher. See "Il comunicato ufficiale sull'esecuzione di Norimberga," *Osservatore Romano,* October 17, 1946, 1: "Tutti i condannati—eccetto due, secondo la propria confessione religiosa, hanno detto al Signore: In manus tuas Domine. Atto di fede, di pentimento, di speranza. Solenne accettazione del castigo umano, fiduziosa offerta di espiazone alla giustizia di Dio, per propiziarsene asieme, l'infinita misericordia. . . . sarebbero morti pentiti non presenti con loro umane colpe presentati al tribunale eterno. [. . .]."

70 "Voci ed echi," "Cronacha di Norimberga," *Osservatore Romano,* October 18, 1946, 1.

71 Donald M. McKale, *Nazis after Hitler: How Perpetrators of the Holocaust Cheated Justice and Truth* (Rowman & Littlefield, 2012), 193ff.

72 NARA, RG 262 (BDC), SS officers, SSO 031A, Arthur Greiser, born 22.1.1897.

73 Catherine Epstein, *Model Nazi: Arthur Greiser and the Occupation of Western Poland* (Oxford University Press, 2010), 120ff., here 330. See also Phayer, *Pius XII, the Holocaust, and the Cold War*, 33ff.

74 "Cardinal Faulhaber Erzbischof von München, München den 19. Juli 1945, Promenadenstrasse 7, An die Amerikanische Militärregierung München Rathaus, Betreff: Ministerialdirektor Dr. Jur. Josef Bühler. z.Z. interniert in Schrobenhausen.", AEMF, NL Faulhaber Signatur 8581.

75 Gnadengesuch für Dr. Josef Bühler ehemal. Staatssekretär im General-Gouvernment. Gez.[eichnet] Cardinal Faulhaber, Erzbischof von München, 14 July 1948, AEMF, NL Faulhaber Signatur 8581, V-16.

76 Gertrude Forster to Papal nunciature in Germany, 10 November 1946, AAV, Segr. Stato, Commissione Soccorsi 261, fasc. 435, f. 4.

77 Note to the II Sezione, 15 gennaio 1947, AAV, Segr. Stato, Commissione Soccorsi 261, fasc. 435, f. 2.

78 Cardinal Hlond to Montini, 14 March 1947, AAV, Segr. Stato, Commissione Soccorsi 261, fasc. 435, f. 10.

79 Vatican Secretariat of State to Muench, 19 April 1947 (spedito 25 April 1947) AAV, Segr. Stato, Commissione Soccorsi 261, fasc. 435, f. 11.

80 Epstein, *Model Nazi*, 330.

81 Dieter Schenk, *Hitlers Mann in Danzig: Albert Forster und die NS-Verbrechen in Danzig-Westpreußen* (Verlag Dietz, 2000), 266ff.

82 "Corte internazionale d'Giustizia penale," *Osservatore Romano*, October 14–15, 1946, 3.

83 Taylor, *The Anatomy of the Nuremberg Trials*, 524; "Discorso di Sua Santità" Pio XII ai nuovi Cardinali, Mercoledì, 20 febbraio 1946, accessed March 18, 2023, https://www.vatican.va/content/pius-xii/it/speeches/1946/documents/hf_p-xii_spe_19460220_la-elevatezza.html.

84 John Q. Barrett, "With Francis at the Vatican (1928 & 1946)," The Jackson List, accessed May 18, 2021, https://thejacksonlist.com/wp-content/uploads/2014/02/20130317-Jackson-List-Francis-Vatican.pdf.

85 Jackson, "The Reminiscences of Robert H. Jackson," 1534.

86 "Cronaca di Roma," *Osservatore Romano*, February 20, 1946, 2.

87 The cardinals stayed as guests of Hudal in the Anima College, with the exception of Frings, who was put up elsewhere, against his will: "Mir wurde eröffnet, ich sollte im Campo Santo wohnen. Das war nicht ganz nach meinen Wünschen. Ich wäre lieber in die Anima gezogen, in der ich in den Jahren 1913 und 1914, als ich in Rom studierte, gelebt hatte." Frings, *Erinnerungen*, 73; Gerald Steinacher, *Nazis auf der Flucht: Wie Kriegsverbrecher über Italien nach Übersee entkamen* (Fischer, 2020), 145.

88 Robert I. Gannon, *The Cardinal Spellman Story* (Doubleday, 1962), 293.

89 Peter Loeffler, ed., *Bischof Clemens August Graf Galen: Akten, Briefe und Predigten 1933–1946*, 2d ed. (Ferdinand Schöningh, 1996), doc. 528, v. II, 1262–1263.

90 Heinrich Portmann, *Cardinal von Galen: By His Chaplain*, trans. and with an introduction by R. L. Sedgwick (Jarrolds, 1957), 204.

91 [Delegation], Cologne at Cardinal Frings' House, 17 October 1946, 17.20 hours, Historische Archiv des Erzbistums Köln (AEK), CR II 25.18,8 / 186.
92 Nicholas Stargardt, *The German War: A Nation Under Arms, Citizens and Soldiers 1939–1945* (Basic Books, 2015), 559.
93 Burckhardt to Max Huber 27 February 1946, UB Basel Nachlass Burckhardt, Bll 46 h Dossier 2, 3 Teil 1. The Papal Nuncio alluded to here was likely Msgr. Philippe Bernardini in Bern.
94 „Bischof Hudal von der Anima in Rom, März 1949", AEMF, NL Faulhaber, Signatur: 8504 (Entnazifizierung—Dr. Hans Frank). Hudal tried to find a German language publisher in Argentina for Frank's memoir.
95 Peter C. Kent, *The Lonely Cold War of Pope Pius XII: The Roman Catholic Church and the Division of Europe, 1943–1950* (McGill-Queen's University Press, 2002), 148.
96 "Commander Rome Describes His Audience with Pope Pius." *The Baltimore Sun*, March 25, 1946, 26.

Chapter 4. The Good Nazi

1 NARA, RG 242, BDC, NSDAP Zentralkartei, Roll To87, Ernst von Weizsäcker, Mitgl.-Nr. 4814617.
2 NARA, RG 242, BDC, SS officers, Roll 234B, 621 ff. Ernst von Weizsäcker, born 25 May 1882.
3 NARA, RG 242, BDC, SS officers, Roll 234B, 621 ff. Ernst von Weizsäcker, born 25 May 1882. Weizsäcker received his SS *Totenkopfring* and SS *Ehrendegen*. For Weizsäcker's version of his SS and Nazi membership, see his memoirs: Ernst von Weizsäcker, *Erinnerungen* (P. List, 1950), 152.
4 Note Di Meglio, 9 Luglio 1943, Vatican, AA.EE.SS., Pontificato: Pio XII, Parte: I (1939–1948), Serie: Germania, Posizione: 866, "Processo contro il barone Weizsaecker" f. 14r-14v.
5 Letter of credence to Pius XII [June 1943], Vatican, Fondo: AA.EE.SS., Pontificato: Pio XII, Parte: I (1939–1948), Serie: Germania, Posizione: 866—Dott. Ernesto Barone von Weizsaecker, Ambasciatore presso la Santa Sede, Data 1943–1951, f. 9 e f. 10.
6 Kertzer, *The Pope at War*, 294–302, here 295. Jobst Knigge, *Der Botschafter und der Papst: Weizsäcker und Pius XII. Die deutsche Vatikanbotschaft 1943–1945* (Verlag Dr. Kovač, 2008); Eckart Conze, Norbert Frei, Peter Hayes, and Moshe Zimmermann, eds., *Das Amt und die Vergangenheit: Deutsche Diplomaten im Dritten Reich und in der Bundesrepublik* (Karl Blessing Verlag, 2010), 388ff.
7 Hudal, *Römische Tagebücher*, 224–25.
8 Note [Tittmann?] May 8, 1945, AAV Segr. Stato, Commissione Soccorsi 370, fasc. 565, f. 054r.
9 *Il Tempo*, 19 July 1945 and *Stars and Stripes*, 19 July 1945: AAV, Segr. Stato, Commissione Soccorsi 370, fasc. 565, on this topic see f. 219r ff.
10 Note Vatican Secretariat of State summarizing a meeting with Weizsäcker, 19 July 1945, AAV, Segr. Stato, Commissione Soccorsi 370, fasc. 565, f. 223r.
11 Weizsäcker, *Erinnerungen*, 382.

12 Pacelli remained Vatican Secretary of State after his election as Pope Pius XII. Monsignors Montini and Tardini held the title *sostituto* (Italian for "substitute"), a designation that often puzzled Vatican outsiders, including the international press and lawyers for Nazi war criminals, who struggled to understand what a "substitute" was. English-language publications frequently translate *sostituto* as "undersecretary of state," which roughly corresponds to similar positions in other diplomatic services and is easier for readers to grasp. The Vatican role does not perfectly align with this title but comes close.

13 Harold H. Tittmann, assistant to the Honorable Myron C. Taylor to Monsignor Montini, Secretariat of State of His Holiness, Vatican City, 5 August 1945, AAV, Segr. Stato, Comm. Soccorsi 265, fasc. 581. f. 003r.

14 Memorandum, June 28, 1945, NARA, RG 59, Entry 1068, Box 6, Decimal File 1944–45, 711. German Diplomats in V.C. [Vatican City]. (note "original left with Msgr. Montini on June 28, 1945").

15 Darcy G. Osborne to Winston Churchill, British Legation to Holy See, July 12, 1945, NARA, RG 59, Entry 1068, Box 6, Decimal File 1944–45 711. German Diplomats in V.C. [Vatican City].

16 Vatican Secretariat of State to His Britannic Majesty's Minister to Holy See. July 16, 1945, NARA, RG 59, Box 6, Entry 1068, Decimal File 1944–45 711. German Diplomats in V.C. [Vatican City].

17 British Legation to the Holy See, July 12, 1945, NARA, RG 59, Entry 1068, Box 6, Decimal File 1944–45, 711. German Diplomats in V.C. [Vatican City].

18 Tittmann to Montini, November [8], 1945, NARA, RG 59, Entry 1068, Box 6, Decimal File 1944–45, 711. German Diplomats in V.C. [Vatican City].

19 Knigge, *Der Botschafter und der Papst*, 169.

20 The town priest of Taormina (Mons. D. Salvatore Cacopardo) to Montini, 2 May 1945, AAV Segr. Stato Comm. Soccorsi 368, fasc. 515, f. 382r, 383r. AAV, Segr. Stato, Comm. Soccorsi 368, Varia 515: Rimpatrio diplomati tedeschi—XI Weizsaecker et al—Wollenweber: convertito al cattolicesimo durante la sua detenzione a Taormina.

21 Montini to Neuhäusler, 25 August 1946, AAV, Segr. Stato, Comm. Soccorsi 370, fasc. 565, f. 408r.

22 Note Vatican Secretariat of State, 6 June 1945, AAV, Segr. Stato, Comm. Soccorsi 370, fasc. 565, f. 108r.

23 Paraphrase. For Ambassador Murphy, (SECRET), July 21, 1945. NARA, RG 59, Entry 1068, Box 6, Decimal File 1944–45 711. German Diplomats in V.C. [Vatican City].

24 D. G. Osborne, British Legation to Holy See, to Winston Churchill, July 12, 1945, NARA, RG 59, Entry 1068, Box 6, Decimal File 1944–45, 711. German Diplomats in V.C. [Vatican City].

25 Savingram No. 2, Osborne, British Legation to the Holy See, Rome, January 2, 1946. My dispatch No. 235.1945. NARA, RG 59, Entry 1068, Box 17, Decimal File 1947, 711.4 Weizsäcker.

26 Pope Pius XII to Weizsäcker, Easter of 1946 (for reference only), NARA, RG 238, War Crimes Records Collection, United States against Ernst von Weizsäcker, M897, Microfilm, Roll 119, Ex. 376, Doc. 439.

27 Vatican Secretariat of State to Tittmann, 22 April 1946, AAV, Segr. Stato, Comm. Soccorsi 370, fasc. 565, f. 333r.

28 Conze et al., eds., *Das Amt und die Vergangenheit*, 388; Weizsäcker, *Erinnerungen*, 384.

29 Letter Weizsäcker to Allied authorities, 24 May 1946, AAV, Comm Soccorsi, 370, fasc. 565, f. 358r.

30 Giovanni Montini, Vatican Secretariat of State, Vatican, 23 August 1946 to Baron von Weizsäcker, NARA, RG 238, War Crimes Records Collection, United States against Ernst von Weizsäcker, M897, Microfilm, Roll 119, Ex. 375, Doc. 455.

31 Vatican letter of protection for Weizsäcker, valid until September 30th, 1946, AAV, Comm Soccorsi 370, fasc. 565, f. 414r.

32 "Wir bitten Sie, sich davon überzeugt zu halten, dass Unsere teilnehmende Sorge dem Werden einer wahren europäischen Befriedigung unentsagt zugewandt bleibt. Innerhalb dieses grossen Rahmens eines erneuerten Europas wird Deutschland immer auf Unsere verständnisvolle Förderung rechnen dürfen in seinem Bestreben, die Grundlage zu seinem Wiederaufstieg zu finden und bei diesem selbst sich des ihm von der Vorsehung bestimmten Platzes bewusst zu sein."

33 Pope Pius XII to Weizsäcker, 1 March 1947 (for reference only), NARA, RG 238, War Crimes Records Collection, United States against Ernst von Weizsäcker, M897, Microfilm, Roll 119, Ex. 377 Doc. 451.

34 One of Weizsäcker's sons was married to the daughter of influential and pro-German Swiss military officer Colonel Ulrich Wille Jr. His father, General Ulrich Wille Sr., was the commander-in-chief of the Swiss Army in WWI.

35 Guardia Svizzera Pontificia, il cappellano, 26 August 1947, Vatican, Fondo: AA.EE.SS., Pontificato: Pio XII, Parte: I (1939–1948), Serie: Germania, Posizione: 866, "Processo contro il barone Weizsaecker" f. 183–717, f. 325.

36 Muench to Montini, 17 September 1947, AAV, Segr. Stato, Comm. Soccorsi 265, fasc. 581. Folder "Barone Ernst Von Weizsaecker. Oggetto: Sua Posizione nei confronti delle autorità alleate e suo processo. Passi in suo favore" 1945–1950, f. 024r, 024v.

37 Secretary of State Holy See to Muench, 22 September 1947, Vatican, Fondo: AA.EE.SS., Pontificato: Pio XII, Parte: I (1939–1948), Serie: Germania, Posizione: 866, "Processo contro il barone Weizsaecker" f. 183–717, f. 328.

38 Conze, Frei, Hayes, and Zimmerman, *Das Amt und die Vergangenheit*, 397.

39 One folder under the label "Trial against the Baron von Weizsäcker" contains around 600 pages and is conserved in the Archivio storico della Segretaria di Stato, Fondo Affari Ecclesiastici Straordinari, Periodo V (Pontificato Pius XII 1939–1958), Parte Prima (1939–1948) Germania, Posizione 866—Dott. Ernesto Barone von Weizsaecker, Ambasciatore presso la Santa Sede, Data 1943–1951, ff. 183–717. The other folder, titled in translation "Baron Ernst Von Weizsaecker. Subject: His position towards the Allied authorities and his trial. Steps taken in his favor," of about 460 pages, is preserved in Archivio Apostolico Vaticano, Segretaria di Stato, Commissione Soccorsi 265, fasc. 581.

40 Nunziatura Apostolica Svizzera, Filippo Bernardini to Montini, 28 October 1947, AAV, Segr. Stato, Comm. Soccorsi 265, fasc. 581. Folder "Barone Ernst Von Weizsaecker. Oggetto: Sua Posizione nei confronti delle autorità alleate e suo processo. Passi in suo

favore" 1945–1950, f. 027r. Commandant of the Swiss Papal Guard Heinrich [de] Pfyffer von Altishofen to Secretariat of State of His Holiness, 9 November 1947, Vatican, Fondo: AA.EE.SS., Pontificato: Pio XII, Parte: I (1939–1948), Serie: Germania, Posizione: 866, "Processo contro il barone Weizsaecker" f. 183–717, f. 329.

41 *Basler Nachrichten Abendblatt* nr 460 vom 5. November 1947, Tagesbericht 5 November: „Der Prozess v. Weizsäcker": „Menschenjäger Kempner der ihm auf den Fersen sitzt und ihn an den Galgen Ribbentrops befördern möchte", Vatican, Archivio storico della Segretaria di Stato, Fondo Affari Ecclesiastici Straordinari, Periodo V (Pontificato Pius XII 1939–1958), Parte Prima (1939–1948) Germania, Posizione 866—Dott. Ernesto Barone von Weizsaecker, Ambasciatore presso la Santa Sede, Data 1943–1951, "Processo contro il barone Weizsaecker" f. 183–717, f. 320 and f. 330 and note on f. 324: „visto dal S. Padre" 11 XI. 1947 I sec oer riserv.

42 According to Berlin Document Center (BDC) records (these are captured Nazi records that were assembled and systematically organized by the U.S. military for trial and denazification purposes), it would appear that his wife Marianne had joined the Nazi party in 1936, two years before her husband. Marianne Freifrau von Weizsäcker, born 8 August 1889, Mitgliedsnummer 3762854, NARA, RG 242 BDC, NSDAP-Ortsgruppe, Roll Y059.

43 Marianne von Weizsäcker to Pius XII, handwritten letter, 17 November 1947, AAV, Segr. Stato, Comm. Soccorsi 265, fasc. 581. Folder "Barone Ernst Von Weizsaecker. Oggetto: Sua Posizione nei confronti delle autorità alleate e suo processo. Passi in suo favore" 1945–1950, f. 047r.

44 Secretariat of State of His Holiness to Myron Taylor, 7 December 1947 AAV, Segr. Stato, Comm. Soccorsi 265, fasc. 581. Folder "Barone Ernst Von Weizsaecker. Oggetto: Sua Posizione nei confronti delle autorità alleate e suo processo. Passi in suo favore" 1945–1950, f. 051r.

45 The Office of Personal Representative of the President to His Holiness, Nota Verbale, 18 December 1947, AAV, Segr. Stato, Comm. Soccorsi 265, fasc. 581. Folder "Barone Ernst Von Weizsaecker. Oggetto: Sua Posizione nei confronti delle autorità alleate e suo processo. Passi in suo favore" 1945–1950, f. 058r.

46 Vatican Secretariat of State to Muench, 7 December 1947, AAV, Segr. Stato, Comm. Soccorsi 265, fasc. 581. Folder "Barone Ernst Von Weizsaecker. Oggetto: Sua Posizione nei confronti delle autorità alleate e suo processo. Passi in suo favore" 1945–1950, 025r.

47 Nota 28 Decembre 1947, Il Barone von Braun, Vatican, Fondo: AA.EE.SS., Pontificato: Pio XII, Parte: I (1939–1948), Serie: Germania, Posizione: 866, "Processo contro il barone Weizsaecker" f. 183–717, f. 332.

48 Sigismund von Braun to Pius XII, Vatican City, 9 January 1948, Vatican, Fondo: AA.EE.SS., Pontificato: Pio XII, Parte: I (1939–1948), Serie: Germania, Posizione: 866, "Processo contro il barone Weizsaecker" f. 183–717, f. 335- f. 337. See Brown-Fleming, *The Holocaust and Catholic Conscience.*

49 "Dati in favore del barone Von Weizsaecker ex ambasciatore di Germania presso la S. Sede", signed D. De Marchi, 6 January 1948, Vatican, Fondo: AA.EE.SS., Pontificato: Pio XII, Parte: I (1939–1948), Serie: Germania, Posizione: 866, "Processo contro il barone Weizsaecker" f. 183–717, f. 339 ff. here 340 f.

50 Cicognani to Tardini in Rome, 25 December 1947, Vatican, Fondo: AA.EE.SS., Pontificato: Pio XII, Parte: I (1939–1948), Serie: Germania, Posizione: 866, "Processo contro il barone Weizsaecker" f. 183–717, ff. 361
51 Giuseppe Di Meglio in Madrid, letterhead Nunciatura Apostólica en España, to Tardini, 15 May 1948, Vatican, Fondo: AA.EE.SS., Pontificato: Pio XII, Parte: I (1939–1948), Serie: Germania, Posizione: 866, "Processo contro il barone Weizsaecker" f. 183–717, f. 411r-413v.
52 NARA, RG 238, War Crimes Records Collection, United States against Ernst von Weizsäcker, M897, Microfilm Roll 1. At the beginning of the roll is a list of all the affidavit materials submitted for the defense.
53 Dr. Anton Weber, Leiter der römischen Zweigstelle des St. Raphaelsvereins dem amerikanischen Militärgericht, 15 January 1948 (Opera Raffaele, Via Pettinari, Roma), NARA, RG 238, War Crimes Records Collection, United States against Ernst von Weizsäcker, M897, Microfilm Roll 119, Ex 326, Doc 53.
54 Eidesstattliche Erklärung, Dr. Paul Georg Berndorff, Erzbischöflicher Kaplan und Geheimsekretär Sr. Eminenz Kardinal Frings, Köln, dem amerikanischen Militärgericht in Nürnberg 9 April 1948, NARA, RG 238, War Crimes Records Collection, United States against Ernst von Weizsäcker, M897, Microfilm Roll 118, Ex 179, Doc 281.
55 Alois Hudal, Bischof der deutschen Nationalkirche und Vorsitzender der Gemeinde der Katholiken deutscher Sprache in Rom dem amerikanischen Gericht, 30 January 1948, NARA, RG 238, War Crimes Records Collection, United States against Ernst von Weizsäcker, M897, Microfilm Roll 118, Ex 189, Doc 103.
56 Steinacher, *Humanitarians at War*, 130–31.
57 Letter Weizsäcker children: Prof. Dr. Carl Friedrich Freiherr von Weizsäcker, Adelheid Gräfin zu Eulenburg, geb. Freiin von Weizsäcker, Richard Freiherr von Weizsäcker to Pius XII („Euer Heiligkeit"), Nuremberg, 17 April 1948, Vatican, Fondo: AA.EE.SS., Pontificato: Pio XII, Parte: I (1939–1948), Serie: Germania, Posizione: 866, "Processo contro il barone Weizsaecker" f. 183–717, f. 401–403.
58 Vatican, Archivio storico della Segretaria di Stato, Fondo Affari Ecclesiatici Straordinari, Periodo V (Pontificato Pius XII 1939–1958), Parte Prima (1939–1948) Germania, Posizione 866—Dott. Ernesto Barone von Weizsaecker, Ambasciatore presso la Santa Sede, Data 1943–1951—ff. 183–717, f 404: "30 April 1948: In una lettera personale l'avv. Warren E. Magee mi scrive: 'Sua Santità si e degnato prendere in considerazione la mia richiesta di una Sua nota personale circa il Barone von Weizsaecker. Alla fine dell'udienza mit permisi informare Sua Santità che io sarei rimasto a Roma ancora pochi giorni. Inoltre dichiarai che avrei considerato come un grandissimo onore di portare con me in Germania la nota'; Carroll."
59 Note, dell'Acqua prot. [20 May 1949] "Il brevissimo autografo di risposta del 2 maggio 1948 dice: 'Abbiamo volentieri gradito il Suo scritto (inviatoci a suo tempo), nel quale Ella chiedeva aiuto per la sorte di suo marito. La sua stimata famiglia *può esser sicura della Nostra pertecipazione come della Nostra preghiera affinché la [la] benedizione di Dio regni su di essa. Dal Vaticano, 2 maggio* 1948,'" Vatican, Fondo: AA.EE.SS., Pontificato: Pio XII, Parte: I (1939–1948), Serie: Germania, Posizione: 866, "Pro-

cesso contro il barone Weizsaecker" f. 183–717, f. 484. „Der geehrten Frau Baronin Marianne von Weizsäcker in Lindau am Bodensee. Wir haben Ihr seinerzeitiges Schreiben, in dem Sie angesichts der Lage Ihres Herrn Gemahls um Hilfe warben, gerne entgegengenommen. Ihre werte Familie darf Unserer Teilnahme sicher sein wie Unseres Gebets, dass in allem Gottes Segen über ihr walte. Aus dem Vatican, den 2. Mai 1948" Note, Vatican, Fondo: AA.EE.SS., Pontificato: Pio XII, Parte: I (1939–1948), Serie: Germania, Posizione: 866, "Processo contro il barone Weizsaecker" f. 183–717, f. 407.

60 Magee to Pius XII, 3 May 1948, "His Holiness Pope Pius XII The Vatican", 5 May 1948 [stamped], Vatican, Fondo: AA.EE.SS., Pontificato: Pio XII, Parte: I (1939–1948), Serie: Germania, Posizione: 866, "Processo contro il barone Weizsaecker" f. 183–717, f. 408.

61 Monsignor [Walter] Carroll notes, 4 June 1948; Vatican, Fondo: AA.EE.SS., Pontificato: Pio XII, Parte: I (1939–1948), Serie: Germania, Posizione: 866, "Processo contro il barone Weizsaecker" f. 183–717, f. 423.

62 Monsignor [Walter] Carroll notes, 4 June 1948; handwritten note: "6.VI.48 Veder se [?] informare Mr. Taylor del tenore—della prudenza—delle dichiarazioni fatte. GBM [Giovanni Battista Montini]". Vatican, Fondo: AA.EE.SS., Pontificato: Pio XII, Parte: I (1939–1948), Serie: Germania, Posizione: 866, "Processo contro il barone Weizsaecker" f. 183–717, f. 423.

63 Pope Pius XII to Marianne von Weizsäcker, 2 May 1948, NARA, RG 238, War Crimes Records Collection, United States against Ernst von Weizsäcker, M897, Microfilm Roll 119, Ex 413, Doc 438.

64 Muench to Tardini, 23 June 1948, Vatican, Fondo: AA.EE.SS., Pontificato: Pio XII, Parte: I (1939–1948), Serie: Germania, Posizione: 866, "Processo contro il barone Weizsaecker" f. 183–717, f. 430. "La difesa termina citando una frase del Santo Padre circa la necessità di adoperarsi in ogni modo per la pace, per concluder che l'opera del W[eizsäcker] per salvaguardare la pace e poi per riaverla merita plauso." Internal note about defense of Weizsaecker, [11 July 1948], Vatican, Fondo: AA.EE.SS., Pontificato: Pio XII, Parte: I (1939–1948), Serie: Germania, Posizione: 866, "Processo contro il barone Weizsaecker" f. 183–717, f. 449.

65 "Von Weizsaecker acquittal seen after priest testifies on his Vatican reports to shorten war", *NCWC News Service*, 19 July 1948, report by correspondent Max Jordan, Vatican, Fondo: AA.EE.SS., Pontificato: Pio XII, Parte: I (1939–1948), Serie: Germania, Posizione: 866, "Processo contro il barone Weizsaecker" f. 183–717, f. 457.

66 Cicognani to Tardini, 21 Ottobre 1948; attached article "This Changing World", in *The Evening Star*, 19 October 1948, Vatican, Fondo: AA.EE.SS., Pontificato: Pio XII, Parte: I (1939–1948), Serie: Germania, Posizione: 866, "Processo contro il barone Weizsaecker" f. 183–717, f. 462; f. 463.

67 Brown-Fleming, *The Holocaust and Catholic Conscience*, 8.

68 Office Muench to Secretary of State of the Holy See, 14 January 1949, AAV, Segr. Stato, Comm. Soccorsi 265, fasc. 581. Folder "Barone Ernst Von Weizsaecker. Oggetto: Sua Posizione nei confronti delle autorità alleate e suo processo. Passi in suo favore" 1945–1950, f. 083r, 083v.

69 Ulrich Raulff, *Kreis ohne Meister. Stefan Georges Nachleben* (C. H. Beck 2010), 403; Philipp Glahé, *Amnestielobbyismus für NS-Verbrecher: Der Heidelberger Juristenkreis und die alliierte Justiz 1949–1955* (Wallstein, 2024); K. Singer and U. Frevert, *100 Jahre Hellmut Becker (1913–2013)—Dokumentation der Ausstellung zu Leben und Werk im Max-Planck-Institut für Bildungsforschung [Online-Publikation]* (Max-Planck-Institut für Bildungsforschung, 2014), https://doi.org/10.14280/08241.29; Philipp Glahé, "The Heidelberg Circle of Jurists and Its Struggle against Allied Jurisdiction: Amnesty-Lobbyism and Impunity-Demands for National Socialist War Criminals (1949–1955)," *Journal of the History of International Law* 22, no. 1 (October 2019): 1–44.

70 Norbert Frei, *Adenauer's Germany and the Nazi Past: The Politics of Amnesty and Integration* (Columbia University Press, 2002), 134.

71 See Mark Roseman, *The Villa, The Lake, The Meeting: Wannsee and The Final Solution* (Penguin UK, 2002).

72 Marianne Weizsäcker to Monsignore [Muench?], 1 March 1949, AAV, Segr. Stato, Comm. Soccorsi 265, fasc. 581. Folder "Barone Ernst Von Weizsaecker. Oggetto: Sua Posizione nei confronti delle autorità alleate e suo processo. Passi in suo favore" 1945–1950, f. 084r.

73 Frei, *Adenauer's Germany and the Nazi Past*, 151.

74 Visitator Apostolicus in Germania (Office Muench) to Secretary of State of the Holy See, 14 January 1949, AAV, Segr. Stato, Comm. Soccorsi 265, fasc. 581. Folder "Barone Ernst Von Weizsaecker. Oggetto: Sua Posizione nei confronti delle autorità alleate e suo processo. Passi in suo favore" 1945–1950, f. 083r, 083v.

75 Note typed in German, likely from Becker "Im Falle Weizsaecker" AAV, Segr. Stato, Comm. Soccorsi 265, fasc. 581. Folder "Barone Ernst Von Weizsaecker. Oggetto: Sua Posizione nei confronti delle autorità alleate e suo processo. Passi in suo favore" 1945–1950, f. 088r.

76 Letterhead Segretaria di Stato di Sua Santità 24 April 1949, Comm Sec. Cifrat. all Dell'Acqua, note on top: Zabkar AAV, Segr. Stato, Comm. Soccorsi 265, fasc. 581. Folder "Barone Ernst Von Weizsaecker. Oggetto: Sua Posizione nei confronti delle autorità alleate e suo processo. Passi in suo favore" 1945–1950, 087r.

77 "E qui espressa preghiera informare Cardinale Arcivescovo di New York che Signor Weizsaecker, già Ambasciatore Germania presso la Santa Sede dal luglio 1943 alla fine della guerra, è stato condannato alcuni anni carcere, nonostante avanzata età. Si vorrebbe ottenere che Generale Clay con confermasse sentenza. Veda Vostra Eccellenza as conveniente et possibile segnalare o appoggiare tale desiderio." Montini telegram to Washington, 28 April 1949, AAV, Segr. Stato, Comm. Soccorsi 265, fasc. 581. Folder "Barone Ernst Von Weizsaecker. Oggetto: Sua Posizione nei confronti delle autorità alleate e suo processo. Passi in suo favore" 1945–1950, f. 089r. Se also Note, Bellotti 21.V.49: "In seguito a richiesta fatta dal difensore di Weizsaecker, avv. Magee, di un interessamento presso il Gen. Clay affinche non confermasse la sentenza di condanna di W., la II sezione ha telegrafato a Washington—cifrato N. 3268 del 28.IV.49—invitando a farne parola al Card. Spellman, affinche, se crede, costui faccia presente tale richiesta." Vatican, Fondo: AA.EE.SS., Pontificato: Pio XII, Parte: I (1939–1948), Serie: Germania, Posizione: 866, "Processo contro il barone Weizsaecker" f. 183–717, f. 492.

78 Cicognani with a message from Spellman to Montini, 11 July 1949, AAV, Segr. Stato, Comm. Soccorsi 265, fasc. 581. Folder "Barone Ernst Von Weizsaecker. Oggetto: Sua Posizione nei confronti delle autorità alleate e suo processo. Passi in suo favore" 1945–1950, f. 124r.

79 Magee to Pope Pius XII, 3 May 1949, AAV, Segr. Stato, Comm. Soccorsi 265, fasc. 581. Folder "Barone Ernst Von Weizsaecker. Oggetto: Sua Posizione nei confronti delle autorità alleate e suo processo. Passi in suo favore" 1945–1950, f. 138r.

80 Marianne Weizsäcker to Pope Pius XII, 2 May 1949, AAV, Segr. Stato, Comm. Soccorsi 265, fasc. 581, folder "Barone Ernst Von Weizsaecker. Oggetto: Sua Posizione nei confronti delle autorità alleate e suo processo. Passi in suo favore" 1945–1950, f. 128r.

81 „Il criminale Von Weizsaecker benedetto da Sua Santità. Una portavoce di Hitler nelle grazie di Pio XII" in: *L'Unità*, 14 Maggio 1949, page 3, Vatican, Fondo: AA.EE.SS., Pontificato: Pio XII, Parte: I (1939–1948), Serie: Germania, Posizione: 866, "Processo contro il barone Weizsaecker" f. 183–717, f. 476.

82 Note, dell'Acqua prot. [20 May 1949] Vatican, Fondo: AA.EE.SS., Pontificato: Pio XII, Parte: I (1939–1948), Serie: Germania, Posizione: 866, "Processo contro il barone Weizsaecker"–f. 183–717, f. 484.

83 Press review, Anno XIX Bollettino N. 107, 14 Maggio 1949, sabato. Vatican, Fondo: AA.EE.SS., Pontificato: Pio XII, Parte: I (1939–1948), Serie: Germania, Posizione: 866, "Processo contro il barone Weizsaecker" f. 183–717, f. 478.

84 [Notes] Per S.E.R. Mons. Montini, 15 May 1949 (URGE), e 16 May 1949, Dell'Acqua 2961/49, Vatican, Fondo: AA.EE.SS., Pontificato: Pio XII, Parte: I (1939–1948), Serie: Germania, Posizione: 866, "Processo contro il barone Weizsaecker" f. 183–717, f. 481.

85 "Storici del fronte", in: *Osservatore Romano*, 16–17 Maggio 1949, page 2. Vatican, Fondo: AA.EE.SS., Pontificato: Pio XII, Parte: I (1939–1948), Serie: Germania, Posizione: 866, "Processo contro il barone Weizsaecker" f. 183–717, [f. 482].

86 "Il processo Weizsaecker e le 'rondini' del Papa", in: *L'Unità*, 20 May 1949, page 3; Vatican response: "Historica e historicus", in *Osservatore Romano*, 21 May 1949, page 1. Vatican, Fondo: AA.EE.SS., Pontificato: Pio XII, Parte: I (1939–1948), Serie: Germania, Posizione: 866, "Processo contro il barone Weizsaecker"–f. 183–717, f. 485; f. 489.

87 Caso Weizsaecker—a list of the interventions taken by the Holy See in favor of Weizsaecker put together by D. Zabkar, 17 January 1950–AAV, Segr. Stato, Comm. Soccorsi 265, fasc. 581. Folder "Barone Ernst Von Weizsaecker. Oggetto: Sua Posizione nei confronti delle autorità alleate e suo processo. Passi in suo favore" 1945–1950, 277r.

88 Muench to Montini, 28 February 1950, AAV, Segr. Stato, Comm. Soccorsi 265, fasc. 581, folder "Barone Ernst Von Weizsaecker. Oggetto: Sua Posizione nei confronti delle autorità alleate e suo processo. Passi in suo favore" 1945–1950, f. 299r.

89 Muench to John J. McCloy, 27 February 1950, AAV, Segr. Stato, Comm. Soccorsi 265, fasc. 581, folder "Barone Ernst Von Weizsaecker. Oggetto: Sua Posizione nei confronti delle autorità alleate e suo processo. Passi in suo favore" 1945–1950, f. 300r and 301r.

90 Montini to Muench, 15 March 1950, AAV, Segr. Stato, Comm. Soccorsi 265, fasc. 581, folder "Barone Ernst Von Weizsaecker. Oggetto: Sua Posizione nei confronti delle autorità alleate e suo processo. Passi in suo favore" 1945–1950, f. 303r.

91 Note, 10 Februray 1950, (VSP [Visto dal Santo Padre?] 12.2.1950) AAV, Segr. Stato, Comm. Soccorsi 265, fasc. 581, folder "Barone Ernst Von Weizsaecker. Oggetto: Sua Posizione nei confronti delle autorità alleate e suo processo. Passi in suo favore" 1945–1950, f. 297r.

92 Weizsäcker to Pius XII , 22 October 1950, AAV, Segr. Stato, Comm. Soccorsi 283, fasc. 989, f. 468r, 468 v.

93 "La morte di von Weizsaecker", in: *L'Osservatore Romano*, 6–7 August 1951, n. 181. Vatican, Fondo: AA.EE.SS., Pontificato: Pio XII, Parte: I (1939–1948), Serie: Germania, Posizione: 866, "Processo contro il barone Weizsaecker"–f. 183–717, f. 712. "Weizsäcker in der Nähe Stuttgarts beerdigt. Der Papst lässt sein Beileid übermitteln. Kein Vertreter der Stuttgarter Regierung", in *Frankfurter Allgemeine*, 9 August 1951: "Im Auftrage von Papst Pius XII. richtete Kardinal Montini am Mittwoch an die Witwe des Verstorbenen folgendes Beileidstelegram: „Mit Anteilnahme vom Hinscheiden Freiherrn von Weizsäckers erfahren, übermittle Ich Ihnen, wie Ihrer Familie des Heiligen Vaters inniges Mitempfinden an diesem Schmerz und versichere Sie persönlichen Gebetes gedenkend." Vatican, Fondo: AA.EE.SS., Pontificato: Pio XII, Parte: I (1939–1948), Serie: Germania, Posizione: 866, "Processo contro il barone Weizsaecker"–f. 183–717, f. 715.

94 Kim C. Priemel and Alexa Stiller, "Introduction," in *Reassessing the Nuremberg Military Tribunals: Transitional Justice, Trial Narratives, and Historiography*, ed. Kim C. Priemel and Alexa Stiller (Berghahn Books, 2012), 9; and Dirk Pöppmann, "The Trials of Robert Kempner: From Stateless Immigrant to Prosecutor of the Foreign Office," in *Reassessing the Nuremberg Military Tribunals: Transitional Justice, Trial Narratives, and Historiography*, ed. Kim C. Priemel and Alexa Stiller (Berghahn Books, 2012), 24–46.

95 Pöppmann, "The Trials of Robert Kempner," 41.

96 Letter Landesbischof Wurm to Dr. Robert Kempner, 5 May 1948, in: Memorandum by the Evangelical Church in Germany on the Question of War Crimes Trials before American Military Courts Published for the Council of the Evangelical Church in Germany by Bishop D. Wurm, Church President D. Niemöller DD. DD. and Prelate D. Hartenstein [Not for publication Printed in Numbers n. 973] Gust. Stürner, Waiblingen-Stuttgart 1949, 29.

97 Landeskirchliches Archiv Stuttgart (LKAS), Wurm papers, USHMM, Reel 61, Bueschel 290, Wurm to Kempner 5 June 1948.

98 For a good overview of the controversy, see Konrad Frei's study *Adenauer's Germany and the Nazi Past*, 108ff.

99 See Richard Tüngel, "Wurm Gegen Kempner," *Zeit* 22, May 27, 1948, accessed October 28, 2024, http://www.zeit.de/1948/22/wurm-gegen-kempner.

100 Robert Ingrim, an Austrian-American lawyer, journalist, and monarchist, strongly criticized Kempner: Kempner would not judge based on individual guilt, but collective. LKAS, Wurm papers, USHMM, Reel 61, Bueschel 290, Robert Ingrim, "Die Kempner von Nürnberg", in *Die Weltwoche* (Zurich), 17 September 1948.

101 Robert M. W. and Ruth Benedicta Kempner papers, United States Holocaust Memorial Museum Archives, Washington, DC, box 162, folder "Ruth Kempner, Biographical documents 1962–1982", Copy Baptismal Certificate, St. Philomena's Church, Lansdowne, Pa. August 9, 1956, Ruth Benedicta Kempner born July 8, 1904 was baptized on April 7, 1954 by Rev. Thomas J. B. Lawlor.

102 USHMM. Kempner collection, Box 162, F 5.

103 Pascalina regarding the Hochhuth affair: „Ja, ich habe alles gelesen, englisch und deutsch und italienisch und danke Ihnen und Ihrem Herrn Gemahl von Herzen. Lassen Sie nur ja nicht nach, man kann einfach nicht begreifen, wie ein so verlogenes Stück, so besucht werden kann. Nach Italien kam es noch nicht und Papst Paul hat bei der Einweihung des Denkmals für unseren Heiligen Vater sehr schön gesprochen, aber diese schlechten Leute lesen nur das Schlechte. Sollte ich bald etwas hören, schreibe ich Ihnen sofort wieder. Viel Liebes von Ihrer dankbaren. Sr. M. Pascalina" USHMM Archives, Kempner papers, Box 162, Folder "Letters of Sister Pascalina to Ruth Kempner", Pascalina Lehnert to Benedikta Kempner, 14 March 1964.

104 USHMM Archives, Kempner papers, box 56, Typewritten manuscript with corrections by hand. The German version of this article apparently was published as Robert M. W. Kempner, "Papst Pius XII. als Gegner des Nationalsozialismus. Seine Hilfsaktionen für Juden," *Aufbau* (New York) 24 (October 17, 1958): 31–32.

105 Cardinal Bea's secretary P. Stefan Schmidt S.J. in the name of the cardinal to Benedicta Kempner, 9 December 1964, USHMM Archives, Kempner papers, Box 56, Folder "newspapers 1950–64", Folder 1 of 2.

106 Kempner apparently sent a copy of the German version of this 1958 article defending Pius XII to Cardinal Frings signed with "with high regards." USHMM Archives, Kempner papers, Box 56, Folder Clippings & correspondence regarding Pius XII, Church complicity." Kempner to Frings, 17 October 1958.

107 Robert M. W. Kempner, *Ankläger einer Epoche: Lebenserinnerungen*. In Zusammenarbeit mit Jörg Friedrich, Frankfurt am Main: Ullstein 1983, 395. See also Diary Faulhaber, Entry from 15 December 1948, Nachlass Faulhaber 10027, Seite 140. https://www.faulhaber-edition.de/. The diary entry suggests that it may have referred to the Weizsäcker case.

108 Kempner, *Ankläger einer Epoche*, 36.

109 Weinke, *Nürnberger Prozesse*, 96.

Chapter 5. Germans as Victims

1 *Rechtsbewusstsein und Rechtsunsicherheit* [1946], AEK, CR II 25.18,7; Brown-Fleming, *The Holocaust and Catholic Conscience*, 82.

2 Brown-Fleming, *The Holocaust and Catholic Conscience*, 83; see also Suzanne Brown-Fleming, "Granting Absolution: Vatican Nuncio Aloisius Cardinal Muench and the Catholic Clemency Campaign," *Kirchliche Zeitgeschichte* 19, no. 2 (2006), 361; Gerald J. Steinacher, "Le pape contre Nuremberg Procès des crimes de guerre nazis, le Vatican et la question de la justice après la guerre," *Revue d'Histoire de la Shoah* (automne 2023) (the title of this issue is "Vatican, Église et Shoah: Renouveau historiographique autour des archives Pie XII"): 301–321 (English version: "The Pope against Nuremberg: Nazi War Crime Trials, the Vatican, and the Question of Postwar Justice," available at https://

shs.cairn.info/journal-revue-d-histoire-de-la-shoah-2023-2?lang=en); Gerald J. Steinacher, "Forgive and Forget? The Vatican and the Escape of Nazi War Criminals from Justice," *S:I.M.O.N.—Shoah: Intervention. Methods. Documentation* 9 (2022): 1, 4–28.

3 See Hubert Wolf unter Mitarbeit von Ingrid Lueb, *Clemens August Graf von Galen: Gehorsam und Gewissen* (Herder 2006) and Daniel Utrecht, *The Lion of Münster: The Bishop Who Roared Against the Nazis* (Tan Books, 2016); Beth A. Griech-Polelle, *Bishop von Galen: German Bishops and National Socialism* (Yale University Press, 2022).

4 "Muenster Prelate Assails 'Russians'," *The New York Times*, April 7, 1945, 4.

5 (Graf Galen) [handwritten]; „Predigt bei einer Münsterischen Wallfahrt nach Telgte am 1 Juli 1945 Regina pacis, ora pro nobis!", AEK,CR II 25.18,3 / 69 ff.

6 Fritz Rene Allemann, „Deutsche Bilanz 1945: Ein Bischof sagt nein," *Die Tat*, October 26, 1945, 2. A typewritten copy of this article can also be found in Fring's papers, AEK, CR II, 25,18,7.

7 The world took notice and showed little understanding. Even the famous German writer Thomas Mann from his exile in the United States criticized the bishop harshly for his words; Wolf, *Clemens August Graf von Galen*, 136–37.

8 „Rechtsbewusstsein und Rechtsunsicherheit: Rede des Kardinals Graf v. Galen in Rom, März 1946 ohne Verlag 1946" 20 Blatt maschinenschriftlich, Stadtbibliothek München am Gasteig.

9 "Cronaca di Roma," *Osservatore Romano*, February 20, 1946, 2.

10 [Kapitularvikar Franz Vorwerk], "Rechtsbewusstsein und Rechtsunsicherheit", in *Kirchliches Amtsblatt für die Diözese Münster* 80 (1946), Nr. 20, Art. 149, 91, dated 26 June 1946, Archives of the diocesis of Münster. The statement is dated June 14, 1946, and it appeared on the frontpage of this edition of the *Amtsblatt*. Special thanks to Dr. Heinz Mestrup from the archives of the dioceses of Münster for helping me with this research. The pamphlet is also not listed in Peter Loeffler (ed.), *Bischof Clemens August Graf Galen: Akten, Briefe und Predigten 1933–1946*, 2nd ed. (Ferdinand Schoeningh, 1996).

11 Utrecht, *The Lion of Muenster*, 379.

12 Frings to Jaeger, 8 December 1945, AEK, CR II 25.18, 7 / 251.

13 Frings to Jaeger, 8 December 1945, AEK, CR II 25.18, 7 / 251.

14 Jaeger to Frings, 15 December 1945, AEK, CR II 25.18,7 / 243.

15 Regarding Jaeger, see Wolfgang Stüken, *Hirten unter Hitler: Die Rolle der Paderborner Erzbischöfe Caspar Klein und Lorenz Jaeger in der NS-Zeit* (Klartext 1999); Johannes Vutz, Josef Meyer zu Schlochtern (Eds.), *Jaeger: Ein Erzbischof in der Zeit des Nationalsozialismus* (Münster: Aschendorff Verlag, 2020); Christian Kasprowski and Nicole Priesching (eds.), *Lorenz Jaeger als Kirchenpolitiker* (Brill—Schöningh, 2021).

16 Dieter Riesenberger, *Der Paderborner Dompropst Paul Simon (1882–1946): Ein Beitrag zur Geschichte des Nationalsozialismus, der Oekumene und der Nachkriegsjahre in Paderborn* (Bonifatius, 1992), 54ff. On the issue of authorship, see also Utrecht, *The Lion of Muenster*, 363ff.

17 Jaeger to Pius XII, Paderborn 15 December 1945, in Ulrich Helbach (Bearb.), *Akten deutscher Bischöfe seit 1945 Westliche Besatzungszonen 1945–1947*, vol. 1 (Ferdinand Schoeningh, 2012), 313–16.

18 For a positive, rather uncritical view of Frings, see Norbert Trippen, *Josef Kardinal Frings (1887–1978). Band I. Sein Wirken für das Erzbistum Köln und für die Kirche in Deutschland* (Ferdinand Schoeningh, 2003). The author, a Catholic priest, was ordained by Frings. In 1991, Trippen attacked the groundbreaking research of the German historian Ernst Klee that detailed the Catholic Church's (and Frings's) role in helping Holocaust perpetrators escape earthly justice. See "Falsches Bild von der Wirklichkeit," *Rheinische Merkur*, 3 May 1991 AEK, Slg. Personalia, Geistliche, Tr-Tz, Norbert Trippen.

19 Josef Kardinal Frings, *Für die Menschen bestellt: Erinnerungen des Alterzbischofs von Köln Josef Kardinal Frings* (J. P. Bachem Verlag, 1974), 37.

20 Frings, *Für die Menschen bestellt*, 53.

21 Erzbistum Köln, Treffen Frings mit Colonel Hamilton und einem Vertreter von Field Marshal Montgomery, Aufzeichnung, July 1945, AEK, CR II 25.18,4/96.

22 Erzbistum Köln, Treffen Frings mit Colonel Hamilton und einem Vertreter von Field Marshal Montgomery, Aufzeichnung, July 1945, AEK, CR II 25.18,4/96.

23 Spotts, *The Churches and Politics in Germany*, 47.

24 Spotts, *The Churches and Politics in Germany*, 51.

25 Kornberg refers to a 1942 remark by Pius XII to the Austrian bishop Andreas Rohracher; see Kornberg, *The Pope's Dilemma*, 261.

26 Hirtenwort des deutschen Episkopats, Fulda, 23. August 1945, published in *Veröffentlichung der Kommission für Zeitgeschichte* (ed.) Reihe A, Quellen Band 38, *Akten deutscher Bischöfe über die Lage der Kirche VI, 1943–1945*, ed. Ludwig Volk (Mathias Gruenewald Verlag, 1985), 688–94.

27 „Lettera pastorale dell' Episcopato Germanico," *Osservatore Romano*, September 27, 1945, 1.

28 Hirtenwort des deutschen Episkopats, Fulda, 23, 688–694.

29 „Lettera pastorale dell' Episcopato Germanico," *Osservatore Romano*, September 27, 1945, 1.

30 Spotts, *The Churches and Politics*, 90.

31 "Dalla Germania," *Osservatore Romano*, 5 September 1946, 3.

32 Ruff, *The Battle for the Catholic Past*, 16; Rainer Bendel, ed., *Kirche der Sünder—Sündige Kirche? Beispiele für den Umgang mit Schuld nach 1945* (Münster: LIT, 2002); see also Thomas Forster, „Zweiter Kirchenkampf oder Stellvertreterdiskurs? Katholischer Konservatismus und die Interpretation des Katholizismus im Nationalsozialismus nach 1945" in Antonia Leugers, ed., *Zwischen Revolutionsschock und Schulddebatte*,243–282.

33 For more on these statements see: Toi Staff, "In 'confession of guilt,' German Catholic Church admits 'complicity' with Nazis," *Times of Israel*, 2 May 2020, accessed July 25, 2022, https://www.timesofisrael.com/german-bishops-said-to-admit-complicity-in-nazi-actions-in-new-report/.

34 Ordinariat des Erzbistums München und Freising an die Hochwürdigsten Bischöflichen Ordinariate Bayerns, 16 January 1947, signed Generalvikar Buchwieser, AEMF, NL Neuhäusler 209.

35 „Aus einem Bericht des Bischofs Dr. Muench, an den amerikanischen Episkopat" in *Glaube und Leben: Katholisches Kirchenblatt für das Bistum Mainz*, Nr. 9, 29 February 1948, Redaktion Bischöfliche Kanzlei Mainz 1, AEMF, NL Neuhäusler 203.

36 NL Neuhaeusler 522, Josef Ferrari to Neuhäusler regarding the case of Catholic layman and Nazi victim Josef Mayr-Nusser, 25 August 1947, signed Josef Ferrari. "[. . .] Die Art und Weise der Darstellung, die unserem Empfinden ganz widerspricht, dürfte entschuldbar sein durch den Zweck, den Alliierten zu zeigen, dass nicht alle Deutschen und auch nicht alle Südtiroler, Nazi waren. Dennoch aber bitte ich, auch im Namen der Witwe, in Zukunft von derartigen Veröffentlichungen Abstand nehmen zu wollen."

37 Michael Phayer, "The Postwar German Catholic Debate Over Holocaust Guilt," *Kirchliche Zeitgeschichte* 8, no. 2 (1995); *Theologie und Ideologie: Die beiden Großkirchen und die Diktaturen*, 426–439, 431.

38 Vatican Secretariat of State to Myron C. Taylor, May 14, 1945, NARA, RG 59, Entry 1068, Box 9, 811.1—von Faulhaber, Cardinal Michael.

39 Ventresca, *Soldier of Christ*, 239. Zeiger's speech at the Catholic Day in Mainz in September 1948 (the first after the Nazi regime) caused a stir with its central thesis: "Germany needs to be missionized!"

40 Letter Frings [to Jaeger], 11 September 1945, AEK, CR II 25.18,4/43.

41 Spotts, *The Churches and Politics*, 57.

42 Vatican, Archivio storico della Segretaria di Stato, Fondo Affari Ecclesiatici Straordinari, Periodo V (Pontificato Pius XII 1939–1958), Parte Prima (1939–1948) Germania, posizione 887, Germania e Austria—Visita del padre Ivo A. Zeiger S.J. ff. 2–226. "Bericht über die Reise des P. Ivo Zeiger S.J. zu dem hochwürdigsten Episkopat Deutschlands und Österreichs 1.-20. Sept. 1945."

43 See R. M. Douglas, *Orderly and Humane: The Expulsion of the Germans after the Second World War* (Yale University Press, 2012); Keith Lowe, *Savage Continent: Europe in the Aftermath of World War II* (Picador, 2012), 230–48.

44 Tomáš Staněk, *Verfolgung 1945: Die Stellung der Deutschen in Böhmen, Mähren und Schlesien* (Böhlau, 2002), 155–157; Benjamin Frommer, *National Cleansing: Retribution against Nazi Collaborators in Postwar Czechoslovakia* (Cambridge: Cambridge University Press, 2005), 43.

45 „An den Alliierten Kontrollrat für Deutschland zu Händen des derzeitigen Vorsitzenden Herrn General Eisenhower." 23 August 1945, Vertraulich! Anlage 3, AEK,CR II 25.18,3 / 287 ff.

46 Spotts, *The Churches and Politics*, 77.

47 The pope's message to Faulhaber and the bishops of Germany, in *Kirchliches Amtsblatt für die Erzdiözese Paderborn*, 1 March 1946. Thanks to Julia Hennig from the Erzbischöfliches Generalvikariat for sending me a copy of this document.

48 Frings to Pius XII, Cologne, 25 November 1945, in Ulrich Helbach (ed.), *Akten deutscher Bischöfe seit 1945 Westliche Besatzungszonen 1945–1947*, vol. 1 (Ferdinand Schoeningh, 2012), 290–94.

49 Fulda Conference of Bishops Petition to Truman signed by Frings (Cologne), Faulhaber (Munich), von Preysing (Berlin), Gröber (Freiburg), Jaeger (Paderborn) and Kolb (Bamberg), 3 July 1946, AEK CR II 25.18,9 / 244.

50 General Clay to von Preysing, 20 July 1946, AEK CR II 25.18,9 / 174. General Clay to von Preysing 15 July 1946, AEK CR II 25.18,9 / 175.

51 „Wir wissen, dass gerade in jenen Gebieten Deutsche furchtbare Verbrechen an den Angehörigen anderer Nationen begangen haben. Aber seit wann ist es erlaubt, an Unschuldigen sich zu rächen und Verbrechen durch Verbrechen zu sühnen? Man soll die wirklich Schuldigen zu unerbittlicher Rechenschaft ziehen. Aber wer will das Massensterben von Kindern, Müttern, alten Leuten verantworten?" Der Erzbischof von Köln, Kanzelverkündigung, 19 February 1946, AEK CR II 25.20b,5/130.

52 "Appunti riservati sulle condizioni berlinesi della zona occupata dei russi (aprile, maggio, giugno 1945)", AAV, Segr. Stato, Commissione Soccorsi 242, fasc. 188, f. 001r-010r.

53 Miriam Gebhardt, *Crimes Unspoken: The Rape of German Women at the End of the Second World War* (Cambridge UK: Polity Press, 2017); Lowe, *Savage Continent*, 51–57. On the situation in the Soviet zone of occupation, see Norman M. Naimark, *The Russians in Germany: A History of the Soviet Zone of Occupation, 1945–1949* (Harvard University Press, 1995), 69ff. Pertaining to the U.S. zone of occupation, see Petra Goedde, "From Villains to Victims: Fraternization and the Feminization of Germany, 1945–1947," *Diplomatic History* 23, no. 1 (Winter 1999): 1–20.

54 For more on the French zone of occupation, see Marc Hillel, *L'occupation française en Allemagne 1945–1949* (Balland, 1983), 83, 108–111. See also Gebhardt, *Crimes Unspoken*, 156.

55 "S.E. Il cardinale Faulhaber informa Mons. Carroll che le truppe marocchine in una sola notte hanno violato piu di 6.000 donne nella città di Stuttgart." 12 June 1945, AAV, Segr. Stato, Commissione Soccorsi 370, fasc. 564, f. 001r-003r.

56 See report "Das Kriegsende und die Franzosenzeit" pages 17 to 30. On page 23, the report notes that police officially verified 1,198 cases of rape over several weeks, which probably should be extended to include an approximately equal number of unreported cases. The report is published in Stadtarchiv Stuttgart (ed.), *Stuttgart in den ersten Nachkriegsjahren* (Klett-Cotta 1995). Letter from Stadtarchiv Stuttgart to the author, February 7, 2023; see also for an overview Hillel, *L'occupation française.*

57 Hirtenwort des deutschen Episkopats, Fulda, 23, 688–694.

58 Spotts, *The Churches and Politics in Germany*, 51.

59 OMGUS Office of Political Affairs Intelligence Branch Berlin, prepared by Colonel W. D. Hohenthal, 14 November 1945, Enclosure to Dispatch from November 19, 1945 by Ambassador Robert Murphy, NARA, RG 59, Entry 1068, Box 8, Decimal File 1944–45.

60 "Between War and Peace" (U.S. Bishop's statement Nov. 18, 1945), NARA, RG 59, General Records of the Department of State Myron Taylor File, Entry 1068, Box 9, Decimal File 1944–45 800 to 811.11

61 Tittmann forwarded a translation of an article of the *L'Osservatore Romano della Domenica* to the State Department, December 3, 1945. NARA, RG 59, General Records of the Department of State Myron Taylor File, Box 9, Entry 1068, Decimal File 1944–45 800 to 811.11.

62 Brown-Fleming, *The Holocaust and Catholic Conscience*, 139–157. For the full English text see Appendix C, *One World in Charity* (Fargo, 1946). See also Spotts, *The Churches and Politics in Germany*, 83.

63 Brown-Fleming, *The Holocaust and Catholic Conscience*, 45.

64 Ericksen, *Complicity in the Holocaust*, 168; Ian Kershaw, *'The Hitler Myth': Image and Reality in the Third Reich* (Oxford: Clarendon Press: 1987); Götz Aly, *Hitler's Beneficiaries: Plunder, Racial War, and the Nazi Welfare State* (New York: Metropolitan Books, 2007), Bendel, ed., *Kirche der Sünder*; Ruff, *The Battle for the Catholic Past*.

65 Andreas Wirsching, „Mehr Nähe als Distanz? Kardinal Michael von Faulhaber und der Nationalsozialismus," in *Distanz und Nähe zugleich? Die christlichen Kirchen im "Dritten Reich,"* ed. Friedrich Wilhelm Graf and Hans Günter Hockerts (NS-Dokumentationszentrum, 2017), 216.

66 Aleida Assmann and Ute Frevert, *Geschichtsvergessenheit–Geschichtsversessenheit: Vom Umgang mit deutschen Vergangenheiten nach 1945* (Deutsche Verlags-Anstalt, 1999), 141.

Chapter 6. Victors' Justice

1 Leugers, ed., *Zwischen Revolutionsschock und Schulddebatte*. See p. 27 in the introduction, where Leugers refers to a contribution by Thomas Forstner in the same volume: „Zweiter Kirchenkampf oder Stellvertreterdiskurs? Katholischer Konservatismus und die Interpretation des Katholizismus im Nationalsozialismus nach 1945," 243–82.

2 Klee, *Persilscheine und falsche Pässe*, 7.

3 Priemel, *The Betrayal*, 169.

4 Heller, *The Nuremberg Military Tribunals and the Origins of International Criminal Law*, 17; Frank M. Buscher, *The U.S. War Crimes Trial Program in Germany, 1946–1955* (Greenwood Press, 1989), 31.

5 Kaiser and Jasch, *Der Holocaust vor deutschen Gerichten*, 28; see also John Mendelsohn, "War Crimes Trials and Clemency in Germany and Japan," in *Americans as Proconsuls: United States Military Government in Germany and Japan, 1944–1952*, ed. Robert Wolfe (Southern Illinois University Press, 1984), 226–59, here 228; see Michael J. Bazyler and Frank M. Tuerkheimer, *Forgotten Trials of the Holocaust* (New York University Press, 2014), 75–100.

6 Evans, *Rituals of Retribution*, 744.

7 Initially, Alfried's father Gustav Krupp was charged, but due to old age and failing health, he was found unfit to stand trial. Thomas Rother, *Die Krupps: Durch fünf Generationen Stahl* (Campus Verlag, 2001), 178.

8 Letter Bertha Krupp to Pius XII, 24 October 1947 [Bluehnbach bei Werfen], AAV, Segr. Stato, Commissione Soccorsi 275, fasc. 681, f. 005r-008v.

9 Letter Fürsterzbischof von Salzburg Andreas Rohracher to Pope Pius XII, 30 October 1947, AAV, Segr. Stato, Commissione Soccorsi 275, fasc. 681, f. 003r.

10 Vatican Secretariat of State (Holy See) to U.S. Representative in Vatican, December 3, 1947 (Seal of the Secretariat of State), NARA, RG 59, Entry 1068, Box 17, Decimal File 1947, 711.4 Krupp Factories Managers (Mrs. Bertha Krupp).

11 Nuremberg Military Tribunals, ed., *Trials of War Criminals before the Nuremberg Military Tribunals*, vol. 9, "The Krupp Case" (U.S. Government Printing Office, 1950), 132.

12 Letter Bertha Krupp to Pius XII, 26 September 1948, AAV,—Segr. Stato, Commissione Soccorsi 275, fasc. 681, f. 028r-031v.

13 Montini, Vatican Secretariat of State to Bertha Krupp von Bohlen und Halbach, 15 November 1948, AAV, Segr. Stato, Commissione Soccorsi 275, fasc. 681, f. 033r.

14 AAV, Segr. Stato, Commissione Soccorsi 275, fasc. 681: Muench to Montini, December 1, 1948, f. 040r-040v and Robert Murphy to Bishop Muench, November 26, 1948, f. 041r.

15 "Asking the pope for help," University of Münster, accessed September 16, 2024, https://www.uni-muenster.de/FB2/en/aph/projekt/index.html.

16 Graf Harald Helmersen-Bosse to Pius XII, 1 August 1948, AAV, Segr. Stato, Commissione Soccorsi 282, fasc. 966, f. 002r-008v.

17 Vatican Secretariat of State to Cardinal Hlond, 30 September 1948, AAV, Segr. Stato, Commissione Soccorsi 282, fasc. 966, f. 13r.

18 Letter Vatican Secretariat of State, to Harald von Helmersen Neuwied 28 September 1948, AAV, Segr. Stato, Commissione Soccorsi 282, fasc. 966, f. 014r.

19 NARA, RG 242 BDC, SS Officers Dossier, Roll number SSo 083 A, Erwin von Helmersen 4. Nov. 1914.

20 Sabine Hildebrandt, Miriam Offer, and Michael A. Grodin, eds., *Recognizing the Past in the Present: New Studies on Medicine Before, During, and After the Holocaust* (Berghahn Books, 2021), 226.

21 Ernst Klee, *Das Personenlexikon zum Dritten Reich: Wer war was vor und nach 1945?* (S. Fischer Verlag, 2003), 244.

22 NARA, RG 242 BDC, SS Officers Dossier, Roll number SSo 083 A, Erwin von Helmersen 4. Nov. 1914, page 729, SS Personalbericht 1940.

23 Bass, *Stay the Hand of Vengeance*, 178.

24 Smith, *The American Road to Nuremberg*, 52.

25 Werner K., WCP Landsberg Affidavit, signed Werner K., Landsberg, 22 January 1948 and confirmed by notary Georg Thüsing, 1 March 1948, AEK, CR II 25.18,12a.

26 Steven P. Remy, *The Malmedy Massacre: The War Crimes Trial Controversy* (Harvard University Press, 2017), 85.

27 For example, during the liberation of the concentration camp Dachau, a number of surrendered SS guards were shot by the U.S. Army. Although understandable, given the horrors of the Nazi camps just encountered by the U.S. servicemen, the shooting of surrendered enemy personnel was and remains a war crime. None of the U.S. soldiers involved were ever prosecuted for these killings.

28 Remy, *The Malmedy Massacre*, 2.

29 Frei, *Adenauer's Germany and the Nazi Past*. See also Felix Bohr, *Die Kriegsverbrecherlobby: Bundesdeutsche Hilfe für im Ausland Inhaftierte NS-Täter* (Suhrkamp Verlag, 2018).

30 Condannati di Landsberg: Processi di Malmedy e Muehldorf, 2 February 1948, AAV, Segr. Stato, Commissione Soccorsi 283, fasc. 989, f. 004r.

31 Max Mueller to Pope Pius XII, 13 June 1948 AAV, Segr. Stato, Commissione Soccorsi 283, fasc. 989, 050r.

32 The Vatican Secretariat of State [Montini?] to Graham Parsons, 5 March 1948 [sent March 8, 1948] AAV, Segr. Stato, Commissione Soccorsi 283, fasc. 989, f. 033r-033v.

33 Note Montini, AAV, Segr. Stato, Commissione Soccorsi 283, fasc. 989, f. 35r.

34 Tomaz Jardim, *The Mauthausen Trial: American Military Justice in Germany* (Harvard University Press, 2012), 207.

35 Letter from Pius XII to the German bishops, 1 March 1948. Addressed by name were Faulhaber, Frings, and Preysing. Published in *Kirchlicher Anzeiger für die Erzdiözese Köln*, Köln, den 1. Mai 1948, 88. Jahrgang, pages 97–105. Special thanks to Dr. Josef van Elten and the archives of the archdiocese of Cologne for sending me a copy of this document.

36 Letter from Pius XII to the German bishops, 1 March 1948, in *Kirchlicher Anzeiger für die Erzdiözese Köln*, Köln, den 1. Mai 1948, 88. Jahrgang, pages 97–105, here 99.

37 "Forgive Germany, Pope urges world," *New York Times*, April 16, 1948, 10.

38 Letter Landsberger [Maximilian (Max) Schmid] to Pius XII, 28 April 1948, AAV, Segr. Stato, Commissione Soccorsi 281, fasc. 910, f. 002r-004r.

39 The Landsberg prison complex also was where Hitler was imprisoned for nine months in 1924, after the failed Beer Hall Putsch.

40 See Phayer, *Pius XII, The Holocaust, and the Cold War*; Goñi, *The Real Odessa*; Frei, *Vergangenheitspolitik*; Bohr, *Die Kriegsverbrecherlobby*; Brown-Fleming, *The Holocaust and Catholic Conscience*; Klee, *Persilscheine und falsche Pässe*; Spotts, *The Churches and Politics in Germany*. For Austria, see Eva Maria Kaiser, *Gottes Hirten und Hitler's Jünger: Der Einsatz der katholischen Bischöfe Österreichs für ehemalige Nationalsozialisten nach 1945* (Böhlau Verlag, 2017).

41 „Eine besondere Tätigkeit erforderte damals die Sorge für die sogenannten Kriegsverbrecher, also Soldaten, denen man irgendein Verbrechen zur Last legte." Josef Kardinal Frings, *Für die Menschen bestellt: Erinnerungen des Alterzbischofs von Köln Josef Kardinal Frings* (J. P. Bachem Verlag, 1974), 50.

42 CR II 25.18,10 / 99 Aufzeichnung Besuch Frings am 6 October 1946 „In diesen Tagen ist ein Urteil gefällt worden, durch das furchtbare Verbrechen, die unter Missbrauch des deutschen Namens begangen wurden, gesühnt werden sollen und in der Tat gesühnt werden. Wir glauben freilich, dass diese Sühne noch vollkommener sein würde, wenn das Urteil von deutschen Richtern und nach deutschen Gesetzen, die zur Zeit der Straftaten galten, gefällt worden wäre. Nachdem das Urteil gesprochen, verlangt das Rechtsbewusstsein aller rechtlich Denkenden, nicht nur in Deutschland, dass nunmehr auch Verbrechen, die anderso geschehen sind, die verdiente Ahndung finden. Sonst würde die Gerechtigkeit, die am Werke ist, trotz aller Objektivität nicht ganz jene Gerechtigkeit mit der Binde vor den Augen sein, die ohne jedes Ansehen der Person vorgeht, sondern würde mehr der Siegesgöttin mit dem gezückten Schwert gleichen, die die Feinde niederschlägt."

43 [Delegation], Cologne at Cardinal Frings' House, 17 October 1946, 17.20 hours, AEK, CR II 25.18,8 / 186.

44 [Delegation], Cologne at Cardinal Frings' House, 17 October 1946, 17.20 hours, AEK, CR II 25.18,8 / 186. On Frings, see Frei, *Adenauer's Germany and the Nazi Past*, 98–99.

45 [Delegation], Cologne at Cardinal Frings' House, 17 October 1946, 17.20 hours, AEK, CR II 25.18,8 / 186.

46 Peter Pfister, *Zeuge der Wahrheit: Johannes Neuhäusler—Ein Leben im Zeichen des Kreuzes* (Karmel Heilig Blut, 1988), 7 and 26. Thanks to Dr. Benita Berning, Archiv und Bib-

liothek des Ezbistums München und Freising for additional information from the 1961 *Amtsblatt* of the dioceses (letter from 29 March 2022).

47 Neuhäusler to Cardinal Francis Spellmann, 22 July 1948, AEMF, NL Neuhäusler 544. AEK CR II 25.18,13, letter to Spellmann, 22 July 1948.

48 Text telegram from Frings to Truman [30 October 1948]; Clay to Frings, 25 September 1948, AAV, Segr. Stato, Commissione Soccorsi 283, fasc. 989, f. 155r and 156r.

49 Hans Eisele and Willi Witteler to Neuhäusler, 1 March 1949, AEMF, NL Neuhäusler 531.

50 Hans Eisele and Willi Witteler to Neuhäusler, 9 March 1949, AEMF, NL Neuhäusler 531.

51 See Robert Sigel, *Im Interesse der Gerechtigkeit. Die Dachauer Kriegsverbrecherprozesse 1945–1948* (Campus-Verlag, 1992). Deputy Theater Judge Advocate's Office War Crimes Branch, United States Forces, European Theater, United States v Dr. Wilhelm Witteler et al., March 1946, Review and Recommendations of the Deputy Theater Judge Advocate, page 74, Internationales Forschungs–und Dokumentationszentrum Kriegsverbrecherprozesse (ICWC), Marburg, File 000-050-0002, accessed May 13, 2022, https://www.online.uni-marburg.de/icwc/dachau/000-050-0002.pdf.

52 Frings an General Clay mit Pro Memoria Fulda Bischofskonferenz betreffend Berufungsinstanz für die amerikanischen Militärgerichte, Fulda, 26 August 1948, AEK CR II 25.18,12 / 112. For the memo, see also Memorandum by the Evangelical Church in Germany on the Question of War Crimes Trials before American Military Courts Published for the Council of the Evangelical Church in Germany by Bishop D. Wurm, Church President D. Niemöller DD. DD. and Prelate D. Hartenstein [Not for publication Printed in Numbers n. 973] Gust. Stürner, Waiblingen-Stuttgart 1949, 40–41.

53 Clay to Frings, 25 September 1948, AEK, CR II 25.18,12/69.

54 Remy, *The Malmedy Massacre*, 149.

55 Apostolic Delegation United States of America to Montini, Signed Cicognani, 9 September 1948, AAV, Segr. Stato, Commissione Soccorsi 283, fasc. 989, f. 89r-91r.

56 Telegram Frings to Vatican, 23 Oktober 1948, AAV, Segr. Stato, Commissione Soccorsi 283, fasc. 989, f. 134r.

57 Montini to Frings, 26 October 1948, AAV, Segr. Stato, Commissione Soccorsi 283, fasc. 989, f. 138r. Also in Vatican Secretary of State, Montini to Frings, 26 October 1948, AEK, CR II 25.18,12/87.

58 Commissariat der Fuldaer Bischofskonferenz, to Frings, signed [Heinrich] Wienken, 21 October 1948, AEK, CR II 25.18,12/89.

59 NCWC News Service 10/25/48 „German bishops appeal to Clay to stay executions", AAV, Segr. Stato, Commissione Soccorsi 283, fasc. 989, f. 235r.

60 Vatican Secretary of State to Franklin C. Gowen, October 25, 1948, NARA, RG 59, Entry 1068, Box 21, 800—Germany—Frings.

61 United States Political Adviser For Germany, Berlin, "Unclassified" [handwritten note: Vatican notified 11-24-48], November 9, 1948, NARA, RG 59, Entry 1068, Box 21, 800—Germany—Frings.

62 Neuhäusler to General Clay, 26 October 1948, AEK, CR II 25.18,13a.

63 Neuhäusler to Frings, 27 October 1948, AEK, CR II 25.18,12/10.

64 „Kommentar der Woche: 'Die Stimme des christlichen Gewissens'" in „CND Christlicher Nachrichtendienst" München, Ausgabe 22, 28 October 1948, 1, AEMF, NL Neuhäusler 83.

65 Frei, *Adenauer's Germany and the Nazi Past*, 113. Muench to Montini, 1 May 1954, AAV, Arch. Nunz. Berlino 159, fasc. 42, Fasc. Kriegsgefangene 1950–1959 II—A—C—15, f. 40; Montini to Muench, 11 May 1954, AAV, Arch. Nunz. Berlino 159, fasc. 42, Fasc. Kriegsgefangene 1950–1959 II—A—C—15, f. 41.

66 Thomas Raithel, *Die Strafanstalt Landsberg am Lech und der Spöttinger Friedhof (1944–1958): Eine Dokumentation im Auftrag des Instituts für Zeitgeschichte München-Berlin* (Oldenbourg, 2009), 66.

67 Vatican Secretariat of State to Muench, 29 Oktober 1948 (draft letter!) AAV, Segr. Stato, Commissione Soccorsi 283, fasc. 989, f. 122r.

68 Muench's office (Rossi) to Montini, 22 October 1948, AAV, Segr. Stato, Commissione Soccorsi 283, fasc. 989, 125r, f. 125v.

69 See AAV, Segr. Stato, Commissione Soccorsi 283, fasc. 989.

70 Neuhäusler to Frings, 9 November 1948, AEK, CR II 25.18,12/58. "Was mir in den letzten Tagen von einigen ‚Sachbearbeitern' von Dachauer Prozessen mitgeteilt wurde, ist erschütternd. Ich verstehe darum immer mehr, dass man eine Appellation fast nicht zulassen kann. Es käme zu viel Unangenehmes auf. Ich werde Ew. Eminenz auch weiterhin auf dem Laufenden halten. In tiefster Ehrerbietung [signed] Neuhäusler Weihbischof"

71 Evans, *Rituals of Retribution*, 745; Jean Edward Smith, ed., *The Papers of General Lucius D. Clay: Germany 1945–1949* (Indiana University Press, 1974), 658–59.

72 Military Governor Lucius D. Clay to Monsignor Opilio Rossi, Vatican Mission Headquarters EUCOM, 11 January 1949, AAV, Segr. Stato, Commissione Soccorsi 283, fasc. 989, f. 252r.

73 William H. Draper, Acting Secretary of the Army to Reverend Edmund A. Walsh SJ, Vice president Georgetown University, 23 December 1948, AAV, Segr. Stato, Commissione Soccorsi 283, fasc. 989, f. 317r.

74 Muench to Montini, 3 November 1948, AAV, Segr. Stato, Commissione Soccorsi 283, fasc. 989, f. 231r.

75 Samuel Cardinal Stritch, Erzbischof von Chicago to Fings (?), 22 November 1948, AAV, Segr. Stato, Commissione Soccorsi 283, fasc. 989, f. 229r.

76 Brown-Fleming, *Muench*, 89; Jerome S. Legge, Jr., "Resisting a War Crimes Trial: The Malmedy Massacre, the German Churches, and the U.S. Army Counterintelligence Corps," *Holocaust and Genocide Studies* 26, no. 2 (Fall 2012): 229–60 (for his Nazi party membership, see 244).

77 Rudolf Aschenauer to Generalvikar der Erzdiözese Köln, Nürnberg, 10 July 1948, AEK, CR II 25.18,12/154.

78 Brown-Fleming, *Muench*, 89.

79 General Clay to Bishop Wurm 19 June 1948, LKAS, Wurm papers, USHMM Reel 61, Bueschel 287–289.

80 Johannes Neuhäusler to Wurm, 23 January 1951, LKAS, Wurm papers, USHMM Reel 62, Bueschel 295.

81 On the „Stille Hilfe" see LKAS, Wurm papers, USHMM Reel 62, Bueschel 294–95. See also Klee, *Persilscheine und falsche Pässe*; and Bohr, *Die Kriegsverbrecherlobby*.

82 See "German War Criminals and the Cold War," in Phayer, *Pius XII, the Holocaust, and the Cold War*, 160ff.

83 Congressional Record Proceedings and debates of the 81st Congress First Session, "American Justice Administered by the Military—Disgrace to United Stations" Remarks of Hon. William Langer of North Dakota in the Senate of the United States Thursday January 27, 1949, AEK, CR II 25.18,14/108 a.

84 Earl, *Nuremberg SS-Einsatzgruppen Trial*, 269–70.

85 Malmedy Massacre Investigation: Report of Subcommittee of the Committee on Armed Services United States Senate. S. Res. 42. Investigation of action of Army with respect to trial of persons responsible for the massacre of American soldiers, battle of the Bulge, near Malmedy, Belgium, December 1944. October 13, 1949 Printed for the use of the Committee on Armed Services, United States Government Printing Office, Washington: 1949, 2.

86 See Neuhäusler to National Council for the Prevention of War in Washington D.C., 20 July 1949, AEMF, NL Neuhäusler 521.

87 Malmedy Massacre Investigation: Report of Subcommittee of the Committee on Armed Services United States Senate, 32.

88 Jerome S. Legge, Jr., "Resisting a War Crimes Trial: The Malmedy Massacre, the German Churches, and the U.S. Army Counterintelligence Corps," 248.

89 Malmedy Massacre Investigation: Report of Subcommittee of the Committee on Armed Services United States Senate, 32.

90 Thomas Alan Schwartz, "John J. McCloy and the Landsberg Cases," in *American Policy and the Reconstruction of West Germany, 1945–1955*, ed. Jeffry M. Diefendorf (Cambridge University Press, 1994), 439.

91 On this topic, see Robert Hutchinson, *After Nuremberg: American Clemency for Nazi War Criminals* (Yale University Press, 2022).

Chapter 7. The Harvest of Souls

1 Flyer titled, "*Is Oswald Pohl a German Dreyfus?*," produced by the defense team, [April] 1951. AEMF, Nachlass Morgenschweis, 15.

2 Ulrike Bachhofer und Angela Achi, "Pragmatischer Umgang mit der Vergangenheit? Kirche und Fluchthilfe," in *Kirche der Sünder—Sündige Kirche? Beispiele für den Umgang mit Schuld nach 1945*, Beiträge zu Theologie, Kirche und Gesellschaft im 20. Jh: 1, ed. Rainer Bendel (LIT, 2002), 50; and Klee, *Persilscheine*, 106.

3 Klee, *Persilscheine*, 101.

4 Jan Erik Schulte, *Zwangsarbeit und Vernichtung: Das Wirtschaftsimperium der SS. Oswald Pohl und das SS-Wirtschafts-Verwaltungshauptamt 1933–1945* (Schöningh, 2001), 432.

5 Leon Goldensohn, *Die Nürnberger Interviews: Gespräche mit Angeklagten und Zeugen*, ed. Robert Gellately (Artemis and Winkler Patmos Verlag Ag, 2005), 406, see also 410.

6 Robert Hutchinson, *After Nuremberg: American Clemency for Nazi War Criminals* (Yale University Press, 2022), 85ff.

7 *"und mit dem gleichen Enthusiasmus, mit dem er sich einst in den Dienst eines Phantoms hingegeben hat nun der kath.[olischen] Religion hingeben will und als Apostel viele mit sich führen möchte zur Kirche."* Morgenschweis to the Bishop of Augsburg, January 8, 1950, "Betreff: Aufnahme in die Kirche des ehemaligen SS-Generals Oswald Pohl," Archiv des Bistums Augsburg (ABA), Bestand, Pfarreiakten/Landsberg am Lech—Mariae Himmelfahrt/Gefangenenanstalt/Personalia 1933–1960, (192).

8 Morgenschweis to the Bishop of Augsburg, January 8, 1950, "Betreff: Aufnahme in die Kirche des ehemaligen SS-Generals Oswald Pohl," Archiv des Bistums Augsburg (ABA), Bestand, Pfarreiakten/Landsberg am Lech—Mariae Himmelfahrt/Gefangenenanstalt/Personalia 1933–1960, (192).

9 "Betreff: Aufnahme in die kath. Kirche," SS General Oswald Pohl, Taufe sub condit. Handwritten letter, Vicariate General of Augsburg, January 16, 1950, ABA, Pfarreiakten/Landsberg am Lech—Mariae Himmelfahrt/Gefangenenanstalt/Personalia 1933–1960, (192).

10 Episcopal Ordinariate Augsburg to the Catholic Pastor of the Penal Institution Landsberg, January 18, 1950, signed by Generalvikar Dr. Doom, AEMF, NL Morgenschweis 16.

11 Protokoll der Taufe, February 12, 1950, "Taufe wurde bedingt wiederholt," signed Morgenschweis, AEMF, NL Morgenschweis, 16. See also Totenbuch Landsberg, numerus currens 302, Oswald Pohl, Execution June 7, 1951 (copy in possession of the author). Thanks to Thomas Raithel from the Institute for Contemporary History in Munich for sharing these records with me. See also Raithel, *Die Strafanstalt Landsberg*.

12 Frings to McCloy, February 12, 1951, AEK, CR II 25.18,27/53.

13 Wurm an Hoher Kommissar für Deutschland betreffend Oswald Pohl, February 14, 1951, LKAS, Wurm papers USHMM Reel 64—Bueschel 306/2.

14 Morgenschweis zu Faulhaber, February 8, 1950, AEMF, NL Morgenschweis, 16.

15 Katholischer Caritasverband Rosenheim an Caritas Erzdiözese München-Freising, Munich, February 4, 1950, AEMF, NL Morgenschweis, 16.

16 Dorothee Schmitz-Köster, *Kind L 364: Eine Lebensborn-Familiengeschichte* (Rowohlt, 2007), 187. Thanks to Father David Gantner, St. Ottilien, and Giles Bennett, Munich, for helping me with this research.

17 Schmitz-Köster, *Kind L 364*, 186.

18 Oswald Pohl, *Credo: Mein Weg zu Gott* (Girnth, 1950).

19 Totenbuch Landsberg, numerus currens 302, Oswald Pohl, Execution June 7, 1951 (copy in possession of the author). Thanks to Thomas Raithel from the Institute for Contemporary History in Munich for sharing these records with me. See also Raithel, *Die Strafanstalt Landsberg*.

20 Morgenschweis to Fräulein Pohl, June 26, 1951, ABA, Pfarreiakten/Landsberg am Lech—Mariae Himmelfahrt/Gefangenenanstalt/Personalia 1933–1960, (192).

21 Morgenschweis to Fräulein Pohl, June 26, 1951, ABA, Pfarreiakten/Landsberg am Lech—Mariae Himmelfahrt/Gefangenenanstalt/Personalia 1933–1960, (192).

22 Letter Morgenschweis to Paul T., September 17, 1951, ABA, Pfarreiakten/Landsberg am Lech—Mariae Himmelfahrt/Gefangenenanstalt/Personalia 1933–1960, (192).

23 Eleonore Pohl, "Landsberg Nr 24/51 Deutschland," letter to the editor, *Der Spiegel* 27/51, July 4, 1951, 34.

24 In a letter to the editor, Eleonore Pohl explained that the original plans for an urn burial fell through, because Pohl became Catholic. As a Catholic, his body should not be cremated and will therefore be buried in Landsberg. This is an interesting reasoning for Pohl's wife, given the fact that by the time of his execution, he had converted to Catholicism barely a year earlier. Eleonore Pohl, "Landsberg Nr 24/51 Deutschland," 34. She was reacting to an earlier report by the German weekly *Der Spiegel*, which stated that the town council of her hometown was against the burial of Oswald Pohl in their cemetery. "Landsberg," *Der Spiegel* 24/51, June 13, 1951, 12–13.

25 "Wem wird das kirchliche Begräbnis verweigert?," *Augsburger Katholische Kirchenzeitung*, February 19, 1950.

26 Katharina von Kellenbach, *The Mark of Cain: Guilt and Denial in the Post-War Lives of Nazi Perpetrators* (Oxford University Press, 2013), 89.

27 Muench to Montini, April 2, 1951, "Oggetto: Oswald Pohl," AAV, Arch. Nunz. Berlino 159, fasc. 42, Fasc. Kriegsgefangene 1950–1959 II—A—C—15, f. 81.

28 Notes Commissione Soccorsi 6.IV.51, AAV, Segr. Stato, Commissione Soccorsi 283, fasc. 989, f. 488r.

29 Muench to Montini, April 3, 1951, AAV, Arch. Nunz. Berlino 159, fasc. 42, Fasc. Kriegsgefangene 1950–1959 II—A—C—15, f. 82.

30 Morgenschweis to Muench, May 7, 1951, AEMF, NL Morgenschweis 15.

31 Vatican Secretariat of State to RA Friedrich Wiehl in Landsberg, April 10, 1951, signed Giovanni Battista Montini, AAV, Segr. Stato, Commissione Soccorsi 283, fasc. 989, f. 500r.

32 Letter Frederick Wiehl to Vatican, 30 March 1951, AAV, Segr. Stato, Commissione Soccorsi 283, fasc. 989, f. 489r-490r.

33 "Der Papst telegrafiert an Rotjacke—Ist Oswald Pohl unschuldig?," in *Münchner Allgemeine*, March 18, 1951, title story frontpage, AEMF, NL Morgenschweis 15.

34 Flyer, produced by defense "*Is Oswald Pohl a German Dreyfus?*", AEMF, NL Morgenschweis 15.

35 Morgenschweis to Pohlmann, March 21, 1951, AEMF, NL Morgenschweis 15.

36 Letter Frederick Wiehl to Vatican, 30 March 1951, AAV, Segr. Stato, Commissione Soccorsi 283, fasc. 989, f. 489r-490r.

37 Muench to Montini, April 25, 1951, AAV, Arch. Nunz. Berlino 159, fasc. 42, Fasc. Kriegsgefangene 1950–1959 II—A—C—15, f. 83.

38 Morgenschweis to Montini, March 28, 1951, AEMF, NL Morgenschweis 15.

39 Montini to Morgenschweis, April 7, 1951, AEMF, NL Morgenschweis 15.

40 On Protestant chaplains in Landsberg, see particularly Kellenbach, *Mark of Cain*.

41 Bachhofer and Achi, "Pragmatischer Umgang mit der Vergangenheit?," 50.

42 James W. Bernauer, ed., *Auschwitz and Absolution: The Case of the Commandant and the Confessor* (Orbis Books, 2024).

43 Steinacher, *Nazis on the Run*, 155–158, 191–192.

44 Phayer, *Pius XII, the Holocaust, and the Cold War*, 165; Brown-Fleming, *The Holocaust and Catholic Conscience*, 94–97.

45 Father Dr. Paulus Sladek to Muench, December 14, 1950, AAV, Arch. Nunz. Berlino 159, fasc. 42, Fasc. Kriegsgefangene 1950–1959 II—A—C—15, f. 53r e 53v.

46 Morgenschweis to Pius XII, April 1, 1948, AEMF, NL Morgenschweiss 90.

47 Letter Landsberger [Maximilian (Max) Schmid] to Pius XII, April 28, 1948, AAV, Segr. Stato, Commissione Soccorsi 281, fasc. 910, f. 002r-004r.

48 Kath. Pfarrer War Criminal Prison Landsberg am Lech Morgenschweis to Apostolic Nunciature, May 11, 1948, request to be forwarded to Pius XII, signed K. Morgenschweis Cath. Priest War Crim. Prison Landsberg (Lech), AEMF, NL Morgenschweis 90.

49 Morgenschweis to the Ordinariate of the bishop of Augsburg, January 28, 1946, "Betreff: Wiederaufnahme in die Kirche der 'Dachauer Verurteilten'," Archiv des Bistums Augsburg (ABA), Pfarreiakten Landsberg am Lech (PfA), Gefängnisanstalt Landsberg, Personalia 1933–1960.

50 Photo of Franz Strasser, "War Criminal with Priest (Original Caption) Franz Strasser, former Nazi official who was recently hanged as a war criminal for the killing of American flyers, is pictured in Landsberg prison shortly before he walked the last mile to the gallows. One of the last to visit the convicted criminal was a German Catholic priest Karl Morgenschweis, shown praying with the condemned man," accessed October 11, 2024, https://www.gettyimages.com/.

51 Morgenschweis to Ordinariate of the bishop of Augsburg, January 28, 1946, "Betreff: Wiederaufnahme in die Kirche: Strasser Franz," Archiv des Bistums Augsburg (ABA), Pfarreiakten Landsberg am Lech (PfA), Gefängnisanstalt Landsberg, Personalia 1933–1960.

52 Klee, *Personenlexikon zum Dritten Reich*, 664.

53 Morgenschweis to Ordinariate of the bishop of Augsburg, June 25, 1946 "Betreff: Wiederaufnahme in die Kath. Kirche der Gefangenen Eichberger Leonhard und Weiss Martin," ABA, Pfarreiakten Landsberg am Lech (PfA), Gefängnisanstalt Landsberg, Personalia 1933–1960.

54 Morgenschweis to Ordinariate of the bishop of Augsburg, June 25, 1946, "Betreff: Wiederaufnahme in die Katholische Kirche der Militärgef.[angenen] Altfudisch Hans [. . .], Giese Heinrich [. . .], Dr. Willi Jobst [. . .]," ABA, Pfarreiakten Landsberg am Lech (PfA), Gefängnisanstalt Landsberg, Personalia 1933–1960. For more background information on Altfudisch, Giese, and Jobst, see Jardim, *The Mauthausen Trial.*

55 Jardim, *The Mauthausen Trial*, 101.

56 Klee, *Personenlexikon zum Dritten Reich*, 288.

57 Klee, *Personenlexikon zum Dritten Reich*, 36–37.

58 Morgenschweis to Ordinariate of the bishop of Augsburg, April 16, 1952, "Betreff: Wiederaufnahme in die Kirche des ehemal.[igen] Gefangenen Dr. Wilhelm Beiglböck," ABA, Pfarreiakten Landsberg am Lech (PfA), Gefängnisanstalt Landsberg, Personalia 1933–1960.

59 Morgenschweis to Ordinariate of the bishop of Augsburg, May 7, 1946 "Betreff: Wiederaufnahme in die kath.[olische] für Kirche Fritz Hintermayer [. . .]," ABA, Pfarreiakten Landsberg am Lech (PfA), Gefängnisanstalt Landsberg, Personalia 1933–1960.

60 Klee, *Personenlexikon zum Dritten Reich*, 257.

61 Morgenschweis to Ordinariate of the bishop of Augsburg, January 13, 1948 "Betreff: Aufnahme in die Kath.[olische] Kirche für Dr. Hoven, Waldemar," ABA, Pfarreiakten Landsberg am Lech (PfA), Gefängnisanstalt Landsberg, Personalia 1933–1960.

62 Priemel, *The Betrayal*, 259; and Klee, *Personenlexikon zum Dritten Reich*, 272. See also Ernst Klee, *Euthanasieim Dritten Reich: Die 'Vernichtung lebensunwerten Lebens'* (Fischer, 2010), 286, 288, 661.

63 Morgenschweis to Ordinariate of the bishop of Augsburg, March 24, 1947, "Betreff: Absolution von der Exc.[ommunicatio] gemäss can. 2319,3 für Frau Drauz [. . .]," ABA, Pfarreiakten Landsberg am Lech (PfA), Gefängnisanstalt Landsberg, Personalia 1933–1960.

64 Klee, *Personenlexikon zum Dritten Reich*, 118.

65 Susanne Schlösser, "Die Heilbronner NSDAP und ihre 'Führer.' Eine Bestandsaufnahme zur nationalsozialistischen Personalpolitik auf lokaler Ebene und ihren Auswirkungen 'vor Ort,'" in *Heilbronnica 2: Beiträge zur Stadtgeschichte*, eds. Christhard Schrenk and Peter Wanner (Quellen und Forschungen zur Geschichte der Stadt Heilbronn 15, 2003), 283–89. See also Susanne Schlösser, "Was sich in den Weg stellt, mit Vernichtung schlagen - Richard Drauz, NSDAP-Kreisleiter von Heilbronn", in *Die Führer der Provinz: NS-Biographien aus Baden und Württemberg*, eds. Michael Kißener and Joachim Scholtyseck (Universitätsverlag Konstanz, 1999), 143–58.

66 Morgenschweis an Seine Hochwürden Msgr. Montini Pro-Staatssekretär Roma—Civita [sic!] Vaticana Staats-Sekretariat May, 18, 1954, signed Karl Morgenschweis, AEMF, NL Morgenschweiss 90.

67 Montini to Morgenschweis July 12, 1954, Gezeichnet JB Montini, AEMF, NL Morgenschweiss 90.

68 Roth to Neuhäusler, December 25, 1945, signed Father Roth, Lagerpfarrer, AEMF, Bistumsarchiv München-Freising, Pastorale Mitarbeiter Nr. 3031, (477).

69 "Seelsorge-Stelle im Kriegsgefangenenlager Dachau, 29. September 1945, Monats-Bericht, Pater Leo K. Roth." AEMF, NL Neuhäusler, Dechanat Dachau Seelsorgeberichte, Nr. 258.

70 Baldelli to Vatican Secretariat of State, July 30, 1947; PCA report dated July 22, 1947, signed Don Carlo Bayer, AAV, Segr. Stato, Commissione Soccorsi 264, fasc. 544, f. 001r-009r.

71 Catholic Priest War Crimes Prison Landsberg, to Ordinariate of the bishop of Augsburg, January 19, 1953, "Hochwürdigster, Hochverehrter Herr Prälat!" AEMF, NL Morgenschweis 90.

72 "Ansprache des HH. Kurat L. Roth am 8. Juni 1958 in der Barackenkirche zu Dachau-Ost.", AEMF, Bistumsarchiv München-Freising, Pastorale Mitarbeiter Nr. 3031 (152).

73 Ordinariat des Erzbistums München und Freising to Korbinian Roth, 19 June 1958, AEMF, Bistumsarchiv München-Freising, Pastorale Mitarbeiter Nr. 3031 (156). Roth repeatedly found himself in trouble with his Church superiors in Bavaria, who wanted to keep quiet about his arrest by the Nazis for being gay. Roth was a strong proponent of turning the former concentration camp Dachau into a memorial honoring the Nazi victims while pointing to the postwar careers of local Nazi officials, making him many enemies. In 1960, he apparently took his own life during a vacation in the Austrian Alps.

74 Bernauer, *Auschwitz and Absolution*, xxii.

75 Klee, *Persilscheine und falsche Pässe*, 108; Frei, *Adenauer's Germany*, 102–3.

76 "Der Bischof im Landsberger Gefängnis," *Augsburger Katholische Kirchenzeitung*, April 23, 1950.

77 "Die sieben Worte Jesu am Kreuze," *Augsburger Katholische Kirchenzeitung*, February 19, 1950.

78 Eugenio Zolli, *Before the Dawn: Autobiographical Reflections by Eugenio Zolli, former Chief Rabbi of Rome* (Ignatius, 2008), 15, 18. The author of the introduction is Arthur B. Klyber, who was himself a converted Jew and longtime "missionary" to the Jews.

79 "Il battesimo del Prof. Zolli," *Osservatore Romano*, February 15, 1945, 2.

80 "Alle origine dell'antisemitismo," *Osservatore Romano*, February 5, 1946, 3.

81 Kertzer, David I., and Roberto Benedetti, "The Vatican's Role in the Finaly Children's Kidnapping Case," *Studies in Christian-Jewish Relations* 15, no. 1 (2020): 1–15, https://doi.org/10.6017/scjr.v15i1.12765.

82 Bernauer, *Auschwitz and Absolution*, xxxi.

83 Kellenbach, *The Mark of Cain*, 29. See also Björn Krondorfer, Katharina von Kellenbach, and Norbert Reck, *Mit Blick auf die Täter: Fragen an die deutsche Theologie nach 1945* (Gütersloher Verlagshaus, 2006).

84 See "Rudolf Höss: Final Declaration, April 12, 1947," in Bernauer, *Auschwitz and Absolution*, 153.

85 Thomas Brudholm, "On the Advocacy of Forgiveness after Mass Atrocities," in *The Religious in Responses to Mass Atrocity: Interdisciplinary Perspectives*, eds. Thomas Brudholm and Thomas Cushman (Cambridge University Press, 2009), 126; Bachhofer and Achi, "Pragmatischer Umgang mit der Vergangenheit?," 51.

86 Pascalina Lehnert, *Ich durfte Ihm dienen: Erinnerungen an Papst Pius XII* (Verlag Johann Wilhelm Naumann, 1982), 102.

87 Kornberg, *The Pope's Dilemma*, 263.

88 Lehnert, *Ich durfte Ihm dienen*, 111.

Chapter 8. Godless Communism

1 J. Graham Parsons to Walter C. Dowling, Division of Southern European Affairs, Department of State, Washington, D.C., March 8, 1948 (TOP SECRET), NARA, RG 59, Myron Taylor File, Entry 1068, Box 21, 846. Anne O'Hare McCormick.

2 Kertzer, *The Pope at War*, 295.

3 Kornberg, *The Pope's Dilemma*, 240.

4 Tittmann, *Inside the Vatican of Pius XII*, 57.

5 Ventresca, *Soldier of Christ*, 220.

6 Chamedes, *A Twentieth-Century Crusade*.

7 British Legation to the Holy See, April 18, 1945, signed D. G. Osborne, NARA, RG 59, Entry 1068, Box 8, Decimal File 1944–45.

8 Myron C. Taylor to State Department, "Subject: Declaration on the organization for world peace of the National Catholic Welfare Conference," April 20, 1945, RG 59, Myron Taylor File, Entry 1068, Box 8, Decimal File 1944–45.

9 Harold H. Tittmann to Secretary of State, July 27, 1945 (Confidential), NARA, RG 59, Entry 1068, Box 8, Decimal File 1944–45.

10 "Pope Sees Danger of New Tyranny In Europe's Chaos," *The New York Times*, June 3, 1945, 1, 22.

11 Summarized translation, Harold Tittmann to Secretary of State, December 11, 1945. NARA, RG 59, Myron Taylor File, Entry 1068, Box 9, Folder 800. Moscow and Vatican.
12 Summarized translation, Harold Tittmann to Secretary of State, December 11, 1945. NARA, RG 59, Myron Taylor File, Entry 1068, Box 9, Folder 800. Moscow and Vatican; "Voci ed echi," *Osservatore Romano,* December 10–11, 1945, 1.
13 "L'enciclica 'Orientales omnes' per il 350' anniversario della unione dei Ruteni alla Sede Apostolica," *Osservatore Romano,* January 20, 1946, 1.
14 Vatican Secretariat of State to Franklin C. Gowen, assistant to the US representative, December 19, 1945, NARA, RG 59, Entry 1068, Box 9, Folder 800—Ukrainians displaced.
15 "L'enciclica 'Orientales omnes' per il 350' anniversario," 1.
16 "Proteste di profughi ucraini contro il conciliabolo scismatico tenuto a Leopoli," *Osservatore Romano,* September 12, 1946, 4.
17 "L'atto di accusa del pubblico ministero ucraino contro i vescovi cattolici," *Osservatore Romano,* October 14–15, 1946, 3.
18 "L'emigrazione dei ruteni ed ucraini profughi in Europa occidentale," *Osservatore Romano,* October 25, 1946, 1.
19 "L'opera di un pittore Croato nel Collegio di S. Girolamo," *Osservatore Romano,* January 14, 1945, 2.
20 "Voci ed Echi," *Osservatore Romano,* September, 16–17, 1946, 1.
21 "La prima udienza a Zagabria," *Osservatore Romano,* October 2, 1946, 1.
22 See the following *Osservatore Romano* articles: "Ancora l'interrogatorio di Mons Stepinac a Zagabria," October 3, 1946, 1; "Il processo di Zagabria," October 6, 1946, 1; "Il Sommo Pontefice inaugura il nuovo anno giuridico della sacra Romana Rota," October 7–8, 1946; "Il processo di Zagabria," October 9, 1946, 1; "Il processo di Zagabria," October 10, 1946, 1.
23 "Sentenza di condanna al processo di Zagabria," *Osservatore Romano,* October 12, 1946, 1.
24 "Dopo il processo di Zagabria," *Osservatore Romano,* January 10, 1947, 1; "La società del Sacro Nome sollecita aiuti per Mons. Stepinac," *Osservatore Romano,* October 20, 1947, 1.
25 Gallagher, *Vatican Secret Diplomacy,* 174.
26 "Sviluppi della persecuzione religiosa in Jugoslavia," *Osservatore Romano,* June 25, 1947, 3.
27 "La morte di un eroico vescovo jugoslavo," *Osservatore Romano,* October 10, 1946, 1.
28 „Dopo il processo di Zagabria," *Osservatore Romano,* October 18, 1946, 1.
29 McCormick, *Croatia under Ante Pavelić,* 38–39.
30 Secretariat of State to Sir Francis d'Arcy Godolphin Osborne His Britannic Majesty's Minster to the Holy See, December 5, 1946, National Archives of England, FO 371/59423, Southern 1947, Yugoslavia.
31 Pino Adriano, Giorgio Cingolani, *La via dei conventi: Ante Pavelić e il terrorismo ustascia dal fascismo alla guerra fredda* (Mursia, 2011), 355. English edition: *Nationalism and Terror: Ante Pavelić and Ustashe Terrorism from Fascism to the Cold War* (Central European University Press, 2018); see also Mark Aaron and John Loftus, *"Ratlines": How the Vatican's Nazi Networks Betrayed Western Intelligence to the Soviets,* (St. Martin's Griffin, 1998), 136–43.
32 „Gli Stati Uniti contro l'ingerenza dell'URSS in Ungheria," *Osservatore Romano,* March 8, 1947, 1.

33 "Voci ed Echi," *Osservatore Romano*, January 3–4, 1949, 2; "Dichirazioni ufficiali indicano il vero fine del sacrilegio arresto," *Osservatore Romano*, January 22, 1949, 1. See also the many articles in the *Osservatore Romano* on Mindszenty: January 10–11, 1949, 1; January 12, 1949, 1; January 13, 1949, 1; January 15, 1949, 1; January 21, 1949, 1; January 24–25, 1949, 1; February 3, 1949, 1.

34 "La vibrante protesta del Card Spellman," *Osservatore Romano*, January 6, 1949, 1.

35 "Continua la dolorosa eco per l'arresto del Card Mindszenty" "Il Messagio, riferendosi alle parole del Cardinal Spellman, che aveva definito l'azione del governo ungherese un'attentatto contro Iddio stesso e i popoli che credono in lui.," *Osservatore Romano*, January 6, 1949, 1.

36 "Fronte religioso nel campo politico," *Osservatore Romano*, May 30, 1948, 1.

37 See Michael Phayer's intervention in "Session One: Pacelli's Personality and the Jews," in *Pius XII and the Holocaust: Current State of Research*, eds. David Bankier, Dan Michman, and Iael Nidam-Orvieto (Yad Vashem, 2012), 28–45, here 34.

38 Alden Hatch, *Pope Paul VI* (Random House, 1966), 85–86.

39 Casella, *La mobilitazione delle organizzazioni cattoliche*, 39–49, 42.

40 See Ericksen, *Complicity in the Holocaust*, 58; Guenter Lewy, *The Catholic Church and Nazi Germany* (Da Capo Press, 2000), 30–31; and Wolf, *Pope and Devil*, 9. For Pius XI, see also Charles R. Gallagher, David I. Kertzer, and Alberto Melloni, eds., *Pius XI and America, Proceedings of the Brown University Conference* (LIT, 2012).

41 J. Graham Parsons to Walter C. Dowling, Division of Southern European Affairs, Department of State, Washington, D.C., March 8, 1948 (TOP SECRET), NARA, RG 59, Myron Taylor File, Entry 1068, Box 21, 846. Anne O'Hare McCormick.

42 J. Graham Parsons to Walter C. Dowling, Division of Southern European Affairs, Department of State, Washington, D.C., March 8, 1948 (TOP SECRET), NARA, RG 59, Entry 1068, Box 21, 846. Anne O'Hare McCormick.

43 J. Graham Parsons, Foreign Service Officer, Assistant to the Personal Representative to the President of the United States to His Holiness Pope Pius XII to the Secretary of State, March 23, 1948, "Subject: Future of Holy See If Communists Gain Control of Italy", NARA, RG 59, Entry 1068, Box 21, 800. Italian Elections.

44 J. Graham Parsons, Foreign Service Officer, Assistant to the Personal Representative to the President of the United States to His Holiness Pope Pius XII to the Secretary of State, March 23, 1948, "Subject: Future of Holy See If Communists Gain Control of Italy", NARA, RG 59, Entry 1068, Box 21, 800. Italian Elections.

45 J. Graham Parsons, Foreign Service Officer, Assistant to the Personal Representative of the President of the United States to His Holiness Pope Pius XII to the Secretary of State, March 23, 1948, "Subject: Future of Holy See If Communists Gain Control of Italy", NARA, RG 59, Entry 1068, Box 21, 800. Italian Elections.

46 "Subject: Future of Holy See If Communists Gain Control of Italy" March 23, 1948 to Secr. State Washington DC signed J. Graham Parsons, Foreign Service Officer, Assistant to the Personal Representative to the President of the United States to His Holiness Pope Pius XII, NARA, RG 59, Entry 1068, Box 21, 800. Italian Elections.

47 Burleigh, *Moral Combat*, 538.

48 "Between War and Peace" (U.S. Bishop's statement Nov. 18, 1945), NARA, RG 59, General Records of the Department of State Myron Taylor File, Entry 1068, Box 9, Decimal File 1944–45, 800 to 811.11.

49 Lehnert, *Ich durfte Ihm dienen*, 125.

50 Michael Phayer, "Canonizing Pius XII. Why did the Pope Help Nazis Escape?," *Commonweal Magazine*, June 23, 2004, 23.

51 Peter C. Kent, *The Lonely Cold War of Pope Pius XII.*

52 "Do we want a Soviet Peace" by Cardinal Francis Spellmann, Reprinted from Cosmopolitan Magazine, November, 1946, AAV, Segr. Stato, Titoli (1936–2005), Anno 1946, Cardinali, 86, f. 002r-003v.

53 „Non abbiamo bisogno di una pace sovietica," *Osservatore Romano*, December 2–3, 1946, 3.

54 Memorandum (enclosure with February 7, 1948) forwarded by the Papal Delegate to the US, Amleto Giovanni Cardinal Cicognani, to Monsignor Howard J. Carroll from the NCWC, 7 February 1948, Catholic University of America, Washington DC, University Archives, NCWC, Box 25, Folder 'Communism Italy 1944–1954'.

55 Memorandum handwritten date February 13, 1948, Catholic University of America, Washington DC, University Archives, NCWC, Box 25, Folder 'Communism Italy 1944–1954'. Part of this memorandum is included in the text of the February 7 enclosure.

56 Andrea Di Michele, *Storia dell'Italia repubblicana (1948–2008)* (Garzanti, 2008), 40–41.

57 J. Graham Parsons to Walter C. Dowling, Division of Southern European Affairs, Department of State, Washington, D.C., March 8, 1948 (TOP SECRET), NARA, RG 59, Entry 1068, Box 21, 846. Anne O'Hare McCormick.

58 "Cronaca di Roma. Conferimento della laure 'honoris causa' a Sua Eccellenza Myron Taylor," *Osservatore Romano*, June 7, 1945, 2.

59 Chamedes, *A Twentieth-Century Crusade*, 247.

60 J. Graham Parsons to Walter C. Dowling, Division of Southern European Affairs, Department of State, Washington, D.C., March 8, 1948 (TOP SECRET), NARA, RG 59, Entry 1068, Box 21, 846. Anne O'Hare McCormick.

61 J. Graham Parsons to Walter C. Dowling, Division of Southern European Affairs, Department of State, Washington D.C., March 13, 1948 (SECRET), NARA, RG 59, Entry 1068, Box 21, 800. Irish Ambassador.

62 J. Graham Parsons to Walter C. Dowling, Division of Southern European Affairs, Department of State, Washington D.C., March 13, 1948 (SECRET), NARA, RG 59, Entry 1068, Box 21, 800. Irish Ambassador.

63 Marco Invernizzi, *Luigi Gedda e il Movimento Cattolico in Italia* (Sguarco Edizioni, 2012), 65.

64 Mario Casella, "La mobilitazione delle organizzazioni cattoliche," in *18 Aprile 1948*, ed. Ernesto Preziosi (AVE, 1999), 39–49, 47.

65 To the Secretary of State from J. Graham Parsons Vatican City, March 6, 1948 (SECRET). NARA, RG 59, Entry 1068, Box 21, 800. Catholic Action (no mass rally).

66 "Subject: Civic Committees, the Vatican-inspired anti-Communist political action weapon in Italy." American Embassy Rome Italy, May 17, 1948 (SECRET), NARA, RG 59, Entry 1068, Box 21, 800. Comitati Civici.

67 "Subject: Civic Committees, the Vatican-inspired anti-Communist political action weapon in Italy." American Embassy Rome Italy, May 17, 1948 (SECRET), NARA, RG 59, Entry 1068, Box 21, 800. Comitati Civici.
68 Memorandum to Mr. Byington from Mr. Parsons, March 10, 1948 (SECRET), NARA, RG 59, Entry 1068, Box 21, 800. Italian Elections.
69 "Subject: Civic Committees, the Vatican-inspired anti-Communist political action weapon in Italy." American Embassy Rome Italy, May 17, 1948 (SECRET), NARA, RG 59, Entry 1068, Box 21, 800. Comitati Civici.
70 "Il sommo pontefice nell'ora grave di ansie e di pericoli traccia la via della salvezza per l'umanità," *Osservatore Romano*, March 29–30, 1948, 1.
71 "Subject: Transmitting Easter Sunday Address of the Pope", J. Graham Parsons to Secretary of State in Washington D.C., March 30, 1948, NARA, RG 59, Entry 1068, Box 21, 800 Easter address of Pope.
72 "Subject: Transmitting Easter Sunday Address of the Pope", J. Graham Parsons to Secretary of State in Washington D.C., March 30, 1948, NARA, RG 59, Entry 1068, Box 21, 800 Easter address of Pope.
73 "Subject: Transmitting Easter Sunday Address of the Pope", J. Graham Parsons to Secretary of State in Washington D.C., March 30, 1948, NARA, RG 59, Entry 1068, Box 21, 800 Easter address of Pope.
74 Report Parsons to Secretary of State Washington D.C. March 26, 1948, NARA, RG 59, Entry 1068, Box 21, 800. Il Quotidiano editorial (American Guarantees).
75 Chamedes, *A Twentieth-Century Crusade*, 256.
76 "Subject: Transmitting Copies of the Pope's Radio Broadcast of June 2, 1948", J. Graham Parsons, Foreign Service Officer, to Secretary of State Washington D.C., June 3, 1948, NARA, RG 59, Myron Taylor File, Entry 1068, Box 21, 800 Radio Broadcast of Pope.
77 "Subject: Transmitting Copies of the Pope's Radio Broadcast of June 2, 1948", J. Graham Parsons, Foreign Service Officer, to Secretary of State Washington D.C., June 3, 1948, NARA, RG 59, Myron Taylor File, Entry 1068, Box 21, 800 Radio Broadcast of Pope.
78 Kent, *The Lonely Cold War of Pope Pius XII*, 242.
79 Matthew 12:30; and "Subject: Transmitting Easter Sunday Address of the Pope", J. Graham Parsons to Secretary of State in Washington D.C., March 30, 1948, NARA, RG 59, Myron Taylor File, Entry 1068, Box 21, 800 Easter address of Pope.
80 "Cardinal Tisserant's Message to Faithful of His Diocesis", A.R.I. Bulletin No. 1, March 18, 1948, NARA, RG 59, Entry 1068, Box 21.
81 "Cardinal Tisserant's Message to Faithful of His Diocesis", A.R.I. Bulletin No. 1, March 18, 1948, NARA, RG 59, Entry 1068, Box 21.
82 Memorandum (Secret) to Major Berrisford H. Walker, Embassy, Rome, From Mr. Parsons, July 9, 1948, "Subject: Vatican Foreign Policy", NARA, RG 59, Entry 1068, Box 21, 800. Vatican.
83 "Catholic Communists to be excommunicated," *The Advocate* (Australia), July 15, 1949, 3.
84 Montini to Myron Taylor, July 11, 1949, NARA, RG 59, Entry 1068, Box 27, 570.3 Excommunication Decree ag.[ainst] Communists.

85 Michael Jones, "German Reds' Bloc in Soviet Zone Held Hurt By Pope's Excommunication of Communists," *New York Times*, July 20, 1949, 10.

86 Katholische Kirche und Kommunismus nach dem Dekret des Heiligen Offiziums vom 1. Juli 1949 und der Declaratio vom 11. August 1949, AEK, CR II 30.1,2 / 17.

87 Katholische Kirche und Kommunismus nach dem Dekret des Heiligen Offiziums vom 1. Juli 1949 und der Declaratio vom 11. August 1949, AEK, CR II 30.1,2 / 17.

88 Kent, *The Lonely Cold War of Pius XII*, 243, 245.

89 Chamedes, *A Twentieth-Century Crusade*, 245.

90 Piotr H. Kosicki, "The Holy See and the Cold War," in *The Vatican and Permanent Neutrality*, ed. J. Marshall Breger and Herbert R. Reginbogin (Lexington Books, 2022), 121–41.

91 Spicer and Carter-Chand, *Religion, Ethnonationalism, and Antisemitism in the Era of the Two World Wars*.

92 Wolf, *Pope and Devil*, 271.

93 Andrea Di Michele, *Storia dell'Italia repubblicana (1948–2008)* (Garzanti, 2008), 33.

94 "Non solo pane," *Osservatore Romano*, January 14, 1944, 1.

Chapter 9. Papal Humanitarianism

1 The PCA was re-named Pontificia Opera di Assistenza (POA) in the 1950s and later became part of Caritas Italiana—at least, this is the takeaway from the Vatican archival research tools for navigating and locating materials (finding aids) on the history of the POA.

2 Matteo Sanfilippo, "Per una storia dei profughi stranieri e dei campi di accoglienza e di reclusione nell'Italia del secondo dopoguerra," *Studi Emigrazione/Migration Studies* 43, no. 164 (2006): 835–56.

3 Pontificia Commissione Assistenza dated January 24, 1945, Ferdinando Baldelli, signed Felice Ricci S.J. Audience Baldelli with Pius XII. January 22, 1945, AAV, POA, Busta 1, fasc. 1, Sottofacsicolo 2, f. nn. "atti importanti 1945".

4 Lehnert, *Ich durfte Ihm dienen*, 103.

5 Baldelli to Montini, January 22, 1945, AAV, Segr. Stato, Comm. Soccorsi 382, fasc. 1133, f. 014r.

6 "Scopi e caratteristiche della PCA" [1947], here 2–3, AAV, POA, Busta 1, fasc. 3, [057].

7 Verbale della PCA sotto la Presidenza di S.E. Mons. Giovanni Montini, 8 February 1945, AAV, Segr. Stato, Comm. Soccorsi 382, fasc.1133, f. 144r-148r, here 147r.

8 Richard von Weizsäcker, *Vier Zeiten: Erinnerungen* (Pantheon, 2010), 367. The building was later confiscated by the Allies and today hosts offices of the French Embassy to the Holy See.

9 Dell'Acqua, April 11, 1946, Archivio Storico—Sezione per i Rapporti con gli Stati—Segretaria di Stato Città del Vaticano, Archivio della Segretaria di Stato per i Rapporti con gli Stati, fondo Congregazione degli Affari Ecclesiastici Straordinari, Pio XII, Stati Ecclesiastici, Pos. 575, f. 2331. See also Valbousquet, *Les âmes tièdes*, 300–302.

10 Dell' Acqua, April 11, 1946, Archivio Storico—Sezione per i Rapporti con gli Stati—Segretaria di Stato Città del Vaticano, Archivio della Segretaria di Stato per i Rapporti

con gli Stati, fondo Congregazione degli Affari Ecclesiastici Straordinari, Pio XII, Stati Ecclesiastici, Pos. 575, f. 2331. See also Valbousquet, *Les âmes tièdes*, 300–302.

11 Steinacher, *Humanitarians at War*; Steinacher, *Nazis on the Run*.

12 Steinacher, *Humanitarians at War*.

13 Papal nuncio Giuseppe Fietta to Montini, 3 December 1946, AAV, Arch. Nunz. Argentina 187, fasc. 871, Folder "Missione R.P. Silva, Salesiano", f. 079r. For the role of Argentina, see Goñi, *The Real Odessa*.

14 Stato della Citta del Vaticano, Governatorato, Missione della Pontificia Commissione Assistenza, Memorandum, 30 November 1946, AAV, Arch. Nunz. Argentina 187, fasc. 871, folder "Missione R.P. Silva, Salesiano" f. 083r-085r, here 085r.

15 "Oggetto: Circa opera svolta dagli inviati della Pontificia Commissione Assistenza" Fietta to Montini, 31 December 1946, AAV, Arch. Nunz. Argentina 187, fasc. 871, folder "Missione R.P. Silva, Salesiano" f. 087r.

16 Baldelli to Fietta, 25 January 1947, AAV, Arch. Nunz. Argentina 187, fasc. 871, folder "Missione R.P. Silva, Salesiano", f. 090r.

17 Cicognani to Fietta, 25 November 1946, AAV, Arch. Nunz. Argentina 187, fasc. 871, folder "Missione R.P. Silva, Salesiano", f. 091r.

18 It was named after a sixteenth-century Venetian statesman.

19 Baldelli to Montini, 7 January 1947, AAV, Segr. Stato, Uff. Migrazione 11, fasc. "Incidente Piroscafo 'Gritty'" f. 272r.

20 See e.g. Montini to papal nuncio in Buenos Aires, 16 January 1947, AAV, Segr. Stato, Uff. Migrazione 11, fasc. "Incidente Piroscafo 'Gritty'" f. 274r.

21 Letter NCWC War Relief Services Rio de Janeiro, Dr. Henry Amiel to Monsignor Edward Swanstrom, 22 January 1947, AAV, Segr. Stato, Uff. Migrazione 11, fasc. "Incidente Piroscafo 'Gritty'" f. 279r-284r.

22 "Prima conversazione con Sir Herbert Emerson, Direttore Generale del Intergovernmental Committee for Refugees", 14 February 1947, AAV, Segr. Stato, Uff. Migrazione 11, fasc. "Incidente Piroscafo 'Gritty'" 291r-293r, for the English version of report see f. 296r-301r, quote here 301r.

23 Vatican Secretariat of State, 14 March 1947, AAV, Segr. Stato, Uff. Migrazione 11, fasc. "Incidente Piroscafo 'Gritty'", f. 308r.

24 Francesco Echarri PCA Section for Foreigners to Montini, 4 March 1947, AAV, Segr. Stato, Uff. Migrazione 11, fasc. "Incidente Piroscafo 'Gritty'", f. 302r.

25 Colloquio con Mons. Landi, signed R., 14 March 1947, AAV, Segr. Stato, Uff. Migrazione 11, fasc. "Incidente Piroscafo 'Gritty'", f. 309r-310r.

26 Note, 2 March 1947, AAV, Segr. Stato, Uff. Migrazione 11, fasc. "Incidente Piroscafo 'Gritty'", f. 314r.

27 For more on Rev. Edward Killion, head of the Vatican Migration Bureau in Geneva, see Steinacher, *Nazis on the Run*, 110.

28 Memorandum by Monsignor Walter Carroll, 2 March 1947, AAV, Segr. Stato, Uff. Migrazione 11, fasc. "Incidente Piroscafo 'Gritty'", f. 336r-337r.

29 Report Walter Carroll to Vatican [Montini?], 28 March 1947, AAV, Segr. Stato, Uff. Migrazione 11, fasc. "Incidente Piroscafo 'Gritty'", f. 351r.

30 Patrick O'Boyle to Montini, 28 April 1947, AAV, Segr. Stato, Uff. Migrazione 11, fasc. "Incidente Piroscafo 'Gritty'", f. 375r.

31 Adriano and Cingolani, *Nationalism and Terror*; Christopher Hale, *Hitler's Foreign Executioners: Europe's Dirty Secret* (History Press, 2011).

32 Col. C. B. Findlay, Director D.P.R. Div. LACAB, director of displaced persons section to Monsignor J. McGeough, 3 March 1947, AAV, Segr. Stato, Migrazione Sez. Alleati 1, fasc. 50, f. 007r.

33 "Britain urges 30,000 Chetniks in Italy be given DP status" Newspaper article 26 Marzo 1947, McGeough to Montini "Appunto per S. E. Mons. Montini", 27 March 1947, AAV, Segr. Stato Migrazione Sez. Alleati 1, fasc. 50, f. 012v-013r.

34 Montini to Cicognani, 2 Aprile 1947, AAV, Segr. Stato Migrazione Sez. Alleati 1, fasc. 50, f. 015r.

35 Note, 30 March 1947, AAV, Segr. Stato Migrazione Sez. Alleati 1, fasc. 50, f. 016r.

36 Cicognani to Montini, 8 April 1947, AAV, Segr. Stato Migrazione Sez. Alleati 1, fasc. 50, f. 018r-019r.

37 Memorandum Conversation at the U.S. State Department, April 2, 1947, with General Hilldring, Assistant Secretary of State, Mr. George Warren, Director of Immigration-U.S. State Department and Mr. Fierst, Assistant to General Hilldring signed Walter S Carroll, AAV, Segr. Stato Migrazione Sez. Alleati 1, fasc. 50, f. 22r.-24r.

38 Memorandum Conversation at the U.S. State Department, April 2, 1947, with General Hilldring, Assistant Secretary of State, Mr. George Warren, Director of Immigration-U.S. State Department and Mr. Fierst, Assistant to General Hilldring signed Walter S Carroll, AAV, Segr. Stato Migrazione Sez. Alleati 1, fasc. 50, f. 22r.-24r.

39 Notes 16 April 1947 ("E A SS in 16.4.47"), AAV, Segr. Stato Migrazione Sez. Alleati 1, fasc. 50, f. 25r.

40 Pierre de L. Boal, Preparatory Commission for the IRO, to James C. Dunn, US ambassador in Rome, 10 September 1947, 'Strictly confidential', NARA, RG 84, Italy, US Embassy Rome, classified General Records, 1947, Entry UD2780, Box 20, Folder 848–IRO. See also James Clement Dunn to Pierre de L. Boal, Preparatory Commission for the International Refugee Organization, Palais des Nations, Geneve, Rome, Italy, 22 September 1947, NARA, RG 84, US Embassy Italy, Rome, classified General Records, 1947, Entry UD2780, Box 20, Folder 848–IRO.

41 W. Hallam Tuck Preparatory Commission for the IRO to Monsignor Walter Carroll, 10 September 1947, AAV, Segr. Stato Migrazione Sez. Alleati 1, fasc. 50, f. 051r.

42 Meeting at Villa Anastasia Monday, 29 September 1947 attended IRO official Prof. [Morton] Royse, Admiral Mentz (director of IRO screening board), Mons. Landi, Mons. McGeough and the undersigned Walter Carroll, AAV, Segr. Stato Migrazione Sez. Alleati 1, fasc. 50, f. 058r.

43 Lettera Pontificia Commissione di Assistenza—Presidenza, Oggetto: Profughi jugoslavi (grigi che non sono eleggibili per l'assistenza IRO), Bardelli to Montini 30 September 1947, AAV, Segr. Stato Migrazione Sez. Alleati 1, fasc. 50, f. 055r.

44 Letter H. W. Emerson to Wing Commander R. Innes PCIRO Geneva, 23 September 1947 with attached memorandum—the memo is labeled "riservato", AAV, Segr. Stato Migrazione Sez. Alleati 1, fasc. 50, f. 060r-062r.

45 "Situation of refugees claimed by Russia, Poland and Jugoslavia", "Situation of 'Grey' Refugees in Italy", no date, AAV, Segr. Stato Migrazione Sez. Alleati 1, fasc. 50, f. 173r.

46 McCormick, *Croatia under Ante Pavelić*, see Chapter 5.

47 Giorgio Magjerec, Collegium San Girolamo to Vatican Secretariat of State, 17 Maggio 1947, attached two memos from Prof. Draganović about "The legal position of Croatian war criminals in Italy", and "Croatian 'war criminals' in MP 32 in Rome", AAV, Segr. Stato Migrazione Sez. Alleati 1, fasc. 50, f. 27r.-039r.

48 "The legal position of Croatian war criminals in Italy", signed Prof. K. Draganović, AAV, Segr. Stato Migrazione Sez. Alleati 1, fasc. 50, f. 028r-032r.

49 Draganović to Montini [?], 5 October 1947, AAV, Segr. Stato Migrazione Sez. Alleati 1, fasc.50, 064r-065r; Appunto, Draganović, 3 October 1947, AAV, Segr. Stato Migrazione Sez. Alleati 1, fasc. 50, f. 063r.

50 Montini to Papal Nuncio in Buenos Aires, 2 September 1947, AAV, Segr. Stato Migrazione Sez. Alleati 1, fasc. 50, 124r; Handwritten memo from Draganović, 30 August 1947, handwritten notes in English "Do this". AAV Segr. Stato Migrazione Sez. Alleati 1, fasc. 50, f. 126r.

51 Ferdinando Baldelli to Montini, 4 October 1947, AAV, Segr. Stato Migrazione Sez. Alleati 1, fasc. 50, f. 067r.

52 Memo to Britannic Minister to the Holy, sent 10 October 1947, handwritten note on memo "visto dal SP [Santo Padre] 8 October 1947", AAV, Segr. Stato Migrazione Sez. Alleati 1, fasc. 50, f. 070r-072r.

53 "Ex Audentia SS.mi die 12 Octob. 47", AAV, Segr. Stato Migrazione Sez. Alleati 1, fasc. 50, f. 076r.

54 "Ex Audentia SS.mi die 12 Octob. 47", AAV, Segr. Stato Migrazione Sez. Alleati 1, fasc. 50, f. 076r.

55 Memo 12 October 1947, AAV, Segr. Stato Migrazione Sez. Alleati 1, fasc. 50, 077r; Nota Verbale, 12 October 1947, AAV, Segr. Stato Migrazione Sez. Alleati 1, fasc. 50, f. 078r-079r.

56 Udienza del 14 October 1947, AAV, Segr. Stato Migrazione Sez. Alleati 1, fasc. 50, f. 080r.

57 Memo, 15 October 1947, handwritten note on the side "Ex Aud., SS.mi in die 16-X-47 Non expedire quanto ai locali della P.C.A.", AAV, Segr. Stato Migrazione Sez. Alleati 1, fasc. 50, f. 084r; Appunto, Magjerec and Draganović, 17 October 1947, AAV, Segr. Stato Migrazione Sez. Alleati 1, fasc. 50, f. 085r.

58 "Ex Audit SS mi die 18—X—1947", AAV, Segr. Stato Migrazione Sez. Alleati 1, fasc. 50, f. 089r.

59 Memo, 19 October 1947, AAV, Segr. Stato Migrazione Sez. Alleati 1, fasc. 50, f. 087r-088r.

60 "Appunto per S.E. Mons. Montini", no date, AAV, Segr. Stato Migrazione Sez. Alleati 1, fasc. 50, 155r; Memo (for Montini?), no date, AAV, Segr. Stato Migrazione Sez. Alleati 1, fasc. 50, f. 154r.

61 Notes „SA M—è opportuno che la Santa Sede parli di questa qualifica "grigi"? Non si puo parlare semplicamente di profughi", AAV, Segr. Stato Migrazione Sez. Alleati 1, fasc. 50, f. 142r.

62 Telegram to Papal Nunciature Buenos Aires, signed Montini, undated, likely Winter 1947, AAV, Segr. Stato Migrazione Sez. Alleati 1, fasc. 50, f. 140r.

63 Telegram from Calleri, Nunciature, Buenos Aires 15 October 1947, AAV, Segr. Stato Migrazione Sez. Alleati 1, fasc. 50, 131r; Letterhead Vatican Secretariat of State, Telegram from Buenos Aires 16 Ottobre 1947, signed Calleri, handwrtitten note: "Visto dal S. Padre", AAV, Segr. Stato Migrazione Sez. Alleati 1, fasc. 50, f. 133r; Telegram from Buenos Aires, 17 October 1947, signed Calleri, AAV, Segr. Stato Migrazione Sez. Alleati 1, fasc.50, f. 134r.

64 "Situation of the 'Greys' in Italy," Report by [Joseph] McGeough, 18 October 1947, handwritten note "Ex Aud. SS die 20-X-47 per i soccorsi ai 'grigi' provede la Pont. Commissione Assistenza, come è stato stabilito . La Segretaria di Stato pensa solo alle eventuali trattative coi governi B. G.", AAV, Segr. Stato Migrazione Sez. Alleati 1, fasc. 50, f. 095r-095v.

65 "Partenza dei grigi da Genova 7 novembre 1947", McGeough, 30 October 1947, handwritten note: "31.X.47 avvertito Mons. Baldelli che provvederà", AAV, Segr. Stato Migrazione Sez. Alleati 1, fasc. 50, f. 097r.

66 "Appunto per S.E. Mons. Montini" McGeough, [October/November 1947], AAV, Segr. Stato Migrazione Sez. Alleati 1, fasc. 50, f. 103r.

67 McGeough to Montini, 25 October 1947, AAV, Segr. Stato Migrazione Sez. Alleati 1, fasc. 50, f. 136r.

68 Montini to Buenos Aires, 25 October 1947, AAV, Segr. Stato Migrazione Sez. Alleati 1, fasc. 50, f. 137r.

69 To Colonel C. B. Findlay, Subject: "Personal report from Major Tennant on visit of Argentine Visa Party to the U.S. and British Zones of Germany", Confidential, handwritten date 24 Decembre 1947, AAV, Segr. Stato Migrazione Sez. Alleati 1, fasc. 50, f. 109r-111r.

70 Appunto Il Sac. Draganović, AAV, Segr. Stato Migrazione Sez. Alleati 1, fasc. 50, f. 158r.

71 Krunoslav Draganović, "Resoconto dei lavori per l'emigrazione dei profughi 'grigi' dall'Italia e dalla Germania in Argentina", 8 April 1948, AAV, Segr. Stato Migrazione Sez. Alleati 1, fasc. 50, f. 194r-195r.

72 Andrea Casazza, *La fuga dei nazisti: Mengele, Eichmann, Priebke, Pavelic da Genova all'impunità* (Il melangolo, 2007).

73 Bardelli, PCA Rome to Monsignor Cicali, Genoa, February 26, 1948 Archivio della Caritas Diocesana—Genoa, Busta 71 "Storia", fasc. "profughi croati note e documenti del cap Bertola 1947–1980".

74 Baldelli to Montini, 15 December 1947, AAV, Segr. Stato Migrazione Sez. Alleati 1, fasc. 50, f. 105r.

75 Ferdinando Baldelli and Francesco Eccharri, PCA Ufficio Stranieri, to Mons. Giuseppe Cicali—PCA Sezione di Genova, 17 December 1947, Archivio della Caritas Diocesana—Genoa, Busta 71 "Storia", fasc. "profughi croati note e documenti del cap Bertola 1947–1980".

76 Siri to Montini, 5 February 1948, AAV, Segr. Stato, Uff. Migrazione, 30 AUXILIUM, fasc. Migrazione 1947, f. 016r; Note, 18 December 1947, AAV, Segr. Stato, Uff. Migrazione, 30 AUXILIUM, fasc. Migrazione 1947, f. 009r.

77 Auxilium, 7 November 1947, Ristoro Genova Principe alla PCA Roma, via Cairoli 117, Roma, "Oggetto: Croati diretti in Argentina", Archivio della Caritas Diocesana—Genoa, Busta 71 "Storia", fasc. "profughi croati note e documenti del cap Bertola 1947–1980".

78 Copia per l'Auxilium 18/11/47 "Oggetto: Croati diretti in Argentina", to Spett. Direzione della Pontificia Commissione di Assistenza Piazza Cairoli 117 Roma, Archivio della Caritas Diocesana—Genoa, Busta 71 "Storia" fasc. "profughi croati note e documenti del cap Bertola 1947–1980".

79 Another report to the Vatican from January 1948 talks about 80 Croatians managed by Draganović and helped by the local PCA Auxilium. Posto di Ristoro di Genova Principe to PCA, Roma, Genova 27/1/1948, "Oggetto: Assistenza Croati", Archivio della Caritas Diocesana—Genoa, Busta 71 "Storia" fasc. "profughi croati note e documenti del cap Bertola 1947–1980".

80 Auxilium Ristoro di Genova Principe, Genova, 10 dicember 1947 to PCA Roma, Oggetto: Assistenza Profughi Croati provenienti da Roma e diretti in Argentina, Archivio della Caritas Diocesana—Genoa, Busta 71 "Storia" fasc. "profughi croati note e documenti del cap Bertola 1947–1980". See Dirección Nacional de Migraciones file 72513/46.

81 „Relazione del Prof. Krunoslav Draganović su problemi emigratori", signed Prof. Sac. Kr. Stef. Draganović, Rome, 20 May 1949, AAV, Segr. Stato Migrazione Sez. Alleati 1, fasc. 50, f. 260r.-265r.

82 „Relazione del Prof. Krunoslav Draganović su problemi emigratori", signed Prof. Sac. Kr. Stef. Draganović, Rome, 20 May 1949, AAV, Segr. Stato Migrazione Sez. Alleati 1, fasc. 50, f. 260r.-265r.

83 David Martin, "Jews, Christians—and 'Collaborators,'" *America* 80 (January 1, 1949): 344–45. See Peter Novick, *The Holocaust in American Life* (Houghton, 1999), 89–90.

84 Novick, *The Holocaust in American Life*, 89–90.

Chapter 10. The Vatican Ratline

1 PCA Sezione Stranieri, Ferdinando Baldelli to Pontificia Commissione Assistenza "Auxilium" Genoa, 14 June 1950, Archivio della Caritas Diocesana—Genoa, Busta 71 "Storia" fasc. "profughi croati note e documenti del cap Bertola 1947–1980".

2 Vatican Secretariat of State, March 27, 1946 to Harold Tittmann, assistant to the personal representative of the President of the United States to His Holiness. PRO, WO 204/11133. See also Goñi, *The Real Odessa*, 327ff.

3 Joseph Hurley to Tardini 26 April 1946, Segr. Stato, Sezione per i Rapporti con gli Stati—Archivio Storico, Fondo Affari Ecclesiastici Straordinari, Pontificato di Pio XII, parte I 1939–1948, Jugoslavia, posizione 147, fasc. f. 6–9.

4 To cite one example among many, Vatican Secretariat of State to British Minister at the Holy See, 26 April 1947, PRO, FO 371/67376, File 97 Yugoslavia.

5 FO 371/67370, Yugoslavia File No 97, pp to 1527: "Yugoslav Quislings: Dragonovic" January 1947 internal notes apparently about the "Andrea Gritti" incident e.g. by A W H Wilkinson [18 January] 1947.

6 Draganović to Vatican Secretary of State, 31 May 1949, AAV, Segr. Stato, Commissione Soccorsi 515, fasc. 1949 Jugoslavi 7, f. 003r.

7 Draganović to Vatican Secretary of State, Appunto ("Urgentissimo"), 31 May 1949, AAV, Segr. Stato, Commissione Soccorsi 515, fasc. 1949 Jugoslavi 7, f. 002r.

8 Appunto, 20 July 1949, AAV, Segr. Stato, Commissione Soccorsi 515, fasc. 1949 Jugoslavi 7, f. 006r.

9 Appunto, Vatican Secretariat of State to the Italian Embassy to the Holy See, 3 June 1949, AAV, Segr. Stato, Commissione Soccorsi 515, fasc. 1949 Jugoslavi 7, f. 005r.

10 [From] PS Comm. Tempesta, "D. Draganovic", Notes, 6 June 1949, AAV, Segr. Stato, Commissione Soccorsi 515, Jugoslavi 8, f. 003r.

11 "Il Draganović è quel sacerdote che sembra essere minacciato di morte. Non à pericoloso dare lettera di Segretaria di Stato che potrebbe dar motivo a dicerie, che la Santa Sede si presta a relazioni fra i fuorusciti e il Ministero dell'Interno Italiano? B". [Barbetta?], Note without date, AAV, Segr. Stato, Commissione Soccorsi 515, fasc. 1949 Jugoslavi 7, f. 014r.

12 Note without date, AAV, Segr. Stato, Commissione Soccorsi 515, fasc. 1949 Jugoslavi 7, f. 015r.

13 "Mi sembra che si debba seguire il parere di Mons. Barbetta. Il Draganović è ricercato, si dice, dagli agenti di Tito. Egli non abita a S. Girolamo degli Illirici ma vive ad un indirizzo non precisato. I sacerdoti del collegio S. Girolamo sono pero' in relazione con lui. Per il loro tramite l'ho fatto avvertire del pericolo che gli sovrasta. Forse è più prudente far venire in Segretaria uno dei sacerdoti del collegio e rimmettergli l'appunto (o gli appunti) i questione su carta non intestata cossichè non apparisca la Santa Sede. 8/8/49" Handwritten note on this document: "Ex Aud. S.S. in die IV-VIII-49—[. . .] Se fare a voce, ma niente in scritto". AAV, Segr. Stato, Commissione Soccorsi 515, Jugoslavi 7, f. 015r.

14 Borgongini Duca to Tardini, 21 September 1949, AAV, Segr. Stato, Commissione Soccorsi 515, fasc. 1949, Jugoslavi 8, f. 004r.

15 It is not easy to find information about Jure Bujanović, though a Josip Bujanović is mentioned in Mark Aarons and John Loftus's *Ratlines*, and by Uki Goñi in *The Real Odessa*. Josip Bujanović was a priest and henchman of the Croatian Fascist leader Ante Pavelić, associated with terrible massacres of Serbs. At the war's end, he fled, first to Austria and then to Italy. Known there as "Popa Jolu," he helped criminals like Ante Pavelić and Dinko Sakic hide in Rome and then flee to South America. He also participated in the postwar attempt to dislodge Marshal Tito's communist regime in Yugoslavia. He eventually settled in Australia but visited Argentina a few times. The available details about Jure Bujanović, including his family name, his background as priest and member of Ustaša, his close alliance with Draganović and Drago Jilek, his prominence as wanted war criminal, and his ultimate refuge in Australia, imply that Jure and Josip (Jolu) Bujanović might be the same person. For a brief biography, see Goñi, *La auténtica Odessa: fuga nazi a Argentina* (Ariel, August 2017). See also Mark Aarons, *War Criminals Welcome: Australia, a Sanctuary for Fugitive War Criminals Since 1945* (Black Inc., 2020); and Ante Delić, "Novi prilozi za istraživanje akcije 'Deseti travnja': nepoznato pismo Ante Pavelića iz srpnja 1948," *Radovi Zavoda Za Povijesne Znanosti Hazu U Zadru* 60 (2018): 385–409.

16 See Pino Adriano, Giorgio Cingolani, *La via dei demoni: Ante Pavelic e il terrorismo ustascia dal Fascismo alla guerra fredda* (Mursia, 2011), 410.

17 Appunto D. Zabkar, 27 September 1949, AAV, Segr. Stato, Commissione Soccorsi 515, Jugoslavi 8, f. 007r.

18 Allegato from Italian authorities dated 13 September 1949, attached to official letter from Borgongini Duca to Tardini, 21 September 1949, AAV, Segr. Stato, Commissione Soccorsi 515, Jugoslavi 8, f. 005r.

19 Appunto D. Žabkar, 27 September 1949, AAV, Segr. Stato, Commissione Soccorsi 515, Jugoslavi 8, f. 007r.

20 Italian Ministry of the Interior, Direz. Generale di P.S., Pel Capo della Polizia Nicolosi, all' Ufficio Speciale di P.S.S. Pietro, 3 February 1950, Oggetto: Bujanović Jure, religiosos jugoslavo, (riservatissima), AAV, Segr. Stato, Commissione Soccorsi 515, Jugoslavi 8, f. 14r.

21 Appunti 22 May 1950 gbm, 24 May 1950 Mis.[uraca?], AAV, Segr. Stato, Commissione Soccorsi 515, Jugoslavi 8, f. 023r.

22 Appunto (maybe from Italian embassy), 12 November 1949, AAV, Segr. Stato, Commissione Soccorsi 515, Jugoslavi 8, f. 011r.

23 Report "Collegio di San Girolamo degli Illirici" 1957, Segr. Stato, Sez Rapporti con gli stati, Archivio Storico, Fondo Affari Ecclesiastici Straordinari, Pontificato Pius XII, Parte II 1949–1958, Posiz. 294, Collegio di San Girolamo degli Illirici, Fasc. f. 61, "Circa la situazione del Collegio di San Girolamo degli Illirici e la nomina del nuovo Rettore nella persona die Mons. Giorgio Koksa", pages 125ff.

24 Appunto 25 October 1949, AAV, Segr. Stato, Commissione Soccorsi 515, Jugoslavi 8, f. 010r.

25 Appunto 22 February 1950 with recommendations from Comm. Tempesta, AAV, Segr. Stato, Commissione Soccorsi 515, Jugoslavi 8, f. 016r.

26 Giovanni Battista Montini, Vatican Secretariat of State, to Mons. Misuraca, 6 March 1950, AAV, Segr. Stato, Commissione Soccorsi 515, Jugoslavi 8, f. 019r.

27 Giovanni Battista Montini, Vatican Secretariat of State, to Mons. Misuraca, 6 March 1950 and handwritten note at the bottom of letter dated 7 March 1950 [Gasperini?], AAV, Segr. Stato, Commissione Soccorsi 515, Jugoslavi 8, f. 019r.

28 Appunto Comm. Socc., 9 March 1950, avertito il Comm. Tempesta, 14 March 1950, AAV, Segr. Stato, Commissione Soccorsi 515, Jugoslavi 8, f. 018r.

29 Krunoslav Draganović, "Promemoria circa l'immigrazione dei profughi dell'Europa in Argentina", 8 March 1948, AAV, Segr. Stato Migrazione Sez. Alleati 1, fasc. 50, f. 190r.

30 „Relazione del Prof. Krunoslav Draganović su problemi emigratori", signed Prof. Sac. Kr. Stef. Draganović, Rome, 20 May 1949, AAV, Segr. Stato Migrazione Sez. Alleati 1, fasc. 50, f. 260r.-265r.

31 ACICR, Titres de voyages CICR, application nr. 84,227, Stangl Paul, Rome, 25 August 1948; Letter of Recommendation PCA—Sezione Stranieri to the ICRC in Rome for Paul Stangl, 17 August 1948. ACICR, Titres de voyages CICR, application nr. 84, 228, Wagner Gustav, Rome, 25 August 1948, letter of recommendation from the PCA for Gustavo Wagner, 17 August 1948.

32 On Hudal, see Johannes Sachslehner, *Hitlers Mann im Vatikan: Bischof Alois Hudal. Ein dunkles Kapitel in der Geschichte der Kirche* (Molden Verlag, 2019); Steinacher, *Nazis on the Run*; Klee, *Persilscheine und falsche Pässe*; and Hans Jakob Stehle, "Bischof Hudal und

SS-Führer Meyer: Ein kirchenpolitischer Friedensversuch 1942/43," *Vierteljahrshefte für Zeitgeschichte* no. 2 (1989): 299–322.

33 Alois Hudal, *Die Grundlagen des Nationalsozialismus: Eine ideengeschichtliche Untersuchung* (Verlag Johannes Günther, 1937).

34 ACICR, Titres de voyages CICR, application nr. 83.023, Otto Pape, Rome, 26 July 1948; Lettera PCA 9538/99, 26 July 1948; see Steinacher, *Nazis on the Run*, 92–93.

35 Notes on Pape, Archivio Storico di Santa Maria dell'Anima, Rome (ASMA), Hudal Papers, Box K23, Document 9; AH 23/9

36 Pfarramt Sterzing, Pfarre Unsere Liebe Frau im Moos 1943–1951: Entry in the baptism register for 13 September 1948 for Erich Priebke baptized by Stadtpfarrer Johann Corradini. For the interaction between Pobitzer, Hudal and Father Johann Corradini to procure travel papers for Otto Pape see the short bio of Pape in the Anima Archives, Rome, ASMA, Hudal Papers, Box K23, Dokument 9; AH 23/9 and statement Corradini, Stadtpfarramt Sterzing, 15 February 1948, ASMA, Hudal Papers, Box K23, Document 10; AH 23/10; See also Guy Walters, *Hunting Evil: The Nazi War Criminals Who Escaped and the Quest to Bring Them to Justice* (Random House, 2009), 174 f; and Steinacher, "Forgive and Forget?," 1, 4–28.

37 Gitta Sereny, *Into that Darkness: An Examination of Conscience* (Vintage, 1983), 289.

38 ACICR, Titres de voyages CICR, application nr. 74988, Walther Ottowitz, Rome, 26 March 1948. Affidavit from Walther Ottowitz, 22 March 1948, confirmation for Walther Ottowitz from Bishop Alois Hudal, 24 March 1948; Lettera PCA signed Francesco Echarri, 23 March 1948; for his Nazi career see: NARA, RG 202, BDC, *Ortsgruppendatei* NSDAP, Walther Ottowitz, born 9 April 1902, joined Nazi Party 1 August 1932, Nazi party membership no. 1,209,702.

39 Hudal recommendation for Ottowitz to Vatican Emigration Office, 21 June 1948, AAV, Segr. Stato, Migrazione Sez. Alleati 4, fasc. 55, f. 12r-12v.

40 Montini to Giuseppe Fietta, Nunzio Apostolico, Buenos Aires, 29 November 1948, AAV, Segr. Stato, Migrazione Sez. Alleati 4, fasc. 55, f. 16r.

41 Walther Ottowitz, Memorandum, Ottowitz gave his address: "c/o Bishop Alois Hudal, via della pace 20, Roma", AAV, Segr. Stato, Migrazione Sez. Alleati 4, fasc. 55, f. 7r-8r.

42 Baldelli to Vatican Secretariat of State, December 4, 1946, AAV, Comm. Soccorsi 382, fasc. 1133, f. 724r-729r. See also L'Attività della Santa Sede dal 15 Dicembre 1945 al 15 Dicembre 1946 (non ufficiale) Tipografia Poliglotta Vaticana 1946, report about the Pontificia Commissione di Assistenza starts at page 111 ff, Facoltà Teologica del Triveneto, Padova, Biblioteca.

43 Andrew Landi, NCWC to Hudal, 17 December 1948, ASMA, Hudal papers, Box K 24, Document 73.

44 Klee, *Persilscheine*, 39

45 See e.g. the correspondence in ASMA, Hudal papers, Box K 46.

46 Dominik Moroder, St. Ulrich (Gröden) to Bischof Alois Hudal, Rome, 26 January 1949, ASMA, Box K 24, Document 852.

47 Dominik Moroder had good reasons to leave, as he was a former SS officer, had been involved in numerous crimes against Italian partisans and Jews, and was closely as-

sociated with Mario Carità, the leader of a notorious Italian gang of SS collaborators and murderers. Cf. Gerald Steinacher, "Spione, Räuber und Mörder: Südtiroler im Sicherheitsdienst des Reichsführers SS in Italien 1943–45," *Geschichte und Region/storia e regione* anno/Jg. 12 (2013): 109–36; for more on Carità see Simon Levis Sullam, *The Italian Executioners: The Genocide of the Jews in Italy* (Princeton University Press, 2018) and Amedeo Osti Guerrazzi, *Gli specialisti dell'odio: Delazioni, arresti, deportazioni di ebrei Italiani* (Giustina, 2021).

48 Gerald Steinacher, "Adolf Eichmann—Ein Optant aus Tramin," in "*Deutsche! Hitler verkauft euch!": Das Erbe von Option und Weltkrieg in Südtirol*, ed. Günther Pallaver and Leopold Steurer (Edition Raetia, 2010), 305–35.

49 Letter Pater Franz Pobitzer to Hudal, 28 March 1950, ASMA, Hudal papers, Box K 25, Document 260.

50 Recommendation letter Hudal, official letterhead Anima, "alle autorita italiane ed argentine" „caldamente posso recommendare il profugo Francisco Noelke, 29 March 1950, ASMA, Hudal papers, Box K 25, Document 261.

51 Application for a Red Cross travel document for Francesco Noelke, Italian Red Cross in Genoa, 1 November 1950. ICRC Geneva, Archive, 'Titres de Voyage CICR 1945–1993', application 100, 958. Gerald Steinacher, *Nazis on the Run*, 50.

52 Application for a Red Cross travel document for Riccardo Klement, ICRC Genoa, 1 June 1950, ICRC Geneva, Archive, 'Titres de Voyage CICR 1945–1993', application 100, 940.

53 Goñi, *The Real Odessa*, 299.

54 Adolf Eichmann, "Meine Flucht, Bericht aus der Zelle in Jerusalem," World Exclusive in *The People*, London, NARA, RG 263 (CIA), War Crimes, CIA Name Files, IWG, Box 14, Eichmann, Adolf, Vol.1

55 Goñi, *The Real Odessa*, 299.

56 Steinacher, *Nazis on the Run*, 49–52; Gerald Steinacher, "'Il Signor Mengele di Bolzano': L'Alto Adige come via di fuga dei criminali nazisti (1945–1951)," in *Dalla liberazione alla ricostruzione: Alto Adige/Südtirol 1945–1948*, ed. Giorgio Mezzalira, Fabrizio Miori, Giovanni Perez, and Carlo Romeo (Edition Raetia, 2013), 33–56; David G. Marwell, *Mengele: Unmasking the "Angel of Death"* (W. W. Norton & Company, 2020), 149–58.

57 Application for a Red Cross travel document for Kremhart Teodoro, ICRC Genoa, 31 October 1949, ICRC Geneva, Archive, 'Titres de Voyage CICR 1945–1993', application 100, 569.

58 Hans [Aichinger?] to Greil, 27 October 1949, ASMA, Hudal Papers, Box K 25, Document 629.

59 Steinacher, *Nazis on the Run*, 125.

60 Stangneth, *Eichmann Before Jerusalem*; Steinacher, *Nazis on the Run*.

61 For local Nazi networks, see Gerald Steinacher, "'A Man with a Wide Horizon': The Postwar Professional Journey of SS Officer Karl Nicolussi-Leck," in *A Nazi Past: Recasting German Identity in Postwar Europe*, ed. David A. Messenger and Katrin Paehler (University Press of Kentucky, 2015).

62 Hans-Ulrich Rudel, *Zwischen Deutschland und Argentinien: Fünf Jahre in Übersee* (Plesse Verlag, [1954]) 46.

63 See my paper "The Vatican and the Escape of Axis War Criminals from Justice" presented at the International Conference "New Documents from the Pontificate of Pope Pius XII and their Meaning for Jewish-Christian Relations: A Dialogue between Historians and Theologians" at the Pontifical Gregorian University in Rome, October 2023. The paper will be published in the upcoming conference volume.

64 Nota Verbale Vatican Secretariat of State to Harold Tittmann, 27 August 1945, NARA, RG 59, Entry 1068, Box 8, 800.

65 Simpson, *Blowback*, 180–81; Klee, *Persilscheine und falsche Pässe*, 29; Steinacher, *Nazis on the Run*, 186; Aarons and Loftus, *Unholy Trinity*, 202–07; Hale, *Hitler's Foreign Executioners*, 380; Howard Margolian, *Unauthorized Entry: The Truth about Nazi War Criminals in Canada, 1946–1956* (University of Toronto Press, 2000), 135; Stephen Dorril, *MI6: Inside the Covert World of Her Majesty's Secret Intelligence Service* (Free Press, 2000), 202.

66 Monsignor Antonino Arata [?], from the Congregation of the Oriental Churches to Montini, 19 July 1947, AAV, Comm Soccorsi 382, fasc. 1133 PCA, f. 738r, 739r.

67 Giovanni Bucko to Pius XII, 2 August 1948, AAV, Segr. Stato, Migrazione Sez. Alleati 6, fasc. 40, f. 2r and letter to Montini, 2 August 1948, f. 6r-7r.

68 North King passenger list, 18 april 1948—includes many Hungarians, AAV, Segr. Stato, Migrazione Sez. Alleati 3, fasc. 98, f. 057r.

69 Francesco Zavatti, "'To Be Assisted Secretly': Catholic Humanitarianism and Romanian Displaced Fascists, 1945–7," *Journal of Contemporary History* 61, no. 1 (2026): 49–75.

70 Telegram PCIRO Rome, 9 March 1948, AAV, Segr. Stato, Migrazione sez. Alleati 3, fasc. 98, f. 003r; Telegram PCIRO Rome, signed Dr. H. Zimmermann, Chief Emigration Branch II, 21 April 1948, f. 056r.

71 Steinacher, *Nazis on the Run*, 88. For Vatja, see also the Freedom of Information Act Electronic Reading Room of the CIA: https://www.cia.gov/readingroom/.

72 Robert Obermair, *Oswald Menghin: Science and Politics in the Age of Extremes* (de Gruyter, 2024), 449.

73 ACICR, Titres de voyages CICR, application nr. 13069 for Ambrosio Menghin, Genoa, 6 April 1948.

74 "International Reactionaries Finance the Settling of Yugoslav Criminals from Italy in South America," *Borba*, January 13, 1947, 2.

75 "Prisma," *Il Quotidiano*, January 22, 1947, 1. See also Archivio Storico-Diplomatico, Ministero Affari Esteri Roma, ASMAE, Affari Politici 1946–1950 Paese: Santa Sede, Busta 6, Da "Il Quotidiano" del 22 gennaio 1947, *Visto dal Vice Direttore Generale*.

76 See *L'Unità*, January 29 and 31, 1947. The *L'Unità* front-page article of January 31 is titled "Per i criminali è facile emigrare: Lettera n. 1241 della Commissione Pontificia."

77 See *Il Quotidiano*, January 22, 1947, and February 1, 2, 4, and 5, 1947; here "Prisma," *Il Quotidiano*, February 1, 1947, 1.

78 Archivio Storico-Diplomatico, Ministero Affari Esteri Roma, ASMAE, Affari Politici 1946–1950, Paese: Santa Sede, Busta 6, Aperte accuse di un giornale jugoslavo al Vaticano; Da "Il Quotidiano" del 5 Febbraio 1947.

79 ASMAE, Affari Politici 1946–1950, Paese: Santa Sede, Busta 6, Ministero degli Affari Esteri D.G.A.P.—Ufficio VII—Santa Sede a Ambasciata presso la Santa Sede. Roma, 5 febbraio 1947, Oggetto: Criminali di Guerra Jugoslavi e Vaticano, Riferimento: Telespresso minist. n.14/02250/13 del 24 gennaio u.s. f.to Jannelli.

80 Archivio Storico-Diplomatico, Ministero Affari Esteri Roma, ASMAE, Affari Politici 1946–1950, Paese: Santa Sede, Busta 6, Santa Sede a Ambasciata d'Italia a Mosca e p.c. D.G.A.P.—Ufficio IV—Sede. Roma, 14 febbraio 1947, Oggetto: Richieste jugoslave al Vaticano circa criminali di guerra, f.to Jannelli.

81 Baldelli to Tardini, 7 February 1947 (Copia dates 12 February 1947), AAV, Segr. Stato, Uff. Migrazione 11, fasc. "Incidente Piroscafo 'Gritty'" f. 303r.

82 Exodus to S. America of Yugoslav war criminals / Five Yugoslavs in Vatican property; Copies of two notes by the Yugoslav government to Vatican Secretariat of State, British Embassy, Belgrade to Foreign Office, February 3, 1947. PRO FO 371/67371, File No. 97.

83 Yugoslav Quislings: Dragonovic; telegram from Mr. Clutton, Belgrade, January 14, 1947. Transmits telegram add'd Caserta No.4. signature: AWH Wilkinson 18/1, PRO, FO 371/67370, File No. 97.

84 Exodus of Yugoslav War Criminals to S. America, Report from Sir. D. Osborne; Holy See, January 31, 1947. PRO FO 371/67371, File No. 97.

85 Hansjakob Stehle, "Pässe vom Papst? Aus neuentdeckten Dokumenten: Warum alle Wege der Ex-Nazis nach Südamerika über Rom führten," *Die Zeit*, May 4, 1984, 9–12 ('Dossier'), 12.

86 Sir D. G. Osborne to Ernest Bevin, (RESTRICTED), Yugoslavia, February 4, 1947. PRO, FO 371/67371, File 97.

87 Aide Memoire, Vatican Secretariat of State, February 3, 1947. PRO, FO 371/67371, File No. 97.

88 Sir D. G. Osborne to Ernest Bevin, (RESTRICTED), Yugoslavia, February 4, 1947. PRO, FO 371/67371, File 97.

89 Note by J.R. Colville 13/2—Foreign Office official. Five Yugoslavs on Vatican property: Exodus of Yugoslav war criminals to S. America; from Sir D. Osborne, Holy See, Foreign Office statements, February 1947 PRO, FO 371/67371, File No. 97. See also Goñi, *The Real Odessa*, 332–33.

90 United States' diplomatic and intelligence reports on the subject date back as early as 1946. See Steinacher, "Forgive and Forget?," 4–28.

91 Vincent La Vista to Herbert J. Cummings, 15 May 1947 (TOP SECRET), NARA, RG 84, Austria, Political Adviser, Gen. Records 1945–55, Entry 2057, box 2, 2.

92 American embassy to the Holy See Memo on movement of undesirable persons with the aid of charitable organizations, undated [filed 1948?], AAV, Segr. Stato, Migrazione Sez. Alleati 5, fasc. 20, f. 3r and 4r.

93 Graham Parsons in Vatican City to the Division of Southern European Affairs, Department of State, Washington DC, 29 August 1947 (TOP SECRET), Vienna Wiesenthal Institute, Simon Wiesenthal Archive, I.1, Rauff, Walter (02).

94 "*Österreichische Zeitung*" – *Zeitung der Sowjetarmee für die Bevölkerung Österreichs*, Donnerstag 19 Mai 1949, Seite 1, AA.EE.SS. Pontificato Pius XII, Parte I (1939–1948), Austria, Posiz. 934, 160; "*Der Abend*", 7 May 1949, AA.EE.SS. Pontificato Pius XII, Parte I (1939–1948), Austria, Posiz. 934, 161.

95 Muench to Tardini, Segr. della S. Congregazione degli Affari Ecclesiastici Straordinari, 19 April 1950, AA.EE.SS. Pontificato Pius XII, Parte I (1939–1948), Austria, Posiz. 934: "Inopportuni articoli di Mons. Hudal in riviste tedesche all'estero" da Kronberg, Reggente Nunziatura, 254r and 254v.

96 Attachment to note 25 giugno 1949, Bishop Alois Hudal, Rektor der deutschen Nationalkirche der Anima „Drei Wünsche, Rom Silvester 1948, An meine lieben Landsleute in Argentinien!", Sonderdruck aus der Zeitschrit „der Weg", Monatshefte zur Kulturpflege und zum Aufbau, Heft 2, 1949, Buenos Aires, Casilla Correo 2398. AA.EE.SS. Pontificato Pius XII, Parte I (1939–1948), Austria, Posiz. 934: "Inopportuni articoli di Mons. Hudal", page 164–165, here 165.

97 Tardini to Muench, 30 April 1950, AA.EE.SS. Pontificato Pius XII, Parte I (1939–1948), Austria, Posiz. 934: "Inopportuni articoli di Mons. Hudal in riviste tedesche all'estero" da Kronberg, Reggente Nunziatura, 275.

98 On the Wächter case, see Philippe Sands, *The Ratline: The Exalted Life and Mysterious Death of a Nazi Fugitive* (St. Martin's Press, 2020).

99 "L'assassino di Dollfuss si faceva chiamare Otto Reinhardt," *Il Giornale d'Italia*, September 3, 1949, 1; "Il caso di O. Wächter," *Il Giornale d'Italia*, September 4, 1949, 1 and 2; "Wächter aveva documenti regolari al nome di Reinhardt rilasciati in altra città italiana," *Il Giornale d'Italia*, September 6, 1949, 4; "Sotto la paterna protezione di Vaticano e Viminale—Il partito nazista ricostituito negli istituti religiosi teutonici," *L'Unità*, September 4, 1949, 2; "I trascorsi di Mons. Hudal protettore del nazista Waechter," *L'Unità*, September 6, 1949, 2; "Il vescovo Hudal sara scomunicato? Per aver violato il segreto di S. Ufficio," *L'Unità*, September 9, 1949, 2; "Il criminale Otto Skorzeny atteso al' istituto di Santa Maria dell'Anima," *L'Unità*, February 18, 1950, 2; "Nella bara di Otto Waechter il cadavere del generale Ritter—sintomico intervista da Monsignor Hudal da un giornale," *L'Unità*, February 22, 1950, 2.

100 "Dopo il caso Wächter," *L'Unità*, September 4, 1949, 2.

101 "Menschenschmuggel-Zentrale München—Illegale Kanäle nach Spanien, Südamerika und den Nahen Osten," *Münchner Abendzeitung AZ*, December 3, 1949, 7. See also a long article „Menschenschmugel blüht trotz Grenzsperre," *Passauer Neue Presse*, December 13, 1949; Hudal is mentioned as a "brown [Nazi] bishop," and a contact person for Nazis on the run in Rome, very similar to the article in the Munich newspaper.

102 Dino De Rugeriis, "Mons. Hudal conferma la morte di O. Waechter," *Il Giornale d'Italia*, February 22, 1950, 1.

103 See, for example, The Associated Press, "2 Church Historians Deny that Vatican Helped Nazis Escape," *The New York Times*, January 30, 1984, A1, A7. Ralph Blumenthal, "Study Reported Shelved," *New York Times*, February 23, 1984, A8.

104 "*Papinski hrvatski zavod svetog Jeronima: (1901–2001): zbornik u prigodi stoljetnice Papinskoga hrvatskog zavoda svetog Jeronima*" ["Pontifical Croatian Institute of Saint Jerome (1901–2001): Collection on the occasion of the Centenary of the Pontifical Croatian Institute of Saint Jerome"], edited by Jure Bogdan, Pontifical Croatian Institute of Saint Jerome, Rome, 2001.

105 Osservazione di Carlo Pacelli sulla PCA, Stato della città del Vaticano, Il consigliere Generale, Roma, April 11, 1945 to Cardinale Raffaello Carlo Rossi, Segretario della S.

Congregazione Consistoriale Palazzo della Cancelleria Roma, AAV, Segr. Stato, Comm. Soccorsi 382, fasc. 1133, f. 033r-037v., here f. 037r-037v.

106 See also Francesco Zavatti, "'To Be Assisted Secretly': Catholic Humanitarianism and Romanian Displaced Fascists, 1945–7," *Journal of Contemporary History* 61, no. 1 (2026): 49–75.

107 Hudal, *Römische Tagebücher*, 21: „All diese Erfahrungen haben mich schließlich veranlasst, nach 1945 meine ganze karitative Arbeit in erster Linie den früheren Angehörigen des NS und Faschismus, besonders den sogenannten 'Kriegsverbrechern' zu weihen, die von Kommunisten und 'christlichen' Demokraten verfolgt wurden."

Epilogue

1 Letter Hudal to Montini, 5 May 1949, ASMA, Hudal papers, Box K 40, Document 76.

2 Letter Segretaria di Stato di Sua Santità, Montini to Hudal, 12 May 1949 (Riservata), ASMA, Hudal papers, Box K 39, Document 199. "Can la Sua pregiata lettera, in data 5 corrente, l'Eccellenza Vostra Reverendissima auspicava, in occasione dell'Anno Santo, una giornata di generale perdono e di larga amnistia. In via del tutto riservata e confidenziale, ho il piacere di comunicarLe che questa Segretaria di Stato, per iniziativa del Comitato Centrale per l'Anno Santo, ha gia fatto, al riguardo, vari passi, presso i diversi Governi. Speriamo che, con l'aiuto di Dio e la buona volontà degli uomini, si possa giungere a qualcosa di concreto. Profito della circostanza per baciarLe il S. Anello e confermarmi con sensi di devoto ossequio." G. B. Montini. I found copies of this correspondence also in the Vatican archives; see AAV, Segr. Stato, Titoli (1936–2005), Anno 1950, Anno Santo posiz. V/3. 142 (2), f. 003r.-004r "S. E. Mons. Luigi Hudal—auspica, in occasione dell'Anno Santo, una giornata di generale perdono e di larga amnistia."

3 The Vatican also discussed the burning problem of whether Protestants were welcome in Rome for the Holy Year. The decision: "Everyone agrees on the usefulness of not closing the door to those who, with right intention, want to approach the true Church," Riunione del Comitato Centrale, 13 December 1949, AAV, Anno Santo 1950, Busta 1, fasc. B.

4 AAV, Anno Santo 1950, Busta 1, fasc. C "Comitato Centrale Anno Santo Prot. N. 647 Segretaria Generale. Fini proposti dal Santo Padre per l'Anno Santo" [July 1948], See also AAV, Anno Santo 1950, Comitato Centrale per l'Anno Santo—adunanza del 23 Luglio 1948, Busta 1, fasc. B.

5 Marco Invernizzi, *Luigi Gedda e il Movimento Cattolico in Italia* (Sguarco Edizioni, 2012), 85; see also Mario Casella, *L'Azione Cattolica Italiana e i 'lontani'* (Velar, 2010), 111–200.

6 Letter Franklin C. Gowen to Secretary of State, Washington D.C., November 14, 1949. NARA, RG 59, Myron Taylor File, Records of the Personal Representative of the President to Pope Pius XII, Entry 1068, Box 27, Decimal File 1949, 350. Amnesty granted by Brazil in Holy Year 1950. The letter of Monsignor Montini from October 19, 1949, is quoted by Gowen. See also the original letter in French from Montini to Gowen, October 19, 1949.

7 Letter Franklin C. Gowen to Secretary of State, Washington D.C., November 14, 1949. NARA, RG 59, Myron Taylor File, Records of the Personal Representative of the

President to Pope Pius XII, Entry 1068, Box 27, Decimal File 1949, 350. Amnesty granted by Brazil in Holy Year 1950. The letter of Monsignor Montini from October 19, 1949, is quoted by Gowen. See also the original letter in French from Montini to Gowen, October 19, 1949.

8 Letter Franklin C. Gowen to Secretary of State, Washington D.C., November 14, 1949. NARA, RG 59, Myron Taylor File, Records of the Personal Representative of the President to Pope Pius XII, Entry 1068, Box 27, Decimal File 1949, 350. Amnesty granted by Brazil in Holy Year 1950.

9 Franklin C. Gowen to Montini, January 10, 1950, NARA, RG 59, Entry 1068, Box 27, 350. Amnesty was granted by Brazil in Holy Year 1950.

10 Statement by Pope to Spanish Ambassador, Subject: Editorial in Catholic Action's Ecclesia: Church Must Extinguish Civil War Hatreds. Madrid, January 26, 1949, To Secretary of State in Washington D.C. copy to Taylor from US Embassy Madrid, NARA, RG 59, Entry 1068, Box 27, 570.3.

11 "Oggetto: Circolari al Corpo Diplomatico e alle Rappresentanze pontifiche", AAV, Segr. Stato, Titoli (1936–2005), Anno 1950, Anno Santo posiz. V/3. 142 (3).

12 „Weihnachtsbotschaft seiner Heiligkeit Papst Pius XII am Tag der Eröffnung der Heiligen Pforte", 23 December 1949, AEK, CR II 30.1,2/8; Pius XII, Radiomessaggio di Sua Santità Pio XII al mondo intero, 23 December 1949, Acta Apostolicae Sedis 42 (1950): 122–33, https://www.vatican.va/archive/aas/index_en.htm; For the English version see Pius XII, Radio Message to the World Given December 23, 1949, 1949 Christmas Message (Washington, DC: National Catholic Welfare Conference, 1949), here 10–11.

13 Bishop Aloisius Muench, Regent, Apostolic Nunciature in Germany, to John J. McCloy, US High Commissioner for Germany, 19 December 1949, NARA, RG 466 HICOG, McCloy papers, Entry 1, 1950, Box 6, Folder D (50) 57. For more on Muench, see Brown-Fleming, *The Holocaust and Catholic Conscience.*

14 John McCloy to Aloisius Muench, Bishop of Fargo, Apostolic Nuncio in Germany, 11 January 1950, NARA, RG 466 HICOG, McCloy papers, Entry 1, 1950, Box 6, Folder D (50) 57.

15 Felix Bohr, *Kriegsverbrecherlobby: Bundesdeutsche Hilfe für im Ausland inhaftierte NS-Täter* (Suhrkamp Verlag, 2018).

16 Muench to Tardini, 13 April 1951, AAV, Arch. Nunz. Berlino 159, fasc. 42, Fasc. Kriegsgefangene 1950–1959 II—A—C—15, f. 003r; Staatssekretär des Auswärtigen Amts to Muench, 10 April 1951, AAV, Arch. Nunz. Berlino 159, fasc. 42, Fasc. Kriegsgefangene 1950–1959 II—A—C—15, f. 004r.

17 Filippo Focardi, *Criminali di Guerra in liberta: Un accord segreto tra Italia e Germania federale, 1949–1955* (Carocci, 2008), 54.

18 Muench to Segretaria di Stato, Carlo Grano, 15 June 1951, AAV, Arch. Nunz. Berlino 159, fasc. 42, Fasc. Kriegsgefangene 1950–1959 II—A—C—15, f. 007r; Montini to Muench 11 May 1954 AAV, Arch. Nunz. Berlino 159, fasc. 42, fasc. Kriegsgefangene 1950–1959 II—A—C—15, f. 041r.

19 Weinke, *Die Nürnberger Prozesse*, 105.

20 Kaiser and Jasch, *Der Holocaust vor deutschen Gerichten*, 89–90.

21 Raithel, *Die Strafanstalt Landsberg*, 66.
22 Frei, *Adenauer's Germany and the Nazi Past*, 177.
23 Weinke, *Die Nürnberger Prozesse*, 105.
24 Atina Grossmann, *Jews, Germans, and Allies: Close Encounters in Occupied Germany* (Princeton University Press, 2009), 24.
25 Karl Jaspers, *Die Schuldfrage* (Lambert Schneider, 1946), 29.
26 Jaspers, *Die Schuldfrage*, 31.
27 Jaspers, *Die Schuldfrage*, 65.
28 Thomas Brudholm, "On the Advocacy of Forgiveness after Mass Atrocities," in *The Religious in Responses to Mass Atrocity: Interdisciplinary Perspectives*, ed. Thomas Brudholm and Thomas Cushman (Cambridge University Press, 2009), 126.
29 Martin Niemöller, *Of Guilt and Hope*, trans. Renee Spodheim (Philosophical Library, 1947), 13–14.
30 As Richard Ned Lebow neatly stated: "[Meanwhile] everyone blamed the Germans for the Holocaust, the Germans blamed the Nazis, and the Nazis blamed Hitler." See Richard Ned Lebow, "The Memory of Politics in Postwar Europe," in The Politics of Memory in Postwar Europe, ed. Richard Ned Lebow, Wulf Kansteiner, and Claudio Fogu (Durham, NC: Duke University Press, 2006), 1–39, here 21. Martin Niemöller did not use these exact words, but he conveyed the same idea. Niemöller, *Of Guilt and Hope*, 13–14.
31 Niemöller, *Of Guilt and Hope*, 17–18.
32 Niemöller, *Of Guilt and Hope*, 76–77.
33 Klee, *Persilscheine und falsche Pässe*, 8: „Gerne wird argumentiert, christliche Barmherzigkeit müsse auch für Nazi-Täter gelten. Nichts dagegen. Doch das Argument dient der Irreführung: NS-Mörder bereuten ja nichts. Sie hatten nach eigenem Bekunden nur ihre Pflicht getan. Ihre Exkulpierung wiegt schwerer als das Schweigen der Kirchen zu Nazi-Verbrechen und Judenmord im Dritten Reich. Die Opfer wurden ein zweites Mal verraten. Ohne Zwang, aus freien Stücken. Das heißt doch wohl: aus Überzeugung."
34 Bernauer, *Auschwitz and Absolution*.
35 David Neuhaus, "Auschwitz Absolution: A Confessor Reflects in Fear and Trembling," in *Auschwitz and Absolution*, 90.
36 Umberto Eco, "Ur-Fascism," *The New York Review of Books*, June 22, 1995, 2.
37 Aleida Assmann, *Das neue Unbehagen an der Erinnerungskultur: Eine Intervention* (C. H. Beck, 2020), 201.
38 Berel Lang, "Holocaust Memory and Revenge: The Presence of the Past," *Jewish Social Studies* 2, no. 2 (Winter, 1996): 1–20; Mark Roseman, "'No, Herr Führer!' Jewish Revenge after the Holocaust: Between Fantasy and Reality," in *Revenge, Retribution, Reconciliation: Justice and Emotions between Conflict and Mediation. A Cross-Disciplinary Anthology*, ed. Laura Jockusch (Hebrew University Magnes Press, 2016), 69–90; Naomi Seidman, "Elie Wiesel and the Scandal of Jewish Rage," *Jewish Social Studies* 3, no. 1 (1996): 1–19, 6.
39 Dina Porat, *Nakam: The Holocaust Survivors Who Sought Full-Scale Revenge* (Blackstone Publishing, 2022).

40 Abraham Sutzkever and Justin D. Cammy, *From the Vilna Ghetto to Nuremberg: Memoir and Testimony* (McGill-Queen's University Press, 2021), 283–84, here 284.

41 See Katarzyna Person, *The Hour of Revenge: Holocaust Survivors and Their Search for Revenge and Retribution* (University of Toronto Press, 2025); Laura Jockusch and Gabriel N. Finder, *Jewish Honor Courts: Revenge, Retribution, and Reconciliation in Europe and Israel after the Holocaust* (Wayne State University Press, 2025).

42 World Jewish Congress, "Statement and Resolution on the Punishment of War Criminals," War Emergency Conference, Nov. 26–30, 1944, WJC, C125/10, 3. See also Jockusch, "Justice at Nuremberg? Jewish Responses to Nazi War-Crime Trials in Allied-Occupied Germany," *Jewish Social Studies: History, Culture, Society* 19, no. 1 (Fall 2012), 107–47.

43 See Jockusch, "Justice at Nuremberg?," 107–47.

44 See Jockusch, "Justice at Nuremberg?"

45 Jockusch, "Justice at Nuremberg?," 132.

46 See Jockusch, "Justice at Nuremberg?," 126.

47 Jockusch, "Justice at Nuremberg?," 123.

48 Jockusch, "Justice at Nuremberg?," 130.

49 Gerald Steinacher, "The Nazi Hunter: Simon Wiesenthal and the *Täterforschung*," in *The Second Austrian Republic*, ed. Marc Landry and Eva Pfanzelter (University of New Orleans Press, 2022), 191–207.

50 Peter Novick, *The Holocaust in American Life* (Houghton, 1999), 85–86.

51 Novick, *The Holocaust in American Life*, 90.

52 VWI-SWA, I.1., JHD, Wiesenthal: „Die Rolle der Jüdischen Historischen Documentation bei der Verfolgung und Bestrafung von Kriegsverbrecher (Das Beispiel Oesterreich)", 25 November 1947, 1.

53 Daniel Philpott, ed., *The Politics of Past Evil: Religion, Reconciliation, and the Dilemmas of Transitional Justice* (University of Notre Dame Press, 2006), 90.

54 Simon Wiesenthal, *The Sunflower: On the Possibilities and Limits of Forgiveness* (Schocken Books, 1998), 182.

55 Quoted in Wiesenthal, *The Sunflower*, 171.

56 Quoted in Brown-Fleming, *The Holocaust and Catholic Conscience*, 1.

57 See Brown-Fleming, *The Holocaust and Catholic Conscience*, 1.

58 Susan Neiman, *Learning from the Germans: Race and the Memory of Evil* (Farrar, Straus and Giroux, 2019).

59 Assmann, *Das Neue Unbehagen an der Erinnerungskultur*, 237.

60 Hudal, *Römische Tagebücher*, 21.

61 (1) Alois Hudal, letter of recommendation, 24 April 1940, AAV, Segr. Stato, Commissione Soccorsi 293, fasc. 28, Razza 1940/28, Morgenstern Ernesto. (2) Letterhead Alois Hudal, letter of recommendation, 10 May 1940, Letter Vatican Segr. State to Hudal, 14 July 1940, Letter Hudal to Vatican Segr. State, 23 July 1940, AAV, Segr. Stato, Commissione Soccorsi 293, Razza 1940/48, Margoliner Herta nata Wolf. During the war in Italy, Hudal helped to hide a few Allied prisoners of war and German deserters, usually Christians, in the Anima. See Sachslehner, *Hitlers Mann im Vatikan*, 160ff. Hudal claimed that,

during the German occupation of Rome, he could not hide Jews in the Anima as he was constantly visited by Nazi officials. See Hudal, *Römische Tagebücher*, 201.

62 Catholic apologists often portray Nazi escape assistance as the actions of individual rogue priests, further asserting that the Papal Aid Commission helped Jews and others—thus once again conflating Nazi victims with Nazi perpetrators. This appears to be the main argument in a book by the lawyer Pier Luigi Guiducci, with a foreword by the Jesuit Father Peter Gumpel; both authors are very close to the Vatican: *Oltre la leggenda nera: Il Vaticano e la fuga dei criminali nazisti* (Mursia, 2015). Gumpel was one of the clerics in charge of the beatification process of Pius XII.

63 See Katharina von Kellenbach, "Schuld und Vergebung: Zur deutschen Praxis christlicher Versöhnung," in Björn Krondorfer, *Mit Blick auf die Täter*, 227–312, 279.

64 "'Forgive Germany,' Pope Urges World," *The New York Times*, April 16, 1948, 10.

65 Stuart Eizenstat, *Imperfect Justice: Looted Assets, Slave Labor, and the Unfinished Business of World War II* (Public Affairs, 2009).

SELECTED BIBLIOGRAPHY

Assmann, Aleida, and Ute Frevert. *Geschichtsvergessenheit—Geschichtsversessenheit: Vom Umgang mit den deutschen Vergangenheiten nach 1945*. Deutsche Verlags-Anstalt, 1999.

Bachhofer, Ulrike, and Angela Achi. "Pragmatischer Umgang mit der Vergangenheit? Kirche und Fluchthilfe." In *Kirche der Sünder—Sündige Kirche? Beispiele für den Umgang mit Schuld nach 1945*, edited by Rainer Bendel. LIT, 2002.

Bass, Gary Jonathan. *Stay the Hand of Vengeance: The Politics of War Crimes Tribunals*. Princeton University Press, 2000.

Bauer, Yehuda. *A History of the Holocaust*. Franklin Watts, 2001.

Bazyler, Michael J., and Frank M. Tuerkheimer. *Forgotten Trials of the Holocaust*. New York University Press, 2014.

Bergen, Doris L. *Between God and Hitler: Military Chaplains in Nazi Germany*. Cambridge University Press, 2023.

Bernauer, James W., ed. *Auschwitz and Absolution: The Case of the Commandant and the Confessor*. Orbis Books, 2024.

Best, Geoffrey. *War and Law since 1945*. Clarendon Press, 1994.

Bohr, Felix. *Die Kriegsverbrecherlobby: Bundesdeutsche Hilfe für im Ausland inhaftierte NS-Täter*. Suhrkamp Verlag, 2018.

Borgwardt, Elizabeth. *A New Deal for the World: America's Vision for Human Rights*. Belknap Press of Harvard University Press, 2005.

Breitman, Richard, Norman J. W. Goda, Timothy Naftali, and Robert Wolfe. *U.S. Intelligence and the Nazis*. Cambridge University Press, 2005.

Brown-Fleming, Suzanne. *The Holocaust and Catholic Conscience: Cardinal Aloisius Muench and the Guilt Question in Germany*. University of Notre Dame Press, 2006.

Brudholm, Thomas. "On the Advocacy of Forgiveness after Mass Atrocities." In *The Religious in Responses to Mass Atrocity: Interdisciplinary Perspectives*, edited by Thomas Brudholm and Thomas Cushman. Cambridge University Press, 2009.

Canosa, Romano. *Le sanzioni contro il fascismo. Processi ed epurazioni a Milano negli anni 1945–47*. Gabriele Mazzotta Editore, 1978.

Caroli, Paolo. *Transitional Justice in Italy and the Crimes of Fascism and Nazism*. Routledge, 2022.

Casazza, Andrea. *La fuga dei Nazisti: Mengele, Eichmann, Priebke, Pavelic da Genova all'impunità*. Il Melangolo, 2007.

Casella, Mario. *L'Azione Cattolica Italiana e i "lontani."* Velar, 2010.

Ceci, Lucia. *The Vatican and Mussolini's Italy*. Brill, 2017.

Chamedes, Giuliana. *A Twentieth-Century Crusade: The Vatican's Battle to Remake Christian Europe*. Harvard University Press, 2019.

Cohen, Gerard Daniel. *In War's Wake: Europe's Displaced Persons in the Postwar Order*. Oxford University Press, 2011.

Connelly, John. *From Enemy to Brother: The Revolution in Catholic Teaching on the Jews 1933–1965*. Harvard University Press, 2012.

Conze, Eckart, Norbert Frei, Peter Hayes, and Moshe Zimmermann, eds. *Das Amt und die Vergangenheit: Deutsche Diplomaten im Dritten Reich und in der Bundesrepublik*. Karl Blessing Verlag, 2010.

Cornwell, John. *Hitler's Pope: The Secret History of Pius XII*. Viking, 1999.

Douglas, R. M. *Orderly and Humane: The Expulsion of the Germans after the Second World War*. Yale University Press, 2012.

Epstein, Catherine. *Model Nazi: Arthur Greiser and the Occupation of Western Poland*. Oxford University Press, 2010.

Evans, Richard J. *Rituals of Retribution: Capital Punishment in Germany 1600–1987*. Oxford University Press, 1996.

Fleming, Brian. *The Vatican Pimpernel: The Wartime Exploits of Monsignor Hugh O'Flaherty*. Gill & Macmillan, 2008.

Focardi, Filippo. *Criminali di guerra in libertà: Un accordo segreto tra Italia e Germania federale, 1949–1955*. Carocci, 2008.

Forster, Thomas. "Zweiter Kirchenkampf oder Stellvertreterdiskurs? Katholischer Konservatismus und die Interpretation des Katholizismus im Nationalsozialismus nach 1945." In *Zwischen Revolutionsschock und Schulddebatte*, edited by Antonia Leugers. Universaar, 2013.

Forsythe, David P. *The Humanitarians: The International Committee of the Red Cross*. Cambridge University Press, 2005.

Frei, Norbert. *Adenauer's Germany and the Nazi Past: The Politics of Amnesty and Integration*. Columbia University Press, 2002.

Gentile, Carlo. *I crimini di guerra tedeschi in Italia: 1943–1945*. Einaudi Editore, 2022.

Goñi, Uki. *The Real Odessa: How Perón Brought the Nazi War Criminals to Argentina*. Granta Books, 2002.

Griech-Polelle, Beth A. *Bishop von Galen: German Bishops and National Socialism*. Yale University Press, 2022.

Hammerschmidt, Peter. *Deckname Adler: Klaus Barbie und die westlichen Geheimdienste*. S. Fischer, 2014.

Heller, Kevin Jon. *The Nuremberg Military Tribunals and the Origins of International Criminal Law*. Oxford University Press, 2011.

Hirsch, Francine. *Soviet Judgment at Nuremberg: A New History of the International Military Tribunal after World War II*. Oxford University Press, 2020.

Holland, James. *Italy's Sorrow: A Year of War, 1944–45*. St. Martin's Press, 2008.

Huener, Jonathan D. *The Polish Catholic Church Under German Occupation: The Reichsgau Wartheland, 1939–1945*. Indiana University Press, 2021.

Hutchinson, Robert. *After Nuremberg: American Clemency for Nazi War Criminals*. Yale University Press, 2022.

Invernizzi, Marco. *Luigi Gedda e il Movimento Cattolico in Italia*. Sguarco Edizioni, 2012.

Jockusch, Laura. "Justice at Nuremberg? Jewish Responses to Nazi War-Crime Trials in Allied-Occupied Germany." *Jewish Social Studies: History, Culture, Society* 19, no. 1 (Fall 2012): 107–47.

Jockusch, Laura, Andreas Kraft, and Kim Wünschmann, eds. *Revenge, Retribution, Reconciliation: Justice and Emotions between Conflict and Mediation. A Cross-Disciplinary Anthology*. Hebrew University Magnes Press, 2016.

Kaiser, Eva Maria. *Gottes Hirten und Hitler's Jünger: Der Einsatz der katholischen Bischöfe Österreichs für ehemalige Nationalsozialisten nach 1945*. Böhlau Verlag, 2017.

Kasprowski, Christian, and Nicole Priesching, eds. *Lorenz Jaeger als Kirchenpolitiker*. Brill | Schöningh, 2021.

Kent, Peter C. *The Lonely Cold War of Pope Pius XII: The Roman Catholic Church and the Division of Europe, 1943–1950*. McGill-Queen's University Press, 2002.

Kertzer, David I. *The Pope and Mussolini: The Secret History of Pius XI and the Rise of Fascism in Europe*. Random House, 2014.

Kertzer, David I. *The Pope at War: The Secret History of Pius XII, Mussolini, and Hitler*. Random House, 2022.

Klee, Ernst. *Persilscheine und falsche Pässe: Wie die Kirchen den Nazis halfen*. Fischer Taschenbuch Verlag, 1991.

Kochavi, Arieh J. *Prelude to Nuremberg: Allied War Crimes Policy and the Question of Punishment*. University of North Carolina Press, 1998.

Kornberg, Jacques. *The Pope's Dilemma: Pius XII Faces Atrocities and Genocide in the Second World War*. University of Toronto Press, 2015.

Krondorfer, Björn, Katharina von Kellenbach, and Norbert Reck, eds. *Mit Blick auf die Täter: Fragen an die deutsche Theologie nach 1945*. Gütersloher Verlagshaus, 2006.

Kühlwein, Klaus. *Pius XII. und die Deportation der Juden Roms*. Peter Lang, 2021.

Leugers, Antonia, ed. *Zwischen Revolutionsschock und Schulddebatte: Münchner Katholizismus und Protestantismus im 20. Jahrhundert*. Theologie Geschichte, Beiheft 7. Universaar, 2013.

Lichtblau, Eric. *The Nazis Next Door: How America Became a Safe Haven for Hitler's Men*. Mariner Books, 2014.

Löffler, Peter, ed. *Bischof Clemens August Graf Galen: Akten, Briefe und Predigten 1933–1946*. 2nd ed. Ferdinand Schöningh, 1996.

Lowe, Keith. *Savage Continent: Europe in the Aftermath of World War II*. Picador, 2013.

Matthäus, Jürgen, and Frank Bajohr. *The Political Diary of Alfred Rosenberg and the Onset of the Holocaust*. Rowman & Littlefield, 2015.

McCormick, Robert B. *Croatia Under Ante Pavelić: America, the Ustaše and Croatian Genocide in World War II*. I.B. Tauris, 2014.

McKale, Donald M. *Nazis after Hitler: How Perpetrators of the Holocaust Cheated Justice and Truth*. Rowman & Littlefield, 2012.

Napolitano, Matteo Luigi. *Pio XII tra Guerra e Pace: Profezia e diplomazia di un papa (1939–1945)*. Città Nuova, 2002.

Neiman, Susan. *Learning from the Germans: Race and the Memory of Evil*. Farrar, Straus and Giroux, 2019.

Novick, Peter. *The Holocaust in American Life*. Houghton Mifflin, 1999.

Pavone, Claudio. *A Civil War: A History of the Italian Resistance*. Verso Books, 2014.

Perin, Raffaella. *The Popes on Air: The History of Vatican Radio from Its Origins to World War II*. World War II: The Global, Human, and Ethical Dimension. Fordham University Press, 2024.

Person, Katarzyna. *The Hour of Revenge: Holocaust Survivors and Their Search for Revenge and Retribution*. University of Toronto Press, 2025.

Phayer, Michael. *Pius XII, the Holocaust, and the Cold War*. Indiana University Press, 2007.

Portmann, Heinrich. *Cardinal von Galen: By His Chaplain*. Translated and with an introduction by R. L. Sedgwick. Jarrolds, 1957.

Power, Samantha. *"A Problem from Hell": America and the Age of Genocide*. Basic Books, 2002.

Priemel, Kim Christian. *The Betrayal: The Nuremberg Trials and German Divergence*. Oxford University Press, 2016.

Rashke, Richard. *Useful Enemies: John Demjanjuk and America's Open-Door Policy for Nazi War Criminals*. Delphinium, 2013.

Remy, Steven P. *The Malmedy Massacre: The War Crimes Trial Controversy*. Harvard University Press, 2017.

Riebling, Mark. *Church of Spies: The Pope's Secret War Against Hitler*. Basic Books, 2015.

Riesenberger, Dieter. *Der Paderborner Dompropst Paul Simon (1882–1946): Ein Beitrag zur Geschichte des Nationalsozialismus, der Ökumene und der Nachkriegsjahre in Paderborn*. Bonifatius, 1992.

Roseman, Mark. "'No, Herr Führer!' Jewish Revenge after the Holocaust: Between Fantasy and Reality." In *Revenge, Retribution, Reconciliation: Justice and Emotions between Conflict and Mediation*, edited by Laura Jockusch et al. Hebrew University Magnes Press, 2016.

Ruff, Mark Edward. *The Battle for the Catholic Past: Catholic Memory in Germany, 1945–1980*. Cambridge University Press, 2017.

Sands, Philippe. *East West Street: On the Origins of "Genocide" and "Crimes Against Humanity"*. Vintage Books, 2017.

Sands, Philippe. *The Ratline: Love, Lies and Justice on the Trail of a Nazi Fugitive*. Weidenfeld & Nicolson, 2020.

Sanfilippo, Matteo. "Per una storia dei profughi stranieri e dei campi di accoglienza e di reclusione nell'Italia del secondo dopoguerra." *Studi Emigrazione/Migration Studies* 43, no. 164 (2006): 835–56.

Schenk, Dieter. *Hitlers Mann in Danzig: Albert Forster und die NS-Verbrechen in Danzig-Westpreußen*. Verlag J.H.W. Dietz Nachf., 2000.

Schiessl, Christoph. *Alleged Nazi Collaborators in the United States after World War II*. Lexington Books, 2016.

Smith, Bradley F. *The American Road to Nuremberg: The Documentary Record 1944–1945*. Hoover Institution Press, 1982.

Spicer, Kevin P., ed. *Antisemitism, Christian Ambivalence, and the Holocaust*. Indiana University Press, 2007.

Spicer, Kevin P. *Hitler's Priests: Catholic Clergy and National Socialism*. Northern Illinois University Press, 2008.

Spicer, Kevin P., and Rebecca Carter-Chand, eds. *Religion, Ethnonationalism, and Antisemitism in the Era of the Two World Wars*. McGill-Queen's University Press, 2022.

Spotts, Frederic. *The Churches and Politics in Germany*. Wesleyan University Press, 1973.

Stangneth, Bettina. *Eichmann Before Jerusalem: The Unexamined Life of a Mass Murderer*. Knopf, 2014.

Steinacher, Gerald. "Forgive and Forget? The Vatican and the Escape of Nazi War Criminals from Justice." *S:I.M.O.N.—Shoah: Intervention. Methods. Documentation* 9, no. 1 (2022): 4–28.

Steinacher, Gerald. *Humanitarians at War: The Red Cross in the Shadow of the Holocaust*. Oxford University Press, 2017.

Steinacher, Gerald. "Das Massaker der Fosse Ardeatine und die Täterverfolgung. Deutsch-italienische Störfälle von Kappler bis Priebke." In *Italien, Österreich und die Bundesrepublik Deutschland in Europa: Ein Dreiecksverhältnis in seinen wechselseitigen Beziehungen und Wahrnehmungen von 1945/49 bis zur Gegenwart*, edited by Michael Gehler and Maddalena Guiotto, 291–315. Böhlau Verlag, 2012.

Steinacher, Gerald. "The Nazi Hunter: Simon Wiesenthal and the Täterforschung." In *The Second Austrian Republic*, edited by Marc Landry and Eva Pfanzelter. New Orleans University Press, 2022.

Steinacher, Gerald. *Nazis on the Run: How Hitler's Henchmen Fled Justice*. Oxford University Press, 2011.

Steinacher, Gerald. "Le pape contre Nuremberg: Procès des crimes de guerre nazis, le Vatican et la question de la justice après la guerre." *Revue d'Histoire de la Shoah*, no. 218 (Fall 2023): 301–21.

Steinacher, Gerald. "Vergeben und Vergessen? Kardinal Faulhaber, der Vatikan und die Prozesse gegen NS-Kriegsverbrecher." In *»Wir leben in einer Zeitenwende . . . «: Michael Kardinal von Faulhaber und die katholische Kirche zwischen Monarchie, Diktatur und Demokratie*, edited by Matthias Daufratshofer, Moritz Fischer, and Peer Oliver Volkmann, 221–42. Kohlhammer, 2025.

Stüken, Wolfgang. *Hirten unter Hitler: Die Rolle der Paderborner Erzbischöfe Caspar Klein und Lorenz Jaeger in der NS-Zeit*. Klartext, 1999.

Taylor, Telford. *Anatomy of the Nuremberg Trials: A Personal Memoir*. Knopf, 1992.

Teitel, Ruti. *Transitional Justice*. Oxford University Press, 2000.

Utrecht, Daniel. *The Lion of Münster: The Bishop Who Roared Against the Nazis*. Tan Books, 2016.

Valbousquet, Nina. *Les âmes tièdes: Le Vatican face à la Shoah*. La Découverte, 2024.
Ventresca, Robert A. *Soldier of Christ: The Life of Pope Pius XII*. The Belknap Press of Harvard University Press, 2013.
von Kellenbach, Katharina. *The Mark of Cain: Guilt and Denial in the Post-War Lives of Nazi Perpetrators*. Oxford University Press, 2013.
Vutz, Johannes, and Josef Meyer zu Schlochtern, eds. *Lorenz Jaeger: Ein Erzbischof in der Zeit des Nationalsozialismus*. Aschendorff Verlag, 2020.
Walters, Guy. *Hunting Evil: The Nazi War Criminals Who Escaped and the Quest to Bring Them to Justice*. Broadway Books, 2009.
Weinke, Annette. *Die Nürnberger Prozesse*. C. H. Beck, 2006.
Wiesenthal, Simon. *The Sunflower: On the Possibilities and Limits of Forgiveness*. Schocken Books, 1998.
Wirsching, Andreas. "Mehr Nähe als Distanz? Kardinal Michael von Faulhaber und der Nationalsozialismus." In *Distanz und Nähe zugleich? Die christlichen Kirchen im „Dritten Reich"*, edited by Friedrich Wilhelm Graf and Hans Günter Hockerts. NS-Dokumentationszentrum, 2017.
Wolf, Hubert. *Pope and Devil: The Vatican's Archives and the Third Reich*. Belknap Press of Harvard University Press, 2010.
Wolf, Hubert, with the collaboration of Ingrid Lüb. *Clemens August Graf von Galen: Gehorsam und Gewissen*. Herder, 2006.
Woller, Hans. *Die Abrechnung mit dem Faschismus in Italien 1943 bis 1948*. Oldenbourg Wissenschaftsverlag, 1996.
Zuccotti, Susan. *Under His Very Windows: The Vatican and the Holocaust in Italy*. Yale University Press, 2000.

INDEX

ABOUT THE AUTHOR

Gerald J. Steinacher, PhD, is the James A. Rawley Professor of History at the University of Nebraska–Lincoln and a specialist in modern European history, the Holocaust, antisemitism, fascism, and postwar justice. He has published eighteen books, including *Nazis on the Run* (Oxford University Press, 2011), which received the National Jewish Book Award in the Holocaust category.